Microsoft Tabular Modeling Cookbook

Over 50 tips and tricks for analytical modeling using
Business Intelligence Semantic Models with SQL Server
2012 and PowerPivot

Paul te Braak

[PACKT] enterprise 🞓
PUBLISHING   professional expertise distilled

BIRMINGHAM - MUMBAI

Microsoft Tabular Modeling Cookbook

First published: December 2013

Production Reference: 1171213

Published by Packt Publishing Ltd.
Livery Place
35 Livery Street
Birmingham B3 2PB, UK.

ISBN 978-1-78217-088-4

www.packtpub.com

Cover Image by Neston Simoes (nestonsimoes@ymail.com)

Credits

Author
Paul te Braak

Reviewers
Anindita Basak
Steve Hughes
Cosmin Ioan
Stevo Smočilac

Acquisition Editors
Sam Birch
Edward Gordon

Lead Technical Editor
Ankita Shashi

Technical Editors
Pankaj Kadam
Pramod Kumavat
Adrian Raposo

Project Coordinator
Shiksha Chaturvedi

Copy Editors
Alisha Aranha
Sayanee Mukherjee
Deepa Nambiar
Alfida Paiva
Laxmi Subramanian

Proofreader
Linda Morris

Indexer
Rekha Nair

Graphics
Yuvraj Mannari

Production Coordinator
Nilesh R. Mohite

Cover Work
Nilesh R. Mohite

About the Author

Paul te Braak (ptebraak@abaXdata.com.au) is a leading Business Intelligence Consultant based in Australia. He has been involved in Information Management for over 15 years, with the past 9 years focusing on the Microsoft Business Intelligence stack. His areas of interest include data modeling, data mining, and visualization. He is an active participant in the SQL Server community, speaks at various local and international events, and organizes a regional *SQL Server Saturday*. His blog can be found at www.paultebraak.wordpress.com.

I would like to thank everyone who has contributed to this book. Like most projects, there are many behind-the-scenes people who have assisted me, and I am truly grateful to those people. The book would never have been complete without your help!

Firstly, I'd like to thank my wife for her understanding and acceptance during the project when I spent nights and weekends working. I am sure that my responsibilities at home have decreased (well, they've been removed), and this has afforded me the time to focus on writing.

I would also like to thank Cathy Dumas for recommending me to Packt Publishing at the start of the project, and all the reviewers who have provided their input along the way and looked over my work with an objective view. I would like to thank the members of the community who are always willing to participate in events and forums that help us improve our knowledge.

Finally, I'd like to thank Packt Publishing and all the associated staff (believe me, there have been quite a few) for the opportunity to write for them.

About the Reviewers

Anindita Basak is currently working as a senior system analyst at Sonata Software in the Windows Azure Pro Direct Delivery group of Microsoft. She has worked as a senior software engineer on implementation of various enterprise applications on Windows Azure and Windows phone. She started her journey with Windows Azure in the Microsoft Cloud Integration Engineering (CIE) team and worked as a support engineer in Microsoft India (R&D) Pvt. Ltd. With six years of experience in the Microsoft .NET technology stack, she is solely focused on Cloud and Microsoft Mobility. As an MVB, she loves to share her technical experience and expertise through her blog at http://anindita9.wordpress.com.

She recently worked as a technical reviewer for the books *HDInsight Essentials* and *Microsoft SQL Server 2012 with Hadoop* by *Packt Publishing*.

She holds a B.E in Information Technology from West Bengal University of Technology (formerly IIIT Calcutta). She has attended various business conferences and technology seminars of Microsoft.

I would like to thank my grandpapa Mr. Kanti Das Basak, mom, Anjana, dad, Ajit Kumar Basak, and my affectionate brother, Aditya. Without their help, I can't achieve any goals of my life.

Steve Hughes is a Practice Lead at Magenic. In his current role, he develops strategy and helps guide data, Business Intelligence, collaboration, and data integration development using Microsoft technologies, including SQL Server, SharePoint, and BizTalk. He continues to deliver data and Business Intelligence solutions using these platforms. He has been working with technology for over 15 years with much of that time spent on creating Business Intelligence solutions. He is passionate about using data effectively and helping customers understand that data is valuable and profitable. Steve can often be found at *Professional Association for SQL Server (PASS)* events, where he serves as a regional mentor and is active with the *Minnesota SQL Server User Group (MNPASS)*. He shares his insights about the field on his blog at `http://dataonwheels.wordpress.com`.

I would like to thank my family for their continued support on these projects.

Cosmin Ioan is a data warehouse and Business Intelligence architect with over 16 years' experience in the Information Technology field, spanning development languages, systems administration, RDBMS and OLAP design, architecture, troubleshooting, and scalability on Microsoft, Oracle, and Sybase platforms. He has worked in consultancy and full-time roles for companies, public and private companies alike, such as Motorola, Citrix, Aetna, and Sheridan Healthcorp, chiefly building data warehouse and systems integration solutions, allowing companies to better harness and give meaning to their data assets.

When not working, Cosmin enjoys scuba diving and racquet sports.

Writing a technical book and reviewing one are never easy tasks. Due to inherent time constraints and ever-changing technology advancements, keeping a delicate balance between product depth and breadth, as well as a target audience for covering any one technical product is always a challenging proposition. My thanks to Paul for taking up such a challenge and allowing me to be part of the effort, as well as the nice team at Packt Publishing for their endeavor in publishing quality technical books.

Stevo Smočilac is an associate principal consultant at Magenic, a Microsoft Gold Certified Partner, who specializes in Business Intelligence solutions.

He has over 12 years' experience of working in software development, the last seven of which have focused on designing, implementing, managing, and administrating technical solutions developed using Microsoft SQL Server and the Microsoft Business Intelligence stack. He has been involved in all phases of the BI development lifecycle from envisioning through operational support, and he is passionate about the field of Business Intelligence.

Stevo is currently a Virtual Technology Solutions Professional (V-TSP) for Business Intelligence, a Microsoft Certified IT professional, and holds a B.Tech degree in Information Technology.

Originally from South Africa, he now resides in (the much colder) Northeastern United States with his wife Talya.

www.PacktPub.com

Support files, eBooks, discount offers and more

You might want to visit www.PacktPub.com for support files and downloads related to your book.

Did you know that Packt offers eBook versions of every book published, with PDF and ePub files available? You can upgrade to the eBook version at www.PacktPub.com and as a print book customer, you are entitled to a discount on the eBook copy. Get in touch with us at service@packtpub.com for more details.

At www.PacktPub.com, you can also read a collection of free technical articles, sign up for a range of free newsletters and receive exclusive discounts and offers on Packt books and eBooks.

http://PacktLib.PacktPub.com

Do you need instant solutions to your IT questions? PacktLib is Packt's online digital book library. Here, you can access, read and search across Packt's entire library of books.

Why Subscribe?

- ▶ Fully searchable across every book published by Packt
- ▶ Copy and paste, print and bookmark content
- ▶ On demand and accessible via web browser

Free Access for Packt account holders

If you have an account with Packt at www.PacktPub.com, you can use this to access PacktLib today and view nine entirely free books. Simply use your login credentials for immediate access.

Instant Updates on New Packt Books

Get notified! Find out when new books are published by following @PacktEnterprise on Twitter, or the *Packt Enterprise* Facebook page.

Table of Contents

Preface

In 2010, Microsoft announced a change to its Business Intelligence environment, and said it will focus its development efforts on semantic modeling. At that time, the current technology used for analysis was **SQL Server Analysis Server** (**SSAS**), a technology that relied on disk-based storage and the distinct steps of model development, deployment, and processing—a function usually under the control of IT. The new technology will house all its data in memory and allow the user (or model designer) to change the model in real time and view those changes instantaneously. In addition to this, the platform sought to remove many of the barriers that had existed in the traditional Business Intelligence landscape. It offered a uniform platform for data analysis across an entire organization. The same platform can now be used by an individual user in Excel deployed to SharePoint (for team Business Intelligence) or directly to a server (for corporate Business Intelligence). This will remove a large proportion of the rework that was traditionally involved in Business Intelligence projects and lead to the catchcry "BI to the masses" (meaning that anyone can model a Business Intelligence solution). A free add-in was released for Excel 2010, and the 2012 release of Analysis Server (in SQL Server) included a new storage mode called tabular.

This was an interesting challenge to the traditional methods for implementing Business Intelligence models. Under that structure, Business Intelligence was essentially controlled by an IT department, which used a waterfall methodology and there were distinct phases in an analytical project involving the separation of duties and more importantly, the separation of people. Those that had to use data models were often involved with a back-and-forth battle to make the model work as the business user required.

Tabular models were then introduced and overnight Excel users were able to consume massive amounts of data and create their own analytical models without the need to involve IT (other than access to the data of course!). The product extended the familiar pivot table by allowing users to create pivot tables using many different data sources (and removed the requirements for a pivot table to be sourced from a single data table). More importantly, the ability to create models for the analysis of data was delivered directly to those who needed it most—the analytical end user. The restrictions on analysis and data manipulation that they had previously encountered were removed.

This book is primarily written for those users—individuals who need to answer questions based on large amounts of data. For this reason, we focus on how these users can use that technology to build models in Excel using PowerPivot. We simply don't want to exclude those users who need it the most and do not have access to the more traditional tools developed for corporate BI. Furthermore, these techniques are also directly applicable to corporate tabular models.

Finally, the book looks at how these models can be managed and incorporated into production environments and corporate systems to provide robust and secure reporting systems.

What this book covers

Chapter 1, Getting Started with Excel, covers the basics of the tabular model, that is, how to get started with modeling and summarizing the data. This chapter includes a basic overview of how the tabular model works and how the model presents to an end user (we also look at some general data modeling principles, so that you can better understand the underlying structure of the datasets that you use). In doing so, we look at the basics of combining data within the model, calculations, and the control (and formatting) of what an end user can see.

Chapter 2, Importing Data, examines how different forms of data can be incorporated and managed within the model. In doing so, we examine some common sources of data which are used (for example, text files) and examine ways that these sources can be controlled and defined. We also examine some non-traditional sources (for example, data that is presented in a report).

Chapter 3, Advanced Browsing Features, examines how the model can be structured to provide an intuitive and desirable user experience. We examine a variety of techniques that include model properties and configurations, data structures and design styles, which can be used to control and present data within the model. We also examine how to create some common analytical features (for example, calculation styles, value bounds, ratios, and key performance indicators) and how these can be used.

Chapter 4, Time Calculations and Date Functions, explains how time and calendar calculations are added and used within the model. This chapter looks at defining the commonly used month-to-date and year-to-date calculations, as well as comparative calculations (for example, the same period last year). We also look at alternate calendars (for example, the 445 calendar) running averages and shell calculations.

Chapter 5, Applied Modeling, discusses some advanced modeling functionality and how the model can be used to manipulate its own data thus presenting new information. For example, we look at the dynamic generation of bins (that is, the grouping of data), currency calculations, many-to-many relationships, and stock calculations over time. We also look at how the model can be used to allocate its own data so that datasets that have been imported into the model at various levels of aggregation can be presented under a consistent view.

Chapter 6, Programmatic Access via Excel, explains how the tabular model can open a new world of possibilities for analysis in Excel by allowing the creation of interactive reports and visualizations that combine massive amounts of data. This chapter looks at how Excel and the tabular model can be used to provide an intuitive reporting environment through the use of VBA—Visual Basic for Applications is the internal programming language of Excel.

Chapter 7, Enterprise Design and Features, examines the corporate considerations of the tabular model design and the additional requirements of the model in that environment. We look at the various methods of upgrading PowerPivot model, perspectives, and the application of security.

Chapter 8, Enterprise Management, examines how the model is managed in a corporate environment (that is on SQL Server Analysis Server). This chapter looks at various techniques for deploying the tabular model to a SSAS server and the manipulation of objects once they have been deployed (for example, the addition and reconfiguration of data sources). We look at the addition of new data to the model through petitions and the processing of the model data through SQL Server Agent Jobs.

Chapter 9, Querying the Tabular Model with DAX, shows how to query the model using the language of the tabular model—DAX (Data Analysis Expressions). We look at how to retrieve data from the model and then go on to combine data from different parts of the model, create aggregate summaries and calculations, and finally filter data.

Chapter 10, Visualizing Data with Power View, explains how Power View can be used to analyze data in tabular models. This chapter looks at how to use Power View and how to configure and design a tabular model for use with Power View.

Appendix, Installing PowerPivot and Sample Databases, shows how to install PowerPivot in Excel 2010 and install the sample data used in this book.

What you need for this book

As a book which covers many aspects of tabular modeling, the recipes can be followed using a variety of software that incorporates tabular modeling. Although we focus on PowerPivot in Excel 2010 (this is still the most prevalent installation in corporate environments), the recipes can also be completed in Excel 2013. When recipes focus on server and corporate features, SQL Server Analysis Services 2012 (in tabular storage mode) is used. The complete list of software applications used in this book is:

- ▶ Excel 2010 (with the free PowerPivot add-in)
- ▶ Excel 2013
- ▶ SQL Server Data Tools (installed with SQL Server 2012)
- ▶ SQL Server 2012 (SQL Server Analysis Server Tabular Mode)

Who this book is for

This book is designed for two types of users. First and foremost, it is designed for those users who wish to create tabular models for analysis regardless of whether they create the model for personal use in Excel using PowerPivot or server-based models that are deployed to Analysis Services. For those modelers, we show how to design, create, and manipulate the model so that it can be used to answer the types of questions that appear in business. For these users and consumers of model data, we also show how the model can be used to provide an intuitive and interactive report (both in Excel and Power View). Our goal for these users was to give them the skills so that they can build a model capable of answering their business questions.

The second category of users are those who are responsible for the maintenance of models in corporate environments. These are administrators who must ensure that the corporate model data is up-to-date and secure. For these users we show tricks and techniques to deploy the model and keep it running smoothly.

Conventions

In this book, you will find a number of styles of text that distinguish between different kinds of information. Here are some examples of these styles, and an explanation of their meaning.

Code words in text, database table names, folder names, filenames, file extensions, pathnames, dummy URLs, user input, and Twitter handles are shown as follows: "Each product is identified by a `product_id` value."

A block of code is set as follows:

```
=LOOKUPVALUE
  (Subcategory[Subcategory]
  , Subcategory[product_id],Products[Product ID]
)
```

New terms and **important words** are shown in bold. Words that you see on the screen, in menus or dialog boxes for example, appear in the text like this: "Then on the **PowerPivot** tab, click on the **Create Linked Table** button."

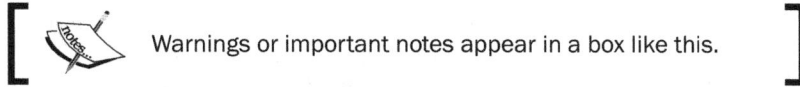

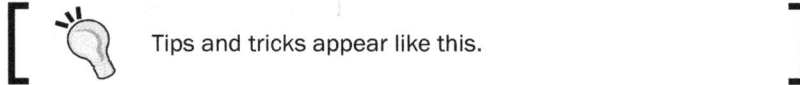

> Warnings or important notes appear in a box like this.

> Tips and tricks appear like this.

Reader feedback

Feedback from our readers is always welcome. Let us know what you think about this book—what you liked or may have disliked. Reader feedback is important for us to develop titles that you really get the most out of.

To send us general feedback, simply send an e-mail to `feedback@packtpub.com`, and mention the book title via the subject of your message.

If there is a topic that you have expertise in and you are interested in either writing or contributing to a book, see our author guide on `www.packtpub.com/authors`.

Customer support

Now that you are the proud owner of a Packt book, we have a number of things to help you to get the most from your purchase.

Downloading the example code

You can download the example code files for all Packt books you have purchased from your account at `http://www.packtpub.com`. If you purchased this book elsewhere, you can visit `http://www.packtpub.com/support` and register to have the files e-mailed directly to you.

Errata

Although we have taken every care to ensure the accuracy of our content, mistakes do happen. If you find a mistake in one of our books—maybe a mistake in the text or the code—we would be grateful if you would report this to us. By doing so, you can save other readers from frustration and help us improve subsequent versions of this book. If you find any errata, please report them by visiting http://www.packtpub.com/submit-errata, selecting your book, clicking on the **errata submission form** link, and entering the details of your errata. Once your errata are verified, your submission will be accepted and the errata will be uploaded on our website, or added to any list of existing errata, under the Errata section of that title. Any existing errata can be viewed by selecting your title from http://www.packtpub.com/support.

Piracy

Piracy of copyright material on the Internet is an ongoing problem across all media. At Packt, we take the protection of our copyright and licenses very seriously. If you come across any illegal copies of our works, in any form, on the Internet, please provide us with the location address or website name immediately so that we can pursue a remedy.

Please contact us at copyright@packtpub.com with a link to the suspected pirated material.

We appreciate your help in protecting our authors, and our ability to bring you valuable content.

Questions

You can contact us at questions@packtpub.com if you are having a problem with any aspect of the book, and we will do our best to address it.

1
Getting Started with Excel

In this chapter, we will cover:

- ▶ Creating the model
- ▶ Managing the appearance of tables and fields
- ▶ Using tabular relationships to filter data
- ▶ Adding fields to tables
- ▶ Linking fields between tables
- ▶ Creating model calculations

Introduction

This chapter is designed as an introduction to **tabular modeling** by using **PowerPivot**. It shows the process by which a user imports data into PowerPivot for Excel, creates relationships between the datasets, and then reports on it.

The data used in this chapter is based on the orders of the fictitious bicycle company (named Adventure Works). Our data includes six datasets and they are:

- ▶ **Product list**: This shows some generic information about the products being sold (for example, the name, color, and size of the product). Each product is identified by a `product_id` value.
- ▶ **Product subcategories list**: This shows a subcategory that a product belongs to. The list shows the `product_id` value and the associated subcategory (by ID and Name).
- ▶ **Product categories list**: This shows the product category that a product belongs to. The list shows the `product_id` value and the associated category (by ID and Name).

> ▸ **Orders list**: This shows what orders have been placed by customers. The list includes an entry for each product that has been ordered. This data simulates a detailed extract from an operational source system.
>
> ▸ **Customer list**: This gives us information about the customer (for example, their names, countries, and states) by customer number.
>
> ▸ **Dates list**: This simply lists consecutive days defining information such as the month name, year, and half-year period of the date.

The tabular modeling lifecycle revolves around three primary steps. These are:

> ▸ Getting the data into the model
>
> ▸ Defining the relationships among tables
>
> ▸ Defining calculations based on business logic

This chapter examines these steps and allows the reader to become familiar with the tabular (PowerPivot) design environment.

Creating the model

An Excel workbook can only contain one tabular model and that one model contains tables of data (which may or may not be related). The first step to create a model is to import data into it. There are many techniques to do this—some techniques have advantages over others but for now, let's only consider the fact that we want to load data that exists in an Excel worksheet into the model.

> The installation instructions for PowerPivot in Excel 2010 are covered in the *Appendix, Installing PowerPivot and Sample Databases*, of this book.

Getting ready

Open the Excel workbook named `SalesBook` which is available from the Packt Publishing website to examine the worksheets within the book. Each sheet contains a dataset for `Products`, `Subcategories`, `Categories`, `Customers`, `Dates`, and `Sales`.

How to do it...

This recipe looks at importing data into the PowerPivot model through linked tables. These are very convenient to use when the data is stored in Excel. Additionally, once the data has been imported into PowerPivot, it retains a connection to the Excel table. This means that, when the data is changed in Excel, it can also be changed in the PowerPivot model.

1. Let's start by importing the product list. Select the **Product List** sheet and select cell A1.

2. Then, on the **PowerPivot** tab, click on the **Create Linked Table** button.

[Excel will automatically highlight the data range.]

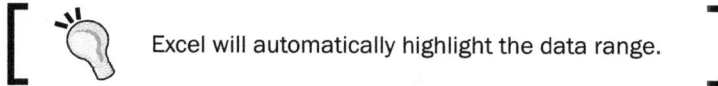

3. A small window will open confirming the data range with a checkbox for table headers. Select the checkbox and press **OK**.

4. The PowerPivot window will open and the data from the **Product List** sheet will be imported. Note that the table appears as a tab which is similar to Excel and is called **Table1**. Also, note that the PowerPivot window is a separate window than the Excel workbook, so that we can return to Excel.

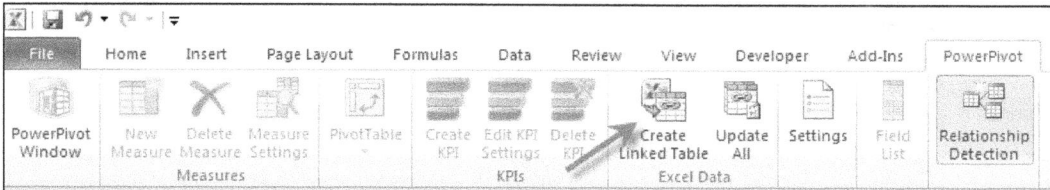

product_id	product_name	colour	size_range	size	Add Column
FR-R92B-58	HL Road Frame - B...	Black	54-58 CM	58	
FR-R92R-58	HL Road Frame - R...	Red	54-58 CM	58	
HL-U509-R	Sport-100 Helmet...	Red	NA	NA	
HL-U509	Sport-100 Helmet...	Black	NA	NA	
HL-U509-B	Sport-100 Helmet...	Blue	NA	NA	
CA-1098	AWC Logo Cap	Multi	NA	NA	
LJ-0192-S	Long-Sleeve Logo...	Multi	S	S	

5. Repeat this process for all the remaining datasets except Customers.

How it works...

When a linked table is created in PowerPivot, Excel creates a named range in the Excel workbook. This is then linked to the PowerPivot model (note that there is a small chain symbol before each of the tables). Also, note that the tables in Excel are formatted with alternate blue coloring. The named ranges can be viewed in Excel by clicking on the **Name Manager** button on the **Formulas** tab.

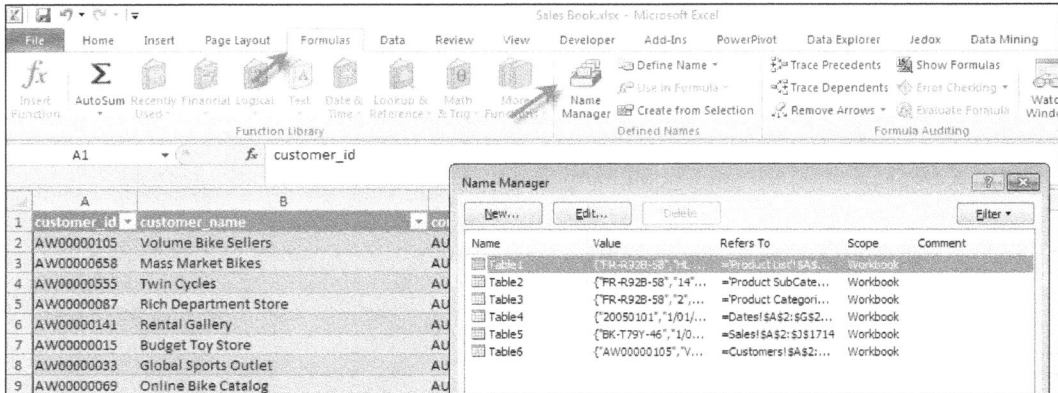

There's more...

A table (table range) is actually an Excel feature that PowerPivot utilizes. A table can be defined in Excel, given a meaningful name and then imported into PowerPivot, so that the name of the table in PowerPivot is the same as the named range in Excel.

Ensure that the Customers sheet is selected in Excel and also any cell in the Customers data is selected. In the **Home** tab, click on the **Format as Table** button, and choose a table style; the style chosen in the following screenshot is a relevant one:

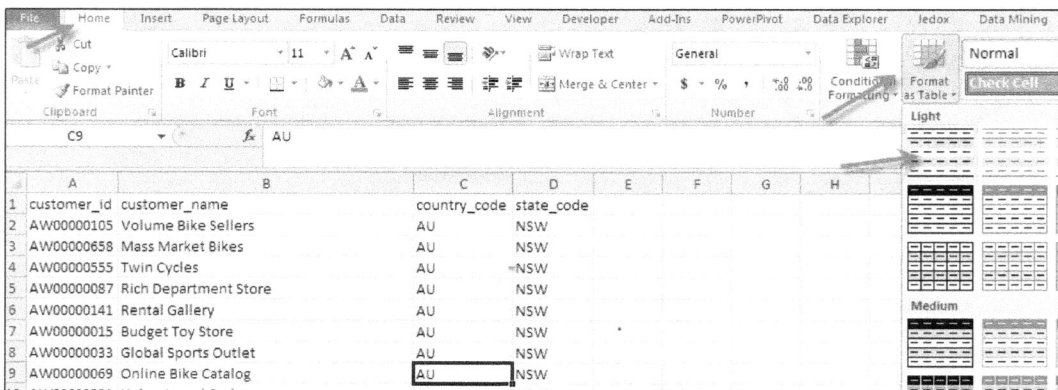

Note that the data is now formatted with alternating colors (based on the selected style). Return to the **Name Manager** window and double-click the table that relates to the `Customers` worksheet. A new window will open allowing you to edit the name, replace the name `Table6` with `Customers`, and click on **OK**. The `Table6` name is replaced by `Customers` in the **Name Manager** window.

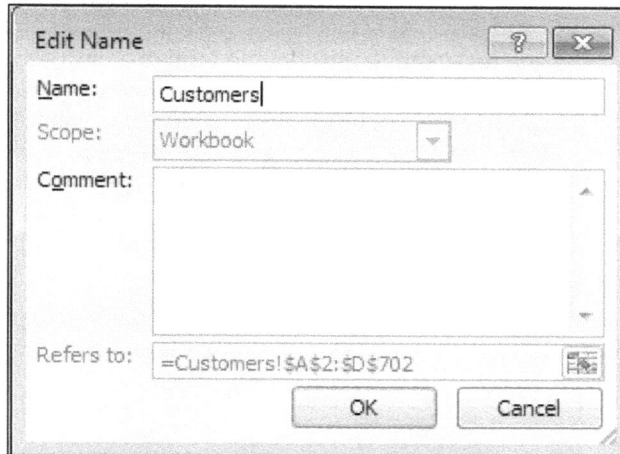

Now, create a linked table in the same manner as we did before and note that the name of the table imported into PowerPivot is `Customers`.

If you want to select an entire table in Excel, simply choose the table name from the **Name Box** drop-down list in the formula bar in the upper-left corner. This is shown in the following screenshot:

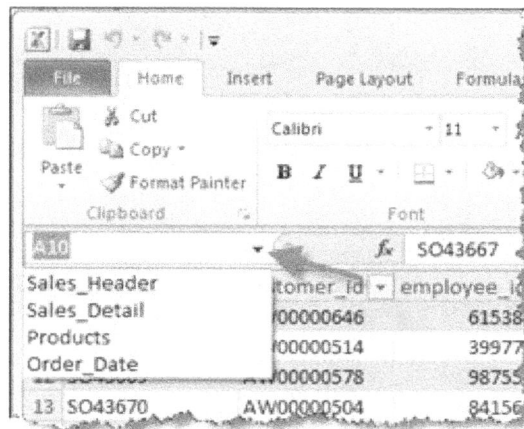

Managing the appearance of tables and fields

A PowerPivot workbook contains two products that allow the user to analyze data. Firstly, there is the xVelocity in-memory analytics engine (the tabular model) which is a columnar database embedded in the workbook. Secondly, there is a client tool that allows the model to be queried, it also displays the results to the user in the form of a pivot table or pivot chart. In Excel 2010, the client tool was restricted to pivot table functionality (for example, a pivot table or pivot chart). In Excel 2013, the tools set has been extended to include Power View. The important distinction here is that the client tool is used to present the model to the user. This recipe shows how to control the way the model is presented to the user.

Getting ready

This recipe uses the model that has already been created in the prior recipe *Creating the model*. If this model has not been created, follow the recipe to ensure that the model has been loaded with data.

How to do it...

Start from an existing model within PowerPivot.

1. Ensure that you are in the PowerPivot window (not Excel), then click on the **PivotTable** button in the **Home** Tab.

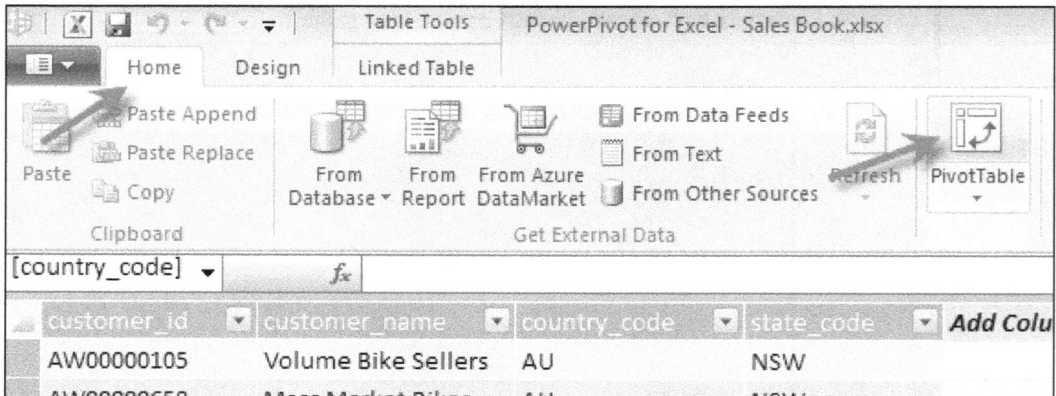

2. PowerPivot will switch back to the Excel window and a dialog will prompt for the location of the new pivot table. Select **New Worksheet** and click on **OK**.

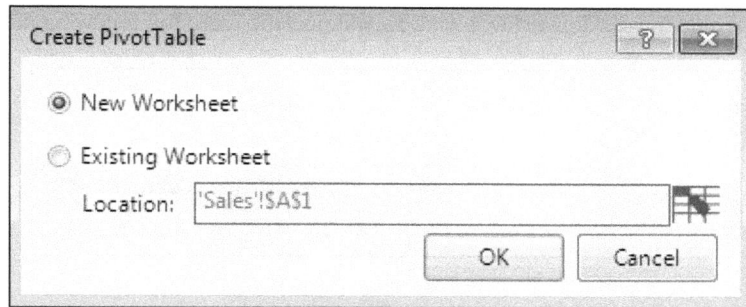

3. Excel will now show **PowerPivot Field List** and a pivot table work area. These are identified by the arrows in the following screenshot. Note that **PowerPivot Field List** shows tables from the model as nodes, with the fields from the model as children.

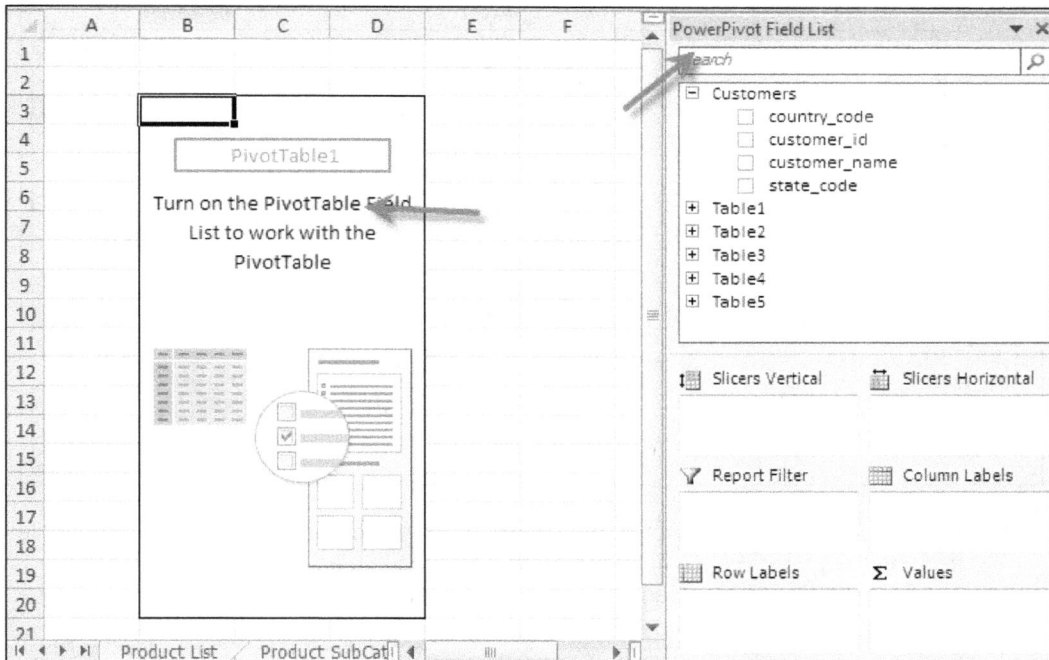

4. Return to the PowerPivot application window and double-click on the `Table1` tab. The name `Table1` will be in a blue background and rename it to `Products`. Repeat this exercise for the other tables (`Subcategory`, `Category`, `Dates`, and `Sales`). The table names in your PowerPivot window will now look like the following screenshot:

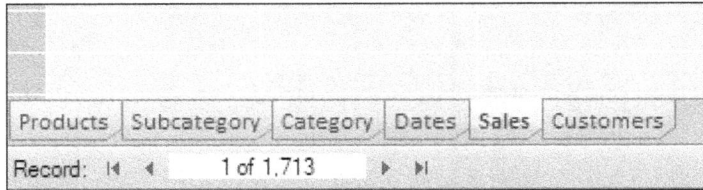

Products	Subcategory	Category	Dates	Sales	Customers

Record: ◄◄ ◄   1 of 1,713   ► ►►

5. Return to Excel and notice that **PowerPivot Field List** has detected a change in the model and prompts the user to refresh. Click on the **Refresh** button and note that the changes in the names of the tables are now reflected in the **PowerPivot Field List** panel.

Before	**After**
PowerPivot Field List ▼ ✕	PowerPivot Field List ▼ ✕
⚠ PowerPivot data was modified [Refresh]	Search 🔎
Search 🔎	⊞ Category
⊟ Customers	⊟ Customers
☐ country_code	☐ country_code
☐ customer_id	☐ customer_id
☐ customer_name	☐ customer_name
☐ state_code	☐ state_code
⊞ Table1	⊞ Dates
⊞ Table2	⊞ Products
⊞ Table3	⊞ Sales
⊞ Table4	⊞ Subcategory

6. Return to the PowerPivot application window and select the `Products` table. Double-click on the `product_id` field and enter `Product ID` as the new name. The field will have a blue background when its name can be changed.

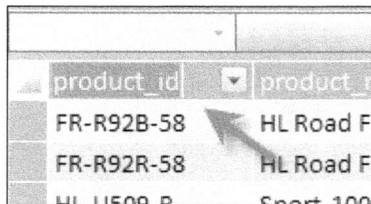

product_id ▼	product_n
FR-R92B-58	HL Road Fr
FR-R92R-58	HL Road Fr
HL-U509-R	Sport-100

7. Return to the PowerPivot window and update the remaining columns to the following names:

Table	Column	New name
Products	product_id	Product ID
Products	product_name	Product Name
Products	colour	Colour
Products	size_range	Size Range
Products	size	Size
Subcategory	subcategory_name	Subcategory
Category	category_name	Category
Dates	date	Day
Dates	year	Year
Dates	month_name	Month
Dates	half_name	Half
Sales	order_number	SO Number
Customers	customer_id	Customer ID
Customers	customer_name	Customer Name
Customers	country_code	Country Code
Customers	state_code	State Code

8. Return to Excel and refresh **PowerPivot Field List**. The column names will now display as those that were entered.

> You can also rename fields by right-clicking on the field and selecting **Rename Column** from the pop-up in PowerPivot. Alternatively, you can double-click on the field name (so that it changes the color of the field) and rename it.

9. Return to the PowerPivot window and select the Sales table. Right-click anywhere on the order_number_line field and select **Hide from Client Tools** in the pop-up window. Select all the fields product_id, order_date, and customer_id by clicking-and-dragging the mouse across the three fields and hide these fields too.

> PowerPivot mimics Excel in the way that you can select multiple fields by dragging your mouse across several columns (with the left button continually pressed). You can also select the first column, hold the *Shift* key, and select the final column.
>
> Unlike Excel, multiple columns cannot be selected by using the *Ctrl* key and selecting multiple fields.

10. Return to the PowerPivot window, refresh **PowerPivot Field List**, and expand the Sales table. Note that these fields no longer appear in the field list.

11. Add the Day field to the pivot by expanding the Dates table and selecting the checkbox next to the Day field. The column will be automatically added to the rows area of the pivot and will be displayed, as shown in the following screenshot:

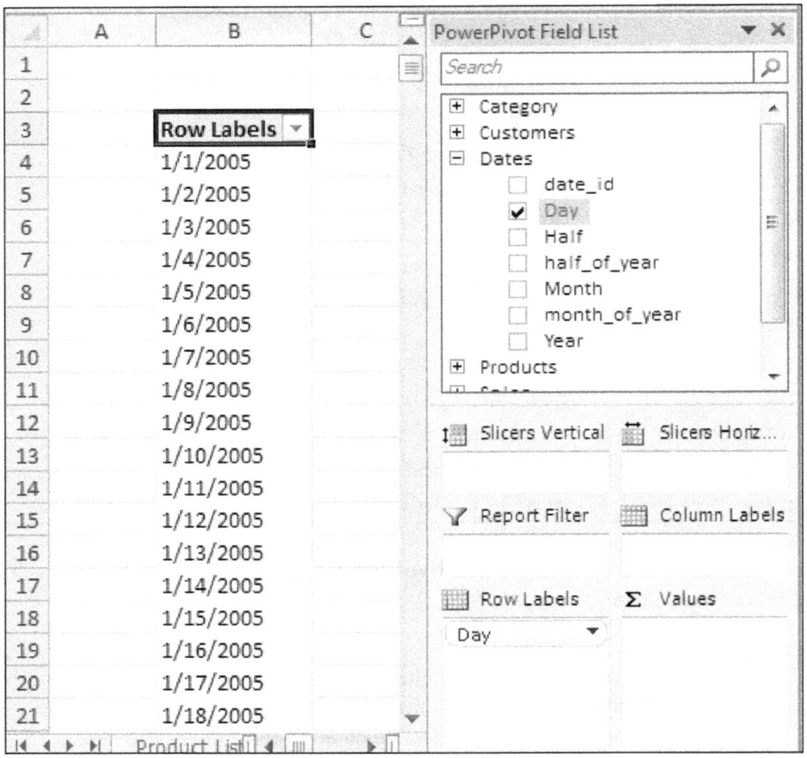

You can achieve the same result by dragging the Day field and dropping it in the **Row Labels** area of the pivot.

12. Return to the PowerPivot window and select the `Day` column. From the format list, select **More Dates Formats...**, and then select the **dd-MMM-yy** format from the list of available formats. The value presented will show a formatted sample of the data. Choose the item that shows **14-Mar-01**.

13. Return to Excel and refresh the pivot table. Note that the **PowerPivot Field List** panel may not indicate the change to the model. However, when the pivot table is refreshed, the data displays the new format.

14. In the `Sales` table, format the columns `unit_price`, `unit_cost`, `tax`, and `total_price` as a whole numeric number by selecting the columns and choosing **Currency** from the **Format** drop-down list.

How it works...

The semantic model defines the metadata structure of the model and includes information such as table names, column names, and data presentation formats. The model designer interacts with the semantic model through its presentation layer in a real-time manner (note that the model did not have to be deployed to a server), so that the changes made in the model are immediately available to the user.

The modeling environment behaves in a What You See Is What You Get (WYSIWYG) manner which means that any changes made to the design environment are reflected in the model that is presented to the user.

There's more...

There are two methods that the model designer can use to examine the structure of the model. So far, we have only examined the data view. The diagram view shows all tables and columns (including hierarchies) that are used within the model and presents them on a design surface. This is shown in the next recipe.

Using tabular relationships to filter data

In addition to table names, column names, and data formats, a semantic model defines how tables within a model relate to each other. This relationship is important because it defines the output of calculations (which are defined in the model). This recipe shows how to create relationships and the effect that these relationships have on the model.

Getting ready

This recipe assumes that the model in the recipe *Managing the appearance of tables and fields* has been created.

The reader should recognize that the model is designed to show sales information by product, date, and customer. This type of modeling scenario is commonly referred to as a **star schema** and is shown in the following diagram. The `Sales` table is referred to as a fact table (since it stores the data facts that we wish to analyze—sales amount, tax amount, and so on) and the other tables are referred to as dimension (subject) tables because they hold descriptive information.

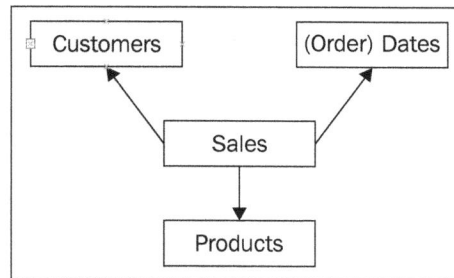

Extending the model further, the `Products` table is linked to the `Subcategory` table, and the `Subcategory` table is linked to the `Category` table. This is shown in the following diagram and is sometimes called a **snowflake schema**, since the dimension tables are not directly connected to the fact table:

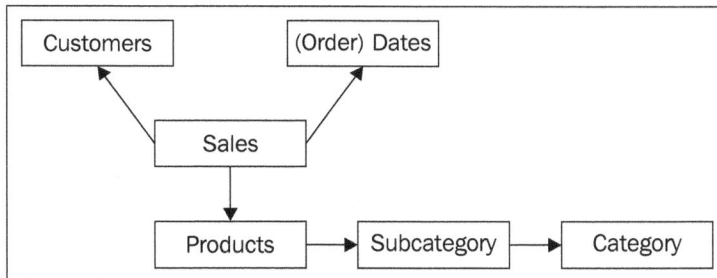

An important point to note, is that each dimension table has a unique identifying field, for example, a product can be uniquely identified in the `Products` table through the `product_id` field. This is commonly referred to as the primary key for the table.

In contrast, the referring column (`product_id` in the `Sales` table) can have many occurrences of the `product_id` field and is commonly referred to as the foreign key.

How to do it...

Start with the workbook that was developed in the prior recipe.

1. Drag the `Product Name` field onto the rows of the pivot table (under the `Row Labels` column) and the **Sales** column `total_price` onto values. Your screen should look like the following screenshot:

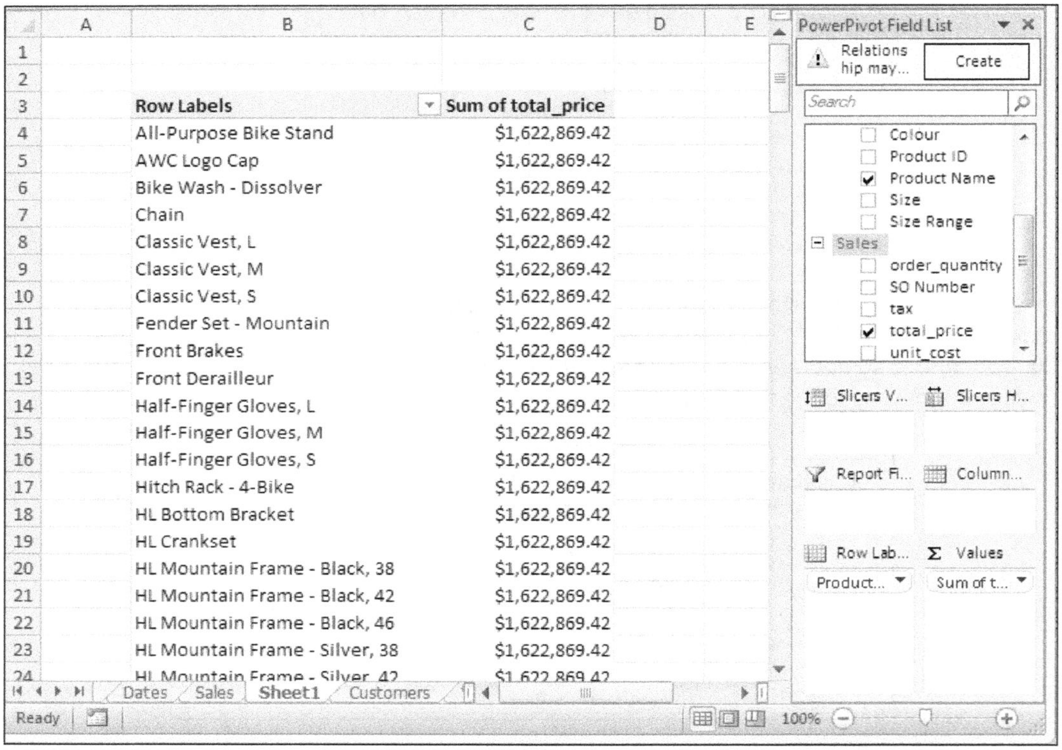

	A	B	C	D	E
1					
2					
3		Row Labels	Sum of total_price		
4		All-Purpose Bike Stand	$1,622,869.42		
5		AWC Logo Cap	$1,622,869.42		
6		Bike Wash - Dissolver	$1,622,869.42		
7		Chain	$1,622,869.42		
8		Classic Vest, L	$1,622,869.42		
9		Classic Vest, M	$1,622,869.42		
10		Classic Vest, S	$1,622,869.42		
11		Fender Set - Mountain	$1,622,869.42		
12		Front Brakes	$1,622,869.42		
13		Front Derailleur	$1,622,869.42		
14		Half-Finger Gloves, L	$1,622,869.42		
15		Half-Finger Gloves, M	$1,622,869.42		
16		Half-Finger Gloves, S	$1,622,869.42		
17		Hitch Rack - 4-Bike	$1,622,869.42		
18		HL Bottom Bracket	$1,622,869.42		
19		HL Crankset	$1,622,869.42		
20		HL Mountain Frame - Black, 38	$1,622,869.42		
21		HL Mountain Frame - Black, 42	$1,622,869.42		
22		HL Mountain Frame - Black, 46	$1,622,869.42		
23		HL Mountain Frame - Silver, 38	$1,622,869.42		
24		HL Mountain Frame - Silver, 42	$1,622,869.42		

PowerPivot Field List

Relationship may... Create

Search

- Colour
- Product ID
- ✔ Product Name
- Size
- Size Range
- ⊟ Sales
  - order_quantity
  - SO Number
  - tax
  - ✔ total_price
  - unit_cost

Slicers V... Slicers H...

Report Fi... Column...

Row Lab... Σ Values
Product... ▼ Sum of t... ▼

Dates / Sales / Sheet1 / Customers

Ready   100%

2. Return to the PowerPivot window and select the `product_id` field and then click on the **Create Relationship** button (in the **Design** tab). A new window will open asking you to define the related (lookup) table and column.

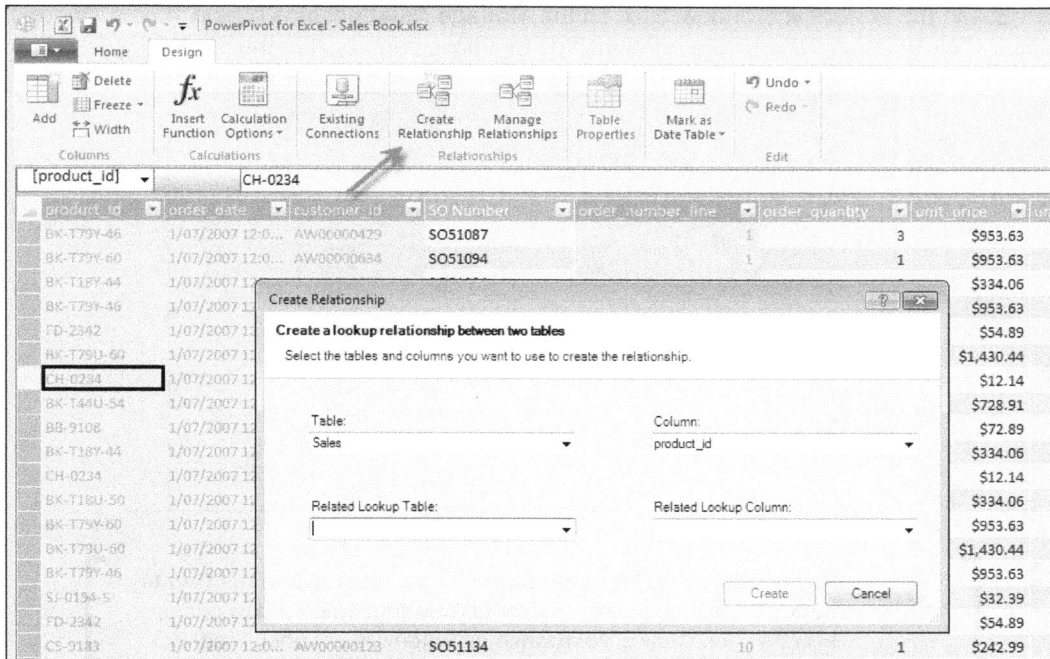

3. Select the **Products** option from the **Related Lookup Table** drop-down list and `Product ID` from the **Related Lookup Column** drop-down list. The **Create** button is now enabled. Click on **Create**.

4. Return to the pivot table and refresh the model. The values for the **Sum of total_price** field have updated to reflect the total for each product.

5. Now, create relationships between the following tables and columns:

Source table	Source column	Related table	Related column
Sales	customer_id	Customers	Customer ID
Sales	order_date	Dates	Day

Downloading the example code

You can download the example code files for all Packt books you have purchased from your account at `http://www.packtpub.com`. If you purchased this book elsewhere, you can visit `http://www.packtpub.com/support` and register to have the files e-mailed directly to you.

6. In the PowerPivot window, click on the **Manage Relationships** button. A new window will open showing all the relationships that have been built in the model.

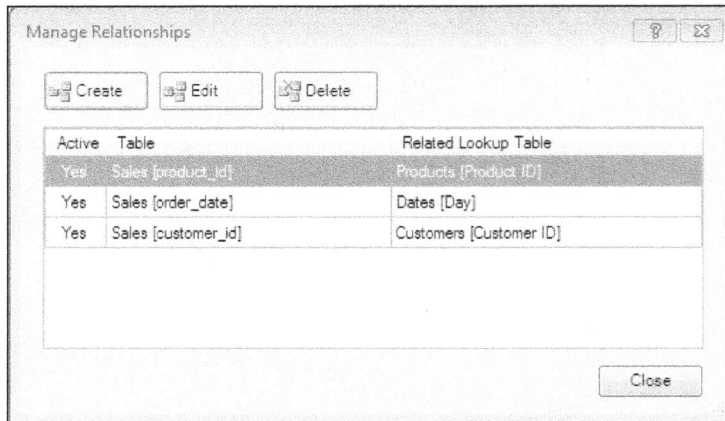

> Relationships can be created using this window. When the **Create** button is clicked, the same **Create Relationships** window opens. However, the **Create Relationships** window is not populated with the source table and columns.

7. Click on the **Diagram View** button in the **Home** menu to switch to the diagram modeling view. Your screen will now show tables and columns (rather than data) and look like the following screenshot. Note that previously defined relationships appear as lines that connect tables.

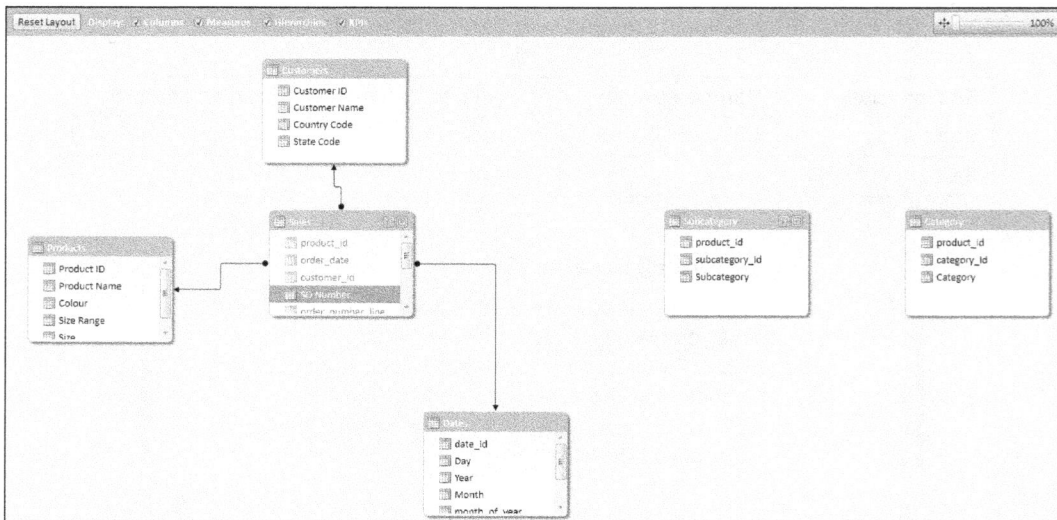

You can also switch between the data and diagram views by toggling the two buttons at the bottom-right side of the PowerPivot application status bar.

8. In the pivot table, replace the `Product Name` field with the `Category` field from the `category` table. The total value (`$1,662,869.42`) is repeated for all categories indicating that there is no relationship between the `Sales` table and `Category` table.

9. From the `Products` table, select the `Product ID` field, and drag it to the `product_id` field of the `Subcateogry` table. A new relationship will be created between `Products` and `Subcategory`. Use this method to create a relationship between the `Products` table and the `Category` table. Refresh the pivot table to ensure that the total value is not duplicated.

10. In the pivot table, drag the `Product ID` field from the `Products` table into the **Values** pane. The pivot table will now show the price and number of products for each category and will look like the following screenshot:

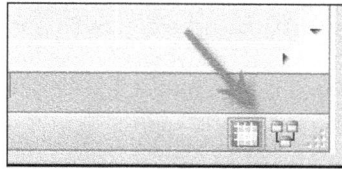

How it works...

The model has been extended to show two things. Firstly, by defining relationships between tables within the model, we have defined the filtering path for the data. This path is used to restrict rows between tables that have a relationship. Secondly, by adding a calculation (**Sum of total_price** and **Count of Product ID**), we have created measures that apply an aggregation function to the model fields. These are special types of measures within PowerPivot and are referred to as implicit measures (because the model implicitly defines a calculation for the field).

Relationships define how one table relates to another. In order to define a relationship, the join must occur on a field that has unique values in one of the tables (this is commonly called a primary key). The table that has the field with unique values is commonly called the **related** table. This can be seen in the diagram view, as shown in the following screenshot with the direction of the arrows on the relationships. Consider the Products table (which has a unique field product_id) that is related to the Sales table (through the product_id field in that table), but only the Products table needs to have a unique product_id. It is also said that the product_id field relates to many records in the Sales table. This can be seen by the direction of the arrow between Sales and Products, the related table has the arrow pointing towards it.

Relationships are important because they define how data is filtered and calculated when it is presented to the user.

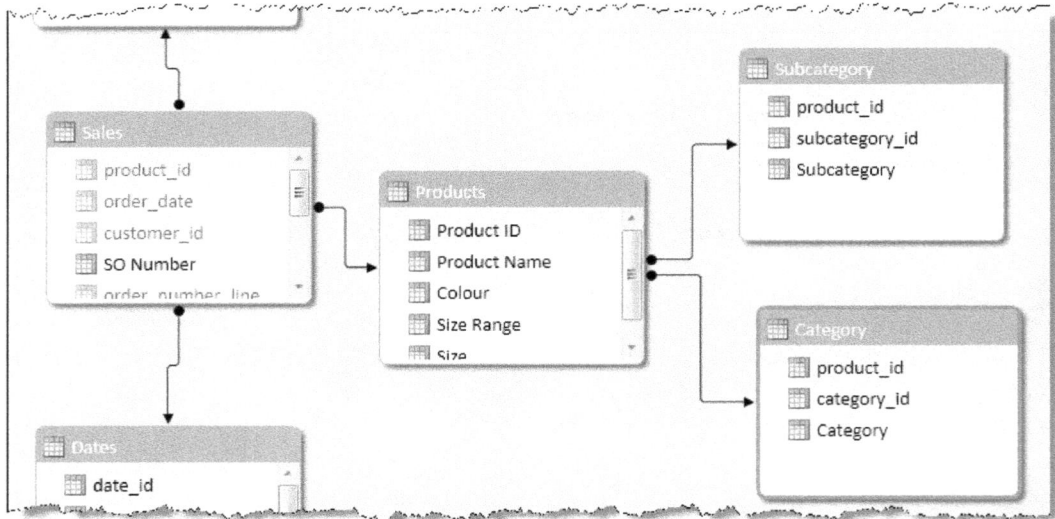

Relationships are the primary mechanisms with the model that are used to filter data and perform calculations. That is, the relationship defines how data is filtered when values are shown to the user. Although this is a new concept, the concept of relationships is important because they have important implications with the way that the model determines what data to show to the user. Consider the pivot table shown in the following screenshot—Subcategory on rows and Sum of total_price, Count of Product ID, and Count of category_id as measures:

	A	B	C	D	E
1					
2					
3		Row Labels	Sum of total_price	Count of Product ID	Count of category_id
4		Bike Racks	$12,424.80	1	197
5		Bike Stands		1	197
6		Bottles and Cages	$362.27	3	197
7		Bottom Brackets	$4,397.84	3	197
8		Brakes	$5,559.30	2	197
9		Caps	$1,029.36	1	197
10		Chains	$850.08	1	197
11		Cleaners	$577.17	1	197

Now, consider the relationship defined in the model. This is summarized in the following screenshot:

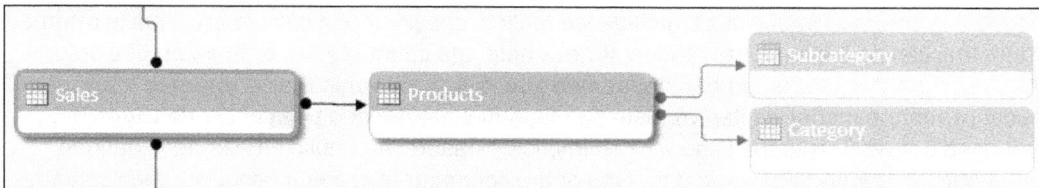

The rows in the pivot show the subcategory which defines a filter for each row (that is a filter for each subcategory). This filter can then be applied to the `Products` table, which in turn is applied to the `Sales` table. It might be better to say that the rows of the `Sales` table are filtered by the `Products` table and then those rows are filtered by the `Subcategory` table. This is why the calculations `Sum of total_price` and `Count of Product ID` show the correct values. The filter on rows of the `Sales` table and rows of the `Products` table can be applied in the direction of the arrows of the relationships.

However, this is not the case when `Subcategory` is shown with data from the `Category` table—a filter will only be applied in the direction that a relationship is created. This is why the calculation `Count of category_id` shows the same number for each subcategory. With the subcategory on rows, a filter is created which can filter the `Products` table but this filter cannot then applied in an upstream manner to the `Category` table.

The application of filters may seem unintuitive at first, especially with a relationship design such as the one among `Products`, `Category`, and `Subcategory`, but in reality the model should be designed so that the filters can be applied in a single direction. There is also, the question of unmatched values between fields used in the relationship and how they are treated by the model. For example, what would happen if we had a `product_id` field in the `Sales` table that did not have a match in the `Products` table? Would this even be allowed in the model? The tabular model handles this situation very elegantly. The model allows this situation (without error), and unmatched values are assigned to a blank placeholder. For example, if there was a product in the `Sales` table and no product in the `Products` table, it would be shown as blank when `Products`, `Category`, or `Subcategory` is used in the pivot.

We have also indicated that the model automatically created implicit measures. The term measure is common in business intelligence tools to specify that a calculated value is returned. Often, this can be a simple calculation, for example, the count of rows or the sum of a field. The important thing to remember is that measure is a single value that is returned from the model (when the model is filtered). Usually, measures are defined by a model designer, but they need not be. This is the case with an implicit measure. An implicit measure is defined automatically, depending on the data type of the column that is being used. Numeric columns are automatically summed, whereas text columns are automatically counted.

There's more...

The aggregation function of an implicit measure is initially set by the underlying data type. However, the user can change this within the pivot table by editing the measure in the pivot table. This can be done in the following manner:

1. Alter the pivot table so that it shows subcategory on rows and `total_profit` as values. By default, the measure will show `Sum of total_profit`. Right-click on the measure and select **Edit Measure...** from the pop-up window.

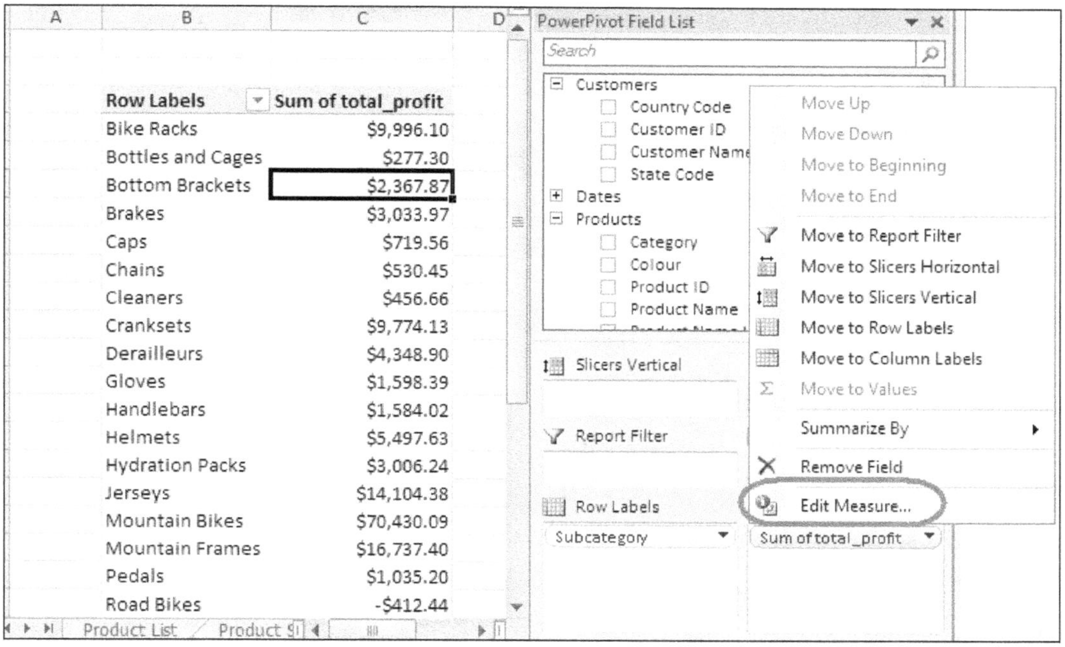

Row Labels	Sum of total_profit
Bike Racks	$9,996.10
Bottles and Cages	$277.30
Bottom Brackets	$2,367.87
Brakes	$3,033.97
Caps	$719.56
Chains	$530.45
Cleaners	$456.66
Cranksets	$9,774.13
Derailleurs	$4,348.90
Gloves	$1,598.39
Handlebars	$1,584.02
Helmets	$5,497.63
Hydration Packs	$3,006.24
Jerseys	$14,104.38
Mountain Bikes	$70,430.09
Mountain Frames	$16,737.40
Pedals	$1,035.20
Road Bikes	-$412.44

2. A new window will open, displaying the aggregation function with the measure. Select **Average** from the function list and change the measure name to `Average Profit`. The **Measure Settings** window should look like the following screenshot:

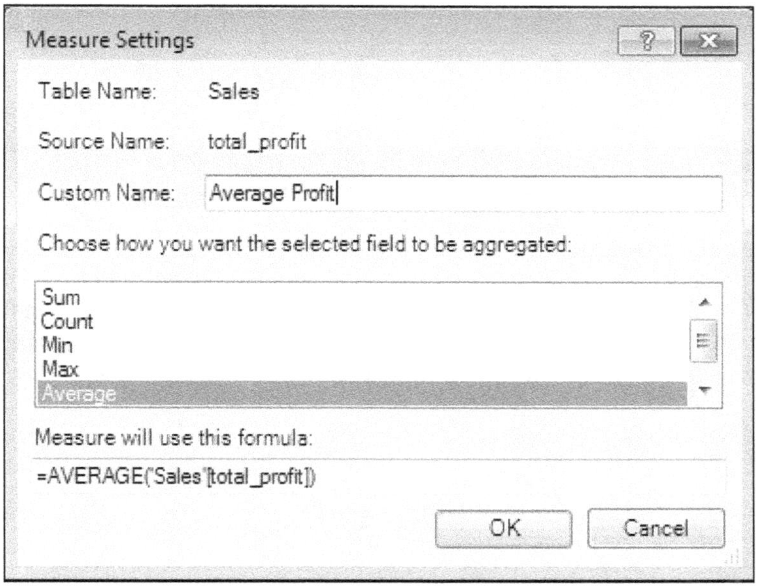

3. Also, notice that a formula is used to define the measure, for `Average Profit`, the formula is `=AVERAGE('Sales'[total_profit])`. Click on the **OK** button and note that the pivot table now contains the new measure `Average Profit`.

Implicit measures that have been created in the model can be seen by exposing the measures in the **Advanced** tab of the PowerPivot window (the **Advanced** tab must be activated). This is shown in the following screenshot:

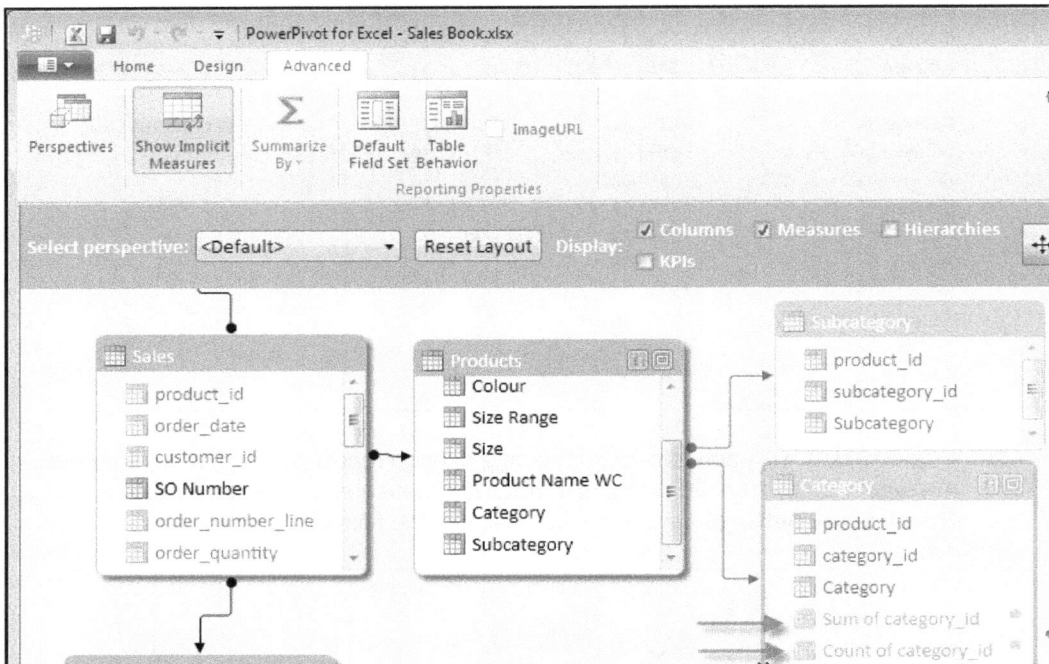

Adding fields to tables

The model designer is often required to add additional fields to tables, so that the information presented to the user is better suited for decision-making purposes. This can include creating new fields that are combinations of other fields within the same table or a calculation that is dependent on data in another table. This recipe looks at the first of these options to create new fields that use other fields within the same table.

Getting ready

The model used in this recipe starts with the model that was created in the previous recipe *Using tabular relationships to filter data*.

How to do it...

1. Switch to the data view in the PowerPivot window and select the `Products` table. Select the `Colour` column by right-clicking on the column header and selecting **Insert Column** from the pop-up menu (note that the entire column must be selected). The new column is inserted to the left of the `Colour` column. Change the name of the **CalculatedColumn1** to `Product Name WC` (product name with code).

Produ..	Product Name	CalculatedColumn1	Colour	Size Range	Size
FR-R92B-58	HL Road Frame - Black, 58		Black	54-58 CM	58
FR-R92R-58	HL Road Frame - Red, 58		Red	54-58 CM	58
HL-U509-R	Sport-100 Helmet, Red		Red	NA	NA
HL-U509	Sport-100 Helmet, Black		Black	NA	NA
HL-U509-B	Sport-100 Helmet, Blue		Blue	NA	NA
CA-1098	AWC Logo Cap		Multi	NA	NA
LJ-0192-S	Long-Sleeve Logo Jersey, S		Multi	S	S

2. Enter the following formula into any cell of the new column.

    ```
    =[Product Name]&" (" & [Product ID] & ")"
    ```

    All rows of the table will be automatically populated.

3. Switch to the `Sales` table. Double-click on the header row of the last column (the current header is **Add Column**) and change the name of the column to `total_profit`. Enter the following formula into any cell of the **Profit** column with the format of the column as currency.

    ```
    =[total_price] - [unit_cost] - [tax]
    ```

> The designer has two built-in functions that enable the easy creation of formulas. If the formula is being typed, an intellisense window will open in the formula bar, and show a list of objects that match what is being typed. Simply navigate to the desired column (or cell in the measure grid) and start typing, then press return to use the provided intellisense option (you can use arrow keys to select a function, table and column). Alternatively, a column or table name can be included in the formula by clicking on the column or table while the formula is being typed.

How it works...

This recipe introduces **Data Analysis Expressions** (**DAX**) as the language that is used in tabular modeling. From this recipe, we can see that the DAX language is very similar to an Excel calculation (there are some noticeable differences which are addressed in chapters). Also, note that in DAX, columns are referred to instead of cells. Furthermore, many Excel functions work exactly the same in DAX as they do in Excel.

In calculating the value for each row, a special filter is applied in the calculation. In these examples where the fields being used in the formula reside on a single row, the filter automatically restricts the value to that of the row. The application of filtering in this manner is commonly referred to as a row filter or a row filter context.

Linking fields between tables

There may be a requirement to create fields in a table that contain data from a separate table. In Excel, this would usually be achieved with a VLOOKUP function.

The sales model that has been developed in this chapter contains three tables which define Products, Subcategory, and Category. When the user browses the model in a pivot table, each of these tables appear as tables in the **PowerPivot Field List** pane. However, in this model, the category and subcategory directly relate to the product and it is our intent to show these fields in the Products table.

Getting ready

This recipe assumes that the sales model created in the *Adding fields to tables* recipe is available and that the appropriate relationships exist among the Product, Subcategory, and Category tables.

How to do it...

Start by opening the PowerPivot window and then perform the following steps:

1. Switch to the data view and create two new columns in the Products table titled Category and Subcategory. In the Category column enter the following formula:

    =RELATED(Category[Category])

2. In the Subcategory column enter the following formula:

    =LOOKUPVALUE
      (Subcategory[Subcategory]
      , Subcategory[product_id],Products[Product ID]
)

> Formulas can be multiline (just like in Excel). To move to the next line when typing simply press *Alt + Enter*.

Hide the Subcategory and Category tables in the model by right-clicking on the tables tab and selecting **Hide from Client Tools** from the pop-up menu. Note that the hidden tables are still visible in the data view and diagram view, although they are now more transparent.

How it works...

These two formulas achieve the same result but in different ways.

The `related` function returns the specified column, based on the relationship within the data model. This can span more than one table (for example, a related table to the `Category` table could be referenced from the `Products` table), however, a relationship must be defined between all the *linking* tables that are spanned by the formula. Furthermore, because the formula relies on these relationships (that is, those defined within the model), the formula will not result in an error since the model enforces the integrity defined by model relationships.

The `LOOKUPVALUE` function is quite different from the `related` function because it does not utilize or rely on a relationship within the model. That is, `LOOKUPVALUE` would still return the same results had the relationship not be defined between the `Products` and `Subcategory` tables. Furthermore, the `LOOKUPVALUE` function can use multiple columns as its reference (to lookup) which may be beneficial when a desired value in another table cannot be related to the source data through a single field. Note that relationships can only be defined on single columns. However, unlike the `RELATED` function, the `LOOKUPVALUE` function may return an error when more than one match can be found in the lookup table.

Both formulas return results by creating a row context filter for each row in the source table.

It is considered best to utilize the relationship wherever possible. Therefore, the use of the `RELATED` function is preferred over the `LOOKUPVALUE` function. Furthermore, the `RELATED` function makes the model simpler for others to understand. However, the `LOOKUPVALUE` function does have some benefits. It allows the value to be determined, based on multiple search conditions. The syntax for `LOOKUPVALUE` is defined as:

```
LOOKUPVALUE ( <result_columnName>
  , <search_columnName>, <search_value>
  [, <search_columnName>, <search_value>]
...)
```

Here, a `result_columnName` column is returned from a target table where search conditions are satisfied. These conditions are defined by a `search_columnName` parameter and a `search_value` parameter. This means that we specify the column (in the lookup table) and the value that should be searched for—this is the field in the current table.

Creating model calculations

The sales model that has been developed in this chapter allows the user to interrogate data from the order list by products, customers, and dates. In doing so, the user can create an implicit measure so that the underlying data is aggregated according to the current filter context. The aggregation function of implicit measures is determined by the underlying data type of the column that is used for the measure. This method offers the user the ability to create and show simple calculations from the model data. However, it does not create a robust model because the calculations aren't readily selectable by the user and the calculation definition is not conformed within the model.

This recipe introduces calculations which are contained within the model and presented to the user as measures. DAX (the tabular model language introduced in *Adding fields to tables* recipe) is used to define measures, so that it can explicitly use these measures in the model. Furthermore, the ability to create measures through a complex DAX allows the model designer a larger degree of flexibility than is involved with implicit measures.

Getting ready

This recipe assumes that the sales model created in *Linking fields between tables* recipe is available and that the appropriate relationships exist among the `Product`, `Subcategory`, and `Category` tables.

By default, a table in **Data View** will have a horizontal line that does not show any data. This is referred to as the **calculation area**. If this is not visible, ensure that the **Calculation Area** button is selected in the **Home** menu.

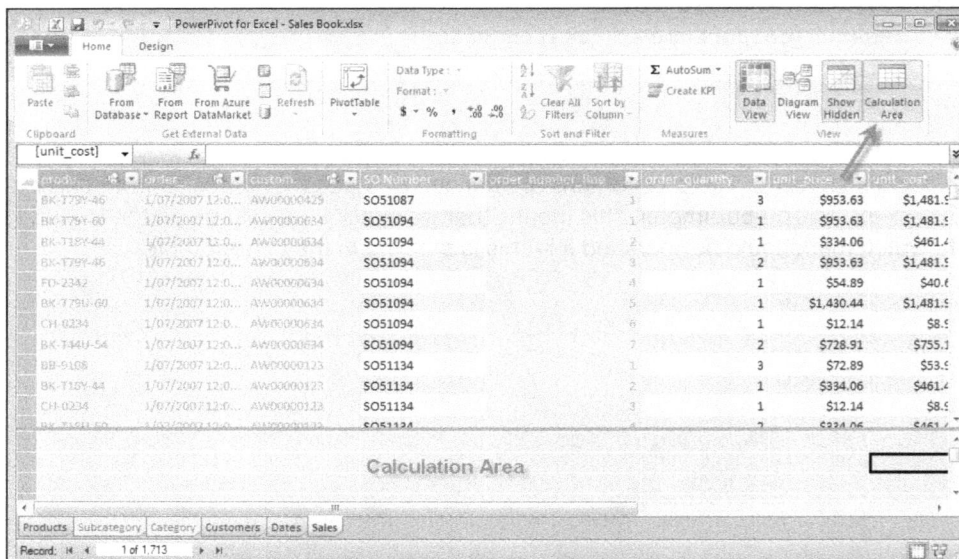

How to do it...

There are many ways to create simple measures. Let's start with the automatic creation of measures.

1. Select any cell in the `order_quantity` field. Then, from the ribbon, select the **SUM** function from the **AutoSum** drop-down. A new calculation will be created in the calculation area as:

   ```
   Sum of order_quantity:=SUM([order_quantity])
   ```

2. In the formula bar, select the name of the measure (`Sum of order_quantity`) and rename it to `Total Order Quantity`. The calculation should now look like this:

   ```
   Total Order Quantity:=SUM([order_quantity])
   ```

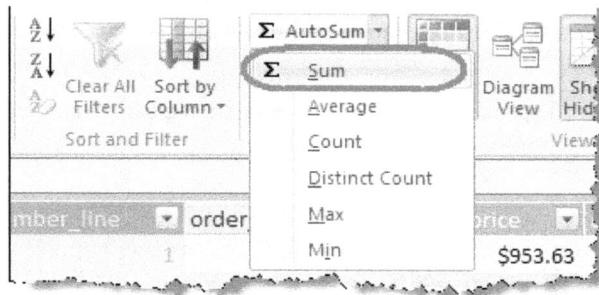

3. Right-click on the calculation, select **Format Cells...** from the pop-up menu, and specify the format as a number format—(decimal number) with zero decimal places and click on the **User 1000 separator (,)** checkbox.

4. Select this group of columns: `unit_cost`, `tax`, `total_price`, and `total_profit`, by selecting the `unit_cost` column and dragging the mouse across to the `total_profit` column.

5. Click on the **AutoSum** button to create your calculations for these columns.

6. Rename the measures to `Total Cost`, `Total Tax`, `Total Price`, and `Total Profit` respectively with the same format as `Total Order Quantity`. Note that the format of the number is inherited as currency.

7. Select the cell in the calculation area under the `unit_price` column and type the formula:

   ```
   Average Price:=AVERAGE([unit_price])
   ```

Intellisence provides a list of formulas available (based on the expression that is entered) and a description of the function, as shown in the following screenshot:

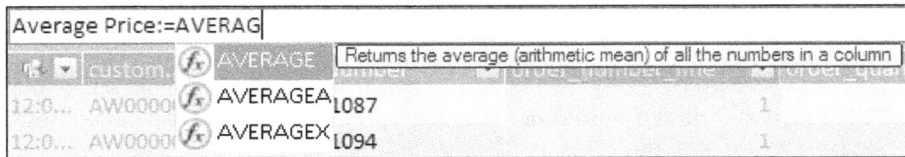

```
Average Price:=AVERAG
```

		AVERAGE	Returns the average (arithmetic mean) of all the numbers in a column

AVERAGEA
AVERAGEX

8. Hide the following fields of the `Sales` table: `order_quantity`, `unit_price`, `tax`, `total_price`, and `total_profit`.

9. Return to the **PowerPivot Field List** pane (in Excel) and refresh the model. Existing implicit calculations that were based on existing fields are removed from the model and the `Sales` table now includes the additional measures which were created. These measures can now be placed in the pivot tables (value) field list.

> Explicit measure cannot be used in a slicer, filter, or as row or column labels.

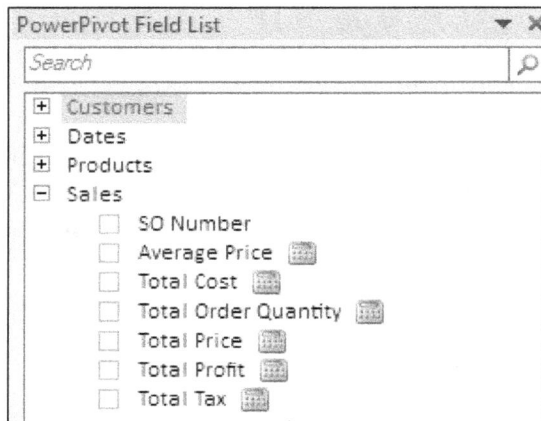

PowerPivot Field List

Search

- Customers
- Dates
- Products
- Sales
  - SO Number
  - Average Price
  - Total Cost
  - Total Order Quantity
  - Total Price
  - Total Profit
  - Total Tax

How it works...

Measures that are created in the calculation area operate in the same manner as implicit measures. That is, the aggregation function is applied to the filtered data specified by the row and filter context within the client tool.

Because the measures are explicitly defined in the model they are called explicit measures and interpreted by the client tool as measures (many client tools detect an explicit measure as a special type of field and treat it differently than a table's standard field or dimension field).

There's more...

By default, the tabular model created in PowerPivot will display the model through a PowerPivot pivot table. This shows the model in its tabular form where measures and columns are shown with respect to the tables that they relate to. For example, the measures created in the *Creating model calculations* recipe appear under the `Sales` table node. In order to compare this (tabular) view with that of a traditional OLAP client, simply do the following:

1. Ensure that a cell within the pivot table is selected.

2. Activate **PivotTable Field List** by clicking on the **Field List** button from the **Options** tab of the **PivotTable Tools** menu.

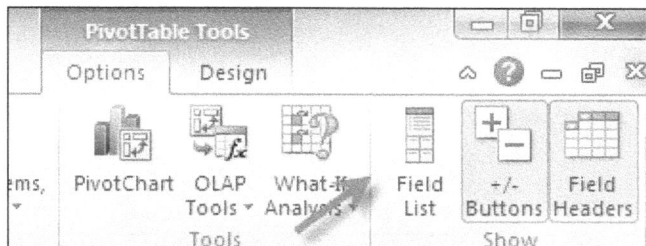

3. The **PivotTable Field List** window opens, which shows the tabular model in the multidimensional (client) format.

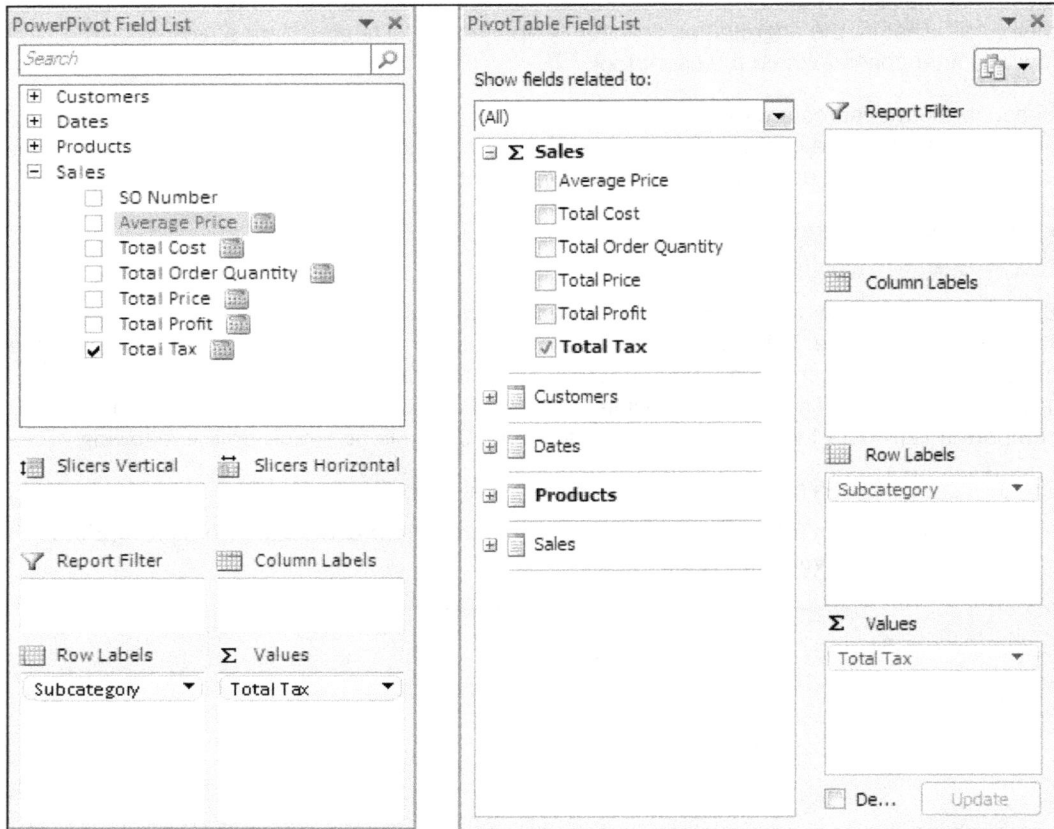

The client tool (**PivotTable Field List**) shows the model in a different format and represents how a client tool interpretation of the model would be shown. Here, the measures are shown in measure groups and are not included as table objects.

2
Importing Data

In this chapter we will cover ways to import data from different types of data sources. This includes:

- ▸ Importing data as text
- ▸ Importing data from databases
- ▸ Managing connections and tables
- ▸ Using data feeds

Introduction

Prior to the introduction of **tabular modeling**, which is now commonly known as **Business Intelligence Semantic Models** (**BISM**), Microsoft relied on its multidimensional storage model (MOLAP) for Analysis Services (analytical) database. In fact, multidimensional refers to a method of storage, which is still a viable option for enterprise business intelligence through **SQL Server Analysis Services** (**SSAS**). The term BISM is not unique to tabular modeling—it also relates to the semantic abstraction of a data model within the MOLAP engine. However, whenever BISM is discussed, it usually relates to tabular modeling (whether that be in PowerPivot or SSAS with a tabular storage mode). The storage engine for tabular modeling is also referred to as **xVelocity**.

Unlike the xVelocity engine of tabular models, the multidimensional model was basically designed to use a relational source (preferably a SQL Server) as its data source. Additionally, the multidimensional engine assumed that data would be provided through a relational and conformed data structure.

In contrast to this requirement for a single source of data, tabular modeling is designed to support many different data sources which can then be combined in the model as a part of the modeling process. This offers the modeler the ability to combine multiple forms of data within a model, and therefore provides a richer modeling experience. By including additional data sources, model development time can also be greatly reduced, because there is no requirement to source the data from a traditional data mart (or data warehouse).

This chapter examines importing of data from various sources, and managing that data once it has been imported.

> The previously discussed statement is not meant to imply that highly optimized models do not require well-structured and conformed databases—they may, when processing times and calculations do not perform satisfactorily. However, one of the benefits of tabular modeling is the ability to apply it at many different levels within an organization. A departmental or subject area solution may be built from an OLTP database, with some information coming from text files, spreadsheets, and other non-traditional (and non-enterprise) sources.

Although there are many data sources available for import (including many different relational database engines), this chapter focuses on some of the more ad hoc ones used by analysts, including text files, reports from reporting services, and data feeds. We also examine how the connection to the database can be managed once it has been created in the tabular model.

Importing data as text

Tabular modeling natively supports the import of files with extensions of text (.txt), comma separated values (.csv), and tab separated values (.tab). Once a file to import has been defined, the user can specify the delimiter (column separator), and the importing interface scans the file to estimate the underlying data types for each column. Finally, the interface finishes the import process by loading the data according to this specification.

Getting ready

A text file to simulate the output file for the sales record header has been created and is available from the online resources for this chapter. This file includes the `sales_order_id`, `customer_id`, `employee_id`, `currency_id`, `customer_po_id`, `sales_territory_id`, `order_dt` (order date), `due_dt` (due date), `ship_dt` (ship date), and `sales_amount` fields.

The file will be imported as a table into PowerPivot (and the tabular model). A screenshot of the file is shown as follows:

```
1    sales_order_id,customer_id,employee_id,currency_id,customer_po
2    SO71774,AW00000609,191644724,USD,PO348186287,4,01-06-2008,10-06
3    SO71779,AW00000149,502097814,USD,PO19633118218,3,01-06-2008,10-
4    SO71783,AW00000024,191644724,USD,PO19343113609,4,01-06-2008,10-
5    SO71787,AW00000509,139397894,USD,PO18038111279,4,01-06-2008,10-
6    SO71794,AW00000678,668991357,CAD,PO17574111985,6,01-06-2008,10-
7    SO71796,AW00000420,191644724,USD,PO17052159664,4,01-06-2008,10-
8    SO71797,AW00000142,399771412,GBP,PO16501134889,10,01-06-2008,10
9    SO71807,AW00000443,668991357,CAD,PO14935135211,6,01-06-2008,10-
10   SO71808,AW00000408,234474252,CAD,PO14761198562,6,01-06-2008,10-
```

How to do It...

Most data imports can be managed from the PowerPivot window:

1. Launch the PowerPivot window.

2. In the **Home** tab, click on the **From Text** button from the **Get External Data** grouping.

3. Call the `Sales Header TXT` connection.

4. Ensure that the file type Comma Separated Files (`.csv`) is selected from the drop-down box.

5. Navigate to the resources listed in *Chapter 2, Importing Data* and select the `02_master.csv` file.

6. Click on **Open**.

7. A new window will open showing the file structure. Ensure that **Comma (,)** is selected from the **Column Separator** drop-down list, and that the **Use first row as column headers** checkbox is ticked.

8. Confirm the import by clicking on **Finish**, as shown in the following screenshot:

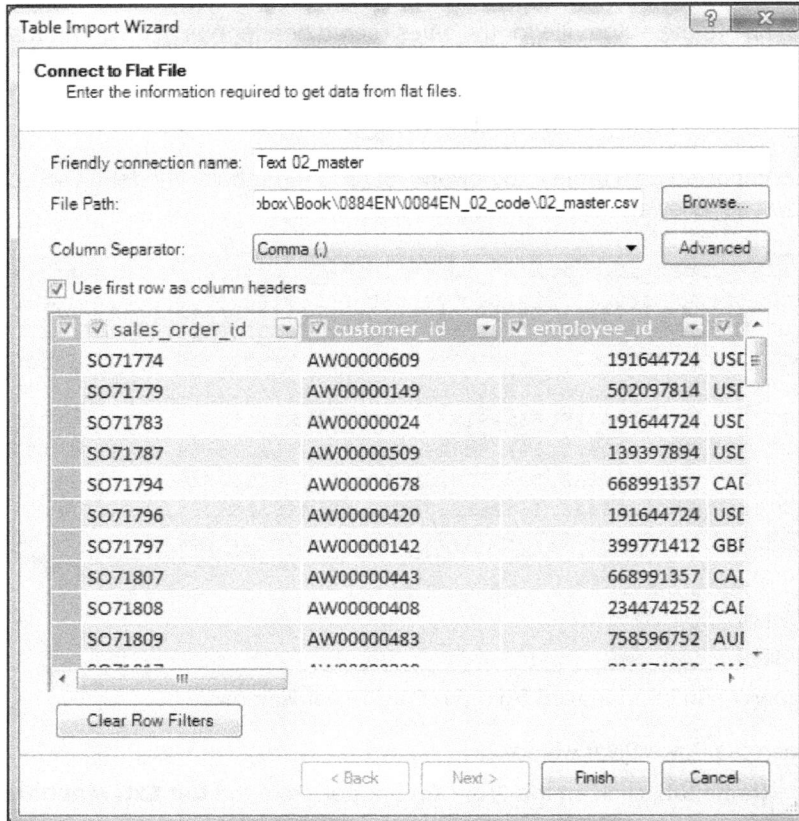

9. The data will load (click on **Close** to exit the **Table Import Wizard** window).

> The Table Import Wizard displays the data that will be imported in columns and rows. Generally, it may be said that this grid is shared across all types of imports. You can choose not to import a particular column by deselecting the column from the header field selection (note that in the preceding screenshot, all columns are selected). Additionally, the amount of data to be imported can be filtered by selecting the drop-down arrow next to a field and applying a filter through the graphical interface. It is considered best practice to import only those columns which are needed in the model, because the extra columns or rows will increase the size of the model.

How it works...

Once the file name has been provided, the **Table Import Wizard** window uses a text driver to scan the first 200 rows of the file and determine the data type of each column. The text driver then uses this definition to import all the data for the file. The columns order_dt, due_dt, and ship_dt have been defined as dates, even though the file did not explicitly specify a date type (after all it is text).

Once the wizard has determined the data types for columns, it will use these types for the entire load. This may create issues where the value within the file does not conform to the data type specifications. In such a situation, the specific value will be discarded from the load. The row will be imported even if all the values are discarded. This type of situation can occur when a numeric value is expected, and a text value is found in the file, or the expected date format for the import cannot be derived from the underlying date value. For example, when the column format is DD-MM-YY, and the value follows the format MM-DD-YY.

The wizard can be defined for different delimiters. Tab, Comma, Semicolon, Space, Colon, and Vertical Bar (Pipe) are supported. This is regardless of the file extension (so you could import a .csv file with a Tab delimiter). However, the importer only allows you to import files that have extensions of .csv, .tab, or .txt. Additionally, you can specify if the first row of the file contains headings (and these are also imported).

There's more...

Although you can specify standard delimiters, the file may contain an unsupported character as its delimiter, and the data format chosen by the wizard may simply be the wrong type for the file. To overcome these issues (or the issues they may create), the text driver defaults (which are defined by the Wizard) can be overridden, so that the input file can be fully defined as load time. This is done by using a defining file titled schema.ini. This file needs to be saved in the same location as the file being imported. This offers the modeler full control over the specification of the import file. Consider the previous text import file with the following changes;

- The delimiter is now a tilde (~)
- The date format is MM-DD-YYYY (note that the local for the machine used in this book specified DD-MM-YYYY)

Repeat the recipe using the `02_master_tilde.csv` file ensuring that the `schema.ini` file exists in the same directory. When the Wizard loads, an information box at the bottom of the window will indicate the presence of a `schema.ini` file, and this file will be used to specify import settings, as shown in the following screenshot:

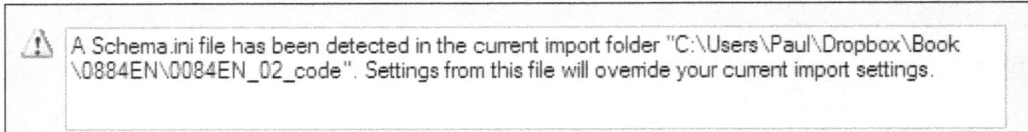

> ⚠ A Schema.ini file has been detected in the current import folder "C:\Users\Paul\Dropbox\Book \0884EN\0084EN_02_code". Settings from this file will override your current import settings.

The `schema.ini` file is a text file and can therefore be examined in notepad—a sample of our file is shown in the next screenshot. In order for it to be used, it must reside in the same folder as the file(s) being imported. The following are some universal notes about the structure of the file that should be mentioned:

- The name of the file for which the schema is to be applied is specified as the first line. Note that the import is specified for a `02_master_tilde.csv` file

- The date format is specified (see the row **DateTimeFormat**) and is applied to each date field

- The delimiter is specified as a tilde

- Each column (by number) can specify a name different from the file's header row

```
[02_master_tilde.csv]
ColNameHeader=True
Format=Delimited(~)
DateTimeFormat=MM-DD-YYYY
MaxScanRows=0
Col1=sales_order_id Text
Col2=customer_id Text
Col3=employee_id Text
Col4=currency_id Integer
Col5=customer_po_id Text
Col6=sales_territory_id Integer
Col7=order_dt DateTime
Col8=due_dt DateTime
Col9=ship_dt DateTime
Col10=sales_amount Double
```

Naturally, there can only be one `schema.ini` file in a directory. However, the same file can be used to specify the format of individual files. This is achieved by simply extending the next specification with the name of the file, as has been done for `02_master_tilde.csv`.

> Further information about the format of the `schema.ini` file can be found at `http://msdn.microsoft.com/en-us/library/windows/desktop/ms709353(v=vs.85).aspx`.

Importing data from databases

Although tabular models support the import of data from a variety of sources, a relational database is still considered to be one of the primary methods of obtaining data. Unlike other sources (such as text files), where the structure may change from time to time, the data from a database is preferred because it conforms to a schema which is expected to remain constant. Furthermore, most operational systems store their data in a relational database format, and therefore, the database becomes a suitable source of data.

Tabular models may extract relational data through a generic connection on the machine, for example, **Open DataBase Connectivity** (**ODBC**), which is a standard method of data access, or by a connection based on a native driver (specific driver) stored in the model.

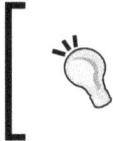

> An ODBC connection also stores a connection within the model. However, the actual connection to the database is managed by the ODBC connection on the machine (rather than the tabular model).

Wherever possible, the native driver should be used, since the driver supports the underlying **Database Management System** (**DBMS**) rather than the generic ODBC standard.

This recipe extracts data from a SQL Server database.

Getting ready

This recipe simulates the loading of the sales data from an operational database, commonly referred to as **Online Transactional Processing** (**OLTP**), based on the following schema:

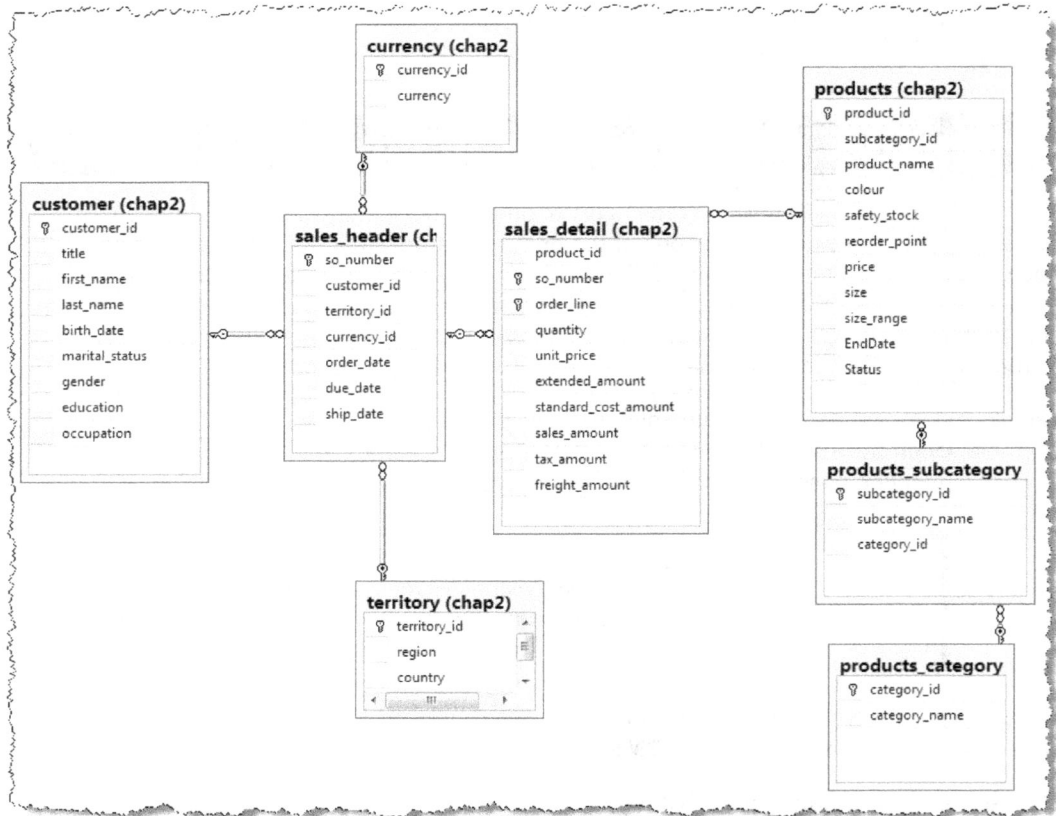

This schema implements a standard invoicing structure where a header record (`sales_header`) contains generic information about the sale, and the detailed records (found in `sales_detail`) collect the line items for the sales. The database implements foreign key constraints to enforce referential integrity.

Our goal for the recipe is to only import all sales (and related information) that occurred in Australian dollars. Australian dollar sales are determined by `currency_id` of AUD in the `sales_header` table.

How to do It...

In order to complete this recipe, the (SQL Server) database should be restored. The information on how to do this is available from the online resources with instructions in the *Appendix, Installing PowerPivot and Sample Databases*. Once this has been completed, we start from the PowerPivot window.

1. Open a new workbook and launch the PowerPivot window.

2. In the **Home** tab, select **From SQL Server** from the **From Database** drop-down list in the **Get External Data** group, as shown in the following screenshot:

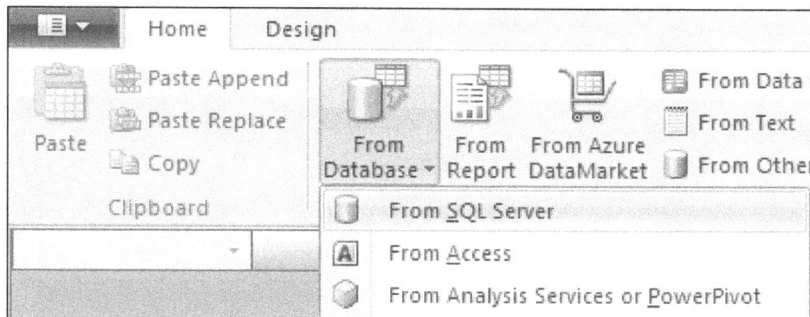

3. The **Table Import Wizard** window opens to create a new connection within the model. Populate the wizard's options with the following values:

Friendly connection name	Sales Data - SQL
Server name	the name of your server
Database name	tabular_modelling

To help with the selection of Servers of Databases, the drop-down boxes can be used. However, while selecting a server, the response of the dropdown may be slow, as all available servers on the network are polled.

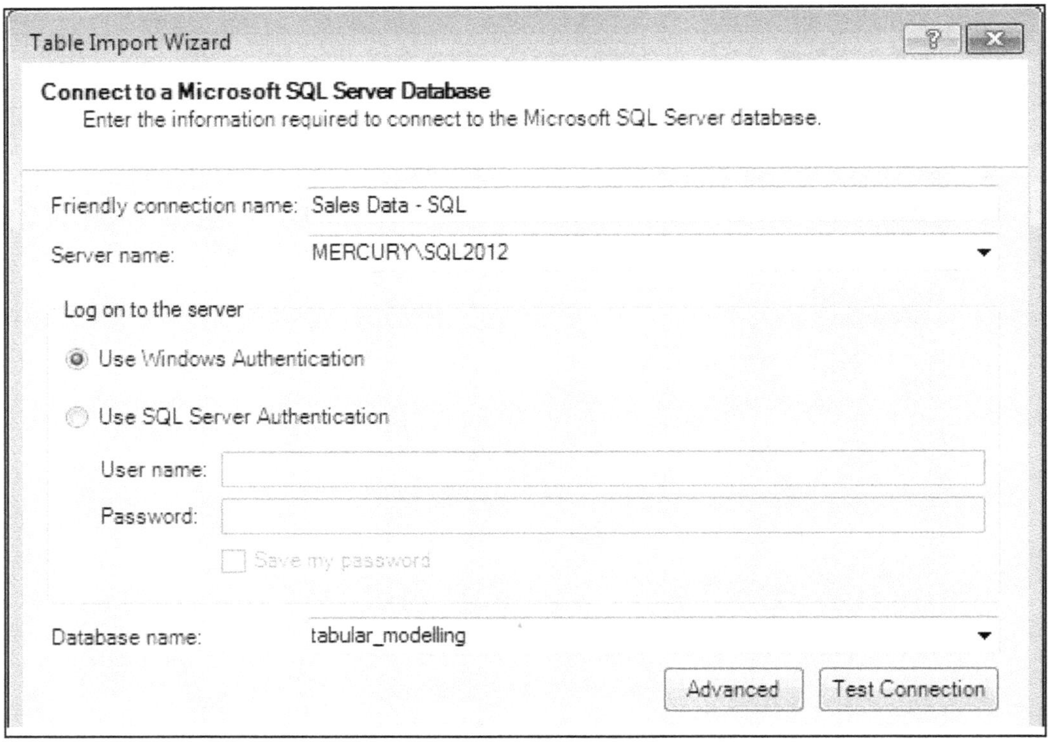

Table Import Wizard

Connect to a Microsoft SQL Server Database
Enter the information required to connect to the Microsoft SQL Server database.

Friendly connection name: Sales Data - SQL

Server name: MERCURY\SQL2012

Log on to the server

◉ Use Windows Authentication

○ Use SQL Server Authentication

User name:

Password:

☐ Save my password

Database name: tabular_modelling

[Advanced] [Test Connection]

---

4. Ensure that you can create a connection to the database by clicking on the **Test Connection** button (a message box should return with the message **Test Connection Succeeded**).

While connecting to a SQL Server, we have two authentication methods to choose from (Windows or a SQL Server). Windows authentication requires your user account to have access to the database (since the database is restored from the online resources, we assume that you have the appropriate permissions), whereas a SQL Server authentication requires a SQL Account (an account on a SQL Server with its own username and password). The preferred method of authentication is always Windows.

5. Click on the **Next** button to specify how to define the data that will be imported. Ensure that the **Select from a list of tables and views to choose the data to import** radio button is selected and click on **Next**.

6. Activate the **sales_detail** field from the Chap2 schema table by checking the checkbox for the sales_detail table. Rename the table to Sales Detail by changing the name in the **Friendly Name** column.

7. With the sales_detail table row still selected, click on the **Select Related Tables** button. This will check the products and sales_header tables. Rename these tables to Products and Sales Header.

		Source Table	Schema	Friendly Name	Filter Details
☐					
☐		currency	chap2		
☐		customer	chap2		
☐		dates	chap2		
☑		products	chap2	Products	
☐		products_category	chap2		
☐		products_subcategory	chap2		
☑		sales_detail	chap2	Sales Detail	
☑		sales_header	chap2	Sales Header	
☐		territory	chap2		

8. Ensure that the sales_header table row is active (the active row is dark blue) and click on the **Preview & Filter** button. A new window will open, which shows the available columns and filters on the table (as a grid). A column can be removed from the import by deselecting it.

9. Restrict the `sales_header` table to import only AUD sales by selecting the AUD `currency_id` from the column's drop-down box and clicking on the **OK** button.

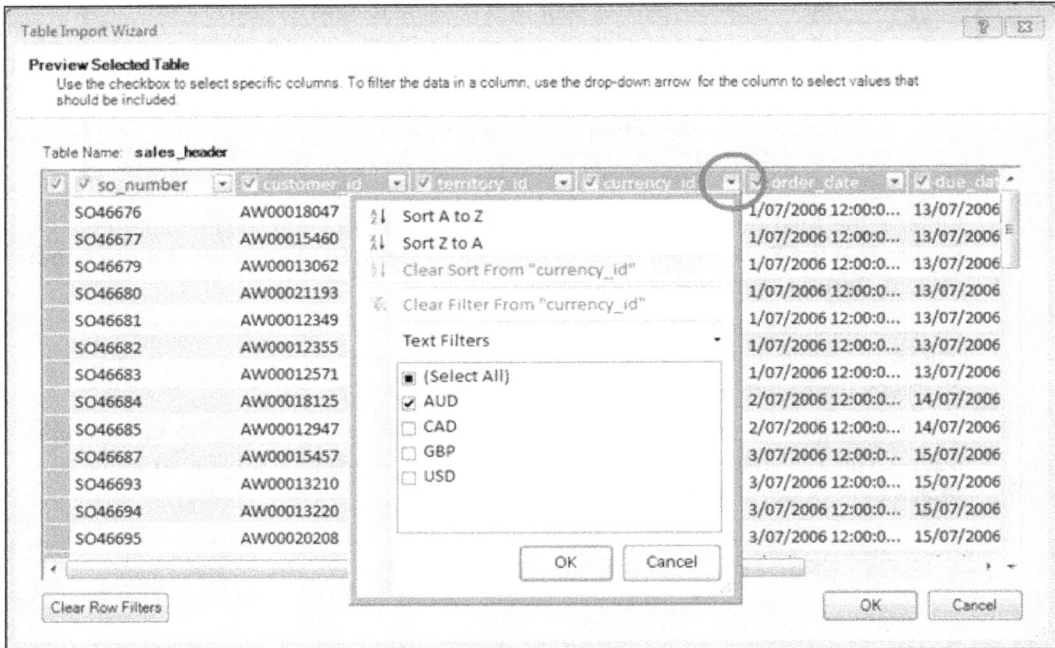

10. Click on **OK** to return to the **Select Tables and Views** dialog box of the **Table Import Wizard** window.

11. Click on the **Finish** button to import the data, and then on **Close** to exit the **Table Import Wizard** window.

12. Switch to **Diagram View** to confirm that relationships have been created between the `Sales Detail`, `Products` and `Sales Header` tables.

13. Create a pivot table which shows `currency_id` from the `Sales Header` table on rows and (the implicit measure) `Sum of quantity` as values.

Row Labels ▾	Sum of quantity
AUD	11886
	45274
Grand Total	**57160**

How it works...

The **Table Import Wizard** window does two things each time it is invoked. Firstly, it creates a connection (which is a definition) within the model to define how the database is connected. Secondly, it creates a table definition for each table that was defined by the Wizard.

We can see that there are two distinct steps. However, since the first step in this process creates a connection when the Wizard is invoked again, and the same connection name is used, an error will be shown. This is because each connection name must be unique. We can demonstrate this by trying to reproduce the steps in this recipe (in the same workbook). Before the **Table Import Wizard** window allows you to select available tables from the connection, the Wizard will prompt you with a message that a data source with the same name already exists (and a different name must be specified in order to continue).

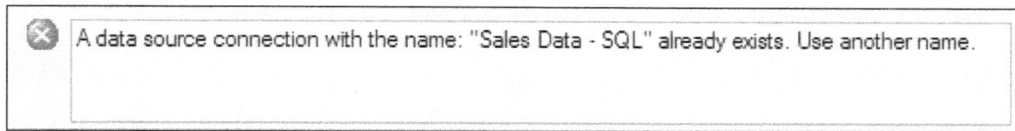

> ⊗ A data source connection with the name: "Sales Data - SQL" already exists. Use another name.

The **Select Tables and Views** window of the import allows you to define the table name within the model (note that the table will be called **Friendly Name** within the model) and filter the data that will be imported. Further, by using the **Select Related Tables** button, the Wizard will include any table that has a foreign key relationship with the selected table. This can be a very useful feature; however, one potential downside of relying on the **Select Related Tables** button for the identification of related objects is that the functionality is non-recursive, and it will apply only to the immediately selected object. This means that the related tables will not be identified. A generic ODBC driver does not allow for the recognition of relationships between tables.

The **Preview Selected Table** window allows you to define new column names and filter the data that is imported for a specific table. However, when a filter is applied to a table, the filter is only applied on the table that is imported—it is not applied to tables related to the table being imported. This means that the data in a table that is related to a filtered table is not filtered simply because its related table is filtered. This is the reason why the pivot of currency_id includes a blank row.

> Tabular models do not allow as much flexibility for defining missing data as multidimensional models do. If the data in one table is missing from another, a missing value (a blank) is substituted into the other table. Unlike the multidimensional model, the label cannot be changed.
>
> In contrast, there is no requirement to explicitly define error handling in tabular modeling. All the data is imported into the model (regardless of any requirement for a related value in another table).

There's more...

The connections that have been created in the tabular model can be seen by clicking on the **Existing Connections** button in the **Design** tab. All connections that exist in the model will be shown under the **Power Pivot Data Connections** group.

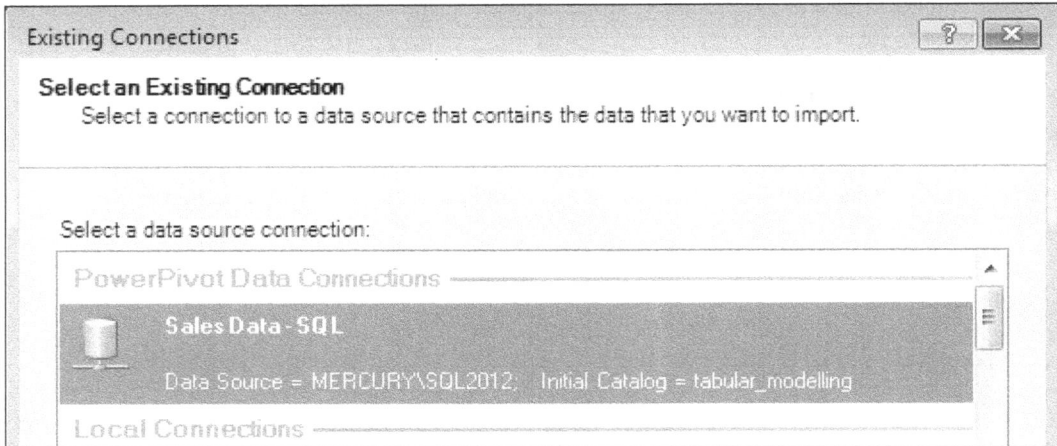

Managing connections and tables

The goal of the model designer should be to produce succinct models that are easily maintainable. This implies the re-use of objects (and structures) wherever possible. We have seen that it is relatively easy to import data into the model; however, the designer should also think about the maintenance of the model in the future. This recipe looks at how an existing model can be extended by adding additional data, and how a table can be altered once inside the model. This recipe is motivated by the maintenance of an existing table—that is, how do we change the import of a table which has already been specified? Additionally, as a point of practice, the modeler should re-use an existing connection that has been created, rather than create additional connections by continually importing tables using the same database settings.

Getting ready

This recipe uses the model that has been created in the prior recipe *Importing data from databases*.

How to do it...

1. Open the workbook that was developed in the recipe *Importing data from databases*, and launch the PowerPivot window.

2. In the **Design** tab, click on the **Existing Connections** button to show the connections in the model.

3. Double-click on the connection **Sales Data – SQL**, ensure that the **Select from a list of tables and views to choose the data to import** radio button is selected, and click on **Next**.

> You can also invoke the **Table Import Wizard** window by clicking on the **Open** button when the connection is selected.

4. Select the `sales_header` table by checking the checkbox next to the table name and click on the **Select Related Tables** button to select all tables that relate to the `sales_header` table.

5. Deselect the `sales_detail` table and click on the **Finish** button to import the remaining tables.

6. Click on the **Close** button to close the **Table Import Wizard** window.

7. Switch to **Diagram View** to ensure that relationships have been created between the `sales_header`, `territory`, `currency`, and `customer` tables.

8. Create a relationship between the `sales_header` and `Sales Detail` tables, and delete the `Sales Header` table that was created in the recipe *Importing data from databases*.

> It is not necessary to correctly identify the source and related tables while defining a relationship. The model makes an estimation about which table is the reference table based on the cardinality of data in both the tables. While defining relationships in the **Diagram View**, PowerPivot will correct an invalid relationship (one which points in the wrong direction) based on this inference.

The `currency` table shows the currency ID in the currency name (as shown in the next screenshot). As the designer, we would like to suffix the `currency_id` field to the name, so that it includes the code within the name. For example, the name **Emirati Dirham** should appear as **Emirati Dirham (AED)**. While we could create a formula for this within the model (see the *Adding fields to tables* recipe in *Chapter 1, Getting Started with Excel*), we want the model to be succinct and only show a single name. In order to do this, we can change the underlying table definition to include a custom calculation. Prior to the change, the table looks as shown in the following screenshot:

currenc...	currency
AED	Emirati Dirham
AFA	Afghani
ALL	Lek
AMD	Armenian Dram
ANG	Netherlands Antillian Guilder
AOA	Kwanza
ARS	Argentine Peso
ATS	Shilling

9. Select the currency table and click on the **Table Properties** button in the **Design** tab. A new **Edit Table Properties** window will open.

10. Change **Table Preview** to a SQL view by selecting **Query Editor** from the view drop-down box.

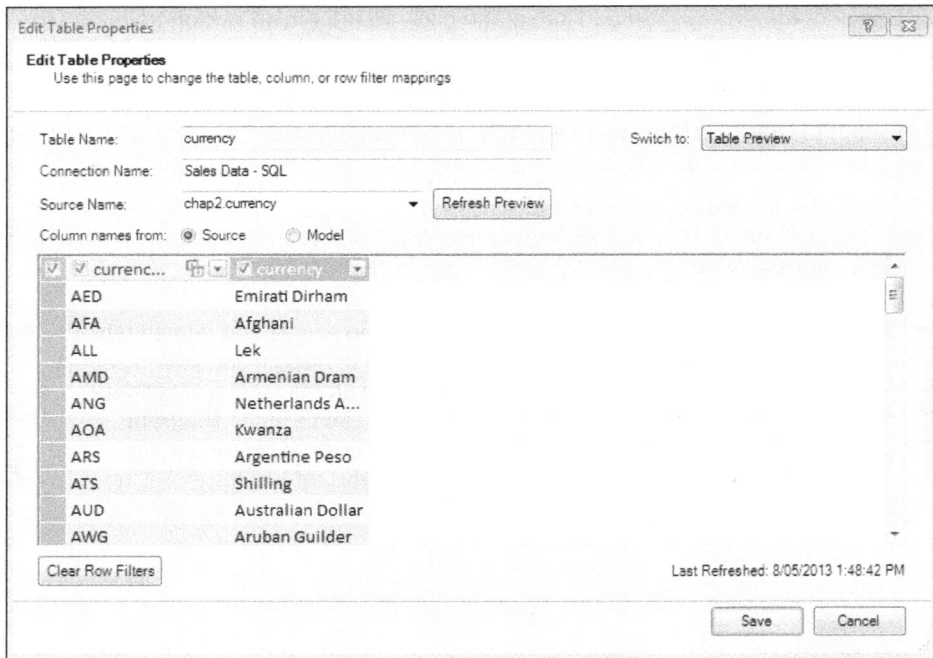

11. Replace the existing query with the following code:

```
SELECT currency_id, currency + ' (' + currency_id + ')'  as
    currency  FROM [chap2].[currency]
```

12. Click on the **Validate** button to ensure that the SQL statement is valid.

13. Click on the **Save** button to reload the data and return to the `currency` table.

How it works...

Importing data through the **Get External Data** group of menu items is done by first creating a new connection and then creating table definitions on the connection. Importing data with these buttons is suitable when there are no existing connections in the model and when new data is required. However, when an existing connection in the model can be used to add additional data sources which use the existing connection, it makes more sense to re-use that connection (rather than creating a new one). This improves model manageability since the number of connections in the model is reduced. If the connection properties change (for example referencing a different server), the property only has to be changed in one connection.

The definition (query) used to define the table can also be edited through its Table Properties.

There's more...

The Table Properties editor includes a query designer which can be used in lieu of writing SQL. In order to use this, click on the **Design** button in the **Edit Table Properties** window. This will invoke the editor (which usually defaults to a text view). However, the developer can click on the **Edit as Text** button in the designer to switch to a visual designer.

> Selecting the visual designer may lead to the loss of the query definition. If this is the case, the user is prompted that this will occur.

The definition of tables within the model holds information about the **Source** and **Model** definitions. **Source** refers to the underlying object (its physical structure), whereas **Model** refers to the semantic definition (what the end user sees). An example of the application of this can be seen when a column is renamed within the model (see the *Managing the appearance of tables and fields* recipe, in *Chapter 1, Getting Started with Excel*). The **Edit Table Properties** window allows us to toggle between these two views of data, by selecting either the **Source** or **Model** radio buttons, as shown in the following screenshot. This is only available for tables that have not been altered by defining a custom SQL.

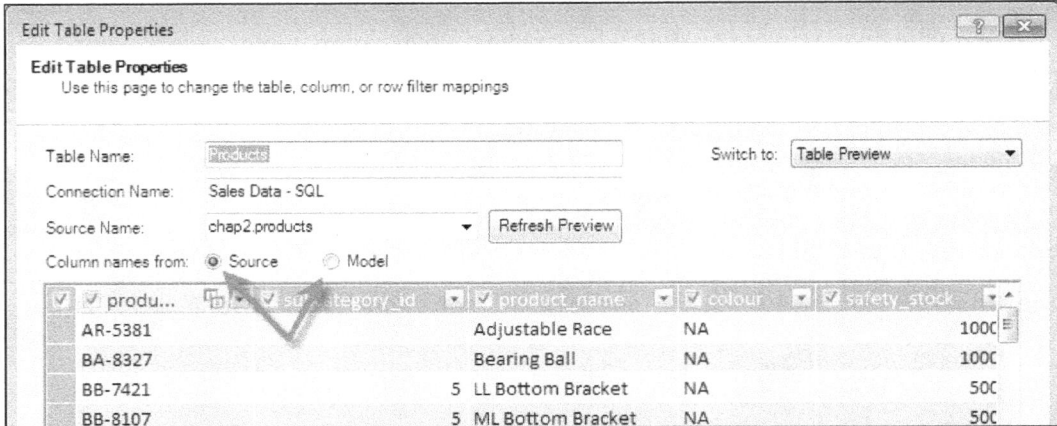

Using data feeds

Data feeds allow a tabular model to consume XML data through an HTTP service—these are called the OData and **.atomsvc** feeds. The feed(s) can be defined to the model through either an OData service (which also can provide data) or a data service document (the `.atomsvc` file) that specifies the URL to the service.

The **Open Data Protocol** (**OData**) is a standard protocol for creating and consuming data over existing technologies such as HTTP. This means that data can be imported into the model as a web service. The ability to use data which is not generated from the corporate environment extends the possible data sources that can be used for analysis. Data may be available for free or purchased from vendors (see `http://datamarket.azure.com/` for both).

Getting ready

This recipe imports some data from an online database called `Northwind`. `Northwind` is a well-known sample database (actually, the data is not that important to us—only the technique used to import it is). We also examine importing data from a reporting services report (which is imported as an `.atomsvc` file).

How to do it...

We firstly examine how to import data using OData and then we examine how to obtain data from a reporting services report.

1. Open a new Workbook and launch the PowerPivot window.

2. Click on the **From Data Feeds** button from the **Get External Data** group.

3. Name the connection `NorthWind`, and use the following data feed URL:

    `http://services.odata.org/Northwind/Northwind.svc/`.

4. Click on **Test** to test the connection, and then click on the **Next** button.

5. The **Table Import Wizard** window will open, here we can select which tables we would like to import.

6. Note that the **Select Related Tables** button is inactive and cannot be used.

7. Highlight the `Products` table and select the **Preview & Filter** button.

8. The Wizard changes to a grid view; however, the table cannot be filtered (there are no filter dropdowns).

9. Click on **Finish** to import the `Products` table.

10. Open a reporting services report and select the **Export to Data Feed** button. This button is identified in the following screenshot:

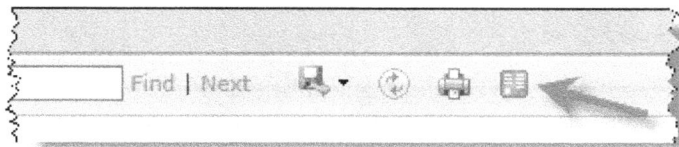

> Unfortunately, we cannot provide specifics about the reporting services report that is required for this recipe. The configuration of reporting services and the associated creation of the report is outside the scope of this book. We do discuss the steps involved which are common to all reporting services reports.
>
> These steps can also be applied to SharePoint lists (which have the same export button).

11. A warning message will prompt to save or open a file with the name of your report and an `.atomsvc` extension.

12. Click on **Save**.

13. Open PowerPivot and import data by clicking on the **From Data Feeds** button.

14. Click on the **Browse** button and navigate to the file which was saved in the previous step. In this case, there is no need to provide the data feed URL.

15. Select the file and click on the **Open** button.

16. This time, the **Table Import Wizard** window lists report objects (Tablix's, lists and charts) as tables that can be imported to PowerPivot.

17. Just like OData feed, there is no ability to filter the data or detect relationships between tables.

How it works...

The OData feed provides a web service which is essentially exposed to the tabular model as an XML feed, and may contain information about the data source, including tables within the source. This file can then be imported to the tabular model.

There's more...

As a web service, the OData feed can provide additional information to the service (such as a requested table, or a record within the table). For example, to specify a connection which only imports the customer's table, we could use the following data feed URL:

```
http://services.odata.org/Northwind/Northwind.svc/Customers
```

Additionally, we may provide the ability to filter and return a specific record. For example, to return a customer record by customer ID, we could use the following data feed URL:

```
http://services.odata.org/Northwind/Northwind.svc/
Customers('ALFKI')
```

When data is imported through an `.atomsvc` file, all data objects within the report are exposed as tables to the Wizard (data objects in the report are controls that present data, that is, Tablix's, lists and charts). The name shown in the Table Import Wizard is the name of the object within the SSRS report.

When exported, the `.atomsvc` file contains a list of objects that existed in the report at the time the file was exported. If the report is changed, and another object is added to the report, the `.atomsvc` file will not be aware that the new dataset has been included, and re-using the file would only show the dataset that existed at the time of export.

Purchased data from the Azure marketplace may require authentication. In this case, the Azure DataMarket Dataset driver should be used.

3
Advanced Browsing Features

This chapter looks at extending the model to provide a positive experience for the user. In this chapter, we will cover:

- ▶ Sorting data
- ▶ Creating hierarchies for drilldown interaction
- ▶ Summing aggregates and row iteration
- ▶ Parent-child hierarchies
- ▶ Creating and using Key Performance Indicators
- ▶ Role playing dimensions and relationships
- ▶ Building ratios

Introduction

The first two chapters of this book focused on the basic modeling principles of relationships and how to import data into the model. This chapter extends those concepts by focusing on the development of the end-user experience. That is, how the user interacts with the model and the experience they have when doing so.

This chapter also examines a fundamental decision that the designer should make when designing the model, that is, the use of role playing dimensions. The choices available through role playing dimensions should be considered by the modeler as part of the initial design.

Sorting data

When data is presented to the user, there is often a requirement to present the members (the individual data values) in a predefined order. Consider months of the year, when the user drills down from a year, they generally expect to see months ordered according to the calendar that they are working with. For example, a natural calendar runs from January to December, whereas a financial calendar may run from October to September.

In tabular modeling, this arrangement is controlled by sorting within column properties.

Getting ready

The workbook used in this recipe is available on the Packt Publishing website (http://www.packtpub.com/).

How to do it...

1. Open the `Sorting Data & Hierarchies.xlsx` workbook and launch the PowerPivot window.
2. Create a linked table that imports the dates worksheet into the PowerPivot model.
3. Hide (hide from Client Tools) the columns `day_of_week`, `day_of_week_name`, `month_of_year`, `quarter_name`, and `semester`.
4. Rename the `month_name` field to `Month Name`.
5. Create a pivot that shows `Month Name` on rows. Note that the members (Months) are sorted alphabetically by default.

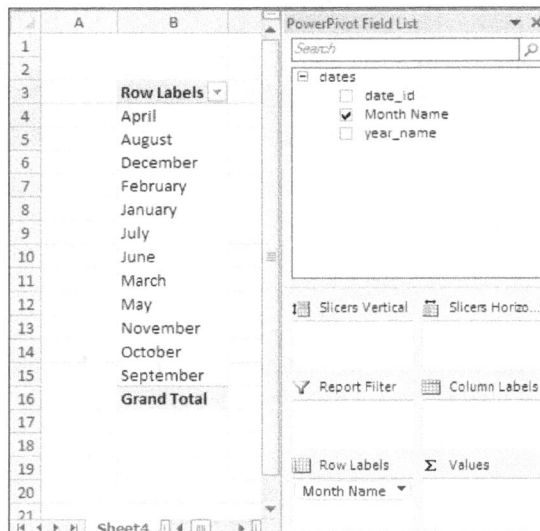

6. Return to the PowerPivot window. Ensure that the **Month Name** column is selected and then select the **Sort by Column** button from the **Home** tab (this is found in the **Sort and Filter** group).

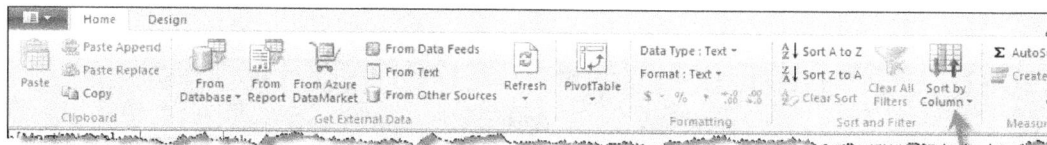

7. A new window opens (**Sort by Column**), which specifies a column (the **Sort** column) that will be sorted by the values of another column (that is, the **By** column). Ensure that the **Sort** column has the value **Month Name** and the **By** column has the value **month_of_year**.

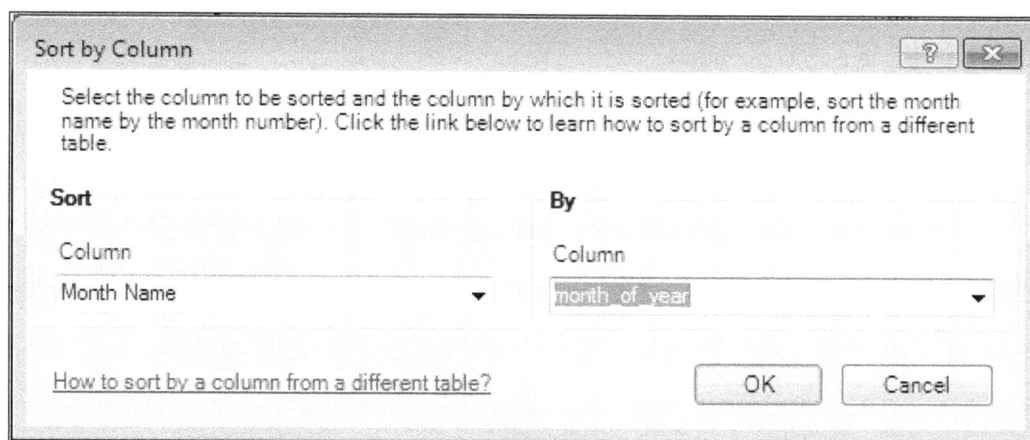

> The field chosen (that is, the field that is being sorted) will be automatically populated based on the field that is selected (or active) in the grid when the **Sort by Column** button is selected.

8. Select **OK** to exit the window.
9. Return to the pivot table in Excel and refresh the model in the pivot table. **Month Name** will now be sorted in calendar month order (January to December).

How it works...

The **By** column defines the order in which the values of the **Sort** column will be displayed. This is a straightforward sort, and may be thought of as attaching a property to the sort column.

The only caveat to this is that the **By** column must be in the same table as the column that is being sorted. If this is not the case, and you wish to sort by a column in another table, the sort order column must be imported (and materialized) in the table (through the RELATED function).

Creating hierarchies for drilldown interaction

Hierarchies allow the model designer to specify navigation paths for the user. Usually, this is done in order to group members of a particular type together. A simple example of this is grouping months of a year together.

Getting ready

This recipe assumes a continuation from the recipe *Sorting data*.

How to do It...

1. Switch to the **Diagram View** of the model.
2. Change the year_name column to Year.
3. Select the Month Name and Year columns by holding down the *Ctrl* key while selecting each column.
4. Right-click the Year column and select the **Create Hierarchy** option, so that a new hierarchy is created within the view.
5. Rename the hierarchy to Month By Year by right-clicking the hierarchy name and selecting **Rename** from the pop-up menu.

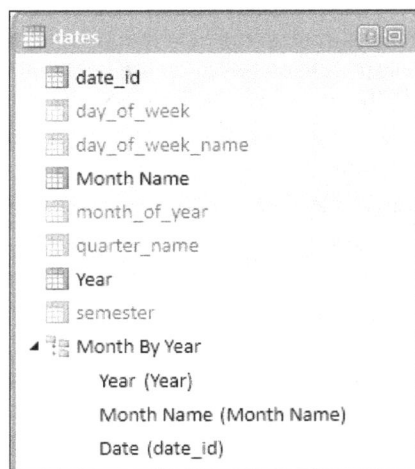

6. Return to Excel and refresh the PowerPivot field list to show the new hierarchy in the **dates** table.

7. Remove the **Months** member from the existing Pivot and add the **Month By Year** hierarchy. Note that all years are shown (since these are the values of the first level).

8. Expand the year (by clicking on the **+** sign next to a year value).

How it works...

The creation of a hierarchy within the model is a metadata definition and not a structural creation within the model. This means that the model does not actually materialize the hierarchy as an object with the tabular database. When a request is made (by the client tool) for members of the hierarchy, the request is effectively the same as a query made against the members of that level (which is subject to restrictions imposed by the parent level).

There's more...

In this recipe, the levels of the hierarchies were automatically detected based on the data within the model and provided the drill path from year to month. Both year and month refer to the levels of the hierarchy and imply the grouping order. If this order is not correct, the levels can be rearranged by selecting the field within the hierarchy and dragging it to a new level. For example, suppose I want to first see months and then years. I can select the Month Name field in the hierarchy and drag it to the required position in the hierarchy. While doing this, the new position is shown by a dark line in the hierarchy.

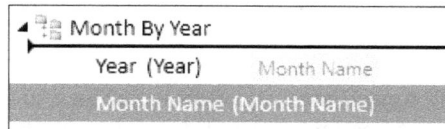

The levels of the hierarchy do not have to be entirely defined when the hierarchy is created. In fact, you could create an empty hierarchy if you wish to, just by right-clicking on the table name (in **Design View**) and selecting **Create hierarchy** from the pop-up menu. Then, to add levels, simply drag the levels into the hierarchy from the table.

The level names in your hierarchy can also be renamed by right-clicking the level (within the hierarchy) and selecting **Rename** from the pop-up menu. The **Design View** will show the hierarchy as the level name followed by the source field (which are enclosed in parentheses), as shown in the following screenshot:

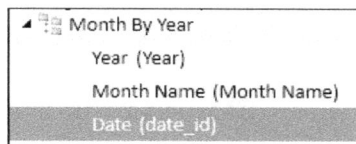

For readers familiar with Analysis Services (OLAP), the addition of hierarchies to dimensions creates performance improvements because the storage engine will use the hierarchical structure in the aggregation of data at higher levels in the hierarchy. For example, the storage engine could provide a yearly total by adding up the months within the year. Of course, this is conditional on the correct design of dimensions and appropriate relationships being defined between hierarchy levels. For a tabular model, there is no such requirement, and there is no performance benefit for creating hierarchies in this way. The choice of hierarchies within the model is a decision of usability for the end user.

Summing aggregates and row iteration

In the recipes so far, we have looked at creating measures based on a simple summation. With these types of calculations, we simply define a measure as the sum of the respective columns. The calculations can then be used by other calculations and the result would be the same as if the calculation had been done within the row and aggregated. For example, if we define a measure of [Sales] and a measure of [COGS] (cost of sales), we could define a new measure as [Profit]:=[Sales]-[COGS]. Alternatively, we could add a column to the Sales table as line_profit with a column formula (SALES-COGS) and sum that column to create the new calculation.

However, in some situations, creating measures based on other measures does not provide the correct result, and it is necessary to determine the result of the calculation for each row and then perform a function on the results. DAX includes some handy functions for achieving this outcome without the need for intermediary columns.

Getting ready

Open the workbook **Summing Aggregates and Row Iteration** and examine the Sales Detail worksheet. This shows the line items for sales but does not include a sales value (selling price) for each line (this amount has been used in previous recipes to determine the sales value but has been removed from this recipe). The unit_price_amount value for each product is shown; however, the sales amount per line is dependent on other fields of the quantity sold and discount given. The sales_amount value for each line is determined by the formula:

```
order_quantity x ( 1 - discount_percent ) x unit_price_amount
```

Our goal is to create this formula without adding additional columns.

How to do it...

Now that we have an understanding of the calculations that we want to create, let's do them in the tabular model. The workbook is available from the online resources.

1. Import the worksheet into the PowerPivot model and create a sales amount calculation as follows:

```
Sales Amount:=
sumx(
Sales_Detail
, [unit_price_amount]*(1-[discount_percent]) * [order_qty]
)
```

2. Create a check measure by performing the calculation manually. Add a column sales_amount to the table with the formula:

```
=[unit_price_amount]*(1-[discount_percent]) * [order_qty]
```

Then, create a measure by summing the sales_amount column

```
Sales Amount Check:=SUM([sales_amount])
```

3. Create a Variance measure with the following formula:

```
Variance:=[Sales Amount]-[Sales Amount Check]
```

4. Add the Variance to a pivot table with sales_order on rows and confirm whether all values are zero.

How it works...

The DAX X functions (SUMX, COUNTX, AVERAGEX, MAXX, and MINX) iterate an expression over a table to determine the result. The syntax for each of these functions is:

```
Function ( <table > , <expression> )
```

In this syntax, the <table> parameter is the data that the function is applied to and the <expression> parameter is the formula that must be determined for each row (of the <table>). As a sidebar, the <table> parameter of the function is not restricted to table names within the model; it can be derived through a function that returns a table.

The aggregate functions (SUM, COUNT, AVERAGE, MAX, and MIN) are performed after the expression has been evaluated (on a row-by-row basis).

Therefore, in this recipe, the use of SUMX simulates the addition of a column (with a formula <expression>) and then performs a SUM on that column after the expression has been evaluated. The expression is:

```
[unit_price_amount]*(1-[discount_percent]) * [order_qty]
```

This formula is applied to each row of the table and then summed to achieve the same result, as if a column was added to the table.

There's more...

It was stated earlier that the <table> parameter within the function is not restricted to table names within the model, and the <table> parameter can be any function that returns a table. This includes filtering functions that restrict table results. For the data that is returned in such a case, the <expression> parameter is still applied against that result.

Consider a situation where we would like to create a measure to show the lowest selling price for Bikes.

1. Extend the model by importing the Products table and creating a relationship between product_id in the Sales_Detail and the Products table.

2. Add the measure Min Sales Price (Bikes) as follows:

```
Min Sales Price (Bikes):=
Minx
(
        FILTER(Sales_Detail
                , RELATED(Products[category])="Bikes"
                )
, [unit_price_amount]
)
```

3. To verify the calculation, create a measure Min Sales Price (Bikes) check that relies on the previous calculations in the model.

```
Min Sales Price (Bikes) check:=Min([unit_price_amount])
```

4. Create a measure variance between the two calculated columns as follows:

```
Min Sales Price (Bikes) Variance:=
[Min Sales Price (Bikes) check]-[Min Sales Price (Bikes)]
```

5. Create a pivot table with a filter on the bikes category and all three measures.

Regardless of what items are placed in the rows and columns, the two calculations for `Min Sales Price` will give the same result, and the variance will be zero.

category	Bikes	.T		
Row Labels	▾ **Min Sales Price (Bikes)**	**Min Sales Price (Bikes) check**	**Min Sales Price (Bikes) Variance**	
Mountain Bikes	113.00	113.00	0	
Road Bikes	296.99	296.99	0	
Touring Bikes	334.06	334.06	0	
Grand Total	**113.00**	**113.00**	**0**	

In this case, the measure `Min Sales Price (Bikes)` works by applying a filter to the `Sales_Detail` table for all products that have a category of bikes (note the use of the `RELATED` function, which has been examined in a previous recipe). Further, by restricting the table to `Bikes` in the calculation, the calculation is not reliant on a PivotTable filter (the `FILTER` function is examined in later recipes).

In order for the calculation `Min Sales Price (Bikes) check` to work as intended (and only show the lowest price for a bike), the pivot table must be filtered by `Bikes`. Therefore, the entire logic of the pivot outcome obtained by creating an additional column, a calculation over that column, and a filter on the pivot table, all of these can be contained in a single formula.

Parent-child hierarchies

Systems often store data in tables that store hierarchical information in a self-referencing (parent-child) relationship. With this design, a field in the table is used to reference the primary key (identifying record) within the same table. A common example of this type of relationship can be found in organizational structures where an employee has a manager field that specifies another employee's record. Another example includes a bill of materials, which defines a product made from subproducts, which may in turn be made up of other products, and so on.

This type of structure is very efficient for storage because the same table can be used for all items within the hierarchy; this allows for easy updates, insertions, and deletions. However, one issue with this type of structure is that the tree of items within the structure is not immediately visible to an end user. A common method to expose the structure is to flatten the relationship into a table, so that each level is exposed as a field within the table. This recipe examines this within the tabular model.

Getting ready

Review the table `Employees`, which shows the manager-employee relationship. The General Manager of the organization (*Ken Sanchez*) is the person who has no manager (`manager_id` is blank). Ken's direct reports have a `manager_id` value equal to Ken's `employee_id` (295847284). This reporting relationship can be continued, as in the following diagram:

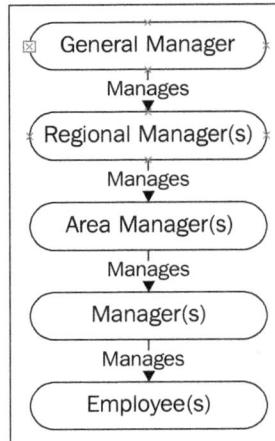

How to do It...

Download the workbook (`Employee.xlsx`) from the online resources.

1. Open the `Employee.xls` workbook and launch the PowerPivot window.

2. Import the table Employee worksheet into the PowerPivot model by creating a linked table.

3. Create a calculated column as `employee_name` with the formula:

   ```
   =[first_name] & "  " & [last_name]
   ```

4. Create a calculated column (`hierarchy_path`) with the formula:

   ```
   =PATH([employee_id],[manager_id])
   ```

   The formula builds a pipe-delimited representation of the hierarchy showing each position from the top level of the hierarchy to the current (row).

5. Add a column to the table titled `General Manager` to store the name of the employee at the first level of the hierarchy. Show the employees name (the highest level of employee) by using the following formula:

```
=LOOKUPVALUE( [employee_name]
, employee[employee_id]
, PATHITEM([hierarchy_path],1))
```

6. Add a column to the table titled `Regional Manager` to store the name of employees who report to the General Manager. Populate this column with the following formula:

```
=IF(ISBLANK(
        LOOKUPVALUE([employee_name], employee[employee_id]
                , PATHITEM([hierarchy_path],2)
                )
        )
    , [General Manager]
            , LOOKUPVALUE([employee_name]
            , employee[employee_id]
            , PATHITEM([hierarchy_path],2)
            )
)
```

7. Add columns for `Area Manager`, `Manager`, and `Employee`. Populate the columns using the same formula as in step 6, increasing the `PATHITEM` value by one each time and referring to the prior column. The formulas are listed in the following table:

Column	Formula
Area Manager	`=IF(ISBLANK(LOOKUPVALUE([employee_name], employee[employee_id], PATHITEM([hierarchy_path],3))), [Region Manager] , LOOKUPVALUE([employee_name], employee[employee_id], PATHITEM([hierarchy_path],3)))`
Manager	`=IF(ISBLANK(LOOKUPVALUE([employee_name], employee[employee_id], PATHITEM([hierarchy_path],4))), [Area Manager] , LOOKUPVALUE([employee_name], employee[employee_id], PATHITEM([hierarchy_path],4)))`
Employee	`=IF(ISBLANK(LOOKUPVALUE([employee_name], employee[employee_id], PATHITEM([hierarchy_path],5))), [Manager] , LOOKUPVALUE([employee_name], employee[employee_id], PATHITEM([hierarchy_path],5)))`

8. Switch to **Diagram View** to create a hierarchy titled `Organisation` with the levels `General Manager`, `Region Manager`, `Area Manager`, `Manager`, and `Employee`, and then hide all the fields in the table.

9. Create a pivot table from the model, add the `Organisation` hierarchy to rows, and expand the nodes. Expanding the level will show what employees report through to the expanded employee. Observe that each member in the hierarchy has a value and that the hierarchy is balanced (there are five levels). Also, note that the hierarchy is balanced through the repetition of employee names. For example, there is a general manager, **Ken Sanchez**, and a regional manager with the same name.

Row Labels	Row Labels
⊟Ken Sánchez	⊟Ken Sánchez
⊞Brian Welcker	⊟Brian Welcker
⊞David Bradley	⊞Amy Alberts
⊞James Hamilton	⊞Brian Welcker
⊞Jean Trenary	⊞Stephen Jiang
⊞Ken Sánchez	⊞Syed Abbas
⊞Laura Norman	⊞David Bradley
⊞Peter Krebs	⊞James Hamilton
⊞Terri Duffy	⊞Jean Trenary
Grand Total	⊞Ken Sánchez
	⊞Laura Norman
	⊞Peter Krebs
	⊞Terri Duffy
	Grand Total

How it works...

The creation of the parent-child hierarchy involves three steps. They are as follows:

1. The normalization of the self-referencing structure, so that all recursive relationships are merged into a single pipe-delimited field. This defines the path from the upper-most level to the current row in the structure (including the current row identifier). This is achieved by using the PATH function (field `hierarchy_path`), as shown in the following screenshot. Note that the root manager (the person with an empty `manager_id` field) has only one level in their `hierarchy_path` (themselves) and the second employee (the one who reports to the root manager) lists the root manager and then themselves:

employee_id	employee_name	manager_id	hierarchy_path
295847284	Ken Sánchez		295847284
112432117	Brian Welcker	295847284	295847284|112432117
481044938	Syed Abbas	112432117	295847284|112432117|481044938
758596752	Lynn Tsoflias	481044938	295847284|112432117|481044938|758596752
502097814	Stephen Jiang	112432117	295847284|112432117|502097814

2. Next, we determine the name of each employee along the path or, each employee in the `hierarchy_path` field based on a position within the field.

    This is achieved through the use of a nested formula. Firstly, the `hierarchy_path` field is stripped into individual positions within the path; this allows each `employee_id` value to be determined by its position. This is done with the following formula:

    ```
    PATHITEM([hierarchy_path],n)
    ```

    Here, n refers to the index position within the path.

> The `PATHITEM` function also includes an optional third parameter, `[TYPE]`. This specifies the return value as either being text or an integer. The allowable values are either a 0 (which is the default) for text, or a 1 for an integer. Since our values are of text type, we have omitted this from the formula.

Next, given the `employee_id` value is returned from the path, the `LOOKUPVALUE` returns the employee's name. This function was examined in the *Linking fields between tables* recipe in *Chapter 1, Getting Started with Excel*. Given a particular `employee_id` value (???), the `LOOKUPVALUE` formula returns the employee's name when it is used as:

```
=LOOKUPVALUE( [employee_name], employee[employee_id], ???)
```

The method also checks that each column in the hierarchy (or level) has an `employee_name` associated with it. This is done by nesting the LOOKUP value in the `IF(ISBLANK())` function. When encompassed by the IF function in this manner, the formula ensures that the name appears on every level in the hierarchy. If there is no `employee_name` found, the `employee_name` of the previous levels is used.

manager_id	hierarchy_path	General M...	Region M...	Area Ma...	Manager
	295847284	Ken Sánchez	Ken Sánchez	Ken Sánchez	Ken Sánc
295847284	295847284|112432117	Ken Sánchez	Brian Welcker	Brian Welcker	Brian We
112432117	295847284|112432117|4810...	Ken Sánchez	Brian Welcker	Syed Abbas	Syed Abb
481044938	295847284|112432117|4810...	Ken Sánchez	Brian Welcker	Syed Abbas	Lynn Tso
112432117	295847284|112432117|5020...	Ken Sánchez	Brian Welcker	Stephen Jiang	Stephen

3. Finally, with the parent-child structure broken down to individual columns that show the employee's name on each level, and a hierarchy is created from the fields that allow the user to drilldown in the client tool (PivotTable).

When viewed through a client tool, the de-normalization of the self-referencing structure gives the illusion of a parent-child hierarchy (that is, a structure that is drillable by the user, which is based on the self-referencing relationship). This technique is often used in this SAS (OLAP) dimension design to improve performance. While this is not a true parent-child hierarchy (the depth of the hierarchy must be specified by the model designer and not by the self-referencing relationship), the method exposes the parent-child structure through a flattened hierarchy.

As a model designer, you must determine the depth of the hierarchy when designing the hierarchy rather than relying on the self-referencing relationship to specify it. Therefore, you need to determine the maximum depth of the current structure. To do this, add a column to the `employee` table titled `path_depth` using the following formula:

```
=PATHLENGTH([hierarchy_path])
```

This shows the number of elements in the hierarchy, or the number of employees within the current (row) employee's reporting path (including themselves). In order to determine the maximum depth of the hierarchy, simply determine the maximum reporting depth by creating a measure as follows:

```
max_path_depth:=MAX([path_depth])
```

This will show that there needs to be five levels.

Since the determination of the hierarchy depth is only required at design time, you can also sort the column in a descending order to find the maximum value (and therefore, the number of levels needed). Simply select the `path_depth` column and click on the **Sort Largest to Smallest** button from the **Home** menu.

Alternatively, you could simply create a measure without the need for additional columns in the table. Simply use the formula:

```
max_required_depth:=
MAXX(employee, PATHLENGTH([hierarchy_path]))
```

There's more...

The creation of a flattened hierarchy to expose a self-referencing relationship provides the modeler with an easy technique to flatten the hierarchy and show it to the user. However, the hierarchy is exposed with balanced levels, where the actual structure may not be balanced.

Consider the situation where we want to show the number of employees within the structure (the count of employees). For example, the structure that shows direct reports as a measure. Add the measure to the model:

```
Number Of Employees (native):=COUNTROWS(employee)
```

> The COUNTROWS function simply returns the number of rows that are present in the table (employee in this case). When used in a pivot, the filtering applied by the pivot shows the number of rows in each cell.
>
> We could achieve the same result (in a slightly long-winded fashion) by adding an additional column (employee_count) to the table and specifying its formula as =1 (1 to represent each employee in the table). Then, the measure Number Of Employees (native) will be:
>
>   :=SUM(employee_count)

When the measure is added to the pivot table, and Brian Welcker's hierarchy is expanded, we can see, as an employee, Brian only reports to Ken Sanchez (the General Manger). Therefore, Brian holds all positions from the Regional Manager to the Employee.

Row Labels ▾	Number Of Employees (native)
⊟ Ken Sánchez	290
⊟ Brian Welcker	18
⊞ Amy Alberts	4
⊟ Brian Welcker	1
⊟ Brian Welcker	1
Brian Welcker	1
⊞ Stephen Jiang	11
⊞ Syed Abbas	2
⊞ David Bradley	9
⊞ James Hamilton	8
⊞ Jean Trenary	10

This is exactly how the hierarchy is designed to act. Note that the table shows this structure.

hierarchy_path ▾	General M... ▾	Region M... ▾	Area Ma... ▾	Manager ▾	Employee ▾
295847284	Ken Sánchez	Ken Sánchez	Ken Sánchez	Ken Sánchez	Ken Sánchez
295847284|112432117	Ken Sánchez	Brian Welcker	Brian Welcker	Brian Welcker	Brian Welcker
295847284|184188301	Ken Sánchez	Laura Norman	Laura Norman	Laura Norman	Laura Norman

There is no *out of the box* method to hide the duplicated names at lower levels of the hierarchy. In the traditional OLAP dimension design, hierarchy levels can be hidden if their name is the same as the parent using the level's **HideMemberIf** property. This property does not exist in tabular modeling. However, the same outcome can be simulated by allowing the client tool to hide empty rows and specifying an empty value for the hierarchy members that are duplicates of their parent.

> By default, pivot tables hide rows with no data (that is, where the data is blank). This can be verified by right-clicking on the pivot table and selecting **PivotTable Options** from the pop-up menu and ensuring that the **Show items with no data on rows** checkbox is deselected.

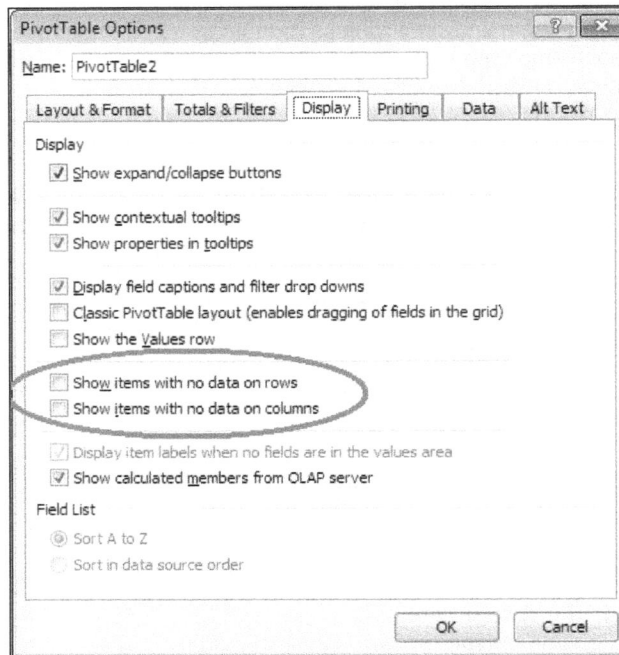

PivotTable Options

Name: PivotTable2

Layout & Format | Totals & Filters | Display | Printing | Data | Alt Text

Display

- ☑ Show expand/collapse buttons
- ☑ Show contextual tooltips
- ☑ Show properties in tooltips
- ☑ Display field captions and filter drop downs
- ☐ Classic PivotTable layout (enables dragging of fields in the grid)
- ☐ Show the Values row
- ☐ Show items with no data on rows
- ☐ Show items with no data on columns
- ☑ Display item labels when no fields are in the values area
- ☑ Show calculated members from OLAP server

Field List

- ◉ Sort A to Z
- ○ Sort in data source order

OK   Cancel

Return to the PowerPivot window and make the following changes:

1. Add the measure `current_browse_depth` to show what level is currently being filtered in the hierarchy:

```
current_browse_depth:=
IF(ISFILTERED([Employee])
        , 5
        , IF(ISFILTERED([Manager])
                , 4
                , IF(ISFILTERED([Area Manager])
                        , 3
                        , IF(ISFILTERED([Region Manager])
                                , 2
                                ,1
))))
```

2. Add a new measure `min_browse_depth` to show the minimum visible depth that is shown by the hierarchy within the Pivot as follows:

```
min_browse_depth:=
MINX(employee
        , PATHLENGTH(employee[hierarchy_path])
)
```

3. Add a new measure to show the employee count as blank where the `current_browse_depth` measure is greater than the exposed browse depth (`min_browse_depth`):

```
Number of Employees (user design):=
IF(employee[current_browse_depth] >
employee[min_browse_depth]
        , BLANK()
        , COUNTROWS(employee)
)
```

4. For illustration purposes, also add the following measure:

```
show_yn:=
IF(employee[current_browse_depth] >
employee[min_browse_depth]
            , "dont show"
            , "show"
)
```

5. Add all these new measures to the pivot.

Here, we can see the interaction of the `current_browse_depth` and the `min_browse_depth` measures within the application of the hierarchy. The `current_browse_depth` measure shows what level of the hierarchy is being viewed in the pivot. The `min_browse_depth` measure shows the highest level of all employees that is encompassed by a hierarchy value.

> Remember that when the hierarchy is placed on rows, each row in the hierarchy is really just grouping employees. The grouping is identified by an employee's name.

Row Labels	current_browse_depth	min_browse_depth	show_yn
⊟Ken Sánchez	1	1	show
⊟Brian Welcker	2	2	show
⊞Amy Alberts	3	3	show
⊟Brian Welcker	3	2	dont show
⊟Brian Welcker	4	2	dont show
Brian Welcker	5	2	dont show
⊞Stephen Jiang	3	3	show
⊞Syed Abbas	3	3	show
⊞David Bradley	2	2	show

When we view the pivot with these fields, we can say that we want to hide those employees within the hierarchy that appear at higher levels in the structure.

Now, replace all the measures shown with the measure `Number of Employees (user design)`. All rows (previously indicated with a Don't show flag) are hidden from the pivot.

Row Labels	Number of Employees (user design)
⊟ Ken Sánchez	290
⊟ Brian Welcker	18
⊞ Amy Alberts	4
⊞ Stephen Jiang	11
⊞ Syed Abbas	2
⊞ David Bradley	9

This method of hiding rows will only work when all the measures for the row are empty. If the native measure (`Number of Employees (native)`) is reintroduced to the pivot, all lower levels of Brian will be shown.

Creating and using Key Performance Indicators

Key Performance Indicators (KPIs) allow the model to implement a logic layer, so that a value can be monitored according to a rule. The outcome of the rule is a simple set of results that indicates how the value is comparing to the expectations, and usually equates to one of the three simple conditions: bad, moderate, or good.

By summarizing logic into the model in this way, the KPI improves model usability as the user is not required to interpret the value in the context of a business situation (or some layer of logic that is applied to the values); this is all managed by the KPI. Furthermore, since the KPI is represented by a state (for example, bad, moderate, or good), the KPI can cover boundary ranges of data. This effectively discretizes data into a conditional state based on the business logic.

Getting ready

This recipe creates a KPI that compares actual sales to budgeted performance. The KPI should indicate an unfavorable outcome if the sales are more than 5 percent from the budget (unfavorable), a warning if the sales are between this and the budget, and a positive indicator if the sales are reported equal to, or greater than the budget. Set up the model by following these steps:

1. Open the KPIs.xlsx workbook and create (PowerPivot) linked tables for the worksheets Budget, Sales_Header, Dates, and Employees.

2. On the Dates table, hide all columns from client tools except for the columns Year and Month of Year. Set the month of the year column to be sorted by the column month_of_year_sort.

3. Hide all of the columns from the Sales_Header and Budgets table.

4. Create relationships between the following tables and columns:

Table	Column	Related Table	Related Column
Sales_Header	employee_id	Employees	employee_id
Sales_Header	order_dt	Dates	date_id
Budgets	employee_id	Employees	employee_id
Budgets	budget_date	Dates	date_id

5. Create the following measures in the Sales_Header table:

Measure Name	Calculation
Sales Amount	Sales Amount:= SUM(Sales_Header[sales_amount])
Budget Amount	Budget Amount:= SUM(Budgets[budget_amount])
Sales Variance	Sales Variance:= [Sales Amount]-[Budget Amount]
Sales Variance %	Sales Variance %:= if(ISBLANK(Sales_Header[Budget Amount]) , BLANK() , Sales_Header[Sales Amount]/Sales_Header[Budget Amount]-1)
Sales KPI	Sales KPI:= SUM(Sales_Header[sales_amount])

6. Create a pivot that shows the month of the year as row labels with the measures (Sales Amount, Budget Amount, Sales Variance, and Sales Variance %). The Pivot should look like the table in the following screenshot:

Row Labels ▾	Sales Amount	Budget Amount	Sales Variance	Sales Variance %
2005 Jul	452,761	486,839	-34,078	-7.00 %
2005 Aug	1,435,864	1,527,515	-91,651	-6.00 %
2005 Sep	1,102,077	1,160,082	-58,005	-5.00 %
2005 Oct	771,018	803,144	-32,126	-4.00 %
2005 Nov	2,201,515	2,269,602	-68,087	-3.00 %
2005 Dec	1,619,718	1,652,775	-33,057	-2.00 %
2006 Jan	659,508	666,170	-6,662	-1.00 %
2006 Feb	1,812,586	1,812,584	2	0.00 %
2006 Mar	1,345,666	1,332,342	13,324	1.00 %
2006 Apr	808,351	792,501	15,850	2.00 %
2006 May	2,143,894	2,081,452	62,442	3.00 %
2006 Jun	941,894	905,667	36,227	4.00 %
2006 Jul	2,197,996	2,093,329	104,667	5.00 %
2006 Aug	3,461,906	3,265,947	195,959	6.00 %
2006 Sep	2,796,662	2,613,703	182,959	7.00 %
2006 Oct	1,693,161		1,693,161	
2006 Nov	2,928,707		2,928,707	

Note that the variance between Actual Sales and Budget Sales has constantly been improving and that Sales Variance % ranges from **-7.00%** in July 2005 to **7.00%** in September 2006. This coincidence is intended, in order to illustrate how the KPI changes over a value range.

How to do It...

In order to add the KPI to the model, perform the following steps:

1. Open the PowerPivot window and right-click on the Sales KPI measure in the Sales_Header table. Select **Create KPI...** from the pop-up menu.
2. Specify the target value as Budget Amount by selecting it from the drop-down box (where the measure radio button is selected).
3. Ensure that the first icon's style set is selected (a border will indicate the selected style).

4. Select the text from the first indicator and type 94.9. Move the other indicator until it reaches **100%**. The KPI dialogue should look like the following screenshot:

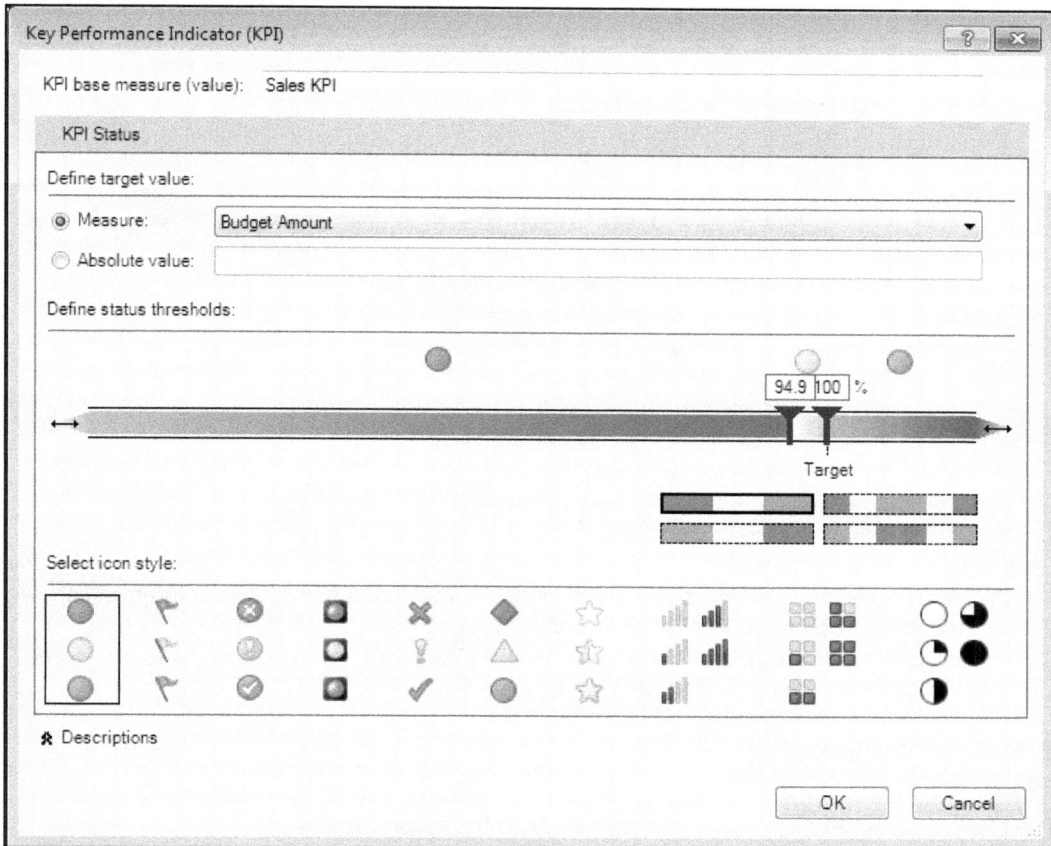

The indicator bars can be slid across the status threshold bar or have values entered directly into the textboxes.

5. Select the **OK** button to complete the process.

6. Return to the Pivot and refresh the model, a new node in the **Sales_Header** table tree will be created titled **Sales KPI**. It has three choices **Value**, **Status**, and **Target**.

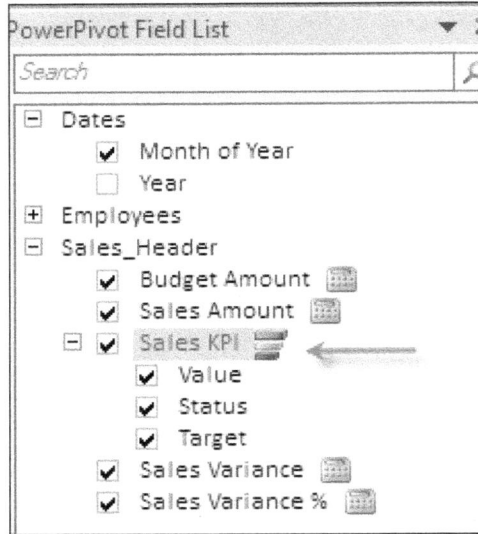

7. Add these three measures to the pivot table. The **Sales KPI Status** column will show as a red cross for sales that have a variance of more than -5 percent, a warning indicator for sales with a variance between -5 percent and 0 percent, and an agreed indicator for the sales that are over budget.

How it works...

The creation of a KPI adds three new measures to the model. These are:

- ▶ **Value**: It holds the value the KPI is based on.
- ▶ **Target**: It holds the value that the `Value` measure is compared to.
- ▶ **Status**: It holds a value that shows how the `Value` measure compares to the `Target` measure (according to the KPI logic). This is an important consideration because the KPI status can also be thought of as a simple condition, which indicates `-1` (for bad), `0` (for moderate), and `1` (for good). The `Status` measure is then converted into an image by the client tool.

We can verify how the KPI status has been translated by the client tool. Outside the pivot table, add a formula that references the `Sales KPI Status` column. The value returned will be either -1, 0, 1.

	A	B	G	H	I	J	K
1		Row Labels ▾	Sales KPI Value	Sales KPI Target	Sales KPI Status		Formula
2		2005 Jul	452,761	486,839	⬤	-1	=I2
3		2005 Aug	1,435,864	1,527,515	⬤	-1	=I3
4		2005 Sep	1,102,077	1,160,082	◯	0	=I4
5		2005 Oct	771,018	803,144	◯	0	=I5
6		2005 Nov	2,201,515	2,269,602	◯	0	=I6
7		2005 Dec	1,619,718	1,652,775	◯	0	=I7
8		2006 Jan	659,508	666,170	◯	0	=I8
9		2006 Feb	1,812,586	1,812,584	⬤	1	=I9
10		2006 Mar	1,345,666	1,332,342	⬤	1	=I10
11		2006 Apr	808,351	792,501	⬤	1	=I11
12		2006 May	2,143,894	2,081,452	⬤	1	=I12
13		2006 Jun	941,894	905,667	⬤	1	=I13
14		2006 Jul	2,197,996	2,093,329	⬤	1	=I14
15		2006 Aug	3,461,906	3,265,947	⬤	1	=I15

The KPI status can be extremely useful when used as a value to filter data. For example, consider the situation where we only want to show data that is considered a bad state (red KPI status). Select the drop-down arrow on the **Row Labels**, then select **Value Filter**, and then **Equals**.

A **Value Filter** window will open. Set the conditions of the window to filter on **Sales KPI Status** for a value of -1. Then, click on **OK**.

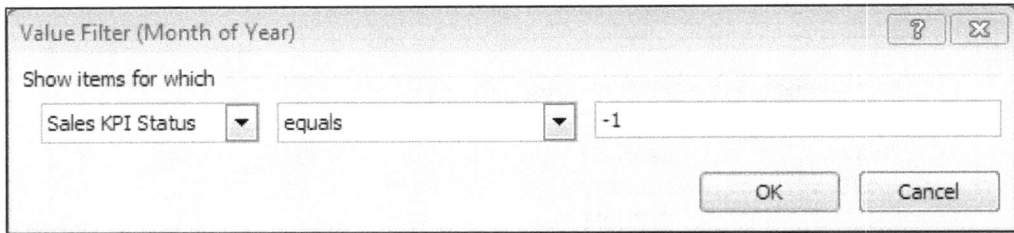

Once this is done, the pivot table will only show the rows with a red KPI indicator.

There's more...

In addition to editing the KPI from the PowerPivot window (right-clicking the **Calculation Area** cell with the KPI formula in it and then selecting **Edit KPI Settings**), the KPI can be edited directly from the workbook by selecting the KPI in the pivot table and selecting **Edit KPI Settings** from the **PowerPivot** tab.

Descriptive information can be added to the KPI by expanding the **Descriptions** section of the **Edit KPI** dialogue. However, the text entered here is not visible from Excel.

The structure of the KPI (for example, what is considered good or bad) can be managed by selecting the appropriate conditional rules under the threshold bar. This also determines the number of threshold indicators that are shown; for example, the following graphic shows the thresholds for an acceptable value (where the KPI value should not deviate too far from a target range):

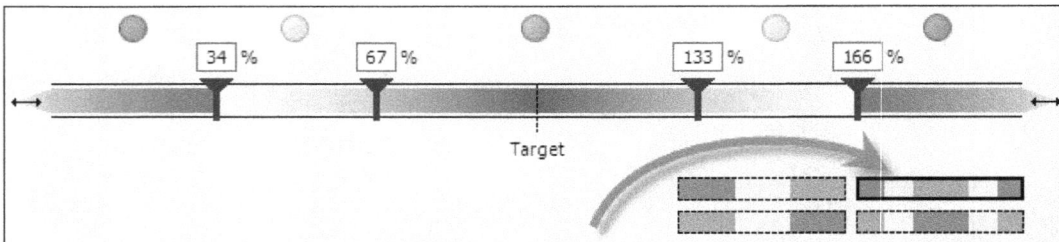

Role playing dimensions and relationships

Role playing dimensions are dimensional structures that are re-used throughout the model. The use of a role playing dimension can simplify model maintenance because only one physical structure is created and it is used many times.

Consider the `Sales_Header` table that has been used in this chapter. It includes three date fields (for `Order Date`, `Due Date`, and `Ship Date`). One date table can be used to reference all three columns.

Getting ready

This workbook model continues with the sales data that has been used so far in this chapter. However, unlike previous models, which focused only on the **Sales Amount** values that were ordered, we show the value of products that were shipped and delivered.

How to do it...

1. Open the workbook `Role Playing.xlsx` and import the `Sales_Header`, `Sales_Detail`, `Products`, and `Dates` tables to a new tabular model.

2. Create relationships between the following tables and fields:

Table	Column	Related Table	Related Column
Sales_Detail	sales_order_id	Sales_Header	sales_order_id
Sales_Detail	product_id	Products	product_id
Sales_Header	order_dt	Dates	date_id
Sales_Header	due_dt	Dates	date_id
Sales_Header	ship_dt	Dates	date_id

3. In design mode, additional relationships between two tables will be shown as dashed lines:

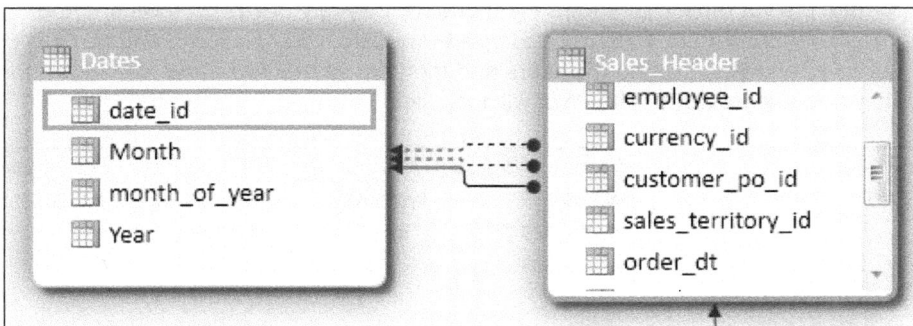

4. Hide the `Sales_Header` table and all the `Sales_Detail` columns from client tools. Then, add the measures `Ordered Amount`, `Shipped Amount`, and `Due Amount` to the model, formatted with no decimal places and comma separation:

```
Ordered Amount:=
CALCULATE (
    SUM([sales_amount]),
 USERELATIONSHIP(Sales_Header[order_dt], Dates[date_id])
)
Shipped Amount:=
CALCULATE (
    SUM([sales_amount]),
 USERELATIONSHIP(Sales_Header[ship_dt], Dates[date_id])
)
Due Amount:=
CALCULATE (
    SUM([sales_amount]),
 USERELATIONSHIP(Sales_Header[due_dt], Dates[date_id])
)
Default Amount:=
SUM([sales_amount])
```

5. In the Dates table:

   1. Sort the `Month` column by the `month_of_year` column.

   2. Create a hierarchy (`Day by Year`) that shows `Year`, `Month`, and `date_id`.

   3. Rename `date_id` to `Date` (within the hierarchy).

   4. Hide all columns in the `Dates` table.

   5. Format the `date_id` column as `14 March 2001`.

6. Create a pivot table that shows the hierarchy `Day by Year` on rows and the measures `Ordered Amount`, `Shipped Amount`, `Due Amount`, and `Default Amount` on rows. Expand the years and months, so that the dates are shown for July and August 2005. The Pivot will look like:

Row Labels	Ordered Amount	Shipped Amount	Due Amount	Default Amount
⊟ 2005	8,065,435	8,065,435	8,065,435	8,065,435
⊟ July	489,329	489,329	489,329	489,329
1 July 2005	489,329			489,329
8 July 2005		489,329		
13 July 2005			489,329	
⊟ August	1,538,408	1,538,408	1,538,408	1,538,408
1 August 2005	1,538,408			1,538,408
8 August 2005		1,538,408		
13 August 2005			1,538,408	
⊞ September	1,165,897	1,165,897	1,165,897	1,165,897

How it works...

The creation of more than one relationship between tables creates a primary (Active) relationship and secondary relationship(s). By default, the Active relationship is used in calculations that are filtered between the two tables.

This can be seen in the pivot table in a way that the default calculation (Default Amount) mimics the measure Ordered Amount. This occurs because the first relationship between the Sales_Header table and the Dates table was between order_dt and date_id (hence, the relationship assumes an Active role).

In order to specify that another relationship should be used in a calculation, we must specify the relationship within that calculation and change the filtering context by including a CALCULATE function. The syntax for USERELATIONSHIP is very simple and automatically determines the lookup table (column) without the need to specify it (as ColumnName1 or ColumnName2). To include USERELATIONSHIP in a formula, simply specify two column names as arguments for the function.

```
USERELATIONSHIP(<columnName1>,<columnName2>)
```

> In order to use the USERELATIONSHIP function, a relationship must be defined between the two columns. The function does not create a relationship, or create a pseudo-relationship, if there is no existing relationship.

There's more...

The Active relationship in the model is indicated in the diagram view by a solid line between two tables. Secondary relationships are shown as a dashed line. This is also visible within the **Manage Relationships** dialogue by the **Active** indicator in the grid.

Active	Table	Related Lookup Table
Yes	Sales_Detail [sales_order_id]	Sales_Header [sales_order_id]
Yes	Sales_Detail [product_id]	Products [product_id]
Yes	Sales_Header [order_dt]	Dates [date_id]
No	Sales_Header [due_dt]	Dates [date_id]
No	Sales_Header [ship_dt]	Dates [date_id]

In order to change the Active relationship, you must first deactivate the current Active relationship and then specify the new Active relationship. In order to do this, edit the relationship and check (or uncheck the **Active** option).

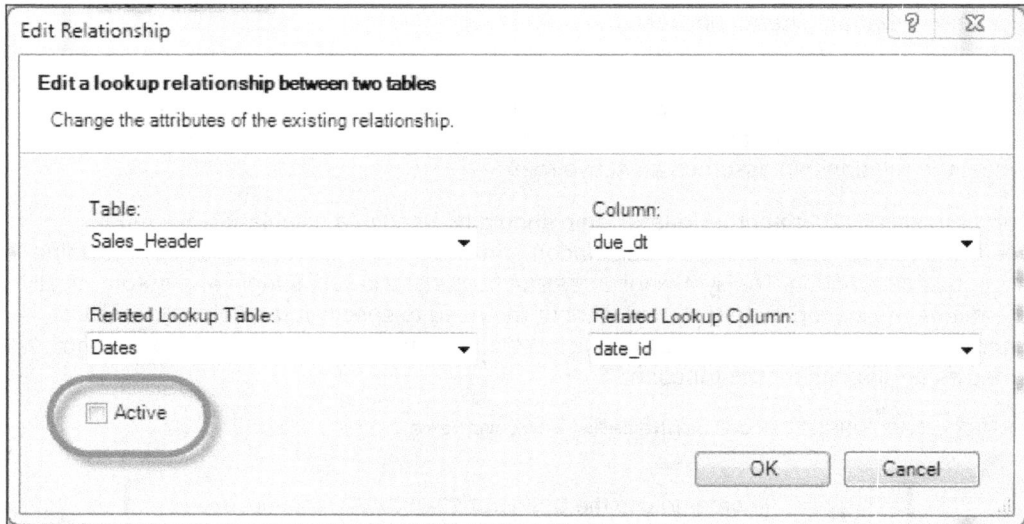

There is no requirement to have an Active relationship between tables in the model. If this is the case and there are no Active relationships defined, any (default) calculations that would otherwise rely on the Active relationship will show duplicated values as if no relationship had existed (see *Linking fields between tables* recipe in *Chapter 1, Getting Started with Excel*).

When editing the model in the Design view, the fields that are active in the relationship are highlighted when the mouse hovers over the relationship. This makes it easy to identify participating fields when browsing the model. Additionally, the relationship can be edited (indicating whether it is active or not) by double-clicking on the relationship line.

Building ratios

We often like to determine the significance of an item within its group, based on its value when compared to the group total. To do that, we use a ratio that indicates the item's importance as a percent age (portion of 100). This recipe examines various techniques for building ratios, based on value data and the presentation of that ratio within the data.

Getting ready

This model continues with the sales data that is being used in previous chapters. Open the Ratios workbook and import the Sales_Header, Sales_Detail, Products, and Dates tables to a new tabular model.

Create relationships between the following tables and fields:

Table	Column	Related Table	Related Column
Sales_Detail	sales_order_id	Sales_Header	sales_order_id
Sales_Header	order_dt	Dates	date_id
Sales_Detail	product_id	Products	product_id

Hide the `Sales_Header` table and all the `Sales_Detail` columns from client tools. Then add the measure `Sales Amount` to the `sales_detail` table:

```
Sales Amount:=SUM([sales_amount])
```

Finally, rename the fields product_name to `Product`, subcategory_name to `Subcategory`, and category_name to `Category`. Then, create a hierarchy (`Product by Category`) that has the levels Category, Subcategory, and Product.

How to do It...

1. Create a measure in the `Sales_Detail` table (`Sales Amount (All Products)`), which shows the value of all product sales. Add the following code:

```
Sales Amount (All Products):=
CALCULATE(Sales_Detail[Sales Amount]
    , ALL(Products))
```

2. Add a measure to the `Sales_Detail` table (`Sales Ratio`), which shows the ratio of the sales against all product sales. Add the measure and format it as a percent age:

```
Sales Ratio:=
[Sales Amount]/[Sales Amount (All Products)]
```

3. Create a pivot with all the three measures as column values and the `Product by Category` hierarchy on rows. Note that the measure `Sales Amount (All Products)` is **80,450,597**, which equals the `Sales Amount` (Grand Total) value. Finally, note that the `Sales Ratio` column correctly shows the value (ratio or mix) for each line.

Row Labels ▼	Sales Amount	Sales Amount (All Products)	Sales Ratio
⊞ -		80,450,597	
⊞ Accessories	541,558	80,450,597	0.67 %
⊞ Bikes	41,360,080	80,450,597	51.41 %
⊞ Clothing	1,191,949	80,450,597	1.48 %
⊞ Components	9,468,393	80,450,597	11.77 %
⊞	27,888,617	80,450,597	34.67 %
Grand Total	**80,450,597**	**80,450,597**	**100.00 %**

4. Create a row filter that only shows the category of `Accessories`, `Bikes`, `Clothing`, and `Components`. Click on the **Row Labels** drop-down arrow and deselect the other categories. Note that the measure `Sales Amount (All Products)` still shows **80,450,597** and that the `Sales Ratio` column does not total to 100 percent.

Row Labels ⊤	Sales Amount	Sales Amount (All Products)	Sales Ratio
⊞ Accessories	541,558	80,450,597	0.67 %
⊞ Bikes	41,360,080	80,450,597	51.41 %
⊞ Clothing	1,191,949	80,450,597	1.48 %
⊞ Components	9,468,393	80,450,597	11.77 %
Grand Total	**52,561,980**	**80,450,597**	**65.33 %**

5. Return to the PowerPivot window and create the following measures. `Sales Amount (Filtered Products)` that should be formatted as numeric and `Sales Ratio (Filtered)` should be formatted as a percent age.

```
Sales Amount (Filtered Products):=
CALCULATE([Sales Amount]
    , ALLSELECTED(Products))

Sales Ratio (Filtered):=
[Sales Amount]/[Sales Amount (Filtered Products)]
```

6. Add these measures to the pivot table. The two new measures show totals for visible cells with the ratio summing to 100 percent.

Row Labels ⊤	Sales Amount	Sales Amount (All P	Sales Ratio	Sales Amount (Filtere	Sales Ratio (Filtered)
⊞ Accessories	541,558	80,450,597	0.67 %	52,561,980	1.03 %
⊞ Bikes	41,360,080	80,450,597	51.41 %	52,561,980	78.69 %
⊞ Clothing	1,191,949	80,450,597	1.48 %	52,561,980	2.27 %
⊞ Components	9,468,393	80,450,597	11.77 %	52,561,980	18.01 %
Grand Total	**52,561,980**	**80,450,597**	**65.33 %**	**52,561,980**	**100.00 %**

How it works...

The calculation of the ratio requires no explanation, as it is simply a numerator divided by a denominator. However, it is worthwhile noting that there is no requirement to check division by zero errors (that is, there is no requirement to check that the denominator equals zero before the division). Expanding the **Accessories** category will show that there are some accessories without sales. These items do not have a sales ratio and do not show an error as one might expect.

The measure which acts as the denominator in the ratio calculations introduces table filtering, which requires further explanation. The normal operation of a measure value in a pivot table is to perform the calculation function at the intersection of the pivot table axis (or the query axis). For example, consider the cell at the intersection of `Accessories` and `Sales Amount`. The value of this cell is effectively obtained by reducing the `Sales_Detail` table to those products that have a category of `Accessories`. Then, a `sum` calculation is performed on the `sales_amount` column to return the value. When the `Accessories` member is expanded in the pivot table (to show measures for `Bike Racks`), the filter is applied so that only sales lines for `Products`, with a Category of `Accessories` and a Subcategory of `Bikes and Racks` is included in the calculation.

The calculation `Sales Amount (All Products)` alters the way this native filtering works. This is done through the use of the `CALCULATE` statement (which specifies that the expression should be evaluated in another context) and subsequent changes to that context. The syntax for the `CALCULATE` function is:

```
CALCULATE(<expression>,<filter1>,<filter2>…)
```

When used within the `Sales Amount (All Products)` formula, the `<filter>`, which is applied (`ALL(Products)`) changes the existing application of the filter created by the row restrictions in the pivot table to `ALL` Products. Therefore, any filter that is applied through the query (or the client tool) is removed when the calculation is evaluated and the calculation is applied to all the products.

The `ALL` function, when used in this manner, simply returns all rows from the `Products` table, thus effectively removing the filter created by the pivot table.

Similarly, the function `ALLSELECTED` is used to restrict the `Products` table to products that are explicitly selected in the pivot.

There's more...

The ability to manipulate how the filter is applied is one of the most powerful features of DAX.

Consider the situation where we would like to provide a nested ratio (as shown in the following screenshot). These types of ratios are often called ratios to parent because they show proportional ratios of their parent in a hierarchy. In this situation, the ratio shows as a percent age of its parent and sums to 100 percent. Here, the measure **Sales Ratio (Nested)** shows the proportion of sales compared to the parent attribute.

For the purposes of this recipe, we will not show the ratio for the products' level of the hierarchy.

Row Labels	Sales Amount	Sales Ratio	Sales Ratio (Filtered)	Sales Ratio (Nested)
⊟ Accessories	541,558	0.67 %	1.03 %	1.03 %
⊞ Bike Racks	197,736	0.25 %	0.38 %	36.51 %
⊞ Bike Stands				
⊞ Bottles and Cages	7,477	0.01 %	0.01 %	1.38 %
⊞ Cleaners	11,188	0.01 %	0.02 %	2.07 %
⊞ Fenders			100 %	
⊞ Helmets	258,713	0.32 %	0.49 %	47.77 %
⊞ Hydration Packs	65,519	0.08 %	0.12 %	12.10 %
⊞ Tires and Tubes	925	0.00 %	0.00 %	0.17 %
⊟ Bikes	41,360,080	51.41 %	78.69 %	78.69 %
⊞ Mountain Bikes	16,016,477	19.91 %	30.47 %	38.72 %
⊞ Road Bikes	14,892,113	18.51 %	28.33 %	36.01 %
⊞ Touring Bikes	10,451,490	12.99 %	19.88 %	25.27 %
⊞ Clothing	1,191,949	1.48 %	2.27 %	2.27 %
⊞ Components	9,468,393	11.77 %	18.01 %	18.01 %
Grand Total	52,561,980	65.33 %	100.00 %	100.00 %

Here, we create another set of measures to show what the sales ratio is for the selected subcategories. Add the following measures:

```
Sales Amount (All Selected Subcategory):=
CALCULATE(
    Sales_Detail[Sales Amount]
    , ALLSELECTED(Products[Subcategory])
)
Sales Ratio (Subcategory):=
[Sales Amount]/[Sales Amount (All Selected Subcategory)]
```

By specifying the `Subcategory` field within `ALLSELECTED`, the filter context for `Products` is forced to the current subcategory (rather than the previous `ALL` Products). When the items shown in the pivot are related to multiple subcategories, as would be the case when the row shows a category, `ALLSELECTED(Products[Subcategory])` returns all Products.

Now, our model contains two ratios, which are expected to be returned depending on the level of the hierarchy that the user is viewing. Firstly, the measure `Sales Ratio (Filtered)` should be shown when the **Accessories** level is being viewed and secondly, `Sales Ratio (Subcategory)` should be shown when the user is at the `Subcategory` level. If the user navigates to **Products**, nothing should be shown.

Unlike MDX (Multidimensional Expressions), DAX does not include the notion of hierarchies (and hierarchy-aware functionality) within calculations; everything must be based on tables and columns. In order to determine which level the user is viewing the hierarchy (or the `Products` table) at, we can check for filtering through the `ISFILTERED` function. For example, to determine if the user is viewing a subcategory, we could simply use `ISFILTERED (Products [Subcategory]`.

The formula for `Sales Ratio (Nested)` is therefore:

```
Sales Ratio (Nested):=
if(ISFILTERED(Products[Product])
    , BLANK()
    , if(ISFILTERED(Products[Subcategory])
    , [Sales Ratio (Subcategory)]
    , [Sales Ratio (Filtered)]
    )
)
```

4
Time Calculations and Date Functions

Often, our models need to display data within the context of time relationships. Therefore, in this chapter, we'll be covering:

- ▶ Calculating running totals–totals to date
- ▶ Month, quarter, and year to date aggregations
- ▶ 445 dates and irregularities
- ▶ Last year and prior period values
- ▶ Relative Time–pivoting around measures
- ▶ Moving averages and last n averages

Introduction

The chapters that have been examined so far treat calculations as a point in time data. That is, some event or occurrence that occurs at a given point in time. Further, the modeling that we have looked at aggregates this data by other tables, which may be thought of as dimensions for analyzing the data.

The ability to manipulate this type of data by dates and date-derived types is one of the most common forms of analysis, and includes a variety of different types of calculations. The most basic form of this analysis is the concepts of trending, and the comparative questions that arise regarding performance against prior periods. This type of analysis always includes the concept of date, and the business implications of a date aggregation (such as month to date value, year to date value, balance to date value, and running balances). Common performance metrics includes trending by time and comparatives to prior periods.

The recipes in this chapter examine how to manipulate and create measures (and define the model) across a date dimension so that this type of analysis can be performed.

Pivotal to date calculations is the concept of the **current date**. The current date is nothing more than a reference point to which a calculation can be based and performed against. Consider the calculation of month to date, this requires a date (current date), otherwise the calculation is meaningless because we cannot calculate a month to date value without a date context. The same current date can then be used to provide year to date, month to date and the like.

Further, the current date as used in a query can be introduced to the tabular filter context in two ways. Firstly, the current date can be set by the report axis (rows or columns) with the current date changing for each row or column for the query. A simple example of this will be the month of the year as columns, where each column represents a change to the filter context. Secondly, the current date can be specified as a report filter where the same value is defined for all the data in the report.

Calculating running totals – totals to date

Running totals are used to provide point-in-time balances where the source data is transactional, and the balance is determined by performing an aggregate on all the values that exist before the current date.

Traditionally, the aggregation of data from the start of the transactional activity has been burdened with performance problems, and model designers have used point-in-time snapshots to reduce the number of calculations required. However, the xVelocity engine in tabular models is very efficient at managing this type of transaction and a simple calculation based on all prior data, could be a viable option when determining totals to date in your model. This recipe shows you how to add a running total to a model.

Getting ready

This recipe determines balances to date for data, and continues with the same type of sales data that has been used in prior chapters. Open the workbook `Sales Book - Time Calcs.xls` and import the `Sales Header`, `Sales Detail`, `Products`, and `Dates` worksheets into a new PowerPivot model. Create the following relationships within the model:

Table	Column	Related Table	Related Column
Sales_Header	order_dt	Dates	date_id
Sales_Detail	sales_order_id	Sales_Header	sales_order_id
Sales_Detail	product_id	Products	product_id

Hide the `Sales_Header` table from the client tools and all the columns from the `Sales_Detail` table.

In the `Products` table hide all fields except for `Product`, `Category`, and `Subcategory`. Create a hierarchy called `Product by Category` and include the levels `Category`, `Subcategory`, and `Product`.

In the `Dates` table, rename the fields `year_cal`, `month_name_cal`, and `date_id` to `Year`, `Cal Month`, and `Date`. Then, create a hierarchy titled `Calendar Dates` and include those columns (in that order) as levels. Set the **Sort by Column** of `Cal Month` to `month_id_cal` and then, hide the column from the client tools.

Finally, rename the field `Cal Month` in the calendar day's hierarchy to `Month`. Hide the fields `date_id`, `month_id_445`, `month_id_cal`, `month_name_445`, `qtr_id_445`, `qtr_445`, and `year_445` from the client tools. The `Dates` table should appear as shown in the following screenshot:

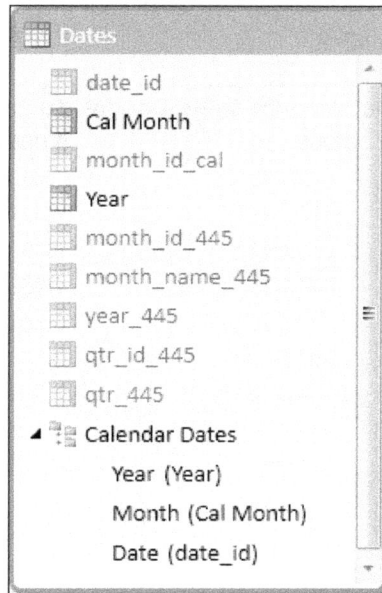

How to do it...

Our recipe starts by creating a generic sales calculation. This can then be used by another calculation that alters the query context to provide a running total.

1. In the `Sales_Detail` table, add the formula `Sales Amount` measure, which sums the `Sales_Detail.sales_amount` column.

   ```
   Sales Amount:=SUM([sales_amount])
   ```

2. Add another measure to show the accumulating balance of the sales amount as follows:

```
Sales Amount (To Date):=
  CALCULATE(Sales_Detail[Sales Amount]
  , FILTER(all(dates)
  , Dates[date_id]<=MAX(Dates[date_id]))
)
```

3. Add a new measure to the `Sales_Detail` table to show the expected result of the `MAX(DATE)` component of the `Sales Amount (To Date)` calculation:

```
Max Date:=MAX(Dates[date_id])
```

4. Create a pivot with the `Calendar Dates` hierarchy on rows and the `Sales Amount`, `Sales Amount (To Date)`, and `Max Date` measures. Expand the `Years` **2005** and **2006** to the `Months` level. Your pivot should look something like the following screenshot:

Row Labels ⊤	Sales Amount	Sales Amount (To Date)	Max Date
⊟ 2005	8,065,435	8,065,435	31-Dec-05
⊞ Jul	489,329	489,329	31-Jul-05
⊞ Aug	1,538,408	2,027,737	31-Aug-05
⊞ Sep	1,165,897	3,193,634	30-Sep-05
⊞ Oct	844,721	4,038,355	31-Oct-05
⊞ Nov	2,324,136	6,362,491	30-Nov-05
⊞ Dec	1,702,945	8,065,435	31-Dec-05
⊟ 2006	24,144,430	32,209,865	31-Dec-06
⊞ Jan	713,117	8,778,552	31-Jan-06
⊞ Feb	1,900,789	10,679,341	28-Feb-06
⊞ Mar	1,455,280	12,134,621	31-Mar-06

How it works...

The calculation for `Sales Amount (To Date)` is a good example to demonstrate how a DAX measure can contort the filter context, which is created by the query. Further, the concepts of a current date that were discussed in the introduction are shown through the creation and use of the measure `Max Date`. In this scenario, the current date is materialized to the user as `Max Date`.

We can rationalize that the current date should be the maximum date of the filter context. If we have selected a month (an entire month as an attribute), we would rationalize that the current date should be the last day of the month. The expected result of `MAX(Dates([date_id]))` as part of the calculation returns the maximum date from the applied (date) filter—the filter in this case is applied as a result of the row values. When the filter context controlled by the query is a `Year` (as in the 2005 value of the pivot), the formula simply returns the last date of that year.

It may also be beneficial to recognize that because of the use of the hierarchy, the Month level of the hierarchy automatically got filtered by Years in the preceding level of the hierarchy. If we were to replace the Pivots row hierarchy with the Cal Months attribute, we would see the last date for all months of the filter context (for example, the last date in January, or all January months). This is important because months (as far as running totals are concerned) should be considered within a year—and this is exactly what the hierarchy provides. The following screenshot illustrates the previously discussed feature:

Row Labels ▾	Max Date
Jan	31-Jan-10
Feb	28-Feb-10
Mar	31-Mar-10
Apr	30-Apr-10
May	31-May-10
Jun	30-Jun-10
Jul	31-Jul-10
Aug	31-Aug-10
Sep	30-Sep-10
Oct	31-Oct-10
Nov	30-Nov-10
Dec	31-Dec-10
Grand Total	**31-Dec-10**

The CALCULATE function is used to alter the filter context, which is natively provided by the query. What we want to do, is firstly remove any date filter from the SUM calculation, and then reapply it so that the new filter context includes the current date and all dates prior to it. This is achieved through the use of the FILTER function within the calculate command, as shown in the following code:

```
FILTER(ALL(dates), Dates[date_id]<=MAX(Dates[date_id]))
```

The FILTER function that restricts rows returned by a table according to the <filter> predicate and follows the syntax is as follows:

```
FILTER(<table>,<filter>)
```

When used within our CALCULATE statement, the result of the FILTER function is all rows from the Dates table that are less than (or equal to) the current date. This is achieved by removing any filters on the Dates table (that is selecting ALL(Dates) as the <table> argument) and then applying a new filter that enforces the predicate whereby the Dates.date_id is less than or equal to the current date.

Month, quarter, and year to date aggregations

Month to Date (MTD), **Quarter to Date (QTD)**, and **Year to Date (YTD)** aggregations are arguably the most common aggregation functions performed on transactional data over time periods. The calculations implicitly include a business context to the end user because the user understands the start and end of the period that is used within the calculation. Consider the phrase Year to Date. Within this term, we assume an aggregation of periods in the current year to the current date. But without an understanding of when the year starts (or ends), the term is meaningless.

This recipe looks at how to build these *to-date* measures within a tabular model.

Getting ready

This recipe follows from the prior recipe *Calculating running totals – totals to date*, and assumes that the workbook from that recipe is completed.

How to do it...

Period to date calculations require that the model has a `Dates` table. This is simply a table that the tabular model can use to reference as a range of dates.

1. Mark the `Dates` table as a date table by selecting the **Mark as Date Table** button from the `Design` tab and specifying the date (column) as the `date_id` field, as shown in the following screenshot:

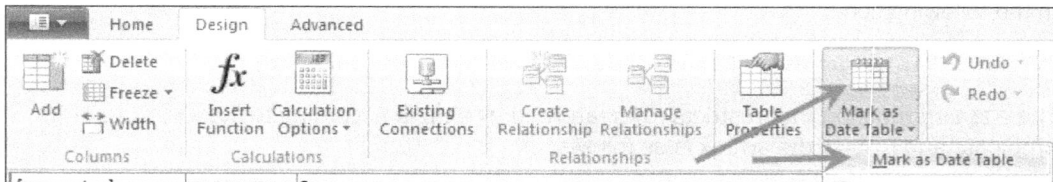

2. Add the `Sales Amount (QTD)` and `Sales Amount (YTD)` measures for the accumulating Sales Amount (QTD and YTD). These should be added in the `Sales_Detail` table, as shown in the following code:

```
Sales Amount QTD:=TOTALQTD([Sales Amount], Dates[date_id])
Sales Amount YTD:=TOTALYTD([Sales Amount], Dates[date_id])
```

3. Create a pivot table from the model, which shows the `Calendar Dates` hierarchy on rows, and the measures `Sales Amount` and `Sales Amount YTD` on columns. Expand the `Years` **2005** and **2006** so that the pivot table looks like the following screenshot:

Row Labels ⊤	Sales Amount	Sales Amount YTD
⊟ 2005	8,065,435	8,065,435
⊞ Jul	489,329	489,329
⊞ Aug	1,538,408	2,027,737
⊞ Sep	1,165,897	3,193,634
⊞ Oct	844,721	4,038,355
⊞ Nov	2,324,136	6,362,491
⊞ Dec	1,702,945	8,065,435
⊟ 2006	24,144,430	24,144,430
⊞ Jan	713,117	713,117
⊞ Feb	1,900,789	2,613,906
⊞ Mar	1,455,280	4,069,186
⊞ Apr	882,900	4,952,086
⊞ May	2,269,117	7,221,203
⊞ Jun	1,001,804	8,223,006
⊞ Jul	2,393,690	10,616,696

The `Sales Amount YTD` holds the cumulative balance of the transaction values. The accumulated value restarts in January each year.

How it works...

The totals to date functions (which includes `TOTALYTD`, `TOTALQTD`, and `TOTALMTD`) evaluate a calculation over the range of dates according to the requirements of the function (where requirements are presented as an `<expression>`). That is, if the function is `TOTALYTD`, the function will accumulate dates according to the current date, and perform a calculation for all dates that occur up to, and including the current date. It is not necessary to define the current date for this formula because it is implied by the relationship within the model. The syntax for these functions follows the same format:

```
TOTALYTD
    (<expression>,<dates>[,<filter>][,<year_end_date>])
```

Since `<year_end_date>` is not required for the month to date calculations, the function `TOTALMTD` excludes this parameter.

In just the same way as the other calculations have used an existing measure as the basis of the calculation, the use of `[Sales Amount]` in this calculation is equivalent to including the qualified measure in place of `<expression>`. Therefore, the two calculations `TOTALYTD([Sales Amount], Dates[date_id])` and `TOTALYTD(sum(sales_amount), Dates[date_id])` are the same.

There's more...

If there is no `<year_end_date>` supplied (as in the previous code), the function defaults to an end date of December 31. It is relatively simple to replace this with another date using the example (for a year end of June 30) as:

```
Sales Amount YTD(30 Jun):=
    TOTALYTD([Sales Amount], Dates[date_id],"30 Jun")
```

445 dates and irregularities

Manufacturing and retail companies often use a special type of calendar, which ensures that all months have an equal number of days. This is commonly called a **445 calendar**, which indicates that a month is made of 4 weeks, with the next month comprising 4 weeks, and the final month (in the quarter) comprising of 5 weeks. The next quarter follows the same pattern of 2 x 4 weeks and then a 5-week month.

Month names in the 445 calendar do not always equate to the calendar month. The 445 calendar month of January may run into February, and December may run into January (in fact this is frequently the case). Further, the week can start on any day of the calendar week, and a 445 calendar's month never end on the same calendar day of a month.

Although there are variations of this pattern (454 and 544), the concepts and implications of the calendar are the same. It poses a challenge in the model because a year does not start or end on the same date, and the months do not align with the calendar months. This recipe examines month to date, quarter to date, and year to date calculations under a 445 calendar.

Getting ready

This recipe builds on the workbook used in the prior recipe (*Month, quarter, and year to date aggregations*). Examine the `Dates` table; the table aligns each day to a month and year in the 445 calendar.

How to do it...

Unlike the period to date calculations that were addressed in the previous recipe, the 445 calendar cannot rely on end dates. Our method must rely on the metadata of the calendar.

1. Launch the PowerPivot window.

2. On the `Dates` table, set the **Sort by Column** of `month_name_445` to `month_id_445`.

3. Create a hierarchy titled `445 Dates` and include the fields `year_445`, `month_name_445`, and `date_id`. Rename the hierarchy levels to `Year`, `Month`, and `Date`. The `Dates` table should look something like the following screenshot:

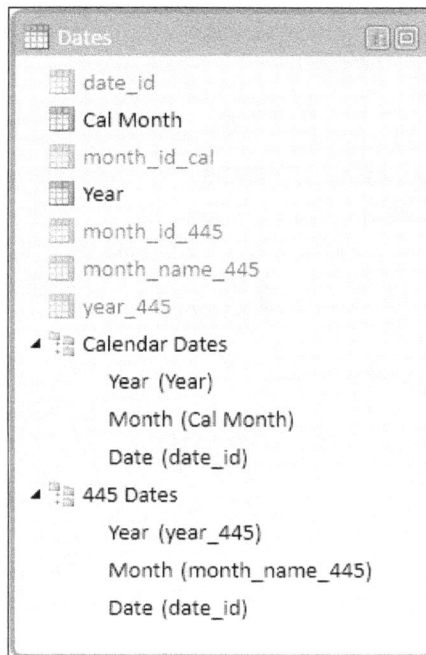

4. Add the following measures to the `Sales_Detail` table:

```
First Date of Period:=FIRSTDATE(Dates[date_id])
Last Date of Period:=LASTDATE(Dates[date_id])
Sales Amount 445 YTD:=CALCULATE([Sales Amount]
   , Filter(ALL(Dates)
   , Dates[year_445]=MAX(Dates[year_445])
   && Dates[date_id]<=MAX(Dates[date_id])
   )
)
```

The placement of measures within tables is at the discretion of the modeler. Measures such as `First Date of Period` and `Last Date of Period` may be better placed in the `Dates` table in larger models (since they are natively associated with a `Dates` subject area). Placing measures in tables that they are associated with may make sense from a tabular modeling point of view (since the measures will appear in the appropriate subject area); however, the multidimensional representation of this will create many measure groups, which may be overwhelming for the user. However, measure names must be unique within the model.

Alternatively, the modeler may choose to create an empty table and then create all measures there. This will only expose one measure group to the client tool, which may provide a simpler interface for the end user.

5. Format the measure `Sales Amount 445 YTD` as a numeric type (comma separated at no decimal places) and the short date dd-mm-yy.

6. Create a pivot table with the hierarchy `445 Dates` on rows and expand the **2006** year to the `Month` level. Add the following measures to columns: `Sales Amount`, `Sales Amount 445 YTD`, `First Date of Period`, and `Last Date of Period`. The pivot table will look as shown in the following screenshot:

Row Labels ▾	Sales Amount	Sales Amount 445 YTD	First Date of Period	Last Date of Period
⊞ 2004			01-Jan-05	02-Jan-05
⊞ 2005	8,778,552	8,778,552	03-Jan-05	01-Jan-06
⊟ 2006	23,431,313	23,431,313	02-Jan-06	31-Dec-06
⊞ Jan			02-Jan-06	29-Jan-06
⊞ Feb	1,900,789	1,900,789	30-Jan-06	26-Feb-06
⊞ Mar	2,338,180	4,238,969	27-Feb-06	02-Apr-06
⊞ Apr		4,238,969	03-Apr-06	30-Apr-06
⊞ May	2,269,117	6,508,086	01-May-06	28-May-06
⊞ Jun	3,395,493	9,903,579	29-May-06	02-Jul-06
⊞ Jul		9,903,579	03-Jul-06	30-Jul-06
⊞ Aug	3,601,191	13,504,770	31-Jul-06	27-Aug-06
⊞ Sep	4,687,513	18,192,283	28-Aug-06	01-Oct-06
⊞ Oct		18,192,283	02-Oct-06	29-Oct-06
⊞ Nov	3,053,816	21,246,100	30-Oct-06	26-Nov-06
⊞ Dec	2,185,213	23,431,313	27-Nov-06	31-Dec-06
⊞ 2007	32,202,669	32,202,669	01-Jan-07	30-Dec-07
⊞ 2008	16,038,063	16,038,063	31-Dec-07	28-Dec-08

How it works...

The addition of the measures `First Date of Period` and `Last Date of Period` demonstrates the issues that are associated with 445 calendars. Namely, the inconsistent ending dates for months and years. Because there is no *defining* end date, it would not be possible to achieve the YTD aggregation through the `TotalYTD` function.

The `FIRSTDATE` and `LASTDATE` functions have a simple syntax, with the output being the expected first and last date for the dates that are passed through the `<dates>` argument. Since each cell in the pivot applies a different (date) filter (that is a filter, based on the dates held at the consolidated (row) levels), the function simply returns the first (and last) date for all dates within the bounds of the row items. Remember that the rows are filtered by both `Years` and `Months`. This is conceptually the same as the use of `MIN` and `MAX` functions.

```
FIRSTDATE(<dates>) , LASTDATE(<dates>)
```

The measure `Sales Amount 445 YTD` works by adjusting the `Dates` filter context in the same way that we would logically rationalize the aggregation problem. That is, give me all dates within the current year which are before (or equal to) the current date. Note that the current year is implied by its association to the current date within the 445 hierarchy. Therefore, we must remove the existing filter from the `Dates` table (that is, the one created by the query) and reapply it according to the 445 chosen year. This is achieved with the following code:

```
Filter(ALL(Dates)
  , Dates[year_445]=MAX(Dates[year_445])
  && Dates[date_id]<=MAX(Dates[date_id])
)
```

Last year and prior period values

One of the most common forms of comparison for a value is that of a base value to prior periods. The idea of a prior period generally takes either of the following two forms:

► Comparison to a different period which relates to the current period—for example, comparison with the last month

► Comparison to the same period with a year offset—for example, this month last year

Both forms of this calculation are conceptually the same—it is only the offset that is applied in the calculation that is different. Consider the situation of determining a value for the last month. Here, we perform a base calculation with a monthly offset from the current date. For the last year value, we perform the same base calculation with a 12-month offset. Of course, the 12-month offset can be simplified as one year, but the calculation is the same.

Furthermore, by considering a base calculation in the context of a current date, the logic of prior period calculations can be applied to any base calculation. The calculation is generally irrelevant—we are only adapting the filter context used in the measure, so that the current date used by the base calculation (or base measure) is relative to the date supplied by the client (query).

Getting ready

This recipe continues from the *445 dates and irregularities* recipe.

How to do it...

We will create measures for `Sales Amount LM` (Sales Amount Last Month), `Sales Amount LY` (Sales Amount Last Year), and `Sales Amount YTD LY` (Sales Amount YTD Last Year).

1. Open the workbook `Sales Book - Time Calcs.xls`. Since the model in this book has been used in a previous recipe, the tables are imported, formatted, and have hierarchies defined. The model also includes the base measure `Sales Amount`.

2. Create the following measures in the `Sales_Detail` table with a numeric, comma separated with no decimal places:

```
Sales Amount LM:=CALCULATE([Sales Amount]
  , DATEADD(Dates[date_id], -1, MONTH)
)

Sales Amount LY:=CALCULATE([Sales Amount]
  , DATEADD(Dates[date_id], -1, YEAR)
)

Sales Amount YTD LY:=
  CALCULATE(Sales_Detail[Sales Amount YTD]
  , DATEADD(Dates[date_id], -1, YEAR)
)
```

> The benefits of a reusable shell measure should be apparent. All these measures are based on the [Sales Amount] measure. If our model requires a change so that [Sales Amount] is be calculated in a different way, a change will only be required in one measure. Since all other (sales-based) measures rely on [Sales Amount], all changes would be propagated throughout the model.

3. Create a pivot with the `Calendar Dates` hierarchy on rows and the measures (`Sales Amount, Sales Amount LM, Sales Amount LY, Sales Amount YTD`, and `Sales Amount YTD LY`) on columns. Expand the `Years` for **2005** and **2006** so that the `Months` level is shown. The pivot should look as shown in the following screenshot:

Row Labels ⊤	Sales Amount	Sales Amount LM	Sales Amount LY	Sales Amount YTD	Sales Amount YTD LY
⊟ 2005	8,065,435	6,362,491		8,065,435	
⊞ Jul	489,329			489,329	
⊞ Aug	1,538,408	489,329		2,027,737	
⊞ Sep	1,165,897	1,538,408		3,193,634	
⊞ Oct	844,721	1,165,897		4,038,355	
⊞ Nov	2,324,136	844,721		6,362,491	
⊞ Dec	1,702,945	2,324,136		8,065,435	
⊟ 2006	24,144,430	23,662,161	8,065,435	24,144,430	8,065,435
⊞ Jan	713,117	1,702,945		713,117	
⊞ Feb	1,900,789	713,117		2,613,906	
⊞ Mar	1,455,280	1,900,789		4,069,186	
⊞ Apr	882,900	1,455,280		4,952,086	
⊞ May	2,269,117	882,900		7,221,203	
⊞ Jun	1,001,804	2,269,117		8,223,006	
⊞ Jul	2,393,690	1,001,804	489,329	10,616,696	489,329
⊞ Aug	3,601,191	2,393,690	1,538,408	14,217,887	2,027,737
⊞ Sep	2,885,359	3,601,191	1,165,897	17,103,246	3,193,634

How it works...

It is easy to see that our calculations work. In August 2005, the `Sales Amount LM` value ($489,329) is the July amount (last month amount). In July 2006, the value also appears as the `Sales Amount LY` value. This is repeated for comparisons of measures `Sales Amount YTD` and `Sales Amount YTD LY`.

For the measures `Sales Amount LM` and `Sales Amount LY`, the base measure used was `Sales Amount`. Remember that this measure is simply the sum of `sales_amount`, and represents the sum within the current filter context. For a monthly value (or a cell in the `Sales Amount` column), this is just the dates within that month. Consider the intersection of `Sales Amount` (July 2005)—value of $489,329—the filter context here is simply `Years` of 2005 and the months of July—that is, dates in July 2005.

Now consider the formula `Sales Amount LM` in the context of the cell of Aug 2005. The formula for the cell is as follows:

```
CALCULATE([Sales Amount], DATEADD(Dates[date_id], -1, MONTH))
```

In Aug 2005, the current date (filter context) is all dates in Aug 2005, the native filter context for the cell will be all the dates in the month.

The `DATEADD` function follows the ensuing syntax:

```
DATEADD(<dates>,<number_of_intervals>,<interval>)
```

It also returns a table of the dates shifted, that is, `<number_of_intervals>` by the `<interval>`. The formula `Sales Amount LM` reduces these dates by one month. The interval can be one of the values `YEAR`, `QUARTER`, `MONTH`, or `DAY`.

Therefore, the dates returned through the `DATEADD` function are all the dates in July (2005) and these are the date(s) used within the `<expression>` of the `CALCULATE` statement.

This principle is applied in all other calculations.

There's more...

The *Month, quarter, and year to date aggregations* recipe, introduced the concept of the `Dates` table. The definition of this table is important in DAX because the table is used as a reference for date-based calculations. Note that the first argument of the `DATEADD` function is a column of dates. In this situation, we have used a date column that existed in the `Dates` table which had a relationship that was used in the model. This is a natural choice, since the `Dates` table includes a continuous list of dates, and this is a requirement of the function argument. There is no requirement however, to have any relationships between the model and the `dates` column used in the function. In fact, we could use any column of dates.

Further, the range of `<dates>` that is provided to the `DATEADD` function does affect its outcome and this should be considered by the modeler when considering the range of dates to include in a `Dates` table (whether it is used as a dimension or not).

Add the following measures to the `Dates` table:

```
Min Date:=CALCULATE(MIN([date_id]))
Min Date LY:=CALCULATE([Min Date], DATEADD(Dates[date_id],
  -1, YEAR))
```

Put these measures on a pivot table with the `Calendar Dates` hierarchy on rows, and then expand **2005** and **2006** as shown in the following screenshot:

Row Labels ▼	Min Date	Min Date LY
⊟ 2005	01-Jan-05	
⊞ Jan	01-Jan-05	
⊞ Feb	01-Feb-05	
⊞ Mar	01-Mar-05	
⊞ Apr	01-Apr-05	
⊞ May	01-May-05	
⊞ Jun	01-Jun-05	
⊞ Jul	01-Jul-05	
⊞ Aug	01-Aug-05	
⊞ Sep	01-Sep-05	
⊞ Oct	01-Oct-05	
⊞ Nov	01-Nov-05	
⊞ Dec	01-Dec-05	
⊟ 2006	01-Jan-06	01-Jan-05
⊞ Jan	01-Jan-06	01-Jan-05
⊞ Feb	01-Feb-06	01-Feb-05

The values returned for `Min Date LY` are constrained by the values in the `Dates` table. Notice that the first and earliest date that is in the `Dates` table is **01-Jan-05**. We know this because it is based on the value of `Min Date`. Also, note that the earliest date for the measure `Min Date LY` is **01-Jan-05** (the same earliest date as `Min Date`). If we examine the date in the `Dates` table, we also find that this is the earliest date in the table.

Since the `DATEADD` function is dependent on the `Dates` table (its date field is required as the first argument in the function), the value returned from the function can never be a date that does not exist in these dates. The `Dates` table used in models should therefore, have a range that will cover the expected requirements of measures.

You might expect that `DATEADD` performs a calculation against the `Date` type, but this is not the case.

Relative Time – pivoting around measures

A **Relative Time** dimension is an example of a **Utility** dimension, a dimension that does not directly join to the data being analyzed, and is not directly used to slice and dice data. Rather, the Utility dimension assists the modeler (and user) by making the presentation of the model more user-friendly. An example of this is allowing the user to select a measure to show in the pivot they create (or report), by allowing them to select a dimension member (that is, the measure name from a list of options).

Consider the following screenshot, which shows a very simple proforma report with `Years` and `Months` on rows, and the product categories on columns. A Utility dimension allows the user to select the measure that they wish to see in the report data area. They do not have to alter the pivot table by dragging a measure to the `Values` section of the pivot table layout.

> A proforma can be thought of as a shell report layout. In the following screenshot, we can see the expected layout of the report. All we have to do is populate it with some measure value.

This principle can also be used in most reporting tools as shown in the following screenshot:

Measure Name	All		
Test			
Row Labels	Accessories	Bikes	Clothi
⊟ 2005			
⊞ Jan			
⊞ Feb			
⊞ Mar			
⊞ Apr			
⊞ May			
⊞ Jun			
⊞ Jul			
⊞ Aug			
⊞ Sep			
⊞ Oct			
⊞ Nov			
⊞ Dec			
⊟ 2006			
⊞ Jan			
⊞ Feb			

Additionally, the user can use the Utility dimension to stack values into the pivot table (or any report). This recipe looks at how to create a Utility dimension for measure selection in a tabular model.

Getting ready

This recipe continues with the model that was developed in the *Last year and prior period values* recipe. The model already contains multiple measures (such as `Sales Amount`, `Sales Amount (To Date)`, and `Sales Amount YTD`). We will create a Utility dimension for the user to select which measure they want to see in the reports.

How to do it...

This recipe starts by creating the Utility dimension.

1. Launch the PowerPivot window and import the Excel named range `Measure_Name` on the sheet `Measure Name` into the tabular model.

2. Hide the field `measure_id` from the client tools.

3. Create a new measure in the `Measure_Name` table (`Dynamic Measure`) to determine what measure name is filtered and return the appropriate measure:

```
Dynamic Measure:=
  if (COUNTROWS (VALUES ('Measure Name'))<>1
  , BLANK()
  ,  SWITCH (VALUES ('Measure Name' [measure_id])
  , 1, Sales_Detail [Sales Amount]
  , 2, Sales_Detail [Sales Amount (To Date)]
  , 3, Sales_Detail [Sales Amount YTD]
  , 4,  Sales_Detail [Sales Amount YTD(30 Jun)]
  , 5, Sales_Detail [Sales Amount LM]
  , 6, Sales_Detail [Sales Amount LY]
  , 7, Sales_Detail [Sales Amount YTD LY]
  )
)
```

4. Create the pivot table (as shown previously) with the `Calendar Dates` hierarchy on rows (expand the `Years` **2005** and **2006**) and `Category` (from the `Products` table) on columns. Add the `Measure Name` field as a pivot filter and the measure `Dynamic Measure` as a value.

5. Test that changing the filter changes the values in the pivot.

6. Alter the pivot by removing `Category` from the columns and placing `Measure Name` on columns. Set the **Sort by Column** filter so that only `Sales Amount`, `Sales Amount LM`, and `Sales Amount LY` are shown. The pivot will look as shown in the following screenshot:

Dynamic Measure	Column Labels ⊤		
Row Labels ⊤	Sales Amount	Sales Amount LM	Sales Amount LY
⊟ 2005	8,065,435	6,362,491	
⊞ Jul	489,329		
⊞ Aug	1,538,408	489,329	
⊞ Sep	1,165,897	1,538,408	
⊞ Oct	844,721	1,165,897	
⊞ Nov	2,324,136	844,721	
⊞ Dec	1,702,945	2,324,136	
⊟ 2006	24,144,430	23,662,161	8,065,435
⊞ Jan	713,117	1,702,945	
⊞ Feb	1,900,789	713,117	
⊞ Mar	1,455,280	1,900,789	
⊞ Apr	882,900	1,455,280	
⊞ May	2,269,117	882,900	
⊞ Jun	1,001,804	2,269,117	
⊞ Jul	2,393,690	1,001,804	489,329
⊞ Aug	3,601,191	2,393,690	1,538,408
⊞ Sep	2,885,359	3,601,191	1,165,897

How it works...

The method of providing a value based on the Utility dimension revolves around two steps. Firstly, we ensure that only one value is selected in the Utility dimension (in whatever filter context is provided by the query) and secondly, we determine which value (or measure) is to be returned based on the selected measure (value).

Ensure that only one value selected is contained within the `IF` function. This is used to return a `BLANK()` function if more than one value is selected as the measure to display.

The use of `COUNTROWS(VALUES('Measure Name'))<>1` as the first argument for the `IF` function simply returns the number of rows from the table that are selected in the query (filter) context. If more than one value is selected, `BLANK()` is returned, otherwise the selected measure is evaluated and returned.

[Constructing the `IF` function in this way (so that, the true part of the statement returns `Blank()` as the first argument) allows us to put the more complex parts of the formula at the end of the `IF` statement. This can help to reduce the clutter of the formula and make it more readable.]

Secondly, if a single row is selected, the `SWITCH` statement will determine what `measure_id` is chosen, and return the measure associated with that `measure_id` (remember that this may happen for each cell in the pivot results). The `SWITCH` statement has the following syntax:

```
SWITCH
(<expression>
  , <value>, <result>
  [, <value>, <result>]
[, <else>]
)
```

Once a `measure_id` value is known, it is easy to see how this is used by `SWITCH`—the real measure is outputted as the `<result>`. Note the `<value>` and `<result>` arguments of the `SWITCH` statement in the preceding formula.

```
, 1, Sales_Detail[Sales Amount]
, 2, Sales_Detail[Sales Amount (To Date)]
, 3, Sales_Detail[Sales Amount YTD]
, 4,  Sales_Detail[Sales Amount YTD(30 Jun)]
, 5, Sales_Detail[Sales Amount LM]
, 6, Sales_Detail[Sales Amount LY]
, 7, Sales_Detail[Sales Amount YTD LY]
```

Finally, it is worth pointing out the use of the `VALUES()` function within the `SWITCH` statement. The `SWITCH` statement will only be evaluated when one row from the `Measure Names` table is selected. Therefore, we are guaranteed that only one row is returned by the `VALUES()` function, and this is the `measure_id` value of the selected measure.

Moving averages and last n averages

Moving averages are often used in analysis for two purposes.

Firstly, they are used to remove volatility from single point values. By including a number of prior observations, a smoother estimation of the volatile point is defined.

Secondly, they remove volatility and can provide the general (and expected) trend movement (just as any consecutive set of numbers are an indicator of trend). Since a daily value may include prior N periods, the value of N is often used to support long-term or short-term trends. For example, a trend based on 30 days may be considered a long-term trend, whereas a trend based on five days may be used to provide a short-term trend. This type of smoothing, and a mix of long- and short-term trends is often used in charting analysis for stock prices.

This recipe shows how to perform last N calculations over stock data. The data is from the Australian Stock Exchange between January 1993 and December 2006. There are approximately 2.5 million value {StockCode, TradingDate} combinations for almost 3,000 stock codes.

Getting ready

Open the workbook Stock Trades and note the three tables (Stocks, Trading History, and Dates). Stocks is a table that lists stock codes. This could include other characteristics such as the stock name, industry, and market. However, for our purposes the field StockCode is sufficient to identify a stock. The table Trading History shows the closing value (CloseValue) for the stock on a given day, and the table Dates is a sequential date table (from January 1, 2003 to December 31, 2006). Dates shows the Year, Month Name, and Month_Sort for each date.

We are going to create a measure that shows the last 10-day average of the closing price.

How to do it...

Start by defining the relationships with the model.

1. Create a relationship between the column TradeDate in Trading History, and TradeDate in the Dates table. Create a relationship between the StockCode column in the Trading History table and the StockCode in the Stocks table. The diagram of the model is quiet simple and should look like the following screenshot:

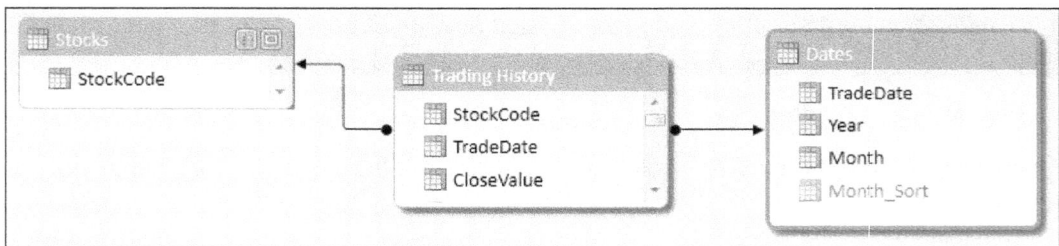

2. In the Dates table, set the **Sort by Column** of the Month field to Month_Sort and hide the Month_Sort field (from the client tools).

3. In the `Dates` table (and the **Design** tab), define the field `TradingDate` as a `Dates` date field by clicking on the **Mark as Date Table** button and specifying `TradingDate` as the date field, as shown in the following screenshot:

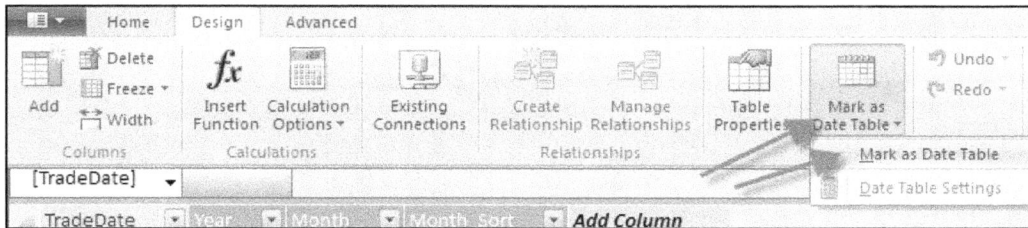

4. In the `Trading History` table, define a measure `Avg Value` (average value) with a two decimal (comma separated) number format as shown in the following code:

```
Avg Value:=AVERAGE([CloseValue])
```

5. In the `Trading History` table, define a measure which shows the maximum date from the `Dates` table filtered perspective. This is the current date. (format the measure as a date March 14, 2001):

```
Max Date:=MAX(Dates[TradeDate])
```

6. In the `Trading History` table, define a measure that shows the date of the day which is 10 days before the current date. Format the measure as a date (March 14, 2001):

```
Max Date -10:=CALCULATE([MAX Date]
    , DATEADD(Dates[TradeDate],-9,DAY)
)
```

7. In the `Trading History` table, define the measure, which holds the average value for the past 10 days' trading. Format the measure with a numeric (comma separated), two decimal place format:

```
Avg Value (10 Running):=CALCULATE([Avg Value]
    , DATESBETWEEN(Dates[TradeDate]
    , 'Trading History'[Max Date -10]
    , 'Trading History'[Max Date]
    )
)
```

8. Create a pivot table with `TradeDate` (from the `Dates` table) on rows, using the `StockCode` (from `Stocks`) table as a filter. Include the measures `Max Date`, and `Max Date -10`. The pivot will look like the following screenshot:

StockCode	All	
Row Labels	**Max Date**	**Max Date -10**
01-Jan-93	01-Jan-93	
02-Jan-93	02-Jan-93	
03-Jan-93	03-Jan-93	
04-Jan-93	04-Jan-93	
05-Jan-93	05-Jan-93	
06-Jan-93	06-Jan-93	
07-Jan-93	07-Jan-93	
08-Jan-93	08-Jan-93	
09-Jan-93	09-Jan-93	
10-Jan-93	10-Jan-93	01-Jan-93
11-Jan-93	11-Jan-93	02-Jan-93
12-Jan-93	12-Jan-93	03-Jan-93
13-Jan-93	13-Jan-93	04-Jan-93

9. Create an additional pivot table with the same format as the prior one, but only include the measures `Avg Value` and `Avg Value (10 Running)`. Filter the pivot table to only show `StockCode` AAC. Your pivot will look like the following screenshot:

StockCode	AAC	
Row Labels	**Avg Value**	**Avg Value (10 Running)**
10-Aug-01	0.99	0.99
11-Aug-01		0.99
12-Aug-01		0.99
13-Aug-01	0.96	0.98
14-Aug-01	0.96	0.97
15-Aug-01	0.94	0.96
16-Aug-01	0.92	0.95
17-Aug-01	0.93	0.95
18-Aug-01		0.95
19-Aug-01		0.95
20-Aug-01	0.93	0.94

How it works...

The formula for `Avg Value (10 Running)` works by calculating three calculations within the formula. These are the current date (`Max Date`), the date 10 days prior to the current date, and the value of the average between these two dates.

The determination of the current date is achieved through the use of (Max Date). Max Date returns the highest date from the current filter context in the Dates table (note that we filter by Dates on pivot rows). This is required so that a scalar (single date) can be determined from whatever filter context is applied to the model. Logically, this should be the last date of whatever period is provided by the filter context.

In the pivot that shows TradingDate and Max Date, we can see that Max Date returns the same day as the row filter (that is, Trading Date). However, the pivot may not be filtered by TradingDate. In this situation we still need to determine a date to base our calculations on, and therefore select the last date (for whatever Dates period is selected). Please review the *Calculating running totals – totals to date* recipe for further explanation on the logical use of Max Date.

Once a value for the current date is determined, we can use it to determine what the date was 10 days prior (to the current date). This introduces the DATEADD function, which has the following syntax:

```
DATEADD(<dates>,<number_of_intervals>,<interval>)
```

For this formula, <dates> specifies the dates column in the model, which should be a continuous range of dates. Since most of the models will have a Date dimension (most models require analysis by date), we can simply use the date field of this table for this purpose (although any range of dates will suffice).

It is also important to identify that the return value for the formula is dependent on the range of dates provided by the <dates> argument. Notice that there is no return value for the first 10 dates (a blank Max Date -10 value) in the first pivot table. The <number_of_intervals> argument for the function is self-explanatory; however, the <interval> argument defines the number of periods and must be a value of the set (year, quarter, month, day).

Finally, the measure Avg Value (10 Running) calculates the average CloseValue between these two dates. Here, the filter context that is applied by the pivot is changed through the use of the keyword CALCULATE and controlled by the DATESBETWEEN function. The DATESBETWEEN function returns a set (table) of dates based on a <dates> column and a start and end date. This syntax for DATESBETWEEN is simply as follows:

```
DATESBETWEEN(<dates>,<start_date>,<end_date>)
```

Although this measure has calculated each component of the formula individually, there is no requirement to do so. That is, there is no requirement to specify AVG Value, Max Date, and Max Date -10 as measures, and then use them in the Max Avg Value (10 Running) formula. We achieve exactly the same result by combining all the components into the same formula.

Therefore, the following alternate formula also works:

```
Avg Value (10 Running):=CALCULATE(AVERAGE([CloseValue])
  , DATESBETWEEN(Dates[TradeDate]
  , CALCULATE(MAX(Dates[TradeDate])
  , DATEADD(Dates[TradeDate],-9,DAY))
  , MAX(Dates[TradeDate])
  )
)
```

There's more...

Having a fixed value for N periods usually raises one issue from the end user: "Can I have a different number of periods?" The best way to overcome this is by allowing the end user a means to specify the number of historical days that they wish to include in their calculation. This is achieved through the use of a Utility table (or dimension) that allows the user to select the number of periods that they wish to review.

The formula for N periods then interprets the selected value from this table and uses that as the basis for the prior number of days.

To briefly reiterate, a Utility dimension is the one that performs a function other than the expected slicing and dicing of data. That is, its primary purpose is not to filter data, but to assist in model presentation. Please see the *Relative Time – pivoting around measures* recipe, for a further explanation and implementation.

In order to use this so that it allows the user to specify the number of periods they wish to include in their N periods, perform the following steps:

1. Import the table on the worksheet `Periods` into the model. The name for this table range is defined, and the data area will be imported as `Periods`.

2. Add another measure to the `Trading History` table as follows:

```
Dynamic N AVG:=
  if(not(HASONEVALUE(Periods[Number Of Periods]))
  , BLANK()
  , CALCULATE( 'Trading History'[AVG Value]
  , DATESBETWEEN(Dates[TradeDate]
  , CALCULATE(MAX(Dates[TradeDate])
  , DATEADD(Dates[TradeDate],-1*VALUES(Periods[Number Of
  Periods])+1,DAY))
  , max(Dates[TradeDate])
  ))
  )
```

3. Add this measure to the pivot with `Year` and `Number of Periods` as the pivot filters. Set the `Year` as **2005**. The pivot should look like the following screenshot:

Year	2005			
StockCode	AAC			
Number Of Periods	All			
Row Labels		Avg Value	Avg Value (10 Running)	Dynamic N AVG
01-Jan-05			1.56	
02-Jan-05			1.57	
03-Jan-05		1.61	1.58	
04-Jan-05		1.63	1.59	
05-Jan-05		1.61	1.59	
06-Jan-05		1.61	1.60	
07-Jan-05		1.60	1.61	
08-Jan-05			1.61	
09-Jan-05			1.61	
10-Jan-05		1.66	1.62	
11-Jan-05		1.65	1.62	
12-Jan-05		1.63	1.63	
13-Jan-05		1.67	1.63	
14-Jan-05		1.67	1.64	
15-Jan-05			1.64	

Since the `Periods` table is not linked to any other table, the `PowerPivot` field list will display a warning message about relationship definition, as shown in the following screenshot. This is nothing to be concerned about, since the `Periods` table is not connected to the model.

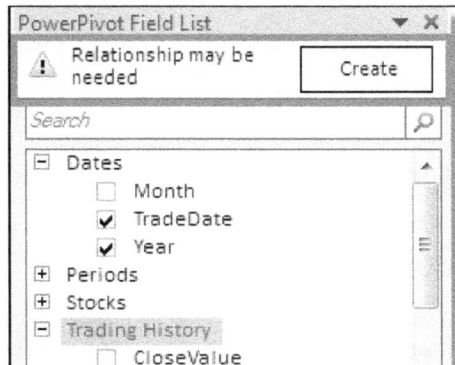

The new calculation includes two important additions to the prior one. Firstly, there is a check for selection on `Number of Periods`. If there are no periods selected (as is currently the case), the measure returns a blank value—although we could return the average value (`Avg Value`) to indicate that the value is an average. This check is achieved with the following code:

```
if(not(HASONEVALUE(Periods[Number Of Periods]))
, BLANK()
```

> Previously (in the recipe *Relative Time – pivoting around measures*), we used `COUNTROWS` to achieve the same result; however, this method is equally valid and shows that the same outcome can be achieved in different ways.

The function `HASONEVALUE()` simply checks for a filter on the `Number of Periods` column in the `Periods` table. If there is more than one period selected, the value `BLANK()` is returned as the output for the measure `Dynamic N Avg`.

Although the negation of `HASONEVALUE` (through the use of `not()`) is not technically required, it assists with the logic of the entire formula. That is, it is simpler to read `BLANK()` as the first return value (the `TRUE` condition) in the `IF` function, rather than the intended formula. Of course, the choice is entirely up to you.

Secondly, the number of periods that the user intends to evaluate is returned through the use of a `VALUES` function. The `VALUES` function has a very simple syntax as follows:

```
VALUES(<column>)
```

This returns the distinct values from the `<column>` reference. Since we know that there is only one value selected, we can use this value as the basis of the N periods in the standard formula. Note that we know there must be only one value in the values function because of the branch that was chosen by the `IF` function.

Previously, the measure `[Max Date -10]` was hardcoded with a fixed value as the following code:

```
DATEADD(Dates[TradeDate],-9,DAY)
```

Now, the value (`-9`) is simply replaced by reference to the value that the person has chosen as follows:

```
-1*VALUES(Periods[Number Of Periods])+1
```

Just as a prior measure, `Avg Value (10 Running)` used nested measures to remove complexity, so could the measure `Dynamic N AVG`. We could separate out each part of the calculation into its own measure and combine these into a final formula.

5

Applied Modeling

In this chapter, we'll be covering more complex modeling concepts such as:

▶ Grouping by binning and sorting with ranks

▶ Defining many-to-many relationships

▶ Using the last non-empty function for stock data

▶ Performing currency calculations

▶ Allocating data at different levels

Introduction

This is the final chapter that examines the foundations of tabular modeling (at least from the modelers point of view). The following chapters will examine the techniques used to manage the model in a corporate environment and include recipes on subjects such as data refreshes, partitioning, security, query modes, and perspectives. The final chapters will examine querying the model and creating visualizations using Power View (and the Power View settings required by the model).

In order to provide a familiar model which can be used in the later chapters, this chapter is a little different from the previous chapters because it progressively builds the model that is used throughout the rest of the book. Each recipe is intended to demonstrate a particular technique; however, they need to be followed in order so that the final model is completed. If this is not suitable, each completed recipe can also be found in the downloadable resources available on the Packt Publishing website.

Grouping by binning and sorting with ranks

Often, we want to provide descriptive information in our data, based on values that are derived from downstream activities. For example, this could arise if we wish to include a field in the `Customer` table that shows the value of the previous sales for that customer or a *bin grouping* that defines the customer into banded sales. This value can then be used to rank each customer according to their relative importance in relation to other customers.

This type of value adding activity is usually troublesome and time intensive in a traditional data mart design as the customer data can be fully updated only once the sales data has been loaded. While this process may seem relatively straightforward, it is a recursive problem as the customer data must be loaded before the sales data (since customers must exist before the sales can be assigned to them), but the full view of the customer is reliant on loading the sales data. In a standard dimensional (star schema) modeling approach, including this type of information for dimensions requires a three-step process:

1. The dimension (reseller customer data) is updated for known fields and attributes. This load excludes information that is derived (such as sales).

2. Then, the sales data (referred to as fact data) is loaded in data warehouse. This ensures that the data mart is in a *current state* and all the sales transaction data is up-to-date. Information relating to any new and changed stores can be loaded correctly.

3. The dimension data which relies on other fact data is updated based on the current state of the data mart.

Since the tabular model is less confined by the traditional star schema requirements of the fact and dimension tables (in fact, the tabular model does not explicitly identify facts or dimensions), the inclusion and processing of these descriptive attributes can be built directly into the model.

> The calculation of a simple measure such as a historic sales value may be included in OLAP modeling through calculated columns in the data source view. However, this is restrictive and limited to simple calculations (such as total sales or n period sales). Other manipulations (such as ranking and binning) are a lot more flexible in tabular modeling (as we will see).

This recipe examines how to manipulate a dimensional table in order to provide a richer end user experience. Specifically, we will do the following:

- Introduce a calculated field to calculate the historical sales for the customer
- Determine the rank of the customer based on that field
- Create a discretization bin for the customer based on their sales
- Create an ordered hierarchy based on their discretization bins

Getting ready

Continuing with the scenario that was discussed in the *Introduction* section of the chapter, the purpose of this chapter is to identify each reseller's (customer's) historic sales and then rank them accordingly. We then discretize the `Resellers` table (customer) based on this. This problem is further complicated by the consideration that a sale occurs in the country of origin (the sales data in the `Reseller Sales` table will appear in any currency). In order to provide a concise recipe, we break the entire process into two distinct steps:

- ▸ Conversion of sales (which manages the ranking of `Resellers` based on a unified sales value)

- ▸ Classification of sales (which manages the manipulation of sales values based on discretized bins to format those bins)

How to do it...

Firstly, we need to provide a common measure to compare the sales value of `Resellers`. Convert sales to a uniform currency using the following steps:

1. Open a new workbook and launch the **PowerPivot Window**.

2. Import the text files `Reseller Sales.txt`, `Currency Conversion.txt`, and `Resellers.txt`.

> The source data folder for this chapter includes the base `schema.ini` file that correctly transforms all data upon import. When importing the data, you should be prompted that the `schema.ini` file exists and will override the import settings. If this does not occur, ensure that the `schema.ini` file exists in the same directory as your source data. The prompt should look like the following screenshot:

⚠ A Schema.ini file has been detected in the current import folder "F:\Drop Box\Dropbox\Book \0884EN\0884EN_05_code". Settings from this file will override your current import settings.

Although it is not mandatory, it is recommended that connection managers are labeled according to a standard. In this model, I have used the convention `type_table_name` where `type` refers to the connection type (`.txt`) and `table_name` refers to the name of the table. Connections can be edited using the **Existing Connections** button in the **Design** tab.

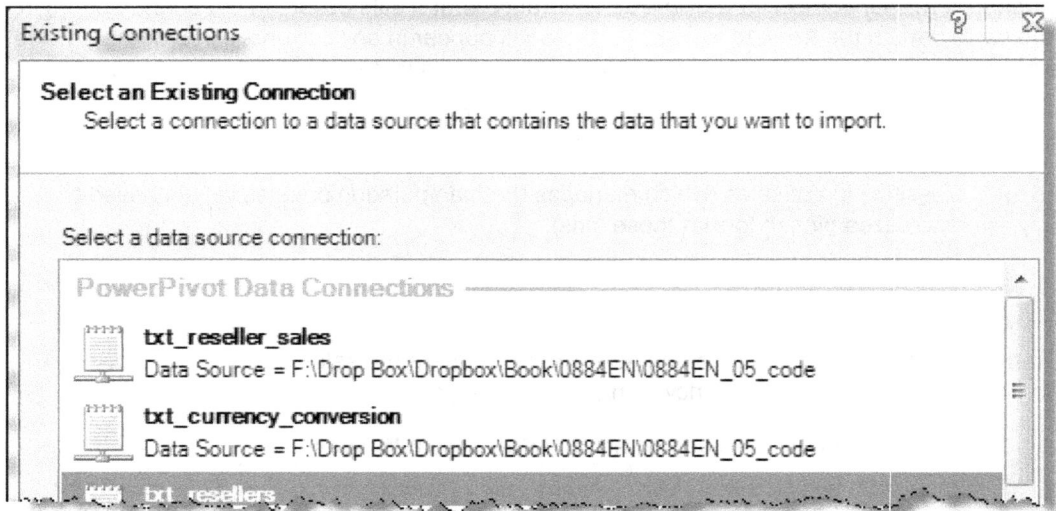

3. Create a relationship between the `Customer ID` field in the `Resellers` table and the `Customer ID` field in the `Reseller Sales` table.

4. Add a new field (also called a calculated column) in the `Resellers Sales` table to show the gross value of the sale amount in USD. Add `usd_gross_sales` and hide it from client tools using the following code:

```
= [Quantity Ordered]
* [Price Per Unit]
*LOOKUPVALUE
(
'Currency Conversion'[AVG Rate]
,'Currency Conversion'[Date]
,[Order dt]
,'Currency Conversion'[Currency ID]
,[Currency ID]
)
```

5. Add a new measure in the `Resellers Sales` table to show sales (in USD). Add `USD Gross Sales` as:

```
USD Gross Sales := SUM ( [usd_gross_sales] )
```

6. Add a new calculated column to the `Resellers` table to show the `USD Sales Total` value. The formula for the field should be:

   ```
   = 'Reseller Sales' [USD Gross Sales]
   ```

7. Add a `Sales Rank` field in the `Resellers` table to show the order for each resellers `USD Sales Total`. The formula for `Sales Rank` is:

   ```
   =RANKX(Resellers, [USD Sales Total])
   ```

8. Hide the `USD Sales Total` and `Sales Rank` fields from **client tools**.

   Now that all the entries in the `Resellers` table show their sales value in a uniform currency, we can determine a grouping for the `Reseller` table. In this case, we are going to group them into 100,000 dollar bands.

9. Add a new field to show each value in the `USD Sales Total` column of `Resellers` rounded down to the nearest 100,000 dollars. Hide it from client tools. Now, add `Round Down Amount` as:

   ```
   =ROUNDDOWN([USD Sales Total],-5)
   ```

10. Add a new field to show the rank of `Round Down Amount` in descending order and hide it from client tools. Add `Round Down Order` as:

    ```
    =RANKX(Resellers,[Round Down Amount],,FALSE(), DENSE)
    ```

11. Add a new field in the `Resellers` table to show the 100,000 dollars group that the reseller belongs to. Since we know what the lower bound of the sales bin is, we can also infer that the upper bin is the rounded up 100,000 dollars sales group. Add `Sales Group` as follows:

    ```
    =IF([Round Down Amount]=0 || ISBLANK([Round Down Amount])
    , "Sales Under 100K"
    , FORMAT([Round Down Amount], "$#,K")  & " - "
    & FORMAT(ROUNDUP([USD Sales Total],-5),"$#,K")
    )
    ```

12. Set the `Sort By Column` of the `Sales Group` field to the `Round Down Order` column. Note that the `Round Down Order` column should display in a descending order (that is, entries in the `Resellers` table with high sales values should appear first).

13. Create a **hierarchy** on the `Resellers` table which shows the `Sales Group` field and the `Customer Name` column as **levels**. Title the hierarchy as `Customer By Sales Group`.

14. Add a new measure titled `Number of Resellers` to the `Resellers` table:

    ```
    Number of Resellers:=COUNTROWS(Resellers)
    ```

15. Create a pivot table that shows the `Customer By Sales Group` hierarchy on the rows and `Number of Resellers` as values. If you created the `usd_gross_sales` field in the `Reseller Sales` table, it can also be added as an implicit measure to verify values. Expand the first bin of `Sales Group`. The pivot should look like the following screenshot:

Row Labels	Number of Resellers	Sum of usd_gross_sales
⊟ $800K - $900K	4	3,381,382
Brakes and Gears	1	882,276
Excellent Riding Supplies	1	853,851
Metropolitan Bicycle Supply	1	828,127
Totes & Baskets Company	1	817,128
⊞ $700K - $800K	7	5,067,477
⊞ $600K - $700K	7	4,505,011
⊞ $500K - $600K	13	7,121,157
⊞ $400K - $500K	27	11,760,112
⊞ $300K - $400K	26	9,160,253

How it works...

This recipe has included various steps, which add descriptive information to the `Resellers` table. This includes obtaining data from a separate table (the USD sales) and then manipulating that field within the `Resellers` table. In order to provide a clearer definition of how this process works, we will break the explanation into several subsections. This includes the sales data retrieval, the use of rank functions, and finally, the discretization of sales.

The next section deals with the process of converting sales data to a single currency.

The starting point for this recipe is to determine a common currency sales value for each reseller (or customer). While the inclusion of the calculated column `USD Sales Total` in the `Resellers` table should be relatively straightforward, it is complicated by the consideration that the sales data is stored in multiple currencies. Therefore, the first step needs to include a currency conversion to determine the USD sales value for each line. This is simply the local value multiplied by the daily exchange rate. The `LOOKUPVALUE` function is used to return the row-by-row exchange rate. (See the *Linking fields between tables* recipe in *Chapter 1, Getting Started with Excel*, for an explanation of this function.)

Now that we have the `usd_gross_sales` value for each sales line, we define a measure that calculates its sum in whatever filter context it is applied in. Including it in the `Reseller Sales` table makes sense (since, it relates to sales data), but what is interesting is how the filter context is applied when it is used as a field in the `Resellers` table. Here, the **row filter context** that exists in the `Resellers` table (after all, each row refers to a reseller) applies a restriction to the sales data. This shows the sales value for each reseller.

For this recipe to work correctly, it is not necessary to include the calculated field `usd_gross_sales` in `Reseller Sales`. We simply need to define a calculation, which shows the gross sales value in USD and then use the row filter context in the `Resellers` table to restrict sales to the reseller in question (that is, the reseller in the row).

The *Summing aggregates and row iteration* recipe in *Chapter 3, Advanced Browsing Features*, have explained how the X functions use row iterations to calculate aggregates based on row-by-row calculations. Here, it is obvious that the exchange rate should be applied on a daily basis because the value can change every day. We could use an X function in the `USD Gross Sales` measure to achieve exactly the same outcome. Our formula will be:

```
SUMX
(
'Reseller Sales'
, 'Reseller Sales'[Quantity Ordered]
* 'Reseller Sales'[Price Per Unit]
* LOOKUPVALUE
(
'Currency Conversion'[AVG Rate]
, 'Currency Conversion'[Date]
,'Reseller Sales'[Order dt]
,'Currency Conversion'[Currency ID]
,'Reseller Sales'[Currency ID]
)
)
```

Furthermore, if we wanted to, we could completely eliminate the `USD Gross Sales` measure from the model. To do this, we could wrap the entire formula (the previous definition on `USD Gross Sales`) into the `CALCULATE` statement in the `Resellers` table's field definition of `USD Gross Sales`. This forces the calculation to occur at the current row context.

Why have we included the additional fields and measures in `Reseller Sales`? This is a modeling choice. It makes the model easier to understand because it is more modular. Additionally, the *Performing currency calculations* recipe is used to dynamically calculate values in any chosen currency. This would otherwise require two calculations (one into a default currency and the second into a selected currency) and the field `usd_gross_sales` is used in that calculation.

Now that sales are converted to a uniform currency, we can determine the importance by rank. `RANKX` is used to rank the rows in the `Resellers` table based on the `USD Gross Sales` field. The simplest implementation of `RANKX` is demonstrated within the `Sales Rank` field. Here, the function simply returns a rank based on the value according to the supplied measure (which is of course `USD Gross Sales`).

However, the RANKX function provides a lot of versatility and follows the syntax:

```
RANKX(<table>
, <expression>[, <value>[, <order>[, <ties>]]]
)
```

After the initial implementation of RANKX in its simplest form, the arguments of particular interest are the `<order>` and `<ties>` arguments. These can be used to specify the sort order (whether the rank is to be applied from highest to lowest or lowest to highest) and the function behavior when duplicate values are encountered. This may be best demonstrated with an example. To do this, we will examine the operation of rank in relation to Round Down Amount.

When a simple RANKX function is applied, the function sorts the columns in an ascending order and returns the position of a row based on the sorted order of the value and the number of prior rows within the table. This includes rows attributable to duplicate values. This is shown in the following screenshot where the Simple column is defined as RANKX(Resellers, [Round Down Amount]). Note, the data is sorted by Round Down Amount and the first four tied values have a RANKX value of 1. This is the behavior we expect since all rows have the same value. For the next value (700000), RANKX returns 5 because this is the fifth element in the sequence.

Round...	Simple	DENSE	INVERSE DENSE
800000	1	1	9
800000	1	1	9
800000	1	1	9
800000	1	1	9
700000	5	2	8
700000	5	2	8
700000	5	2	8

When the DENSE argument is specified, the value returned after a tie is the next sequential number in the list. In the preceding screenshot, this is shown through the DENSE column. The formula for the field DENSE is:

```
RANKX(Resellers, [Round Down Amount],,,DENSE))
```

Finally, we can specify the sort order that is used by the function (the default is ascending) with the help of `<order>` argument of the function. If we wish to sort (and rank) from lowest to highest, we could use the formula as shown in the INVERSE DENSE column. The INVERSE DENSE column uses the following calculation:

```
RANKX(Resellers, [Round Down Amount],,TRUE,DENSE)
```

After having specified the `Sales Group` field **sort by column** as `Round Down Order`, we may ask why we did not also sort the `Customer Name` column by their respective values in the `Sales Rank` column? Trying to define a sort by column in this way would cause an error as it is not a one-to-one relationship between these two fields. That is, each customer does not have a unique value for the sales rank.

Let's have a look at this in more detail. If we filter the `Resellers` table to show the blank `USD Sales Total` rows (click on the drop-down arrow in the `USD Sales Total` column and check the **BLANKS** checkbox), we see that the values of the `Sales Rank` column for all the rows is the same. In the following screenshot, we can see the value `636` repeated for all the rows:

Custom...			Customer Type		Customer Name		Reseller Type		USD Gross Sales		Sales Rank		
AW00000671	591		Reseller		Contoso		Ltd.					636	
AW00000329	315		Reseller		Unicycles		Bicycles					636	
AW00000689	249		Reseller		Consumer Equipm...		Specialty Bike Shop					636	
AW00000619	518		Reseller		Strong Metal Manu...		Specialty Bike Shop					636	
AW00000589	198		Reseller		Hiatus Bike Tours		Specialty Bike Shop					636	
AW00000565	381		Reseller		Metallic Paint and ...		Sp	All Resellers with $0 Sales share the same Rank					636	
AW00000547	382		Reseller		Curbside Sporting ...		Specialty Bike Shop					636	
AW00000537	14		Reseller		Preferable Bikes		Specialty Bike Shop					636	
AW00000507	592		Reseller		Global Sporting Go...		Specialty Bike Shop					636	
AW00000465	17		Reseller		Expert Cycle Store		Specialty Bike Shop					636	

> Allowing the client tool visibility to the `USD Sales Total` and `Sales Rank` fields will not provide an intuitive browsing attribute for most client tools. For this reason, it is not recommended to expose these attributes to users. Hiding them will still allow the data to be queried directly (see the *Retrieving data from a single table* recipe in *Chapter 9, Querying the Tabular Model with DAX*, on querying the tabular model directly).

Discretizing sales

By discretizing the `Resellers` table, we firstly make a decision to group each reseller into bands of 100,000 intervals. Since, we have already calculated the `USD Gross Sales` value for each customer, our problem is reduced by determining which bin each customer belongs to.

This is very easily achieved as we can derive the lower and upper bound for the `Resellers` table. That is, the lower bound will be a rounded down amount of their sales and the upper bound will be the rounded up value (that is rounded nearest to the 100,000 interval). Finally, we must ensure that the ordering of the bins is correct so that the bins appear from the highest value resellers to the lowest.

For convenience, these steps are broken down through the creation of additional columns but they need not be—we could incorporate the steps into a single formula (mind you, it would be hard to read). Additionally, we have provided a unique name for the first bin by testing for 0 sales. This may not be required.

The rounding is done with the ROUNDDOWN and ROUNDUP functions. These functions simply return the number moved by the number of digits offset. The following is the syntax for ROUNDDOWN:

```
ROUNDDOWN(<number>, <num_digits>)
```

Since we are interested only in the INTEGER values (that is, values to the left of the decimal place), we must specify <num_digits> as -5.

The display value of the bin is controlled through the FORMAT function, which returns the text equivalent of a value according to the provided format string. The syntax for FORMAT is:

```
FORMAT(<value>, <format_string>)
```

Field ordering (more specifically, the order of elements with fields) is examined in the *Sorting data* recipe in *Chapter 3, Advanced Browsing Features*.

There's more...

In presenting a USD Gross Sales value for the Resellers table, we may not be interested in all the historic data. A typical variation on this theme is to determine the current worth by showing the recent history (or summing recent sales). This requirement can be easily implemented into the preceding method by swapping USD Gross Sales with recent sales. To determine this amount, we need to filter the data used in the SUM function. For example, to determine the last 30 days' sales for a reseller, we will use the following code:

```
SUMX(
  FILTER('Reseller Sales'
  , 'Reseller Sales'[Order dt]>
  (MAX('Reseller Sales'[Order dt])-30)
  )
  , USD SALES EXPRESSION
)
```

Defining many-to-many relationships

Many-to-many relationships appear in a number of modeling situations. Perhaps, the most common scenario and explanation is that of a bank account and their owners. In this situation, a bank account can have many owners who are equally responsible for the balance. However, the owners can have different accounts. The challenge faced in tabular modeling is that the relationship includes a direction that does not actively filter the fact data. The use of the bridge table breaks the standard downstream filtering that is usually applied in a star schema.

This recipe demonstrates how to create the many-to-many relationship by extending the previous recipe to include store ownership. In this example, a reseller can be owned by one or more owners. Furthermore, each owner has an ownership interest (as a percentage interest in a reseller).

The following are the standard types of questions that the model is expected to answer:

- How many stores does an owner have?
- What is the owner's interest (ownership proportion) of the store(s)?
- What is the total value (both apportioned and unapportioned) of sales for owners' stores?

Getting ready

This recipe extends the prior recipe (*Grouping by binning and sorting with ranks*) by adding additional data to the model. The new data is a list of owners and the table shows the ownership interest.

The Owners.txt file identifies the owner (employee by ID and name), whereas the ownership interest table, Store Owners.txt, identifies the store, owner, and their interest with a percentage stake.

How to do it...

In building the many-to-many relationship, we first show what the implications of not correctly defining measures are. We then show how to correct measure outcomes using **DAX**. Let's start with the workbook that has been developed so far:

1. Open the model developed in the previous recipe.
2. Import the text files Owners.txt and Store Owners.txt into the model.
3. Create a relationship between Customer ID in the Resellers table and Customer ID in the Store Owners table.

4. Create a relationship between the `Employee ID` column in the `Store Owners` table and the `Employee ID` column in the `Owners` table. The relationship between the `Reseller Sales` table and the `Owners` model should look like the following screenshot:

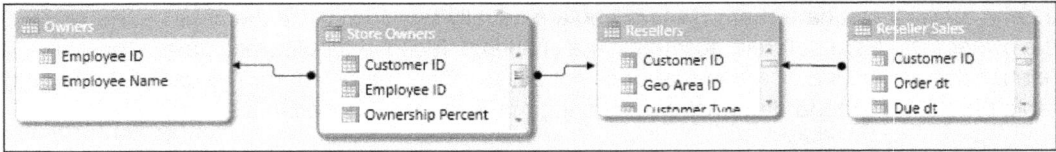

Note that the direction of the relationship between `Store Owners` and `Resellers` breaks the unidirectional filtering path that will otherwise be created, as shown in the following diagram:

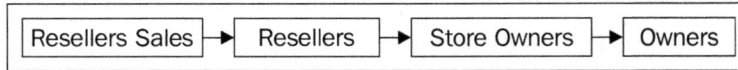

5. Create a pivot table that shows `Store Owners` on rows and the measure `USD Gross Sales`. The pivot will look like the following screenshot:

Row Labels	USD Gross Sales
A. Scott Wright (685233686)	76,989,167
Alan Brewer (470689086)	76,989,167
Alejandro McGuel (761597760)	76,989,167
Alex Nayberg (377784364)	76,989,167
Alice Ciccu (113695504)	76,989,167
Amy Alberts (982310417)	76,989,167

6. Create a measure to show the number of stores owned by an owner. Add the following code to the `Store Owners` table and format it as a (separated by a comma) number with no decimal spaces:

```
Stores Owned := DISTINCTCOUNT('Store Owners'[Customer ID])
```

7. Add the measure `Stores Owned` to the pivot. Filter the pivot so that the first two owners are shown. Then, add the `Customer ID` column from the `Resellers` table as a secondary member on rows—all stores will be shown because the measure `USD Gross Sales (Raw)` appears for every store. Hide the stores that do not have an owner by filtering the pivot to show only the stores that have active owners. Select the `Customer ID` cell in the pivot and then apply a value filter so that `Stores Owned` does not equal to `0`. The pivot will now look like the following screenshot:

Row Labels	USD Gross Sales (Raw)	Stores Owned
⊟ A. Scott Wright (685233686)	76,989,167	8
AW00000186	76,989,167	1
AW00000267		
AW00000308		
AW00000318	76,989,167	1
AW00000448	76,989,167	1
AW00000516	76,989,167	1
AW00000563	76,989,167	1

8. Add a measure to the `Store Owners` table to show average ownership (interest) using the following code. And then, add the `Ownership % (AVG)` measure to the pivot table.

```
Onwership % (AVG):=AVERAGE([Ownership Percent])
```

> We can easily verify that the ownership interest (and stores owned) is correct by selecting an employee (in this case, employee ID of **A. Scott Wright** is 685233686) and filtering the `Store Owners` table within the model. If we do this, the table is reduced to only stores owned by Scott. Have a look at the following screenshot:

Custom...	Employ...	Ownership Percent
AW00000186	685233686	50
AW00000516	685233686	50
AW00000318	685233686	25
AW00000448	685233686	25
AW00000659	685233686	25
AW00000694	685233686	25
AW00000649	685233686	12
AW00000563	685233686	13

> Note that the filter indicator also shows that the column is filtered.

9. Create a measure to show the `USD Gross Sales` value for stores that are owned. Add `Gross Sales (All Owners)` to the `Resellers Sales` table:

```
CALCULATE([USD Gross Sales], 'Store Owners')
```

10. Create a measure to show the USD Gross Sales value for the owners based on their interest percentage in the store. Add Gross Sales (Ownership) to the Resellers Sales table as:

```
CALCULATE(
    SUMX('Store Owners'
    , 'Store Owners'[Ownership Percent]/100
    *[USD Gross Sales])
    , 'Store Owners'
)
```

11. Format both measures as numeric values, separated by a comma, with no decimal places.

12. Hide the unwanted columns from client tools. Hide all columns in the Store Owners and Resellers Sales tables.

13. To verify the results, alter the existing pivot table. Ensure that the USD Gross Sales, Ownership % (AVG), Gross Sales (All Owners), and Gross Sales (Ownership) measures are added to the pivot. Remove Customer ID from the rows. The pivot will look like the following screenshot:

Row Labels	USD Gross Sales	Stores Owned	Gross Sales (All Owners)	Onwership % (AVG)	Gross Sales (Ownership)
A. Scott Wright (685233686)	76,989,167	8	629,433	28	161,999
Alan Brewer (470689086)	76,989,167	2	276,544	38	84,936
Grand Total	76,989,167	10	905,977	30	246,935

14. Create a new pivot that shows sales information for **A. Scott Wright**. Add Customer ID from the Resellers table on the rows and the measures USD Gross Sales (Raw), Gross Sales (All Owners), and Gross Sales (Ownership) on the columns. Add a filter to the pivot (Employee ID from the Owners table) and then filter to Scott. Create a value filter for rows, so that the measure Gross Sales (All Owners) does not equal to 0. The pivot will look like the following screenshot:

Employee Name   A. Scott Wright (6 233686)

Row Labels	USD Gross Sales	Stores Owned	Gross Sales (All Owners)	Onwership % (AVG)	Gross Sales (Ownership)
AW00000186	54,964	1	54,964	50	27,482
AW00000318	3,071	1	3,071	25	768
AW00000448	492,733	1	492,733	25	123,183
AW00000516	784	1	784	50	392
AW00000563	28,408	1	28,408	13	3,693
AW00000649	45,289	1	45,289	12	5,435
AW00000659	665	1	665	25	166
AW00000694	3,520	1	3,520	25	880
Grand Total	629,433	8	629,433	28	161,999

15. Note that Scott's sales `Gross Sales (All Owners)` match the `USD Gross Sales` and that `Gross Sales (Ownership)` are equal to the all owners' sales multiplied by the `Ownership % (AVG)`. Furthermore, note that the totals for Scott match the prior pivot's line items.

How it works...

We have previously seen that the calculation of a measure is a calculation that is performed on data that is restricted by the query context (the pivot table creates this context by the intersections of the pivot table rows and columns). So far in this book, all models have implemented relationships in a unidirectional manner, so that the relationships within the model filter the data that is being used in the calculation. However, the creation of a relationship between the `Store Owners` table and the `Resellers` table does not follow this *outward* pattern and hence the data in the `Resellers Sales` table is not filtered when fields from the `Store Owners` table or `Owners` table are used in the pivot table.

This is the reason why the first pivot table shows duplicate values for the `USD Gross Sales (Raw)` measure. Note that the direction of the relationship between `Resellers` and `Store Owners` is different from the others, as shown in the following screenshot:

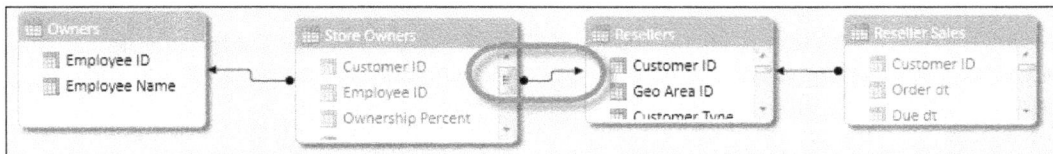

This does not affect the calculations that are performed between tables where the relationship and filter context automatically restrict the rows that the calculation is performed on. Therefore, the measures for `Stores Owned` and `Ownership %` can be automatically derived through any filter that is applied to the `Store Owners` table, since the relationship dictates that the `Store Owners` table is automatically filtered by `Owners`. That is, the number of stores owned will always be derived by the (query) filters which occur between the `Owners` and `Resellers` tables.

If there is no filter applied (forcing all customer IDs to be shown), we only want to count individual stores (that are applicable based on the `Owners` filter) and so, we need to apply the `DISTINCTCOUNT` function to the `Customer ID` column in the `Store Owners` table. The `DISTINCTCOUNT` function performs, as the name suggests, and returns the number of unique values of the provided column. This gives us what we want—the number of unique stores under the current filter context.

While it is possible to use the `COUNTROWS` function for the `Store Owners` table, the value returned will only be correct if there is a filter context on the employee. There is no filter for a total level and, therefore, relying on `COUNTROWS` would give the total number of owners and store combinations, rather than the number of stores.

Now, let's consider the measure `Gross Sales (All Owners)`. The purpose of the measure `Gross Sales (All Owners)` is to show the `USD Gross Sales` measure whenever a valid reseller or owner combination occurs. The value at a dimensions aggregate level (say for example, all owners) should be the full amount without adding the individual detail items.

This is achieved by specifying the bridge table in the calculation for `Gross Sales (All Owners)`. Revisiting the formula, we can see that the filter is applied on the basis of the `Store Owners` table. Thus, the `Boolean` predicate (the part of the `CALCULATE` function that filters the table) is only applied if a row exists in the current queries filter context. In this way, we only show the measure `USD Gross Sales (Raw)` when a row in the queries filter context leaves a row in the `Store Owners` table.

```
Gross Sales (All Owners):=
CALCULATE([USD Gross Sales], 'Store Owners')
```

While the measure `Gross Sales (All Owners)` shows the value of total sales for stores that are owned (by an employee), it does not show how much of those sales the owner is entitled to. In order to determine each owner's ownership interest in sales, we extend the concept that was applied to `Gross Sales (All Owners)` at their ownership interest as defined in the `Store Owners` table. Stated another way, we wish to sum each row's ownership interest of the sales amount multiplied by the `Ownership Percent` field.

We have already seen how `SUMX` can be used to iterate over rows (see the *Summing aggregates and row iteration* recipe in *Chapter 3*, *Advanced Browsing Features*), which is exactly the same principle that is applied in this formula. That is, iterate over each row in the `Store Ownership` table that has been filtered by the query context to and multiply the amount that is shown (see the `Gross Sales (All Owners)` measure) by the rows ownership proportion (that is, by the `Ownership Percent` field).

Using the last non-empty function for stock data

Most OLTP (Operational) systems contain summary tables to record the on hand quantity of stock. This is recorded at the level of detail appropriate to the system (for example, product item and location).

Of course, the current value of any item or location(s) should be determined by aggregating the net movement of all the prior transactions; however, the performance of such a calculation is unacceptably slow in traditional relational environments. Therefore, in order to retain balance history, the snapshots of the quantities are taken at key dates (say for example, the month end).

A similar type of recording process occurs in data marts and data warehouse environments. In these situations, the fact data (table) is commonly referred to as a periodic snapshot because the snapshot of the data is taken at periodic intervals.

For these types of tables, **Stock on Hand** quantities cannot be aggregated across time dimensions because the aggregated value would not give the correct result. Consider a situation where the daily balance of stock is held in a table (that is, there is a record of the balance for every day). While we can easily determine daily balances, we cannot derive a monthly balance by adding up all the daily balances. Instead, we must return the values on the last day of the month. This adjustment is only applicable to aggregations across a date dimension. All other dimensions (for example, stores and products) should aggregate according to the hierarchy that is selected.

SQL Server Analysis Services (**SSAS**) multidimensional modeling includes a special aggregation function (**last non-empty**) to retrieve the latest balance when dates were aggregated. However, there is no such function in tabular modeling and the result has to be determined with DAX.

Getting ready

This recipe builds on the tabular model that was developed in the *Defining many-to-many relationships* recipe. Continuing with the example developed in this recipe, we assume that our resellers have implemented a just-in-time inventory system. When a product is sold, it is ordered from the head office and delivered on the same day (this is a stock movement in for the `Resellers` table). Then, on the sales shipping date, when the product is shipped from the reseller, the stock is transferred out of the store's holdings.

Examine a sample of stock movements (filtered on customer AW00000438 and product BK-R79Y-48). Here, we can trace that the daily balance (QTY_BAL) is incremental and equal to the prior day's balance, and the net effect of QTY_IN and QTY_OUT.

Moveme...	Custom...	Produ...	QTY_IN	QTY_...	QTY_BAL
06-Mar-08	AW00000438	BK-R79Y-48	0	0	1
07-Mar-08	AW00000438	BK-R79Y-48	0	0	1
08-Mar-08	AW00000438	BK-R79Y-48	0	-1	0
01-Jun-08	AW00000438	BK-R79Y-48	2	0	2
02-Jun-08	AW00000438	BK-R79Y-48	0	0	2
03-Jun-08	AW00000438	BK-R79Y-48	0	0	2
04-Jun-08	AW00000438	BK-R79Y-48	0	0	2
05-Jun-08	AW00000438	BK-R79Y-48	0	0	2
06-Jun-08	AW00000438	BK-R79Y-48	0	0	2
07-Jun-08	AW00000438	BK-R79Y-48	0	0	2

How to do it...

As with the previous recipes, we start by adding some additional data to our model.

1. Launch the **PowerPivot Window**.

2. Import the text files `Inventory Balances.txt`, `Products.txt`, and `Dates.txt`.

3. Create a relationship between the `Customer ID` column in the `Inventory Balances` table and the `Customer ID` column in the `Resellers` table.

4. The `Dates` table will act as a date dimension and can also be used to filter the `Reseller Sales` data (this was not included in the previous recipe). Create a relationship between the `Day` field in the `Dates` table and the `Movement Dt` field in the `Inventory Balances` table and a relationship between the `Day` field in the `Dates` table and the `Order dt` in the `Resellers` table.

5. Create a relationship between the `Product ID` field in the `Products` table and the `Product ID` field in the `Reseller Sales` table. Then, create another relationship between the `Product ID` field in the `Products` table and the `Product ID` field in the `Inventory Balances` table.

6. Hide all fields in the `Inventory Balances` table.

7. Set the sort column from `Month Name` to `Month Number` in the `Dates` table and hide `Month Number` from client tools. Then, create a hierarchy titled `Date by Year` that has the levels: `Year`, `Month Name`, and `Day`.

8. Hide all fields in the `Resellers Sales` table from client tools.

9. The model should appear, as shown in the following screenshot (note that we are excluding tables that are not necessary for inventory balances):

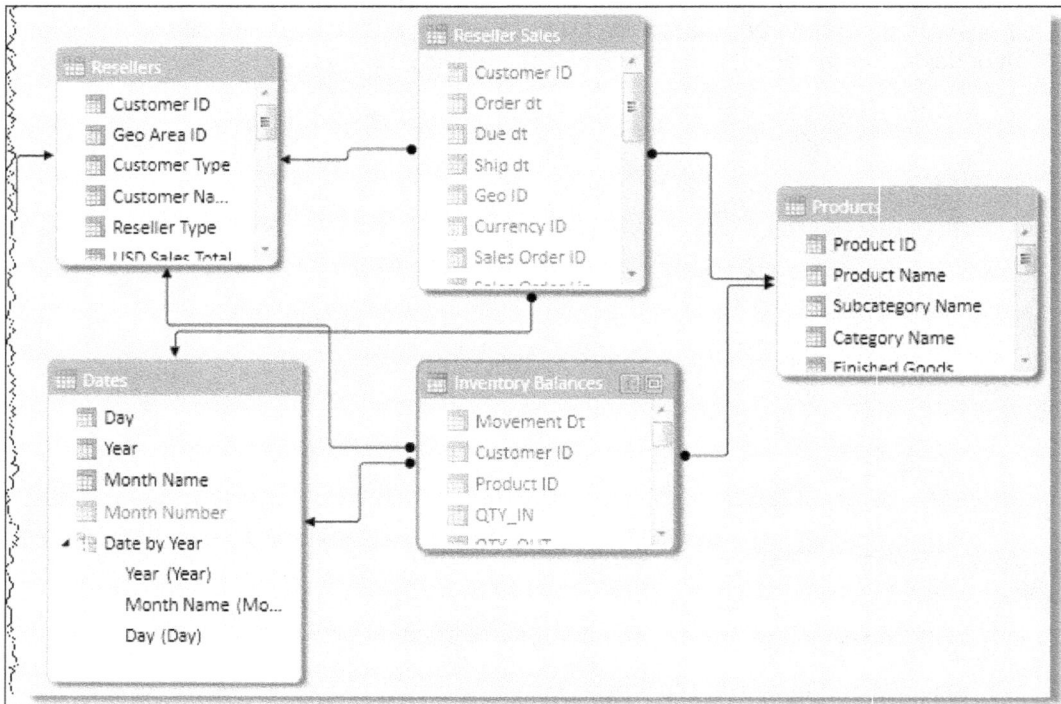

10. Add a measure to the `Inventory Balances` table to calculate the net effect of stock movements. Add `Stock Movement` as follows:

```
Stock Movement := SUM([QTY_IN]) + SUM([QTY_OUT])
```

11. Add a measure to the `Inventory Balances` table to aggregate the value of Stock on Hand. Add `QTY BAL` as follows:

```
QTY BAL := SUM([QTY_BAL])
```

12. Add a measure to the `Inventory Balances` table, which determines the value of Stock on Hand (the stock balance) based on the addition of all historical transactions. Add `Stock Balance (Trans)` as follows:

```
Stock Balance (Trans):=
CALCULATE
(
  [Stock Movement]
  , FILTER(ALL(Dates)
  , Dates[Day]<=MAX(Dates[Day])
  )
)
```

13. Add a measure in the `Inventory Balances` table to show what the last date was, which was associated with any stock movements that is within the current (Date) filter context. Add `Stock Date` and format the date accordingly using the following code:

```
Stock Date:=
LASTNONBLANK('Inventory Balances'[Movement Dt]
, 'Inventory Balances'[QTY BAL]
)
```

14. Add a measure to the `Inventory Balances` table to show the total stock balance at `Stock Date`. This is the last non-empty (or stock balance) aggregation. Add `Stock on Hand` using the following code:

```
Stock On Hand:=
CALCULATE
(
  [QTY BAL]
  , LASTNONBLANK('Inventory Balances'[Movement Dt]
  , 'Inventory Balances'[QTY BAL]
  )
)
```

15. Create a pivot table (which we will refer to as **Pivot 1**) that shows the `Stock on Hand` value for the customer `AW00000438` and the product `BK-R79Y-48` (this was the sample extract shown earlier in the chapter). The pivot should have filters for `Customer ID` and `Product ID`, the `Date by Year` hierarchy on rows, and the `Stock Date` and `Stock on Hand` measures on the columns. Expand the `June 2008` value to look like the following screenshot:

| Customer ID | AW00000438 | |
| Product ID | BK-R79Y-48 | |

Row Labels	Stock Date	Stock On Hand
⊞ 2007	08-Dec-07	0
⊟ 2008	07-Jun-08	2
⊞ March	08-Mar-08	0
⊟ June	07-Jun-08	2
01-Jun-08	01-Jun-08	2
02-Jun-08	02-Jun-08	2
03-Jun-08	03-Jun-08	2
04-Jun-08	04-Jun-08	2
05-Jun-08	05-Jun-08	2
06-Jun-08	06-Jun-08	2
07-Jun-08	07-Jun-08	2
Grand Total	**07-Jun-08**	**2**

16. Create another pivot table (which will be referred to as **Pivot 2**), which shows all the entries in the `Resellers` and `Products` tables. Include the measures `Stock Date`, `Stock on Hand`, and `Stock Balance (Trans)`. The pivot should look like the following screenshot:

| Customer ID | All | |
| Product ID | All | |

Row Labels	Stock Date	Stock On Hand	Stock Balance (Trans)
⊞ 2005	08-Dec-05	0	0
⊞ 2006	08-Dec-06	0	0
⊞ 2007	08-Dec-07	0	0
⊞ 2008	07-Jun-08	10,264	10,264
⊞ 2009			10,264
⊞ 2010			10,264
Grand Total	**07-Jun-08**	**10,264**	**10,264**

How it works...

The `Stock Balance (Trans)` measure in Pivot 2 shows how the `Stock Balance` measure can be calculated by aggregating transactional movements from prior periods. This formula was addressed in the *Calculating running totals – totals to date* recipe in *Chapter 4, Time Calculations and Date Functions*. However, using this technique, one may question whether the balance from the year 2008 should be continued into 2009 because the balance does not relate to the future years—or does it? This question is often argued in reporting teams!

The traditional approach to the last non-empty problem is to return all data on the last date within the current period that is specified by the filter context.

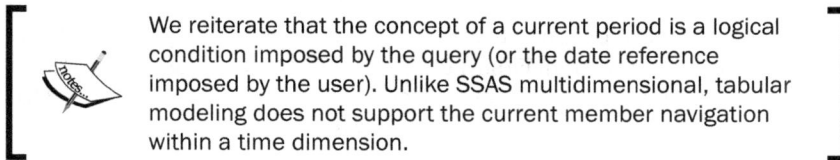

> We reiterate that the concept of a current period is a logical condition imposed by the query (or the date reference imposed by the user). Unlike SSAS multidimensional, tabular modeling does not support the current member navigation within a time dimension.

The measures in Pivot 2 demonstrate how this works through the use of `Stock Date`. The purpose of the measure is to return the last date within the `Inventory Balances` table, within the current filter context, that is, the last non-empty date. Note that this is not the same value as the month end (which is the value that would be returned had a `MAX(Dates[Date])` function been used).

In order to determine the last date of the activity, we rely on the `LASTNONBLANK` function. This simply returns the last value in the `<column>` parameter where the `<expression>` parameter is not blank. Since we are interested in stock balances, we would naturally use the `QTY BAL` measure (since it is the sum of the balance field).

```
LASTNONBLANK(<column>,<expression>)
```

Once this date is determined, we can use the value as the last non-empty date and aggregate the values from the `Inventory Balances` table. This is done by specifying the value as the filter within the `CALCULATE` command. Remember, that the syntax for `CALCULATE` is:

```
CALCULATE(<expression>,<filter1>,<filter2>…)
```

By specifying the `LASTNONBLANK` value as a `<filter>` argument, we automatically apply the filter without the need to completely redefine the queries filter context.

In summary, these formulas work by effectively filtering Stock on Hand records to the last date based on the current filter context.

One may question, why the recipe does not manipulate the `Date` table filter context, for example, trying to filter stock records based on the maximum date in the query filter context. Trying to determine a stock balance in this way creates and reapplies many filters to the `Date` table and can cause undesired results. Consider the logic being applied—I redefine the date filter to determine the last date which had stock, then I try to use this date by removing the queries filter context on the dates table. However, removing the filter changes the filter that is applied when we try to get the last date.

Performing currency calculations

Currency calculations are a unique type of calculation, because the value that is returned to the user needs to be dynamically determined within the model, based on their input (choice of currency). This relies on two dynamic types of data, which can change within the model and therefore may impact the calculation. Firstly, the rate used can be changed (that is, a change to the rate of existing data) or secondly, new currencies can be added or removed to the currency data that requires a new conversion to be created. Unlike the previous calculations that we have seen in this book, the calculation must dynamically determine the rate that is to be applied in conversions based on the available data in the model. Because additional currency data could be added at any time, it is simply not possible to add additional columns to our target table to precalculate a value in a target currency and materialize it in a table. If we wanted to materialize values for each available currency (and extend our tables to add columns for converted values in target currencies), we could determine the value to show in a similar manner, as shown in the *Relative Time–pivoting around measures* recipe in *Chapter 4, Time Calculations and Date Functions*.

The general approach used to determine a value in a target currency is to convert a base currency to a target currency and then aggregate it (according to the query). We have seen how we can iterate over rows using the X aggregations (see the *Summing aggregates and row iteration* recipe in *Chapter 3, Advanced Browsing Features*). This recipe takes that concept one step further by dynamically determining a conversion rate based on a value that the user has chosen.

Getting ready

This recipe extends the model that was built in the recipe titled *Using the last non-empty function for stock data* by creating a currency conversion based on the USD Gross Sales measure. The model includes the table of exchange rates (Currency Conversion) that shows the USD conversion from a currency. These rates appear for every day of history.

Date	Currency ID	AVG Rate	EOD Rate
1/07/2005 ...	AUD	0.64553611774...	0.645161290...
2/07/2005 ...	AUD	0.64271482743...	0.642756138...
3/07/2005 ...	AUD	0.64135454079...	0.641148938...
4/07/2005 ...	AUD	0.63918184723...	0.639631572...
5/07/2005 ...	AUD	0.63828429182...	0.638162093...
6/07/2005 ...	AUD	0.63930443677...	0.639549756...
7/07/2005 ...	AUD	0.63918184723...	0.638895987...

The sales data records its transactions in the source currency where the sale has taken place (see the Reseller Sales table). Therefore, if we wish to calculate a converted amount, we must first determine the USD value of line items by multiplying with the exchange rate applicable to the currency that the sale was recorded in, and then, dividing by the USD value for the target currency.

The *Grouping by binning and sorting with ranks* recipe included the creation of the additional column titled usd_gross_sales to the Resellers Sales table, which shows the value of the sale line in USD. In this recipe, we reproduce this field in a two-step process: firstly, we add the USD conversion rate (the value required to convert the lines value to USD) and then, we add the usd_gross_sales column.

While we could (and have) included this as a single step (see the definition of the usd_gross_sales column in the *Grouping by binning and sorting with ranks* recipe), it may make more sense to have a column value for the USD conversion in every row because it would be used (in a real environment) by multiple measures. For example, a conversion rate would be required for each standard measure such as Gross Sales, Net Sales, Cost of Goods Sold, and Profit. However, in this recipe we only work with Gross Sales.

How to do it...

Since the existing model already includes currency conversion data (used in the *Grouping by binning and sorting with ranks* recipe), the only additional data required for this recipe is a definition table for currency types.

1. Launch the **PowerPivot Window**.

2. Import the `Currency.txt` file into the model.

3. Create a relationship between the `Date` field in the `Currency Conversion` table and the `Day` field in `Dates`.

4. Create a relationship between the `Currency ID` field in the `Currency` table and the `Currency ID` field in the `Currency Conversion` table. The diagram view of your model should look like the following screenshot:

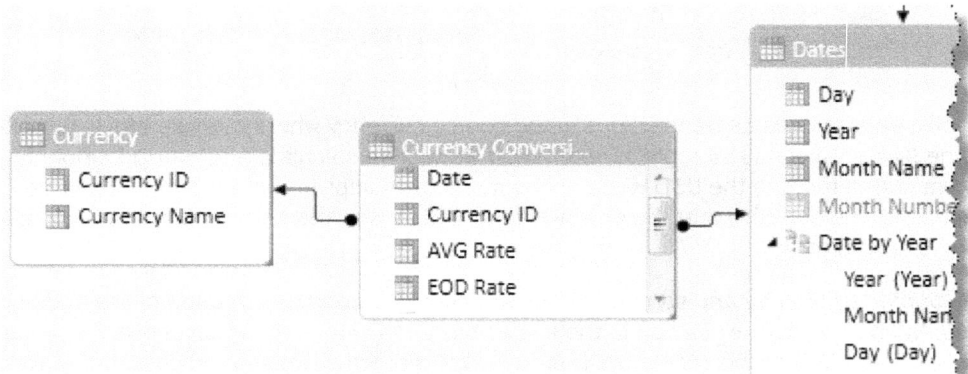

5. Hide all the fields of the `Currency Conversion` table from client tools and add the following measures to show the average daily rate and average end of day rate. Format the measures appropriately.

```
Avg Ex Rate:=AVERAGE([AVG Rate])
Avg EOD Rate:=AVERAGE([EOD Rate])
```

6. Add a new field to the `Resellers Sales` table to show the USD conversion value for the day and a currency applicable to the line (the amount rate which is required to convert each line to a USD value). Add `usd_exchange_rate` as follows:

```
=LOOKUPVALUE('Currency Conversion'[AVG Rate],'Currency
Conversion'[Date],[Order dt],'Currency Conversion'[Currency
ID],[Currency ID])
```

7. Add a new field to the `Resellers Sales` table (alter the formula for the existing field) to show the value of gross sales in USD. Add the field `usd_gross_sales` as follows:

    ```
    =[Quantity Ordered]*[Price Per Unit]*[usd_exchange_rate]
    ```

8. Hide both the fields `usd_exchange_rate` and `usd_gross_sales` from client tools.

9. Add a new measure to the `Resellers Sales` table to show the amount of gross sales in the target currency and format it appropriately. Add the measure `Local Gross Sales` as follows:

    ```
    Local Gross Sales:=
    IF
    (
      NOT(HASONEVALUE(Currency[Currency ID]))
      , [USD Gross Sales],SUMX('Reseller Sales'
      , IF(ISBLANK('Currency Conversion'[Avg Ex Rate])
      , BLANK()
      , [usd_gross_sales]
      / 'Currency Conversion'[Avg Ex Rate])
      )
    )
    ```

10. Create a pivot table (Pivot 1), which shows `Currency Name` on the rows and the measures `USD Gross Sales` and `Local Gross Sales` on the columns.

Row Labels	▼	USD Gross Sales	Local Gross Sales
Afghani		76,989,167	
Algerian Dinar		76,989,167	
Argentine Peso		76,989,167	131,713,977
Armenian Dram		76,989,167	
Aruban Guilder		76,989,167	
Australian Dollar		76,989,167	142,279,185
Azerbaijanian Manat		76,989,167	

11. Create a pivot table (Pivot 2) which shows the conversion of `USD Gross Sales` to its Australian Dollar equivalent by day. Filter the pivot to show a `Currency Name` of Australian Dollar.

12. Add the measure `Avg Ex Rate` (found in the `Currency Conversion` table) to `USD Gross Sales` and `Local Gross Sales` on columns and the `Date by Year` hierarchy (found in the `Dates` table) on rows.

13. Expand the `Date by Year` hierarchy to show the dates for `July 2005`, then filter the date level so that only rows with a `USD Gross Sales` value which is not zero is shown. Select a date value in the pivot, click on the drop-down arrow on **Row labels** and navigate to **Value Filters | Does Not Equal**. Set the value to `0`, the dialog looks like the following screenshot:

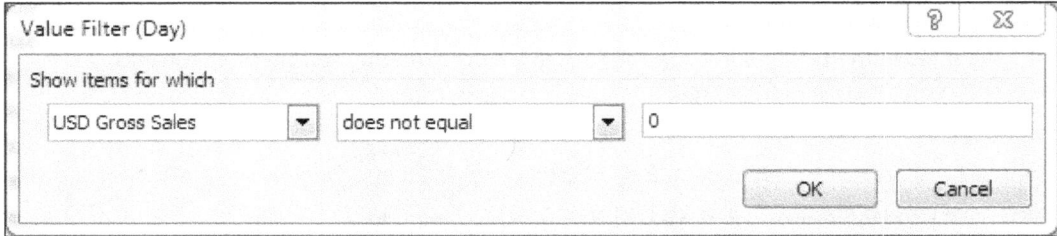

Value Filter (Day)				
Show items for which				
USD Gross Sales	▼	does not equal	▼	0
			OK	Cancel

14. The pivot should look like the following screenshot. Note that the total converted value, `142,279,185`, is the same value as in Pivot 1 (showing that the formula works for aggregated values) and the daily converted value, `01-Jul-05`, of `701,372` is equal to `USD Gross Sales` of `452,761` divided by the exchange rate.

Currency Name Australian Dollar

Row Labels	USD Gross Sales	Avg Ex Rate	Local Gross Sales
⊟ 2005	7,586,983	0.63094	12,154,380
⊟ July	452,761	0.64554	701,372
01-Jul-05	452,761	0.64554	701,372
⊞ August	1,437,493	0.64098	2,242,633
⊞ September	1,102,514	0.66498	1,657,960
⊞ October	771,098	0.62664	1,230,518
⊞ November	2,202,908	0.61091	3,605,940
⊞ December	1,620,209	0.59655	2,715,957
⊞ 2006	23,044,103	0.54882	42,633,657
⊞ 2007	30,821,316	0.51880	59,315,689
⊞ 2008	15,536,766	0.55005	28,175,459
Grand Total	76,989,167	0.55244	142,279,185

How it works...

In the introduction, we discussed the general approach to determining a value in the target currency. That is, we translate a standard USD amount at a rate which is determined by the filter context placed on the `Currency` table (that is, the currency selected by the user). Since this must be calculated on a daily basis, we use the `SUMX` function to iterate over the sales rows and calculate the amount in the target currency for each day.

There are some built-in checks in the measure defining `Local Gross Sales` and it may be best to look at the equation in its entirety. Firstly, the formula can be broken down into some simple pseudocode.

If the user has selected more than one currency, return the USD gross value; otherwise, return the target currency value.

Why must we check for multiple currencies as a first step? We need to check it for two reasons: firstly, what would a conversion into multiple currencies mean?—it is a condition that does not make sense. Secondly, our formula uses an average rate (`Avg Ex Rate`), which will return the daily average across all the selected currencies. This does not make sense either!

The check for multiple (user selected) currencies is achieved through the `NOT(HASONE(VALUE))` part of the equation. This simply returns `TRUE` if the user has selected more than one currency from the currency table.

The calculation of USD gross sales is straightforward, sums the column `usd_gross_sales`. This field should not require any further explanation (see the *Grouping by binning and sorting with ranks* recipe for a full explanation). The only difference in this recipe, is that we materialize the currency USD conversion rate in the `Reseller Sales` table rather than calculating it in a formula. This is because the rate would be used in several calculations had all the measures been added. These measures would include `Gross Sales`, `Discount Amount`, `Net Sales`, `Cost of Goods Sold`, and `Profit`.

Now, we examine the determination of the value in a local or selected currency. This part of the equation is managed by the following code snippet:

```
SUMX('Reseller Sales'
, IF
(
  ISBLANK('Currency Conversion'[Avg Ex Rate])
  , BLANK()
  , [usd_gross_sales]
  / 'Currency Conversion'[Avg Ex Rate])
)
```

In determining the target currency value, the `SUMX` function is used to iterate over each row in the `Reseller Sales` table. Therefore, (provided we have a single target currency) we can satisfy that the measure `Avg Ex Rate` will return the appropriate exchange rate because of the row-by-row iteration and a single target currency.

However, the formula also checks to ensure that an exchange rate can be found, which means, there is the `Avg Ex Rate` measure that can be used. If there is no rate (that is, the rate is `BLANK`), we return nothing, otherwise, we return the converted value. If there was no check and an empty `Avg Ex Rate` measure, the result will display #NUM.

Allocating data at different levels

Often, we have to present two data sources and compare them as if they were one. A typical example of this type of situation is the comparison of budget data to actuals. More often than not, the budgets are prepared at a much higher-level of grain than of actual data.

Consider the sales data that has been used in this chapter. We may define the grain of this as `Reseller`, `Date`, and `Product`. The actual grain of the table is, of course, a lower-level since it includes additional fields such as `Sales Order` and `Geography`, but for our purposes, this is the grain that we have chosen to present to the model user. Now, consider some high-level budget data that simply shows the budgeted sales (`USD Gross Sales`) by `Quarter` and `Year`. Our goal is to incorporate this into the model. Have a look at the following screenshot:

```
1   Year,Quarter,Budget Amount
2   2006,1,4750000.0000
3   2007,1,5913000.0000
4   2008,1,8051000.0000
5   2006,2,5068000.0000
6   2007,2,8039000.0000
7   2008,2,10359000.0000
```

There are two common approaches that are commonly used to solve this problem. Firstly, the original data is arbitrarily assigned to a member within the aggregated value. For example, the entire amount for the year of `2006` and quarter `1 (4,750,000)` may be assigned to `1 January 2006`. The second method involves creating a comparative view within the model that allows the actual data to be reported at the same grain as that of the budget. For this to work, new tables need to be introduced with keys at the higher-level grain, so that the data can be compared in a consistent context. For our budget data, we will add an additional date dimension defined by `Year` and `Quarter`, so that the budget data could be incorporated into the model. A new column can be defined in the actual data (that is in `Resellers Sales`), which defines `Year` and `Quarter` of the sale, and this field can be linked to the new date table. Unfortunately, I now have two date tables (at different levels of grain) and measures, which are not consistent across both. This can be most confusing!

While these methods can provide a solution which incorporates a different grain of data, they lack the ability to fulfill a common desire and recast the aggregated budget data based on historic transactions. Furthermore, the second method can be quite confusing for an end user because there are now more tables in the model to navigate.

The method shown in this recipe is a third alternative. Here, we allocate the higher-level data to lower levels based on values that is based on some gross up value. Of course, that value is the ratio between the detail data sum and the summary data sum. This is conceptually very simple—create a new measure based on our lower-level data, which will equal the total of the higher-level data.

This can aid in the model because variances to the budget can then be examined at any level that exists in the model.

Getting ready

This recipe continues from the previous recipe *Performing currency calculations*.

How to do it...

Since the model only lacks budget information, start by importing the budget data:

1. Import the text file `Reseller Budgets Amounts.txt` into the **PowerPivot Window**.

2. Add a new field to the `Reseller Budget Amounts` table to record the granularity at which the budgets are set (this is the primary key of the table). Add a field `year_quarter_key` with the following formula:

   ```
   =[Year]* 10 +[Quarter]
   ```

   > The new calculated column is an example of a **smart key** and is a common method of key determination in data warehouses. A smart key creates a key based on the business definition.
   >
   > If we were including a product category (or some other textual description) in the key, we would need to convert the values to text and use a delimiter to uniquely identify the key. A pipe symbol (|) or tilde (~) is often used for this purpose.

3. Add a new field to the `Resellers Sales` table that classifies each row with the table at the same grain as that of the budget data. Add a new column `year_quarter_key`:

   ```
   =YEAR([Order dt]) * 10
   + SWITCH(month([Order dt])
   , 1, 1
   , 2, 1
   , 3, 1
   , 4, 2
   , 5, 2
   , 6, 2
   , 7, 3
   , 8, 3
   , 9, 3
   , 10, 4
   , 11, 4
   , 12, 4
   )
   ```

4. Create a relationship between the `year_quarter_key` column in the `Reseller Budget Amounts` table and the `Reseller Sales` table.

5. Add a column to the `Resellers Budget Amounts` table to record the value of USD sales for the given `year_quarter_key` value. Add `usd_gross_sales` as follows:

```
= CALCULATE(SUM('Reseller Sales'[usd_gross_sales]))
```

6. Add a field to the `Resellers Budget Amounts` table that shows the ratio between the budget amount and the USD sales amount. Add `actual_budget_ratio` as follows:

```
= [Budget Amount] / [usd_gross_sales]
```

7. Add a field `actual_budget_ratio` to the `Resellers Sales` table to show what the related `actual_budget_ratio` field for each line is. Add `actual_budget_ratio` as follows:

```
= RELATED('Reseller Budgets Amounts'[actual_budget_ratio])
```

8. Add a field to show what the allocated value of USD sales is—grossed up or down—depending on the `actual_budget_ratio`. Add `usd_gross_sales_budget` as follows:

```
= [actual_budget_ratio] * [usd_gross_sales]
```

> The `usd_gross_sales_budget` field in the `Resellers Sales` table could easily be obtained by combining the `actual_budget_ratio` and `usd_gross_sales` formulas. Including two fields only assists with the explanation. If both fields are combined, the formula will be:
>
> ```
> RELATED('Reseller Budgets Amounts'[actual_budget_ratio])
> * [usd_gross_sales]
> ```

9. Create a measure in the `Resellers Sales` table to show the value of the budgeted amount. Add `USD Gross Sales Budget` and format it appropriately.

```
USD Gross Sales Budget := SUM([usd_gross_sales_budget])
```

10. Hide the `Reseller Budget Amounts` table from client tools.

11. Hide the additional fields: `year_quarter_key`, `actual_budget_ratio`, and `usd_gross_sales_budget` from client tools in the `Resellers Sales` table.

12. Create a pivot table that shows the `Date by Years` hierarchy on rows, `USD Gross Sales` and `USD Gross Sales Budgets` on columns. Expand the year `2005` to show months. The pivot will look like the following screenshot:

Row Labels	USD Gross Sales	USD Gross Sales Budget
⊟ 2005	7,586,983	9,513,000
⊞ July	452,761	587,893
⊞ August	1,437,493	1,866,532
⊞ September	1,102,514	1,431,574
⊞ October	771,098	944,442
⊞ November	2,202,908	2,698,124
⊞ December	1,620,209	1,984,434
⊞ 2006	23,044,103	29,009,000
⊞ 2007	30,821,316	38,782,000
⊞ 2008	15,536,766	18,410,000
Grand Total	76,989,167	95,714,000

How it works...

To aid in the discussion, a screenshot of the `Reseller Budget Amounts` table follows this paragraph. Here, we can see that the `Budget Amount` value for quarter `20053` is `3,866,000`. This is the amount that needs to be apportioned on the basis of actual values in `July`, `August`, and `September` in `2005` (actually, over all dates in this quarter). Note, our budget total of 3,886,000 = 587,893 + 1,866,532 + 1,431, 574. The true sales amount (`usd_gross_sales` and `USD Gross Sales`) for this period is `2,992,767.63`, as shown in the following screenshot:

year_quarter_key	Year	Quarter	Budget Amount	usd_gross_sales	actual_budget_ratio
20053	2005	3	3,886,000.00	2,992,767.63	1.29846365539154
20054	2005	4	5,627,000.00	4,594,215.22	1.22480113023058
20061	2006	1	4,750,000.00	3,817,843.98	1.2441577032143
20062	2006	2	5,068,000.00	4,020,581.46	1.26051419312295
20063	2006	3	10,537,000.00	8,496,592.78	1.2401441696835
20064	2006	4	8,654,000.00	6,709,084.30	1.2898928699978
20071	2007	1	5,913,000.00	5,028,233.76	1.17595964787796

Based on this data, we can easily see how our problem becomes one of allocation. That is, we have existing sales data of `2,992,767.63` (our actual data), but we would like to show a value of `3,866,000`. Therefore, we simply need to gross up the sales data by difference (`actual_budget_ratio`) in order to make both values the same. This is calculated in the `actual_budget_ratio` column.

In the `Reseller Sales` table, the column `usd_gross_sales_budget` calculates the budget value. The field `usd_gross_sales_budget` is derived by `usd_gross_sales`; simply multiplying the existing sales value, `usd_gross_sales`, by the grossed up amount to determine what the budget amount should be. The `USD Gross Sales Budget` measure simply sums up the new column holding the grossed up amounts.

This method should be applicable in most situations. However, a potential reconciliation error can occur when there is no data to base the allocation on. For example, imagine if there were no sales for Q3 of 2003. In this circumstance, there would be no allocation and the USD gross sales budget shown would exclude the Q3 values.

[💡 It is always advisable to reconcile (verify) data shown by the model.]

There's more...

In this recipe, we have so far allocated budget data based on the sales data for the same year. A more common approach to this practice is to allocate the budget based on the data of a previous year. For example, the Q3 values for 2005 would be allocated in the same proportions as the sales data for Q3 of 2004 and the budget data for Q1 of 2006 would be allocated based on the sales during Q1 of 2005. A side benefit of this is that all allocated data can be immediately reconciled since the historic data exists—and the budget allocation can be verified once the allocation has occurred.

The technique that we can use to do this is essentially the same as that shown in this recipe; however, there are two main differences that are worth noting. Firstly, in order to determine the sales value, we must offset the `year_quarter_key` in the `Reseller Sales` table. Secondly, we need to project any calculated budget amount in the `Reseller Sales` table, forward a year since there is an existing relationship between the `Dates` table and the `Reseller Sales` table.

1. Alter the formula for the `year_quarter_key` field in the `Reseller Sales` table to cast the key in the next year. The formula should become:

    ```
    =(YEAR([Order dt])+1) * 10 + SWITCH(month([Order dt])
    , 1, 1
    , 2, 1
    , 3, 1 ...
    ```

2. Add a field to the `Reseller Sales` table to showcast the sales data a year forward. Add `order_dt_ny` as follows:

    ```
    = CALCULATE(DATEADD(Dates[Day], 1 ,YEAR))
    ```

3. Create a secondary relationship between the `Dates` table and `Reseller Sales` based on the `order_dt_ny` in `Reseller Sales` and `Day` in `Dates`.

4. Alter the `USD Gross Sales Budget` measure in `Reseller Sales` to calculate the `SUM` based on the secondary relationship (the relationship between the `Dates` table and `order_dt_ny` in the `Reseller Sales` table). The formula for the gross sales budget is:

```
USD Gross Sales Budget:=
CALCULATE
(
SUM([usd_gross_sales_budget])
, USERELATIONSHIP(
'Reseller Sales'[order_dt_ny]
, Dates[Day]
  )
)
```

5. Hide the new field `order_dt_ny` from client tools.

6. Refresh the pivot and expand the months for 2006. Here, the Q3 budget values have been apportioned over months (marked in red in the following screenshot) so that the total is `10,537,000` (this number is the same value as shown for `20063`, as shown in the preceding screenshot of the `Reseller Budgets Amounts` table).

Row Labels	USD Gross Sales	USD Gross Sales Budget	
⊟ 2005	7,586,983		
⊕ July	452,761		
⊕ August	1,437,493		
⊕ September	1,102,514		
⊕ October	771,098		
⊕ November	2,202,908		
⊕ December	1,620,209		
⊟ 2006	23,044,103	19,191,000	
⊕ January	659,584		
⊕ February	1,812,593		
⊕ March	1,345,667		
⊕ April	808,428		
⊕ May	2,144,494		
⊕ June	1,067,660		
⊕ July	2,214,875	1,594,090	
⊕ August	3,475,686	5,061,156	
⊕ September	2,806,031	3,881,754	10,537,000
⊕ October	1,695,094	1,452,497	
⊕ November	2,929,680	4,149,558	8,654,000
⊕ December	2,084,310	3,051,945	

Note that there is no budget data for 2005 and the first half of 2006. This is because there is sales data that only appears in the second half of 2005 and therefore, nothing to base the allocation against.

If we re-examine this process (in light of the requirement to use prior years' data as the basis for allocation), the method can be explained with the following logic:

1. We have the sales data which relates to a specific period (based on the order date).

2. We have the budget data identified by a period (year and period), which we want to allocate to on the basis of the prior period's sales data.

3. We append a field to the sales, which shows the budget period that the sales row is related to. Since the budget data is to be allocated based on the prior years' sales data, a year in the sales data is offset, so that it refers to a future year in the budget data.

4. The relationship between the budget data and sales data (`year_quarter_key`) can be used to calculate the total sales in the budget period and this can be used to determine what the gross up value should be.

5. The gross up value can then be applied to the sales data using the existing relationship and a calculation that applies the gross up value to the sales value.

6. Now, we have a budgeted allocation amount in our sales data. However, the allocated amount is apportioned on the basis of the following year's budget period. For example, the sales data relating to 2005 has the 2006 budget allocations. What we have to do is force the budget data to appear in 2006, while the sales data appears in 2005. This is managed by casting the row forward a year (using the field `order_dt_ny`) and using this date as the basis for the summation of budget values. The secondary relationship is used to manage this.

6
Programmatic Access via Excel

In this chapter, we will cover:

- ► Connecting pivot tables and Slicers
- ► Using cube functions
- ► Working with worksheet events and VBA
- ► Managing the Slicer through VBA

Introduction

The ability to create a tabular model through PowerPivot opens up countless possibilities for the advanced Excel user and business analyst to develop reporting and analytical solutions. Historically, these types of users start by attacking a business problem by *pulling* data into Excel, creating pivot tables (to summarize data) using some of Excel's built-in programmatic, and form functionality to create solutions.

However, a common problem encountered with this approach is that of scalability. And as the amount of data increased, the ability of Excel to handle the solution decreased. This tipping point need not be very large; further, the requirement of traditional pivot tables to use flattened data required a lot of inefficient data work (usually through VLOOKUP functions, because a traditional pivot table required a single table of data). Obviously, it is a poor use of time when more effort is spent organizing data rather than analyzing it.

The ability of the tabular model to manage large amounts of data, create relationships between that data, and define calculations based on business logic reignites the opportunity for end users to create powerful applications in Excel.

This chapter examines how Excel interacts with the model, and how Excel can be used as a reporting application layer to provide a rich and intuitive reporting environment. Most importantly, the reader should recognize that the model is, for all intents and purposes, its own object within Excel. Excel interacts with it, just as it would with any other OLAP solution.

The outcome of this chapter is to enable the reader to create a reporting workbook with the functionality shown in the following screenshot. It shows two pivot tables and three charts. A Slicer allows the user to select a year, which automatically applies a filter to pivot tables **A** and **B**. The trend line chart also updates for the year, and when the user selects one of the category names (in pivot table **B**), a selected category is shown for one of the trend lines. Also, the selected year is shown highlighted in bar chart **C**. All chart labels and headings are also updated accordingly.

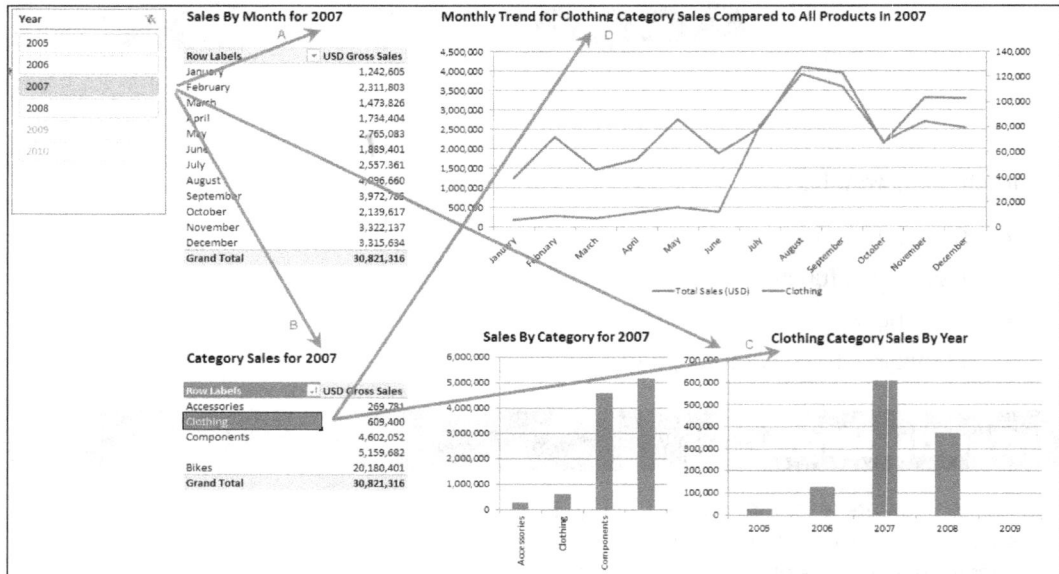

It is important to reiterate that the PowerPivot model is a tabular model hosted in Excel, that an Excel pivot table can connect to as a client. This experience would be exactly the same had the user connected via Excel to the model hosted on a production server (or an OLAP (multidimensional) cube posted in a traditional method of storage for analysis services).

Connecting pivot tables and Slicers

Excel 2010 introduced new functionality into Excel in the form of **Slicer** controls. A Slicer can be thought of as an Excel data control that connects to multidimensional data as a client tool, which has built-in functionality for interacting with pivot tables. Since the tabular model is presented to Excel as a multidimensional model (it is essentially a server model stored in Excel and accessed through Excel's client tools), the pivot table and Slicer can connect to the tabular model.

In fact, the **PowerPivot Field List** is a special field list for interacting with a pivot table based on the tabular model that includes two window groups for horizontal and vertical Slicers, as shown in the following screenshot (the horizontal or vertical position only refers to the Slicers position in relation to the location of the pivot table). This is only available in Excel 2010.

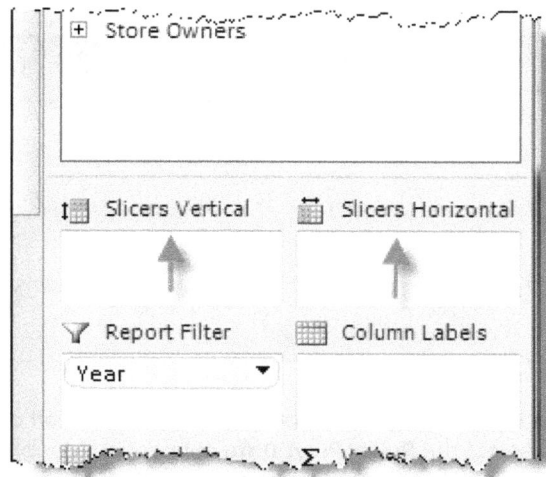

While the Slicer can be attached to a pivot table through the **PivotTable Field list**, the Slicer can also be inserted as an individual control to interact with the model.

A Slicer can only be added to a pivot table using the **PivotTable Field list** when using the **PowerPivot Field list** (or a pivot table that was inserted from a tabular model). If you choose to show the pivot table's default field list (that is, the default list when connecting to a model as a normal client—see the *There's More...* section of the *Creating model calculations* recipe in *Chapter 1, Getting Started with Excel*), you will not see the options for adding Slicers to the pivot. In this case they will have to be added manually.

This recipe shows how to insert a Slicer to your worksheet, use it to access data, and connect it to pivot tables. In addition, we show how to manage and add pivot tables as a client, by referencing an internal tabular model.

Getting ready

This recipe uses the model that was built in the *Allocating data at different levels* recipe in *Chapter 5, Applied Modeling*. All the existing worksheets with pivot tables have been deleted, leaving only a blank sheet in the workbook. If the required recipes have not been completed, the empty workbook with the PowerPivot model can be downloaded (see online resources).

How to do it...

Let us start by adding a pivot table to our worksheet.

1. Insert a pivot table by clicking on the **PivotTable** button from the **Insert** tab, as shown in the following screenshot:

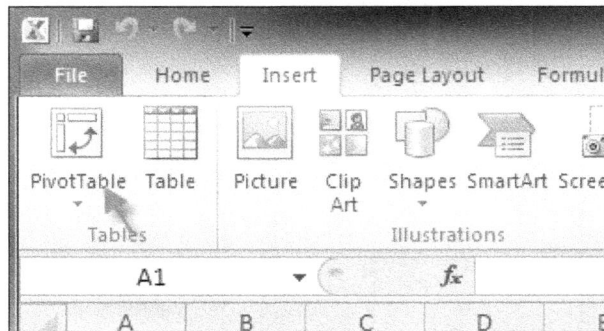

2. The **Create PivotTable** dialogue will open. Choose the **Use an external data source** option and then select the **PowerPivot Data** connection (double-click on the connection or highlight the connection and click on the **Open** button). Place the pivot table in cell D10 (select the location and click on **OK**). This is shown in the following screenshot:

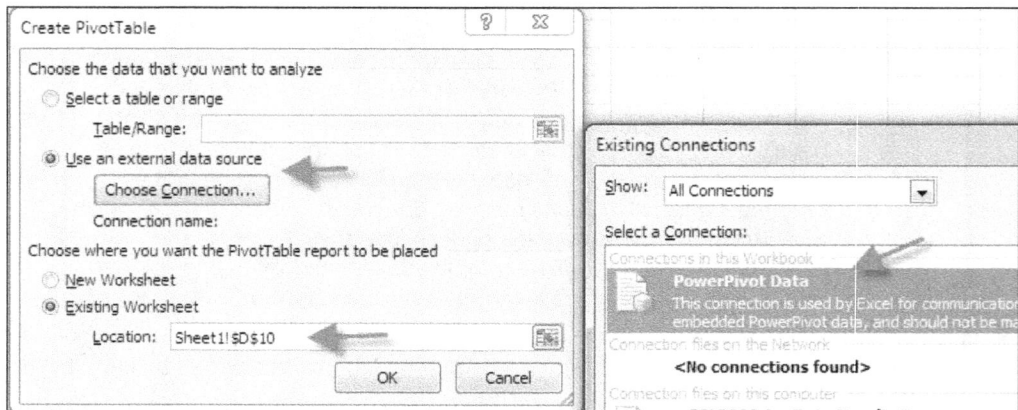

[💡 The location of the pivot table will default to the active cell when the **Insert a PivotTable** button is clicked.]

3. Place the `Month Name` attribute from the `Dates` table on rows, and show the `USD Gross Sales` measure from the `Reseller Sales` table as values.

4. Insert a Slicer into the worksheet by clicking on the **Slicer** button from the **Insert** tab, as shown in the following screenshot:

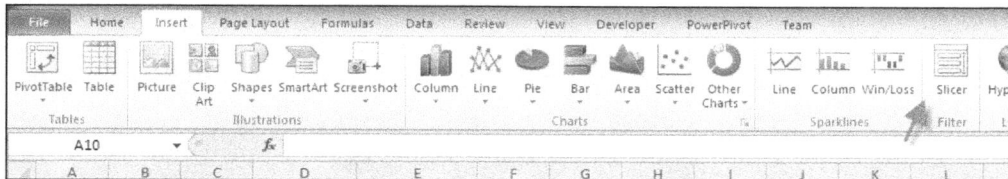

5. When the **Slicer** button is clicked, a (choose) connection window will open. Choose the **PowerPivot Data** connection that exists in the workbook.

6. Once the connection is chosen, a pop-up window will display a list of tables, attributes, and hierarchies that are available in the model. Choose the `Year` attribute from the `Dates` table. More than likely, you will have to expand the **More fields** grouping. Click on **OK** after the **Year** box is checked. The **Slicer** dialogue is shown in the following screenshot:

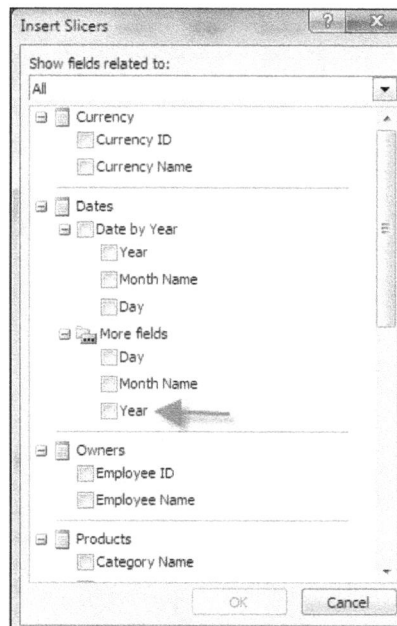

7. A Slicer will appear on the page (as shown in the following screenshot). This contains the data values (or members) for the `Year` attribute in the model. A year can be selected by clicking on the year within the **Slicer**; however, the values in the pivot table will not change.

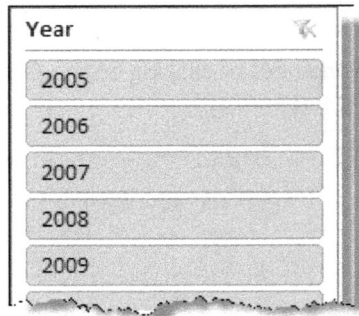

Year
2005
2006
2007
2008
2009

8. When a cell in the pivot table is selected, the **PivotTable Tools** menu is displayed in the ribbon of Excel (this is not shown when the pivot table is not active). Name the pivot table by overwriting the default name given to the pivot table (**PivotTable Tools | Options**). Name the pivot `sales_by_month_all`. This can also be typed directly into the **PivotTable Name** box, as highlighted in the following screenshot:

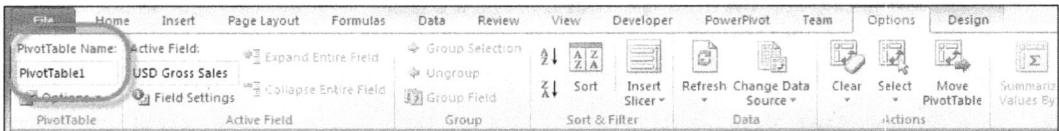

9. Attach the pivot table to the Slicer by clicking on the **PivotTable Connections...** option after right-clicking on the Slicer. This is shown in the following screenshot:

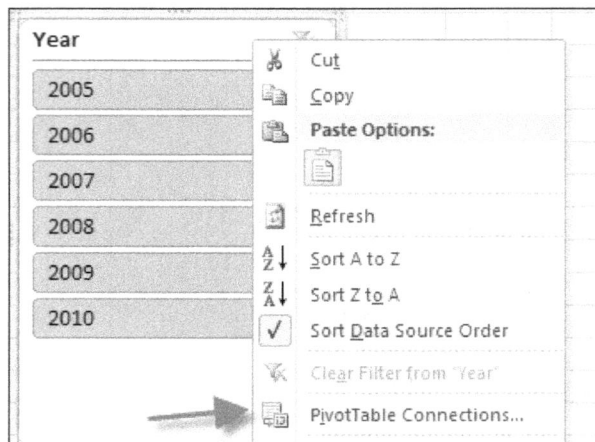

10. When the **PivotTable Connections...** option is clicked on, a dialogue will open showing all pivot tables in the workbook (as shown in the following screenshot). Select the pivot tables that the Slicer is attached to, by checking the pivot table and clicking on the **OK** button.

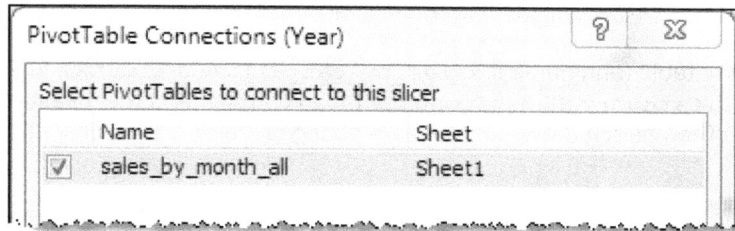

PivotTable Connections (Year)

Select PivotTables to connect to this slicer

	Name	Sheet
☑	sales_by_month_all	Sheet1

> We can see that using a name for the pivot table allows us to easily identify the pivot table in a workbook.

11. When the Slicer is attached to a pivot table (immediately after the **OK** button is clicked on), the members for **2009** and **2010** will gray out. This indicates that there is no data for those years. Further, when a **Year** is selected (by simply clicking on the year) the active year remains blue (all other members white out), and the values in the pivot table change to reflect the selected year.

12. Ensure that all months are shown for the pivot (regardless of data values) by checking the **Show items with no data on rows** option from the **Display** tab in the **Pivot Table Options...** (click on the **Options** button in the **PivotTable Tools** menu to show the **Options** window).

How it works...

There is nothing extraordinary to explain here. The Slicer filters the data for the pivot table(s) that it is attached to.

There's more...

The creation and use of the Slicer does not impede any pivot table functionality, or place any additional requirements on the pivot table. For example, we can create another pivot table below the existing one which has a **Filter** on the `Years` hierarchy of the `Dates` table, and attach the Slicer to this new pivot table. When the value of the Slicer changes, the Filter on the pivot table will automatically change to reflect the value(s) of the Slicer.

> Adding a Filter to a pivot table with an alternate connection to a Slicer is a very convenient way to determine the value of the Slicer. This can then be used to provide descriptive headings (as we will see in the *Working with worksheet events and VBA* and *Managing the Slicer through VBA* recipes).

Create a new pivot table (and name it `sales_by_cat_all`). Add `Year` as a Filter (from the `Dates` table) with `Category Name` (`Products` table) on rows, and the measure **USD Gross Sales** as values. Then attach the Slicer to it—any changes made to the Slicer are reflected by the Filter.

Since this pivot is used in other recipes for this chapter, the first cell of the pivot table should appear in `D25` (you may have to move your pivot table). We also want to show the names of the sales categories in an ascending order (based on **USD Gross Sales**). Right-click on any cell in the pivot and select **More Sort Options** from the pop-up window. That is, right-click on the Cell, and go to **Sort | More Sort Options**. When the **Sort** window opens, ensure that **USD Gross Sales** is selected in the **Ascending (A to Z) by:** listbox (as shown in the following screenshot). Then click on **OK**.

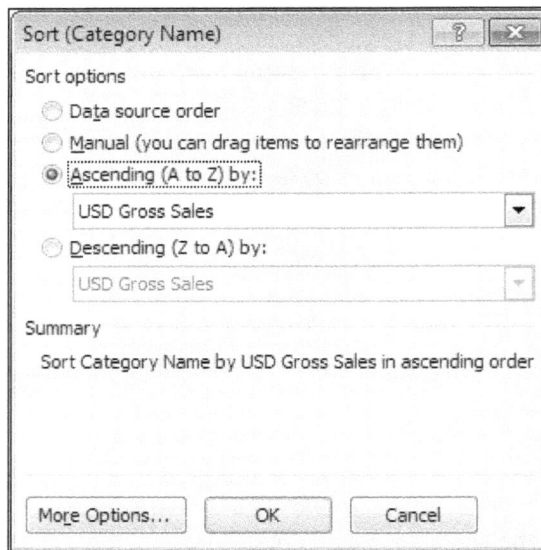

The pivot table field headings will change their icons slightly to indicate that a filter or sort has taken place. Notice that the **Row Labels** button includes an arrow to indicate a Sort. This is shown in the following screenshot:

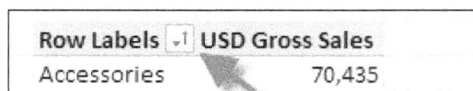

Using cube functions

A pivot table can be a very useful tool for analyzing data. The ability to dynamically drop a hierarchy from the model and expose all members, then sorting, filtering, and restricting those members can be used in a large number of analytical situations. However, one problem with the pivot table is that all the elements of the object (Filters, rows, and columns) are connected and cannot be formatted with the complete discretion of the user. For example, the user cannot insert a row between rows in the pivot table. While there are some options for formatting a pivot table, these mainly relate to styles, and often the user wishes to have a larger amount of control over what they are presenting. Additionally, using the formula that refers to a cell in the pivot table is troublesome, because the pivot table can change and invalidate the formula.

This recipe examines the use of the CUBE FUNCTION formulas, which allows the user to access model data without the restrictions imposed by the pivot table.

Getting ready

This recipe continues from the prior recipe *Connecting pivot tables and Slicers*.

How to do it...

While CUBEFUNCTIONS can be used as any formula and directly typed into the formula bar, it is often more convenient to start with an existing pivot table and inherit that pivot table's structure. The entire pivot table can be replaced with formulas. Let's start by creating a new pivot table.

1. Activate cell H27 and insert a pivot table based on the model data. Put the Years hierarchy on rows and display the **USD Gross Sales** as a measure. Then use the Category Name hierarchy of the Products table as a Filter.

2. Format the pivot table (change its options) so that rows without data are shown (this will show all Years in the model).

3. With the pivot table active, select the **Convert to Formulas** button from the **OLAP Tools** group. This is highlighted in the following screenshot:

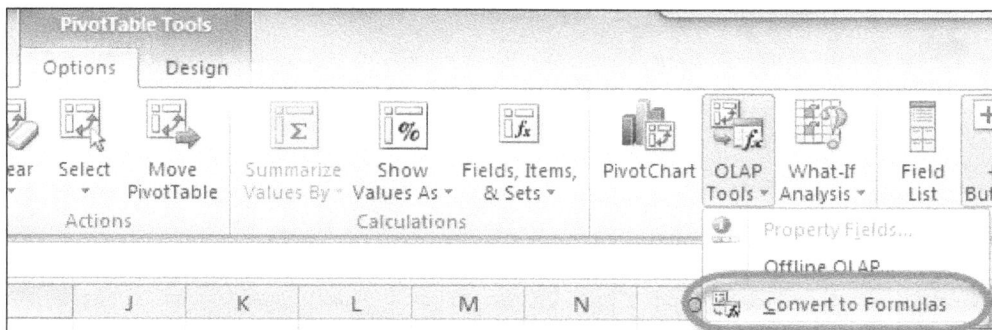

4. A dialogue will open (as shown in the following screenshot) prompting you to check the **Convert Report Filters** option and click on the **Convert** button.

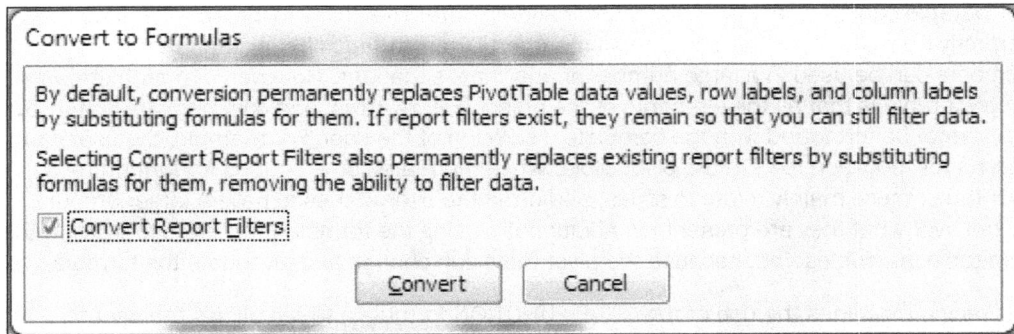

Convert to Formulas

By default, conversion permanently replaces PivotTable data values, row labels, and column labels by substituting formulas for them. If report filters exist, they remain so that you can still filter data.

Selecting Convert Report Filters also permanently replaces existing report filters by substituting formulas for them, removing the ability to filter data.

☑ Convert Report Filters

[Convert]   [Cancel]

---

5. Once this button is clicked, the pivot table will be entirely replaced with formulas. It also loses its formatting and the ability to filter by category.

6. Delete the values from both the cells under **2010** (it does not matter whether cells are shifted up or to the left-hand side).

7. Select the cell that stores year values as a filter in the pivot table `sales_by_cat_all` (cell E25) and call it `name` (that is, define a named range that refers to the cell). Title the **Range** as `selected_year` by selecting cell E25 and typing the name into the **Name Box**. This is shown in the following screenshot:

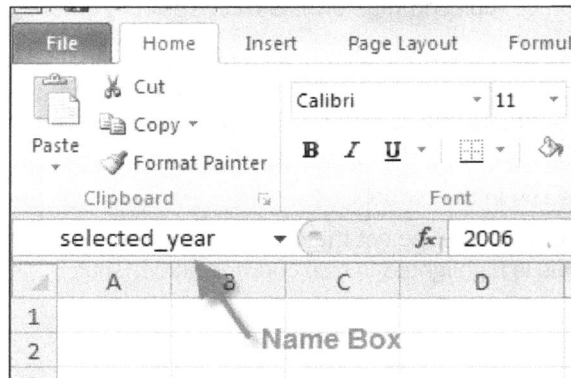

File	Home	Insert	Page Layout	Formula

Cut
Copy ▾
Paste
Format Painter
Clipboard

Calibri   ▾ 11 ▾
B *I* <u>U</u> ▾
Font

selected_year   ▾ f_x 2006

	A	B	C	D
1				
2				

Name Box

> A name can be used to refer to a range of cells (in this case there is only one cell in the range). Alternatively, names can be defined and edited using the **Name Manager** on the **Formulas** tab. See the *Creating the model* recipe in *Chapter 1, Getting Started with Excel*, for more information on using the **Name Manager**.

8. Highlight the cells J28 through to J32 (the first column without a formula) and type the following formula:

   ```
   =IF(selected_year=H30:H34,I30:I34,"")
   ```

9. Instead of pressing the *Enter* key to accept the formula, press *Shift + Ctrl + Enter*.

10. Note that the formula is applied to all the sales that were selected and the formula is enclosed in { }. The formula looks like this:

    ```
    {=IF(selected_year=H30:H34,I30:I34,"")}
    ```

11. Change the year in the Slicer and note that a value is shown for the *active* year in column **J**. Notice how the formula in the following screenshot is surrounded by { }:

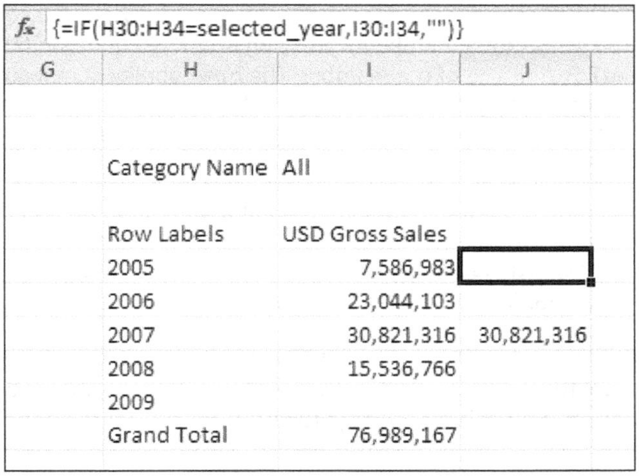

fx	{=IF(H30:H34=selected_year,I30:I34,"")}		
G	**H**	**I**	**J**
	Category Name All		
	Row Labels	USD Gross Sales	
	2005	7,586,983	
	2006	23,044,103	
	2007	30,821,316	30,821,316
	2008	15,536,766	
	2009		
	Grand Total	76,989,167	

How it works...

The first part of this recipe converted the pivot table to formulas. These formulas allow an Excel cell to access data directly from the model without relying on the pivot table. For our purposes, there are two formulas. One formula defines a member (categorical value within the model) as the descriptive or caption name, and the other to return measure values—that is the values that exist at the intersection of members.

The formula in cell H30 shows an example of the CUBEMEMBER function. This function returns the member for the provided member expression. The syntax for the CUBEMEMBER function is as follows:

```
CUBEMEMBER(connection , member_expression , caption)
```

Here the connection parameter refers to the name of the connection of the PowerPivot model—remember that this was called **PowerPivot Data** when we inserted the pivot table in the *Connecting pivot tables and Slicers* recipe.

The member_expression parameter refers to the member_unique_name or member_name for the member being defined. This is a three part name that defines a distinct area in the model and includes the dimension, hierarchy, and member values, and follows the syntax as follows:

```
[table].[hierarchy].[member]
```

In this case, [member] can refer to a key (which is prefixed by an & symbol) or simply the member name (its value). For example, consider the definition of the member for the year 2005. There are two ways to represent the member. These are as follows: [Dates].[Year].&[2005] or [Dates].[Year].[2005].

> The syntax for a member expression is derived from the MDX unique_name of the member. The functionality demonstrated for all recipes in this chapter would work in the exact same manner, had a multidimensional cube been used as a data source.

Finally, the last argument of the CUBEMEMBER formula allows us to specify the display value for the formula (sounds ironic right?). However, we can change what is displayed as the caption. For example we could display Sales for 2005 as the caption even though the caption should display 2005. In both cases, the member still refers to the 2005 year member.

The CUBEVALUE function is used to return a measure (or aggregated value) from the model. The CUBEVALUE function follows a simple syntax, which defines the connection and intersection (as MDX expressions). The syntax for CUBEVALUE is as follows:

```
CUBEVALUE(connection, [member_expression1],
    [member_expression2], …)
```

The CUBEVALUE function is quite flexible in how it can be used to return values. So far we have only used CUBEVALUE by referring to previously defined CUBEMEMBERS. These members can be replaced with strings or defined as an MDX tuple. For example, all the following formulas produce the same result (the USD Gross Sales amount for 2006 and All Accessories):

```
=CUBEVALUE("PowerPivot Data",$I$27,$H31,I$29)
```

Where I$27, $H31, and I$29 are the CUBEMEMBER functions.

```
=CUBEVALUE("PowerPivot Data"
    ,"[Dates].[Year].&[2006]"
    ,"[Measures].[USD Gross Sales]"
    ," [Products].[Category Name].[All]"
    )
=CUBEVALUE("PowerPivot Data"
    ,"(
        [Dates].[Year].&[2006]
    , [Measures].[USD Gross Sales]
    , [Products].[Category Name].[All]
        )"
    )
```

The formula used in column **J** is an array formula and is immediately identifiable by the curly parentheses around the formula. A complete discussion of this type of formula is out of the scope of this book; however, using an array allows ranges to be applied against each other within the formula (as was demonstrated when the formula was created). We could have used the same formula and copied it down (maintaining the correct references of course). Further reading about array formulas can be found at http://office.microsoft.com/en-au/excel-help/introducing-array-formulas-in-excel-HA001087290.aspx.

Working with worksheet events and VBA

For the reporting scenario that was outlined in the *Introduction* to this chapter, the intent is to allow the user to click on a pivot table row item and then have this action create downstream activity affecting other elements on the worksheet. That is, when the user clicks on a category item in the pivot table (the pivot titled sales_by_cat_all), the bar chart showing year-on-year category sales will change to show the selected category.

This type of action may be achieved through various methods—the use of a Filter or Slicer connecting the two pivot tables immediately springs to mind. However, in doing this, the end user is still required to select something from the drop down (Filter) or Slicer. We want to interrogate the clicking action on a part of the spreadsheet to facilitate a change. Furthermore, while the event (recipe) applies to a pivot table, there is no restriction to binding this action to a pivot table. The technique can be applied to any situation where the user selects a cell in the worksheet.

Getting ready

This recipe continues from the worksheet and model that was developed in the prior recipe (*Using cube functions*). In order to do this we use a programmatic component of Excel (**VBA**). In order to access this, the **Developer** tab of the ribbon should be visible. If not, the **Developer** tab can be made visible by checking the **Developer** tab under the **Customize Ribbon** option of **Excel Options**. To launch the **Excel Options** dialogue, select the **Options** button from the **File** menu. This is shown in the following screenshot:

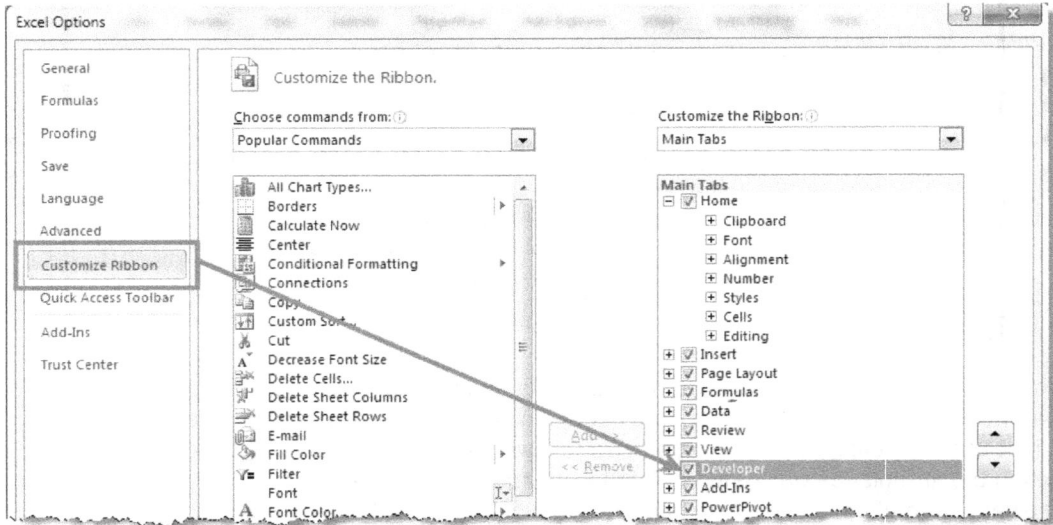

How to do it...

The overview of this recipe is as follows; firstly, we listen for a cell to be selected by the user. Once this occurs, we use the cell to identify if it lies in the pivot table and then (if so), use its value to populate a holding cell (I26 in the following screenshot). Then, the existing CUBE FUNCTIONS can use this value as a reference (as part of the formula). This is demonstrated in the following screenshot:

⏴	C	D	E	F	G	H	I	J
24								
25		Year	2007	⊤				
26								
27		Row Labels ⤓	USD Gross Sales			Category Name	All	
28		Accessories	269,781					
29		Clothing	609,400			Row Labels	USD Gross Sales	
30		Components	4,602,052			2005	7,586,983	
31			5,159,682			2006	23,044,103	
32		Bikes	20,180,401			2007	30,821,316	30,821,316
33		**Grand Total**	**30,821,316**			2008	15,536,766	
34						2009		
35						Grand Total	76,989,167	

Let us start by defining a name for the highlighted cell shown in the preceding screenshot (that is cell I26) as follows:

1. Create a named range for cell I26 by typing category_sel into the **Name Manager** of Excel when cell I26 is selected.

2. Alter the existing CUB EFUNCTION formula in cell I27 (the prior pivot table's Filter location) to refer the value of the range category_sel. Replace the existing formula with the following:

    ```
    =CUBEMEMBER("PowerPivot Data",category_sel)
    ```

3. After this, the existing CUBE FUNCTIONS formulas will be invalidated showing the **#N/A** values. We can correct this by pasting [Products].[Category Name]. [All] into the category_sel cell (I26).

4. Launch the **Visual Basic for Applications** (**VBA**) editor by clicking on the **Visual Basic** button from the **Developer** tab.

5. Activate the code page for `Sheet1` by double-clicking on **Sheet1** from the **VBAProject**. When this occurs, the grayed out background in the image will turn white. If **VBAProject** is not visible, it can be made visible by pressing *Ctrl + R* or by navigating to **View | Project Explorer** from the menu items. You should see something very similar to the following screenshot:

6. Create a subroutine for a selection change event by selecting the event from the drop-down box (as shown in the following screenshot). Select **Worksheet** from the first drop-down box, and **SelectionChange** from the second.

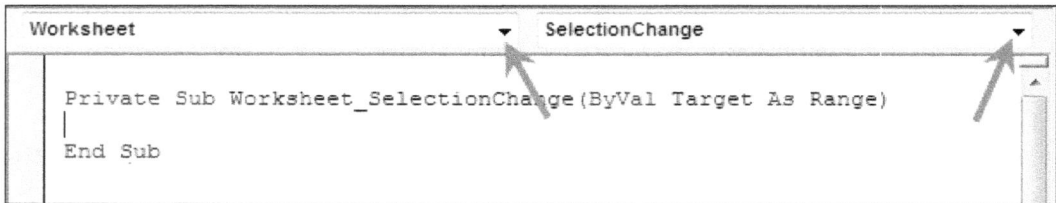

> You can create this automatically by pasting the following code:
>
> ```
> Private Sub Worksheet_SelectionChange(ByVal Target As
>     Range)
> End Sub
> ```

7. Fill the subroutine with the following code:

```
On Error GoTo Err

    If Target.Cells.Count = 1 And _
        Target.PivotTable.Name = "sales_by_cat_all" And _
        Target.PivotField = "[Products].[Category
        Name].[Category Name]" Then
```

```
Sheet1.Range("category_sel").Value =
        Target.PivotItem.Value


    End If


    Exit Sub
Err:
```

> Notice the reference to Sheet1 in the previous code. Here, Sheet1 refers to a workbook class in code, which is the sequentially numbered sheet in the workbook and not the actual name of the sheet. If the sheet had been renamed (for example) to S1, we can still refer to it by the sheet number, that is, Sheet1.
>
> Alternatively, we can refer to it by its name by replacing the Sheet1 prefix with Sheets("name").

8. The code screen should look like the following screenshot:

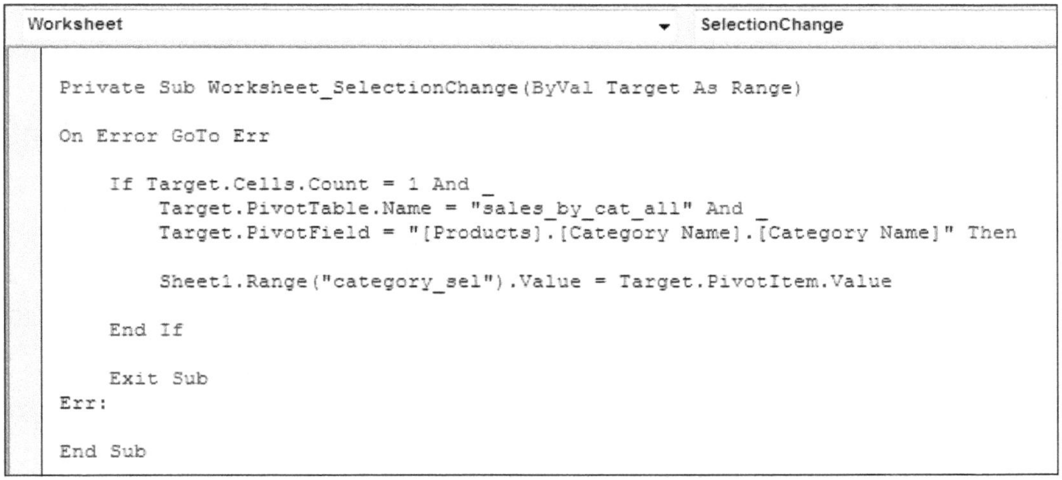

Worksheet	▼ SelectionChange

```
Private Sub Worksheet_SelectionChange(ByVal Target As Range)

On Error GoTo Err

    If Target.Cells.Count = 1 And _
        Target.PivotTable.Name = "sales_by_cat_all" And _
        Target.PivotField = "[Products].[Category Name].[Category Name]" Then

        Sheet1.Range("category_sel").Value = Target.PivotItem.Value

    End If

    Exit Sub
Err:

End Sub
```

9. Close the VBA code window and return to Excel. Test the application by selecting different categories, multiple cells, and so on. When a category is selected, the key will be placed in the `category_sel` range and the CUBE FUNCTIONS will change, as shown in the following screenshot:

	C	D	E	F	G	H	I	J	K	L
24										
25		Year	2007	⊤						
26							[Products].[Category Name].&[Accessories]			
27		Row Labels ▾	USD Gross Sales			Category Name	Accessories			
28		Accessories	269,781							
29		Clothing	609,400			Row Labels	USD Gross Sales			
30		Components	4,602,052			2005	18,599			
31			5,159,682			2006	70,435			
32		Bikes	20,180,401			2007	269,781	269,781		
33		Grand Total	30,821,316			2008	154,128			
34						2009				
35						Grand Total	512,942			

How it works...

The overall operation for this recipe has been discussed from a procedural perspective. That is, we determine the member's unique name (see the *How it works...* section in the *Using cube functions* recipe) for the category that the user has selected, and use this value in the CUBE FUNCTION formula that has been previously created.

In doing this, Excel listens for an event where the user changes their selection (or the active cell(s)). This is (of course) handled through the internal `Worksheet_SelectionChange` routine. Here the argument (`Target`) refers to the cell range that the user has selected.

Once this has occurred, there are several things that the code in the routine (`Sub`) looks for. These occur in unison, and are as follows:

1. A check that the user has only selected one cell (by checking that `Target.Count` equals to `1`).

2. Determining if the cell belongs to the appropriate pivot table (through `Target.PivotTable.Name`).

3. Checking that the user has selected a cell that relates to the `Category` hierarchy (through the `Target.PivotField` property for the selected cell).

The functions that relate to the use of the pivot table should be somewhat self-explanatory, that is, provided with a cell reference (through `Target` or cell chosen), we can determine the name of the pivot table and the hierarchy chosen.

Once we are satisfied that these conditions have occurred (and these are the only conditions that make sense for our scenario), we simply set the value of the named range `category_sel` to the value of the category that has been selected.

The reliance on the existence of a pivot table through the `Target.PivotTable.Name` and `Target.PivotField` functions will throw an error (runtime error) had a pivot table not been selected by `Target`. Therefore, we effectively wrap the `IF` statement in an error catching routine.

There's more...

In addition to the unique member name (or key) for the selected cell, it will be desirable to identify the name (that is, the display name) of the selected cell and combine that with a descriptive graphic for the data. The intent of this will be to produce something similar to the following chart:

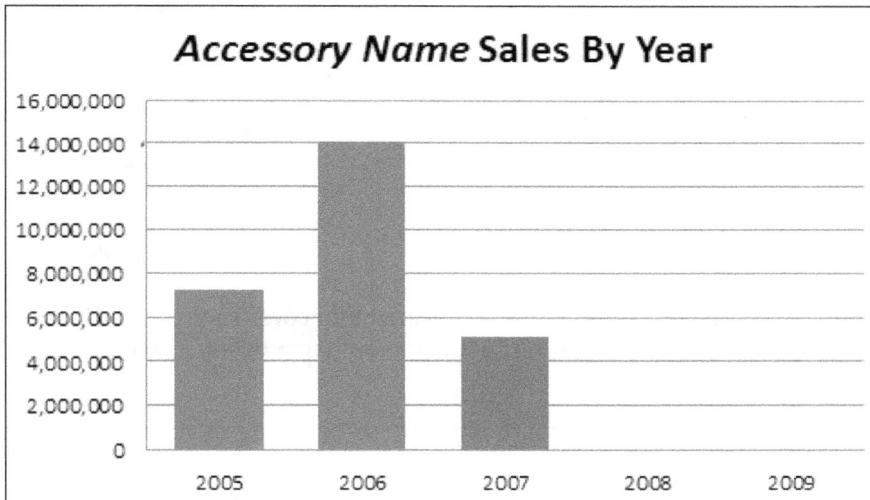

For this chart, the chart title changes depending on the pivot table cell selected (as previously demonstrated) and the color for one of the bars signifies the selected year (as filtered by the pivot table `sales_by_cat_all`).

The creation of the chart is relatively straightforward. Create a bar chart with two series based on the output from the *Using cube functions* recipe, and set the overlap distance for the second series to 100 percent or completely overlapped. This can be set by right-clicking on the second series (in the chart), selecting **Format Data Series...** from the pop-up window, and then sliding the series overlap all the way to the right, as shown in the following screenshot:

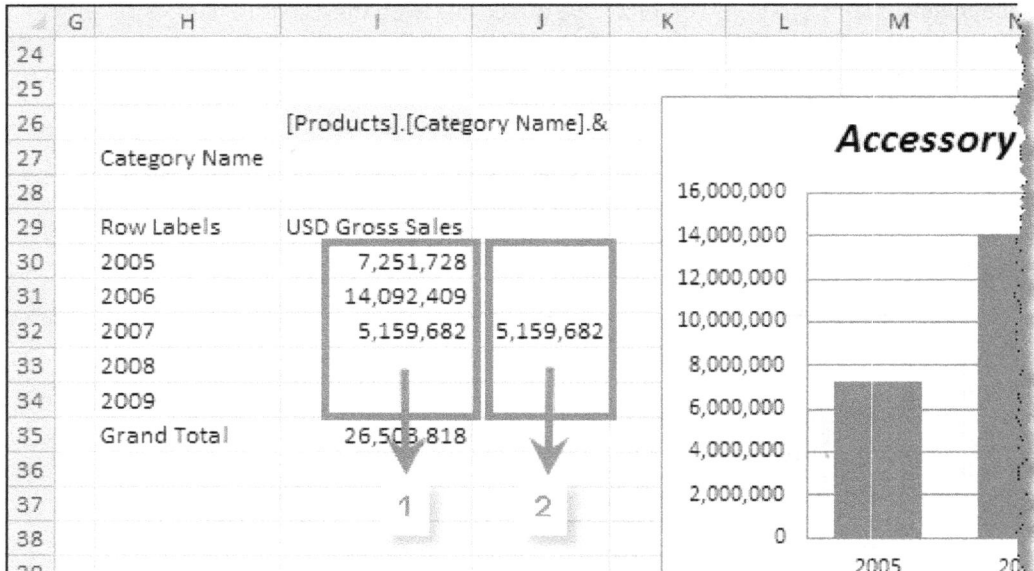

In reality, we are showing two series in the same chart that cover each other (of course, one series is on top of the other). We can control the overlap property as shown in the following screenshot:

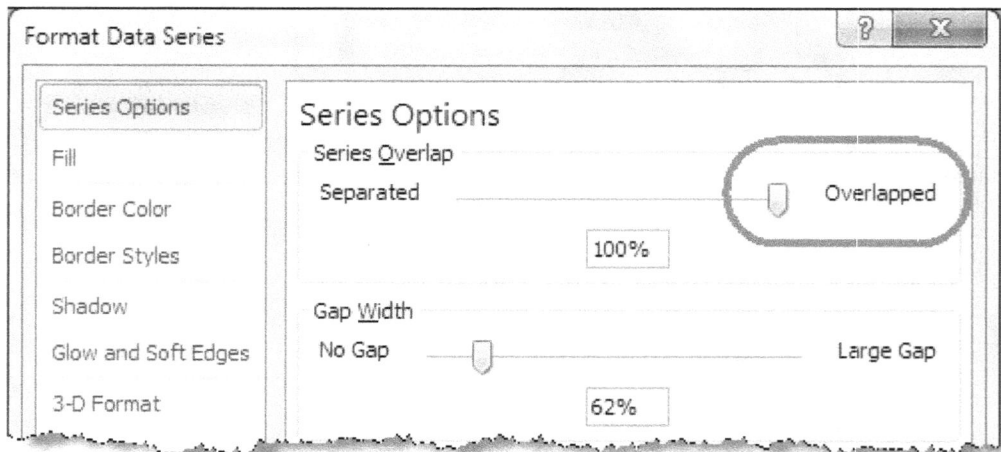

Just as we have named the pivot tables in order to identify them in VBA, we can also name the charts.

> The naming of objects is not necessary from a technical perspective (required in VBA) but it certainly makes it easy to identify them. Other options include identifying a chart by its index within the sheet.

When the chart is selected, the **Chart Tools** ribbon item will be displayed, exposing the **Chart Name:** box in the **Layout** tab. Name the chart `accessory_sales_by_year_chart`, as shown in the following screenshot:

Now, the existing routine for `_SelectionChange` can be altered to dynamically change the title of the chart. Add the following line of code to the routine before the `End If` line:

```
Sheet1.ChartObjects("accessory_sales_by_year_chart").Chart.ChartTi
    tle.Text = Target.PivotItem.Caption & " Sales by Year"
```

It should be relatively straightforward how this code works—we specify the `Text` for the `ChartTitle` within a (required) chart. The actual text is determined by concatenating the *value* of the selected cell to the string `Sales By Year`. We can determine the value in a number of ways (`Target` or `Target.Value` would provide the same result); however, in keeping with the notion of PivotTable properties, the `.Caption` property of `PivotItem` returns the name (value) that the user sees. Recall that the `unique_name` key was determined by the `.value` property.

Finally, it might also be appealing to identify the cell in the pivot table that was selected and highlight it accordingly. This can be done by applying a cell style (based on the existing cell styles in Excel). To do this, we require two lines of code: the first resets existing styles, and the second highlights the selected cell.

The complete code snippet looks like the following code:

```
Private Sub Worksheet_SelectionChange(ByVal Target As Range)

On Error GoTo Err

    If Target.Cells.Count = 1 And _
        Target.PivotTable.Name = "sales_by_cat_all" And _
        Target.PivotField = "[Products].[Category Name].[Category
        Name]" Then

        Sheet1.Range("category_sel").Value =
            Target.PivotItem.Value
        Sheet1.ChartObjects("accessory_sales_by_year_chart")
            .Chart.ChartTitle.Text = Target.PivotItem.Caption & "
            Sales by Year"

        Sheet1.Range("D28:D32").Style = "Normal"
        Target.Style = "Accent1"

    End If

    Exit Sub
Err:

End Sub
```

> When we are clearing the existing formatting from the pivot rows, we use a cell reference (`"D28:D32"`) and not a named reference.

Managing the Slicer through VBA

Managing an array of data based on the CUBE FUNCTION formulas is one method of allowing the end user the ability to interact with the data. Another method is the ability to programmatically interact with the Slicer, and then let the Slicer do the work for you (through its pivot connections).

Accessing the Slicer programmatically can also open up a variety of additional development options since you can access a wide range of information about the source of the Slicer (both its data and elements), in addition to specific members that have been explicitly selected (as in the *Working with worksheet events and VBA* recipe). In this recipe we will be using VBA to determine the value (both the unique name and caption) of a Slicer, and using this value in chart captions and pivot table Filters.

Getting ready

This recipe assumes that the prior recipe *Working with worksheet events and VBA* has been completed. What this recipe does is create a monthly trend chart for a selected category against all categories, as shown in the following screenshot:

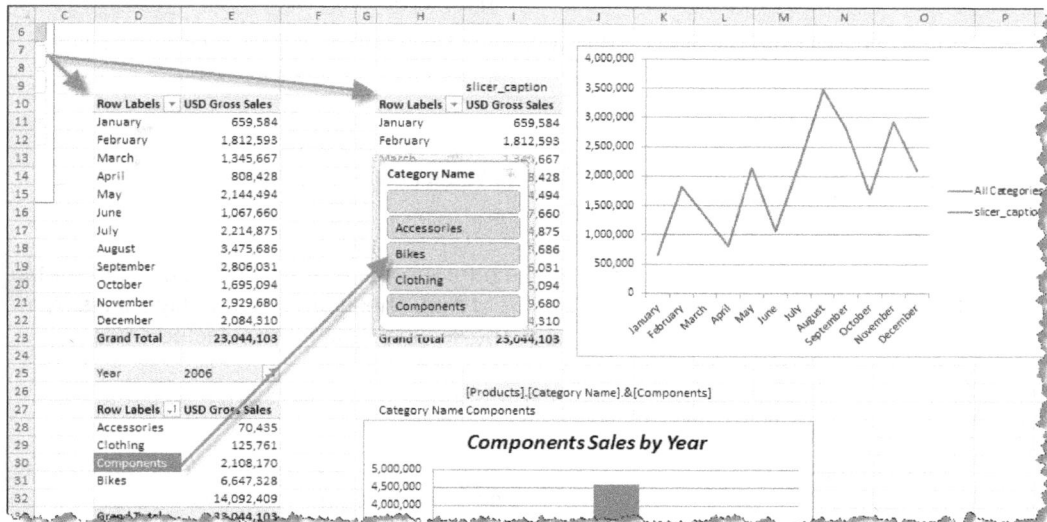

Here, the additional pivot table (for showing the selected category's sales) has a Slicer attached, which is set by the selected cell (of the pivot table `sales_by_cat_all`). The additional line chart is used to compare the monthly sales values of each pivot table. Unlike the previous recipe, we will show all the categories, when the user has not explicitly selected a category within the pivot table.

How to do it...

Start by setting up the worksheet with the required objects.

1. Ensure that the pivot table `sales_by_month_all` (the original monthly pivot table) will show all the items with no data on rows, by checking the **Show items with no data on rows** option from the **Display** tab of the **PivotTables Options**.

2. Copy the pivot table to cell `H10` by highlighting the pivot table, pressing *Ctrl + C*, then selecting cell `H10` and pressing *Ctrl + V*. Rename the pivot table to `sales_by_month_all_sel`.

3. Ensure that the Slicer for the year is attached to both pivot tables. Right-click on the Slicer, select **Pivot Table connections...** and ensure that all pivot tables are connected via the checkbox.

4. Insert a Slicer based on the `Category` field of the `Products` table by clicking on the **Slicer** button from the **Insert** tab.

5. Attach the `Category` Slicer to the pivot table `sales_by_month_all_sel`.

6. Add a cell to record the Slicer value (caption). Create a named range for cell `I9` as `slicer_caption`.

> 💡 It is also a good idea to color the cells, which had user input in a consistent format. In the preceding screenshot they are in off yellow.

7. Insert a line chart using two series as the data ranges. One series has the name `All Categories` and series values from `E11` to `E22`. These are the monthly values from the pivot table `sales_by_month_all`. The second series (the selected category) has a range from `I11` to `I22` (monthly values from the `sales_by_month_all_sel` pivot table). The horizontal (category) axis labels of the series should be set to the month names (of either pivot).

8. Test whether the two lines of the chart change when a new year is selected from the year Slicer, and when a category name is selected from the category name's Slicer. The lines of the chart should move accordingly.

> 💡 Depending on the year and category chosen, the line for the pivot table `sales_by_month_all_sel` may be as close as the horizontal axis, and it may be hard to see any relationship between the two lines. In order to show this relationship clearly, it may help to move the line for the `sales_by_month_all_sel` pivot table, to the chart's secondary axis. Do this by right-clicking on the (chart) line and selecting **Format Data Series...** from the pop-up menu. Then, check the **Secondary Axis** radio button from the **Plot Series On** group, as shown in the following screenshot:

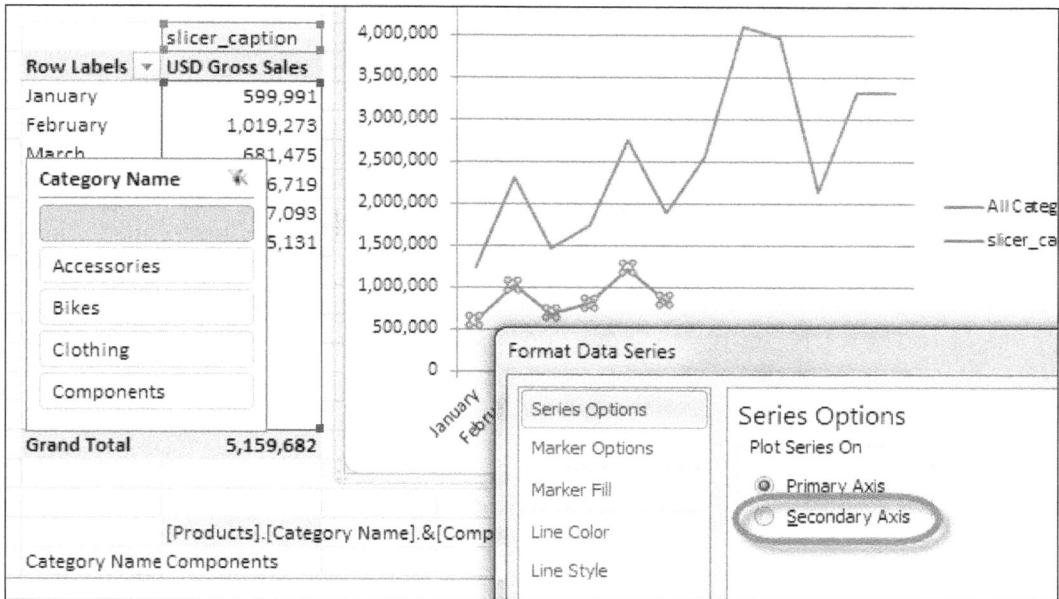

Now let's create a subroutine to set the Slicer for a particular category.

9. Add a new module to our VBA solution. Launch the (VBA) developer window (click on the **Visual Basic** button from the **Developer** tab of the ribbon). Right-click on the project node and navigate to **Insert | Module** from the pop-up window, as shown in the following screenshot:

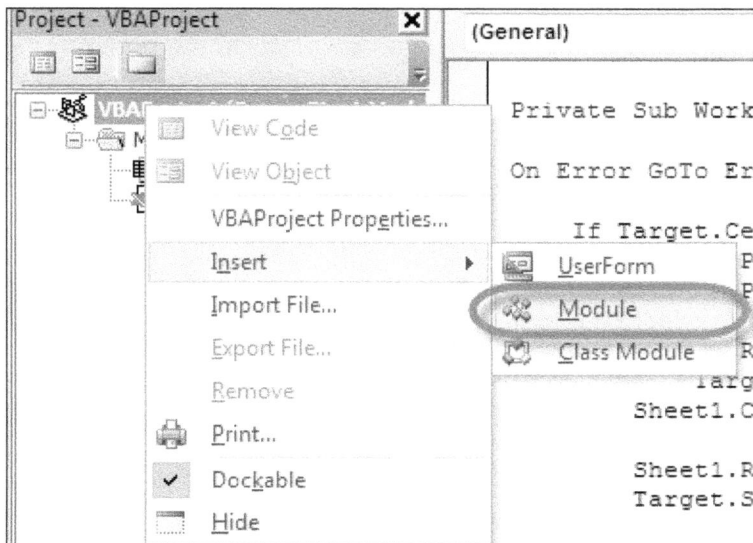

[💡 You can also navigate to **Insert | Module** from the VBA developer's menu.]

10. When the module is added, create a subroutine to set the category name Slicer to the value of the `member_unique_name` key which is passed as an argument to the routine. Add the following subroutine:

```
Public Sub SetSlicer(ByVal SlicerKey As String, _
                    ByVal SlicerName As String)
    Dim sC As SlicerCache
    Set sC = ActiveWorkbook.SlicerCaches
        ("Slicer_Category_Name")

    If SlicerKey <> "" Then
        sC.VisibleSlicerItemsList = SlicerKey
    Else
        sC.ClearManualFilter
    End If

    Sheet1.Range("slicer_caption").Value = SlicerName

End Sub
```

11. Alter the `Worksheet_SelectionChange` event for `Sheet1` to call the new subroutine depending on the cell activities of the user (in `Sheet1`) as follows:

```
Private Sub Worksheet_SelectionChange(ByVal Target As Range)

On Error GoTo Err

    If Target.Cells.Count = 1 And _
        Target.PivotTable.Name = "sales_by_cat_all" And _
        Target.PivotField = "[Products].[Category
        Name].[Category Name]" Then

        Sheet1.Range("category_sel").Value = _
            Target.PivotItem.Value
        Sheet1.ChartObjects
            ("accessory_sales_by_year_chart")
            .Chart.ChartTitle.Text = _
            Target.PivotItem.Caption & " Sales by Year"

        Sheet1.Range("D28:D32").Style = "Normal"
        Target.Style = "Accent1"
```

```
        SetSlicer Target.PivotItem.Value,
            Target.PivotItem.Caption

        Exit Sub

    End If

Err:
SetSlicer "", "All Categories"
End Sub
```

12. Test the new functionality on the worksheet. When any cell within the
    `sales_by_cat_all` pivot table is selected, the Slicer for the category name
    is set, and the chart displays that category (on the secondary axis). If this does
    not occur, the chart shows the trend for `All Categories`.

How it works...

The operation for the worksheet event (`Worksheet_SelectionChange`) was covered in the
Working with worksheet events and VBA recipe. Therefore, it is not necessary to go into any
great depth of how this component works, other than to just say that Excel listens for a change
in the user's cell activity (on `Sheet1`). When the user has selected only one cell within the
desired pivot table range, we can be satisfied that a valid category is selected, and therefore,
we can pass the `category_unique_name` and caption to our Slicer change function. If this
is not the case, we simply remove any Filters that have been set by the Slicer.

The creation of the `SetSlicer` subroutine is also relatively straightforward. Here, we
simply make a reference to the Slicer (through the `SlicerCache` object) and then set its
value (through the `.VisibleSlicerItemsList`). If the user has not selected a single cell
(resulting in the obvious conclusion that no unique category is selected), we simply remove
any filter that is on the Slicer and define the name as `All Categories`.

There are some advantages in creating a public subroutine as we have done in this recipe.
The routine can be called from anywhere in the workbook and will allow code reuse within
the workbook. This technique might have also been applied in the prior recipe *Working with
worksheet events and VBA*.

The routine refers to the Slicer by its name. This can be determined from the worksheet by selecting the **Slicer Settings...** options from the pop-up menu when the Slicer is right-clicked. We can also use this to control how the Slicer appears (for example, whether it has a name or not and what that name is), as shown in the following screenshot:

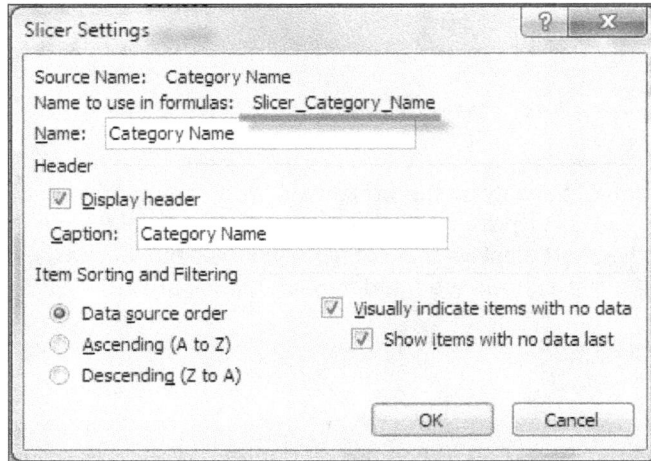

There's more...

In setting the Slicer value we assume a one-way flow of information, that is, that the Slicer will be manipulated (by a known value). However, we may want to obtain data from the Slicer and allow it to be used as any other data range—for example, in a drop-down box. In order to do this, we must read the data from the Slicer. For this intention, we need to be interested only in the following three values:

▶ The number of elements in the Slicer

▶ The caption shown at an **Index Position** *n* of the Slicer

▶ The member_unique_name shown at an **Index Position** *n* of the Slicer

Consider the desired output as shown in the following screenshot:

	A	B	C	D	E	F	G	H	I	J
1										
2	Years Count	6			=SlicerItemCount("Slicer_Year")					
3										
4	**Index Position**	**Index Caption**	**Index Unique Name**							
5	1	2005	[Dates].[Year].&[2005]							
6	2	2006	[Dates].[Year].&[2006]		B Column Forumla					
7	3	2007	[Dates].[Year].&[2007]		=SlicerIndex("Slicer_Year", A5)					
8	4	2008	[Dates].[Year].&[2008]							
9	5	2009	[Dates].[Year].&[2009]		C Column Formula					
10	6	2010	[Dates].[Year].&[2010]		=SlicerIndex("Slicer_Year",A7,"member_unique_name")					
11	7	#REF!	#REF!							

There are only two formulas in this worksheet. The first (`SlicerItemCount`) takes the Slicer name as an argument and returns the number of data members in the Slicer. The second (`SlicerIndex`) takes arguments for the Slicer name, an index position, and (an optional) return type (note that the default return type is the data member caption).

Open the VBA editor and double-click on `Module1` to open it. Then, add the following formulas (lines of code) to the existing subroutine:

```
Public Function SlicerItemCount(ByVal SlicerName As String) As
    Integer

On Error GoTo err_handler

    SlicerItemCount = _
        ActiveWorkbook.SlicerCaches(SlicerName)
        .SlicerCacheLevels(1).SlicerItems.Count

Exit Function

err_handler:
    SlicerItemCount = -1
End Function

Public Function SlicerIndex(ByVal SlicerName As String _
    , ByVal IndexPostition As Integer _
    , Optional ReturnType As String) As Variant

On Error GoTo err_handler

    Dim sl As SlicerCacheLevel
    Set sl =
        ActiveWorkbook.SlicerCaches(SlicerName)
        .SlicerCacheLevels(1)

    If UCase(ReturnType) = "MEMBER_UNIQUE_NAME" Then
        SlicerIndex = sl.SlicerItems(IndexPostition).name
    Else
        SlicerIndex = sl.SlicerItems(IndexPostition).Caption
    End If
    Exit Function

err_handler:
    SlicerIndex = CVErr(2023)

End Function
```

Add a new sheet to the workbook. Cell `B2` (the number of elements in the Slicer) has the formula `=SlicerItemCount("Slicer_Year")`. The formula for the index's caption is given by `=SlicerIndex("Slicer_Year", A5)`, and the formula for the `member_unique_name` is given by the formula `=SlicerIndex("Slicer_Year",A5,"member_unique_name")`.

In both these formulas, **A5** refers to the index position for the data member that we are looking for in the Slicer. Furthermore, the formula will display as functions in Excel's formula bar.

Both formulas work by making reference to the Slicer's `SlicerCacheLevel`. This is actually the hierarchy displayed within the Slicer. Note that both the formulas refer to the `SlicerCache` (the Slicer by name) and then specify `SlicerCacheLevel(1)` in order to reference the actual level of the hierarchy (or perhaps from our point of view, the members within that level).

The Slicers that we have created so far have all been single-level hierarchies (these were commonly referred to as attribute hierarchies in traditional OLAP). However, when a Slicer is created on a drillable hierarchy (or user hierarchy—a hierarchy with multiple levels), a **Slicer Control** is created for each level (within the hierarchy). We can demonstrate this by adding a Slicer for the date-by-year hierarchy (in the `Dates` table). When this is added, three Slicer boxes are created as shown in the following screenshot:

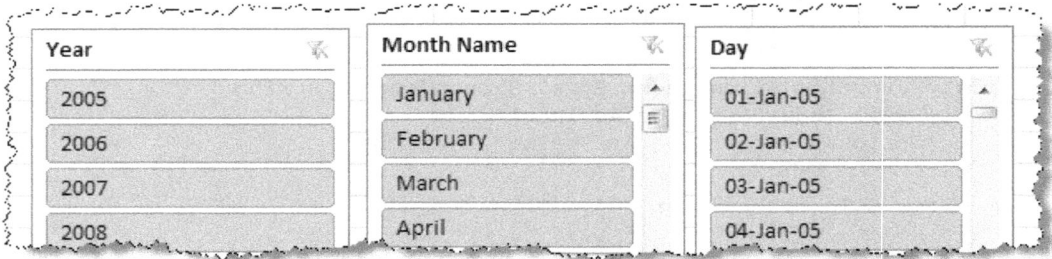

In this situation, the property `SlicerCacheLevel` can be used to identify the data members restricted by each level. That is, the **Year** level is 1, the **Month Name** is 2, and the **Day** is level 3.

7
Enterprise Design and Features

In this chapter, we will cover:

- ▶ Restoring a workbook to Analysis Services
- ▶ Importing models into SQL Server Data Tools
- ▶ Developing models in SQL Server Data Tools
- ▶ Securing data with roles
- ▶ Implementing dynamic security
- ▶ Creating perspectives

Introduction

Creating a tabular model in Excel is a great way of allowing a user to combine a large amount of data, business logic (through calculations and relationships), and semantic information (column names, hierarchies, and tables) into a single, succinct model. This is beneficial to a single user. However, hosting this model in Excel limits the audience that can use the model for analysis (or the output of the model in the case of reports, charts, Pivots, and the like). True, the workbook can be shared among users (say for example, a file share); however, the workbook can only be used by one person at a time and there exists an inherent risk of workbook duplication and the associated risk of workbook proliferation, that is, Excel Hell and multiple versions of the same book with different data.

There are two methods of promoting the Excel tabular model within the organization. Firstly, publishing the workbook to the SharePoint site (commonly referred to as Team BI) or secondly, promoting the model to **SQL Server Analysis Services** (**SSAS**) with its storage in tabular mode. Promoting the tabular model to an Analysis Services database may be considered as the final step in the development cycle of a tabular model. It allows the modeler to include enterprise features in the model (such as perspectives, security, and partitions) and allows a multitude of client tools to query the Model.

Of course, it may not be necessary to promote the model in all situations. However, the designer should always consider the possibility of the current piece of work becoming an enterprise model.

This chapter focuses on moving an Excel model into the SSAS environment and the additional features in design and security that it offers.

> It is not necessary to create a model in Excel and then promote it to an SSAS instance. The model can be completely designed in **SQL Server Data Tools** (**SSDT**). The principles for design in SSDT are exactly the same as in Excel, albeit with a slightly different user interface.

Restoring a workbook to Analysis Services

Once the tabular model has been created in Excel, it can be immediately imported to a SSAS server, thus allowing multiple people to query it and additional (XMLA/MDX) client tools to access it. This recipe shows how to import an existing Excel model to the SSAS (tabular) server.

Getting ready

The workbook used in this recipe is the same as the workbook developed in the *Allocating data at different levels* recipe in *Chapter 5, Applied Modeling*. This is also the same workbook that was used in *Chapter 6, Programmatic Access via Excel*.

In order to import the workbook directly into SSAS, it must be saved with a `.xlsx` (nonmacro) extension.

How to do it...

Let's start and connect to an SSAS server (with the storage in tabular mode).

1. Open SQL Server Management Studio and connect to the Analysis Services (tabular instance).

2. Right-click on the database node and select **Restore from PowerPivot**. This is shown in the following screenshot:

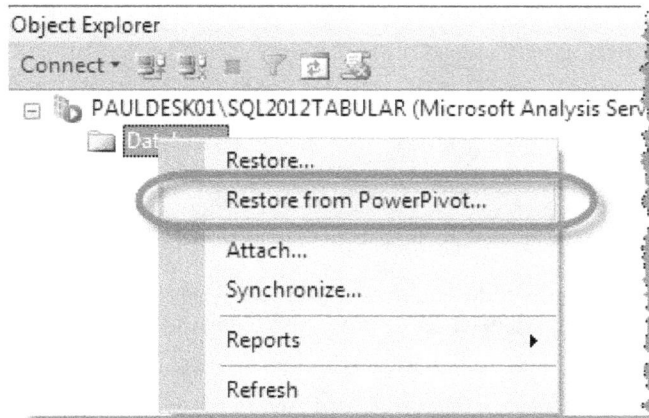

3. Navigate to the file using the **Browse...** button from the **Backup file:** location as shown in the following screenshot. Then select **OK**.

> The directories that can be browsed are a property of the SSAS server. In order to change these, right-click on the server node in **SQL Server Management Studio** (**SSMS**) and select **Properties**. Then, change the value **AllowedBrowsingFolders** to include any needed folders. This is an advanced option and is found under the **General** tab.

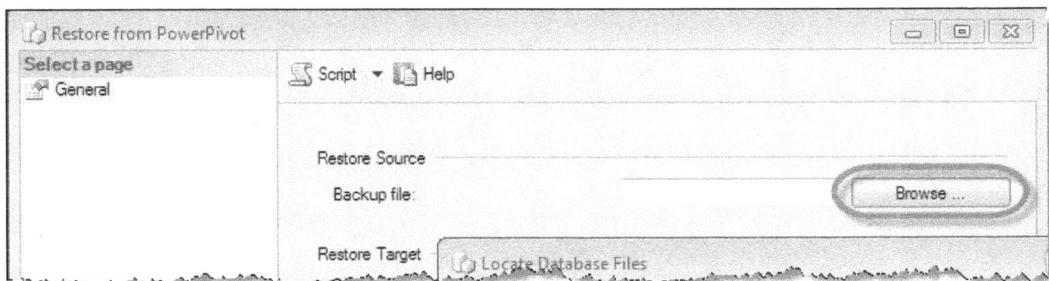

4. Name the database `Import Example`, as shown in the following screenshot, and then click on **OK**:

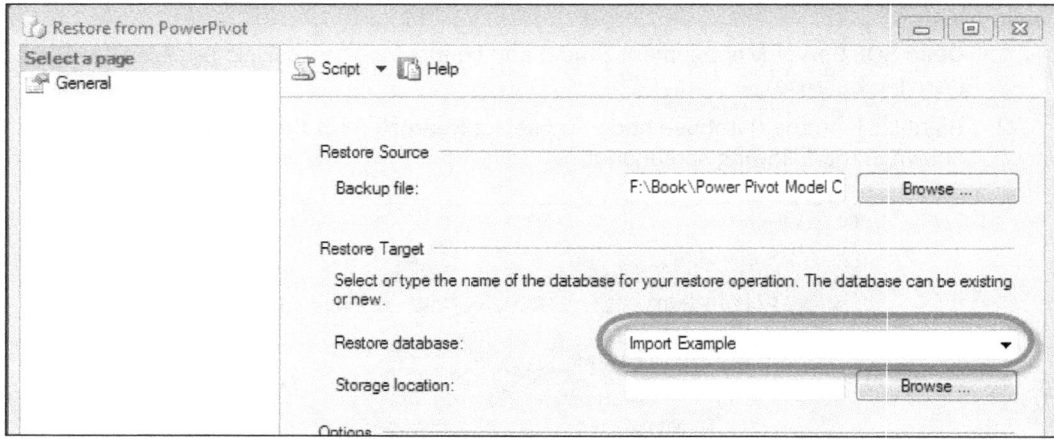

5. Refresh the database node and ensure that the model has been imported. A new database should exist as shown in the following screenshot:

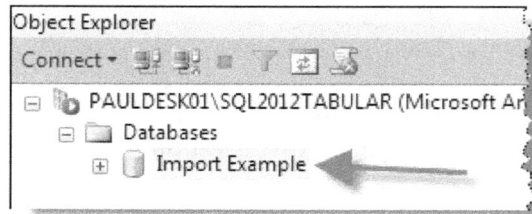

How it works...

Despite the implication that restoring an Excel tabular model is a restore operation (from Analysis Services point of view), it is in fact the execution of an `ImageLoad` (XMLA) command. The standard XMLA to restore a database from a backup is given in the following snippet:

```
<Restore xmlns="...">
  <File>Backup File Name.abf</File>
  <DatabaseName>Target Database</DatabaseName>
  <AllowOverwrite>true</AllowOverwrite>
</Restore>
```

However, the command to import the workbook is shown in the following snippet. In both cases, the namespace declarations are removed for brevity (the full snippets are available from the chapter's resource file XMLA to Import and Restore.XMLA):

```
<ImageLoad xmlns="…"
xmlns:ddl100= "…"
xmlns:ddl200_200="…"
xmlns:ddl100_100="…">
<ddl200_200:ImagePath>Import File Name.xlsx</ddl200_200:ImagePath>
<ddl100:ReadWriteMode>ReadWrite</ddl100:ReadWriteMode>
<DatabaseName>Target Database</DatabaseName>
<DatabaseID>Target Database</DatabaseID>
</ImageLoad>
```

The ImageLoad command loads the Excel tabular database (or model) to a tabular SSAS server. While this is a convenient and quick solution for making a model available to a wider audience, it may have some undesired implications. This includes a general lack of ability to alter the model's semantic design and the creation of default values; for example, a single cube is created with the name Model (right-click on the database **Import Example** and see that only one cube exists with the name Model).

If you are happy to live with these limitations there is no reason why a PowerPivot workbook cannot be imported to the server. However, if you wish to make the model truly enterprise-ready, you may first need to import the model into SQL Server Data Tools (SSDT) and edit the model from there.

There's more...

It is possible to alter the Server Model through XMLA (although not that practical in reality). In order to change the name of the cube, we could script the database out as alter syntax and then change the `<Name>` element in the `<Cube>` path. The command can then be executed and the name of the cube will change. The location of the Name tag can be seen in the following screenshot:

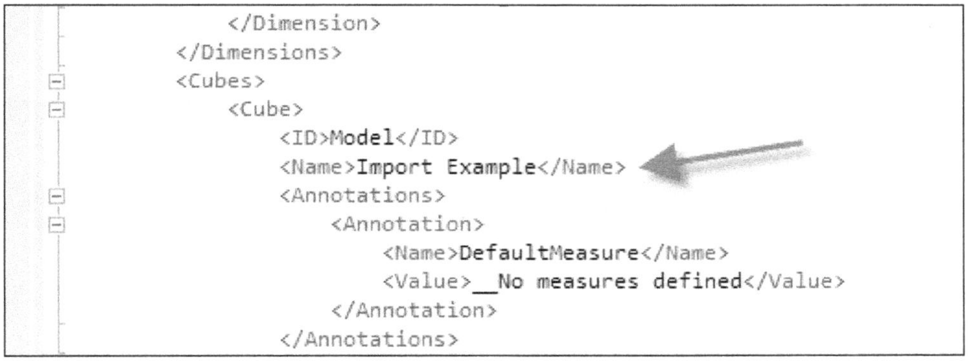

```
            </Dimension>
        </Dimensions>
        <Cubes>
            <Cube>
                <ID>Model</ID>
                <Name>Import Example</Name>    <——
                <Annotations>
                    <Annotation>
                        <Name>DefaultMeasure</Name>
                        <Value>__No measures defined</Value>
                    </Annotation>
                </Annotations>
```

Importing models into SQL Server Data Tools

Importing tabular models hosted in Excel to an SSAS tabular server may be an intermediate step in creating an enterprise-ready tabular database. If an Excel model is to be used as a prototyping mechanism it will more than likely have to be imported with SQL Server Data Tools (SSDT), so that the model can be saved, managed, and verified in a more robust manner. The tabular model can also be built from scratch using SSDT should a more traditional development environment be required, that is one where Excel is not used.

> For the purposes of the tabular model (in as much as the model revolves around table relationships in calculations), there is no difference between developing in Excel through PowerPivot or SSDT. Indeed, on proof of concept and prototyping situations it is often a good idea to sit with the user, using the same tools as they use and build a model with them!

Getting ready

This recipe examines how to import an existing PowerPivot model into SSDT. The workbook is the same as the one used in the *Restoring a workbook to Analysis Services* recipe and is present in the code bundle available at http://www.packtpub.com. Let's start with SSDT.

How to do it...

1. **Open** SQL Server Data Tools from the Microsoft SQL Server 2012 program group.

2. Create a new Project using the menu path **File | New | Project**. Then, select the **Import from PowerPivot** template by navigating to **Business Intelligence | Analysis Services** as shown in the following screenshot:

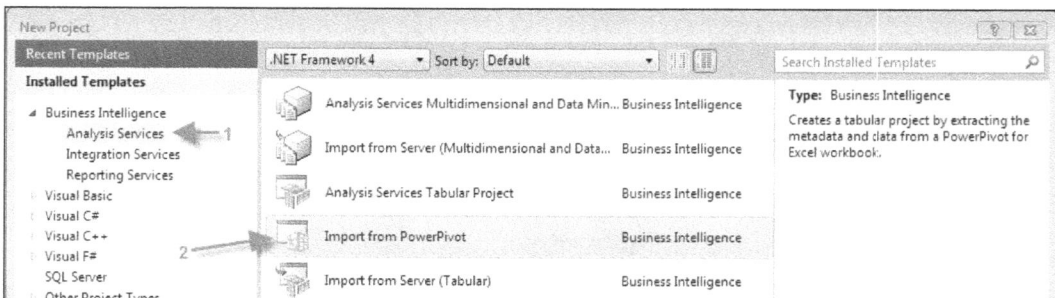

3. You may also want to specify a suitable name for the project; let's call this `Import Example SSDT`, and a different file location to store the project.

4. An open dialogue will display where you can navigate to the Excel workbook, in order to select the appropriate file. Navigate to the directory storing the file `Power Pivot Model Complete.xlsm` (you will have to change the file filter) and click on **Open** once you have selected the file.

> In order to use the SSDT project, we will require a link to a workspace database. This is really a connection to an SSAS server and is discussed in the *How it works...* section of this recipe.

5. SSDT will spend a few moments importing the model (note that the status bar will move from time to time while objects are being imported).

6. When the operation is finished, the project will open in SSDT showing a table view of the model.

How it works...

There is nothing complex associated with the import of the workbook to SSDT. However, the reader should be aware that SSDT requires a connection to a tabular server in order to display the model to the user and to be able to work on that model in SSDT. This is referred to as a workspace database.

If there is no connection available, the import will not complete and no development can occur. The presence of the model in the workspace database can be confirmed by refreshing the model and expanding the **Databases** node in SSMS. Note the GUID appended to the name of the solution in the **Object Explorer** dialog of SSMS, as shown in the following screenshot:

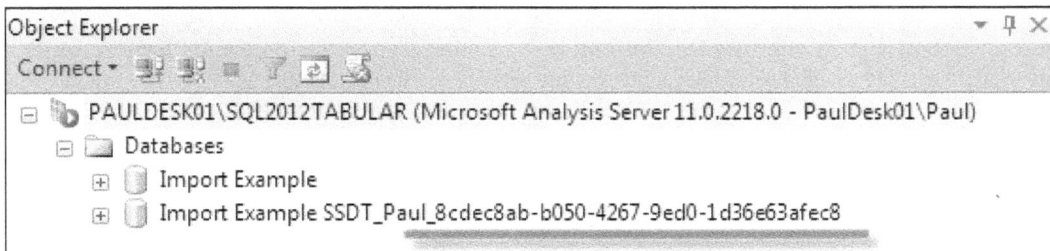

The name of the workspace database (as a read-only property) that is used by the model can be seen from the **Solution Explorer** pane (within SSDT). Right-click on the **Model.bim** file within the **Solution Explorer** pane and select **Properties**. A screenshot of the window that opens up is shown as follows:

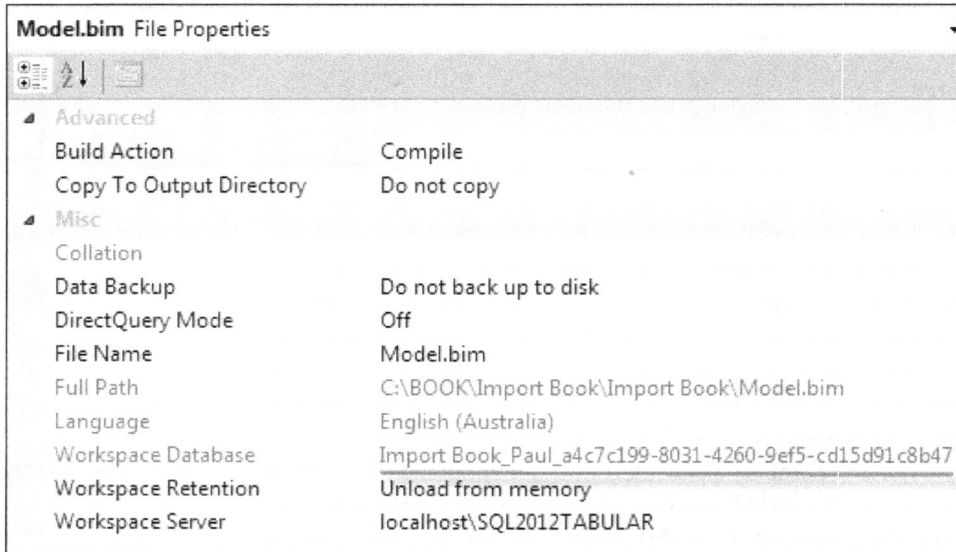

Model.bim File Properties	
▲ Advanced	
Build Action	Compile
Copy To Output Directory	Do not copy
▲ Misc	
Collation	
Data Backup	Do not back up to disk
DirectQuery Mode	Off
File Name	Model.bim
Full Path	C:\BOOK\Import Book\Import Book\Model.bim
Language	English (Australia)
Workspace Database	Import Book_Paul_a4c7c199-8031-4260-9ef5-cd15d91c8b47
Workspace Retention	Unload from memory
Workspace Server	localhost\SQL2012TABULAR

There's more...

The server that is to be used as the workspace database cannot be set when the import occurs. Further, if a tabular server is not available, an import (conversion) will not succeed.

Therefore, the developer should ensure that the server used to store the workspace database was previously connected to SSDT. This can be as simple as creating a new Analysis Services tabular project and setting the Deployment server to the tabular SSAS server. Note that, by default, `localhost` is used as the server and this may not be the case when named instances are used (as is the case).

The server can be set by right-clicking on the properties node (in the **Solution Explorer** pane of SSDT) of the Project and selecting **properties**. The server name can then be set, as in the following screenshot (a workspace database will be created on a local instance called **SQL2012TABULAR**):

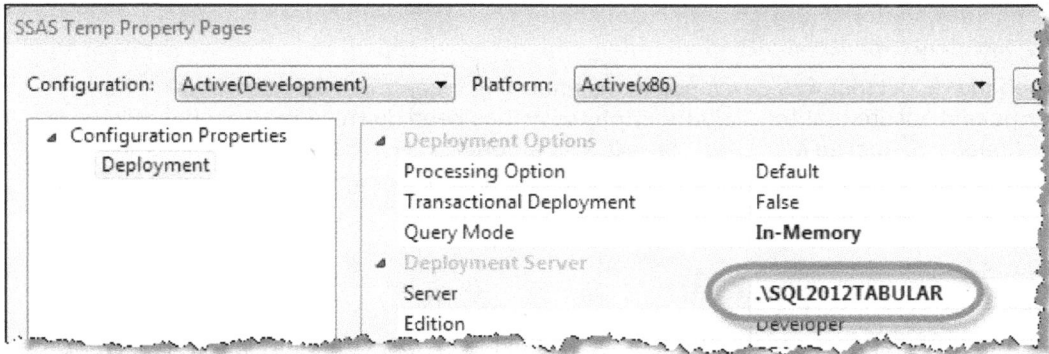

The properties also allow us to specify the **Cube Name** property, so that the default name of model is not shown. This can be set by overwriting the **Cube Name** property as shown in the following screenshot:

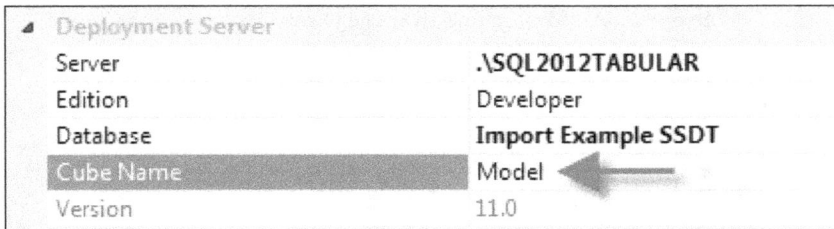

Finally, this technique can be used to import a model that is located on a tabular server. Simply choose the **Import from Tabular Server** template project.

Developing models in SQL Server Data Tools

The modeling environment in SQL Server Data Tools (SSDT) is almost identical to that of PowerPivot. There is more functionality available; for example, the ability to create partitions and apply security to the model. However, the general approach to modeling in SSDT is identical to PowerPivot. That is, the import of data, its definition (tables and columns), and the creation of relationships and measures are the same.

This recipe demonstrates how models can be developed in SSDT by extending the model imported in the *Importing models into SQL Server Data Tools* recipe. Here, we add a Geography table to the model to show the sales region that the purchase occurred in. Later on (see the *Securing data with roles* recipe) this table will be used to secure the model by allowing specific users access to privileged regions.

Getting ready

Open the model that was developed in the *Importing models into SQL Server Data Tools* recipe and ensure that the file `Geography.txt` has been downloaded from the resources for *Chapter 5, Applied Modeling*. There is also a `schema.ini` file, which accompanies this file and overwrites the default import settings. The file `Geography.txt` and `schema.ini` should be located in the same directory.

How to do it...

Start with the SSDT project that was developed in the *Importing models into SQL Server Data Tools* recipe.

1. Click on the **Import From Data Source** button from the toolbar. This is shown in the following screenshot:

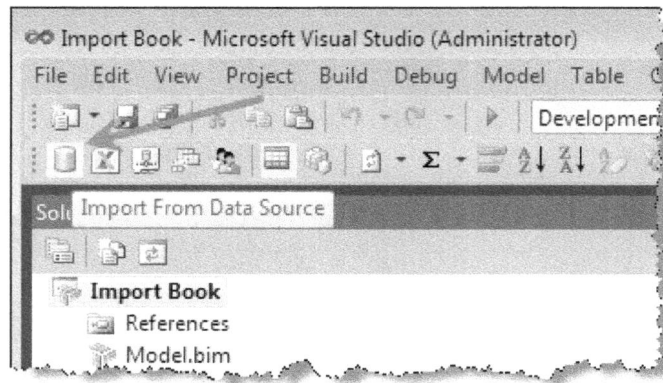

> Alternatively, you can select **Import From Data Source...** from the model's menu group. This action is very similar to the **From Other Sources** button in PowerPivot and displays a variety of data sources that can be imported.

2. Select **Text File** as the **Data Source** and click on **Next**.
3. Navigate to the `Geography.txt` file and select **Open**. A **Table Import Wizard** will open allowing the connection name to be specified (in keeping with the model's standard, the connection should be labeled `txt_geography`). Note also, that the `schema.ini` file has been recognized and the settings in this file will be used instead of the default settings. This is shown in the following screenshot. Click on **Next**.

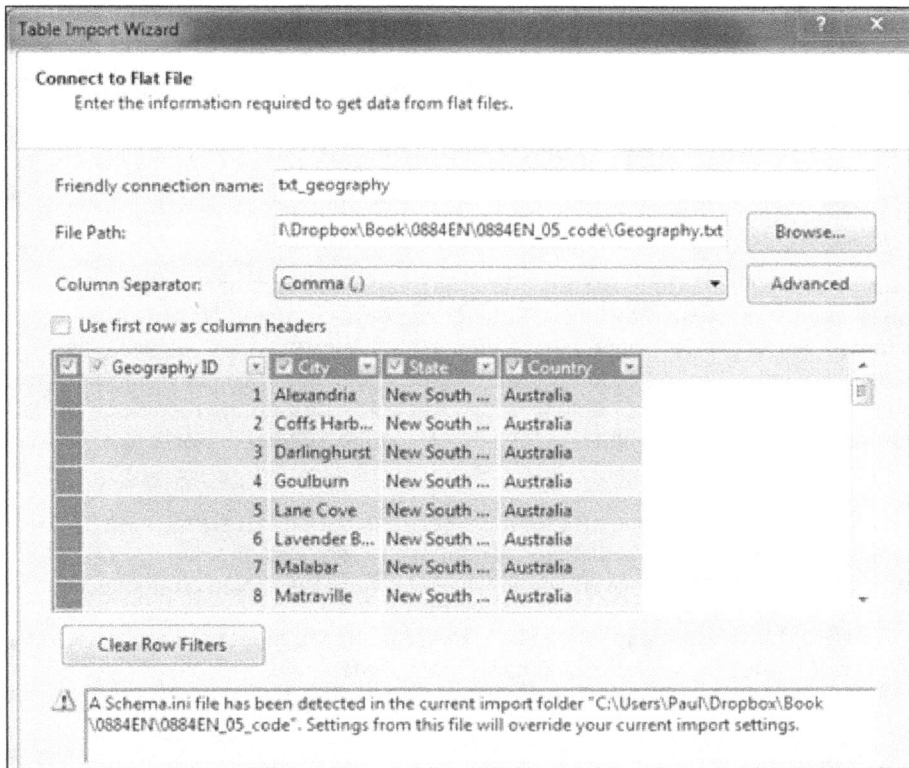

4. A new window will open that specifies the account that will be used to connect to the data source by Analysis Services when the data is processed. Although not recommended (in a production environment), let us assume that the SSAS service account can access the file and use this account for convenience. Select the **Service Account** and click on the **Finish** button. Once the data has been imported, click on the **Close** button. The new table is added to the model.

5. Right-click on the `Geography ID` column heading (in the `Geography` table) and select **Create Relationship** from the pop-up window. When the **Create Relationship** dialog opens, select **Reseller Sales** under **Related Lookup Table** and **Geo ID** under **Related Lookup Column**. Note that an information button appears as shown in the following screenshot. When you hover over the icon, a warning message indicates an incorrect direction for the relationship. Click on **Create** to create the relationship.

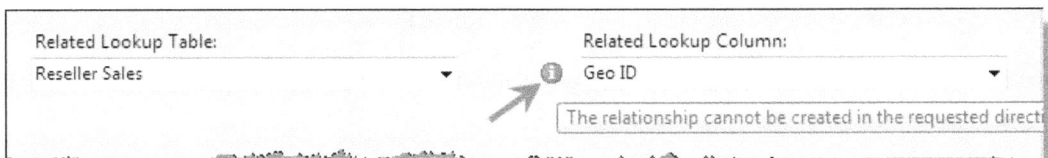

6. Hide the `Geography ID` field in the `Geography` table by right-clicking on the field and selecting **Hide from Client Tools** from the pop-up menu.

7. Switch to the diagram view and locate the `Geography` table. Create a hierarchy by selecting the `City`, `State`, and `Country` attributes from the table, right-clicking and selecting **Create Hierarchy** from the pop-up menu.

How it works...

This process is quite similar to importing a text file into PowerPivot. In fact, the only noticeable exception is that when developing in SSDT, the designer is prompted for an authentication account to connect to the data source (remember that importing a text file will create a new data source). It is important to remember that the design experience is actually managed by a tabular server and SSDT connects to this in displaying data to the modeler. That is, SSDT creates a workspace database on the server and the server connects to a data source through its impersonation settings.

The creation of this relationship is also intuitive because the design surface (SSDT) identifies the cardinality between the two tables and identifies the required direction of the relationship between the two tables. The information message shown in the recipe demonstrates this.

In order to detect this relationship, one side of the relationship must hold only unique values in the column. If it doesn't, a relationship cannot be created.

There's more...

The account used to authenticate to a data source can be changed once the connection has been created. This account is the impersonation setting for the connection and can be managed through the **Existing Connections** dialog. To change the account in an existing connection, click on the **Existing Connections** button from the toolbar. Alternatively, this functionality also exists in the **Model** menu button, as shown in the following screenshot:

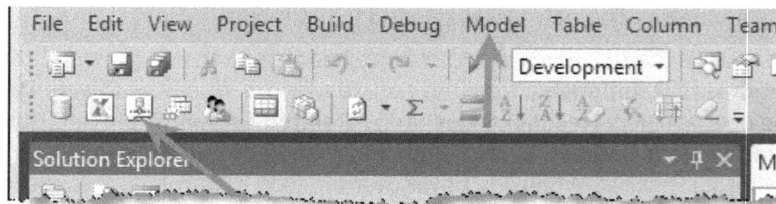

When the **Existing Connections** dialog opens, select the connection (in our case, it is the `txt_geography` connection) and click on the **Edit** button. Then, click on the **Impersonation...** button to select the method and account for impersonation, as shown in the following screenshot:

Edit Connection

Connect to Flat File
Enter the information required to get data from flat files.

Friendly connection name: txt_geography

File Path: C:\Users\Paul\Dropbox\Book\0884EN\0884EN_05_code'   Browse...

Column Separator: Comma (,) ▼   Advanced

☐ Use first row as column headers   Impersonation...

| Geography ID | City | State | Countr: |

Impersonation Information

Specify the credentials used by the Analysis Services server to connect to the data source. These credentials are used by the server when importing and refreshing data.

◉ Specific Windows user name and password
Connects to the data source using the credentials of the user named below.

User Name: Paul

Password:

○ Service Account
Connects to the data source using the credentials of the user running the Analysis Service server.

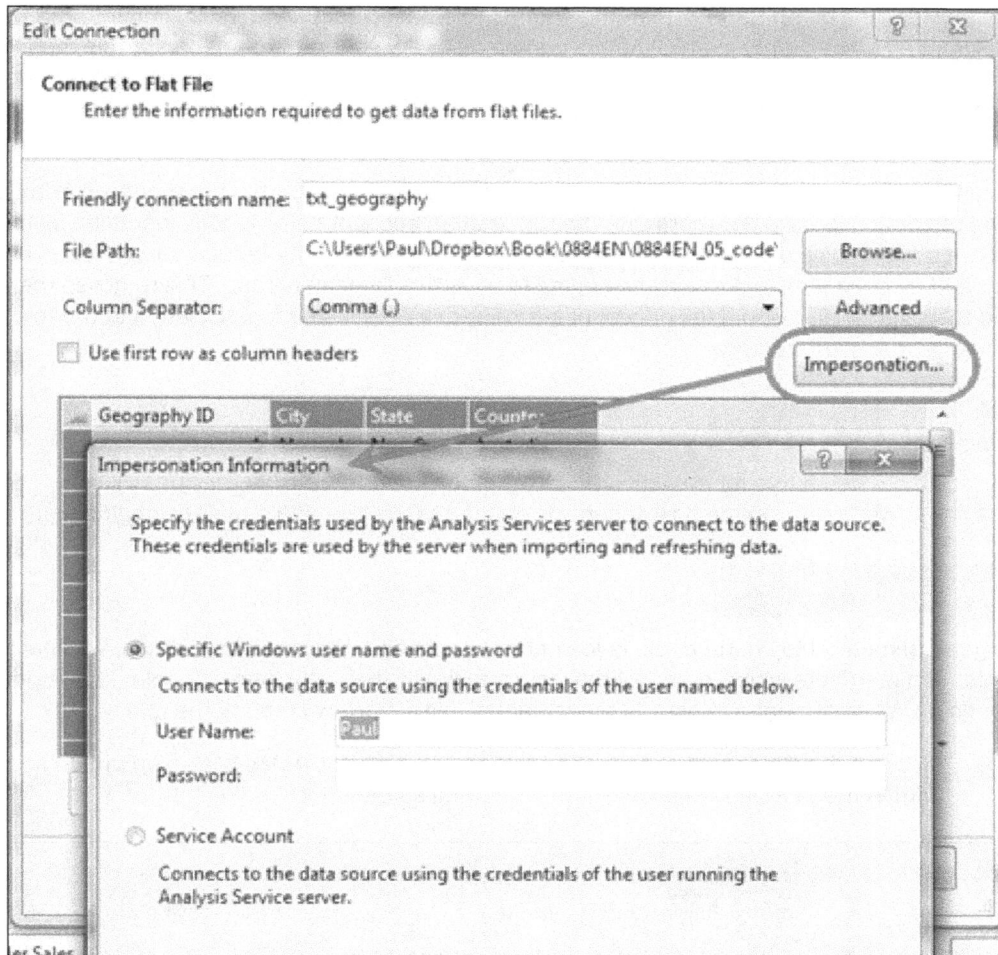

Securing data with roles

Often, there is a desire to restrict the amount of data that a user can see. This can take two forms. Firstly, there may be a need to restrict data because of a security concern, that is, the user should only be able to read information from the model that relates to their area of operating concern. Typical examples of this type of security restrictions are based on geographical areas, reporting, or departmental lines. Restricting data through security is examined in this recipe and the *Implementing dynamic security* recipe in this chapter. Secondly, we may wish to restrict the objects that a user can see when they connect to the server. This is not the application of a security feature, but simply the creation of specific view(s) for the user. This is achieved through the use of perspectives (which is examined in the *Creating perspectives* recipe in this chapter).

Tabular modeling on an SSAS server implements role-based security. This is similar to the way SSAS implements security in an OLAP environment. A very general explanation of this model is that, when the user (or account) connects to the model, they are identified as belonging to one or more roles and the implementation of their security profile is the amalgamation of all roles they belong to.

This allows roles to be defined for different processing operations within the model, in addition to the restriction of data. Furthermore, the role that an account belongs to is identified by that account's Active Directory profile. When the account connects to the tabular server, it can be identified as belonging to a role by belonging to an Active Directory group. This removes the need to assign an individual user account's access to a role; instead, association to the role is managed by Active Directory.

Getting ready

This recipe creates a role for an Active Directory group called TABULAR_SECURITY_AMERICAS. We then examine how security is applied to the role and a user belonging to it.

How to do it...

The general method to create a role is to define the role and its access layer. Then, we specify the domain members who are part of that role and finally the security for the role. This is done through a DAX statement against the model tables. Let's start by creating the role.

1. Click on the **Roles** button from the toolbar. Alternatively, **Roles** is also an option in the **Model** menu group, as shown in the following screenshot:

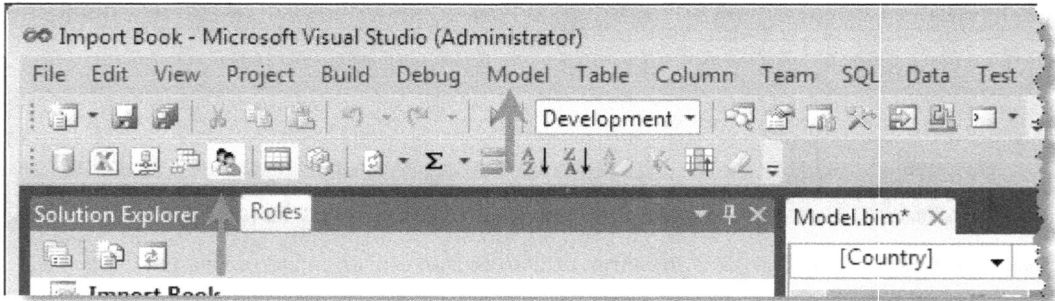

2. The **Role Manager** dialog will open. Create a new role by clicking on the **New** button and name the role AMERICAS. Specify the permissions for the role as **Read** (select **Read** as the permission from the **Permissions** drop-down menu). Although not mandatory, we can also give a description of the role.

3. Assign members (domain users, groups, and principals) to the role by selecting the **Add...** button from the **Members** tab. If the name of the domain member is known, it can be typed directly into the dialog and confirmed with the **Check Names** button. The role should look like the following screenshot:

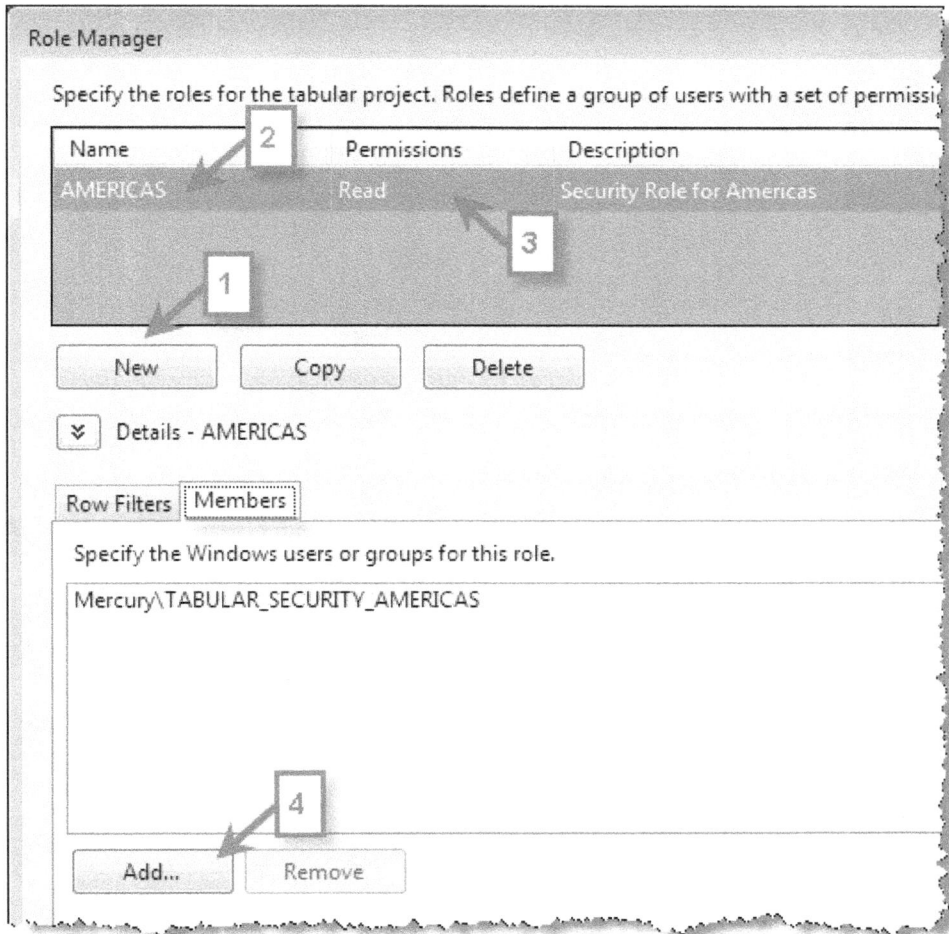

Active Directory groups are not searched by default and the name may not be validated. If this is the case, Domain Groups can be added to the selection criteria by clicking on the **Object Types...** button and checking the **Groups** option. Additionally, a detailed search can be carried out by clicking on the **Advanced** button.

4. Change to the **Row Filters** tab and find the Geography table. Add the following code in the **DAX Filter** column:

```
=[Country] = "United States" || [Country] ="Canada"
```

The **Row Filters** tab should look like the following screenshot:

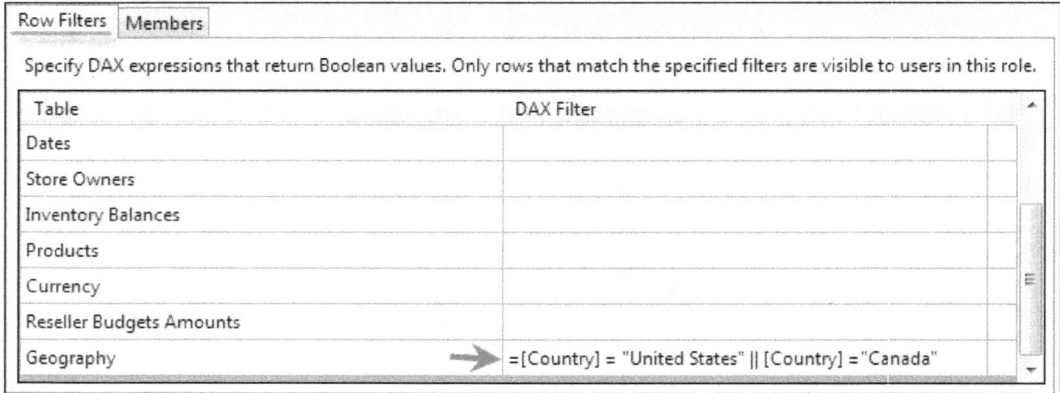

Row Filters	Members

Specify DAX expressions that return Boolean values. Only rows that match the specified filters are visible to users in this role.

Table	DAX Filter
Dates	
Store Owners	
Inventory Balances	
Products	
Currency	
Reseller Budgets Amounts	
Geography	=[Country] = "United States" || [Country] ="Canada"

5. Click on **OK** to create the role.

6. Now that the role has been created we can test it through SSDT. Click on the **Analyze in Excel** button (which is also an option in the **Model** menu group). After this, a dialogue will open allowing you to specify the connecting user. Select **Role** as the method and **AMERICAS** from the drop-down menu. Then click on **OK** to open Excel. This is shown in the following screenshot (note that you need to be an Administrator on the SSAS server to do this):

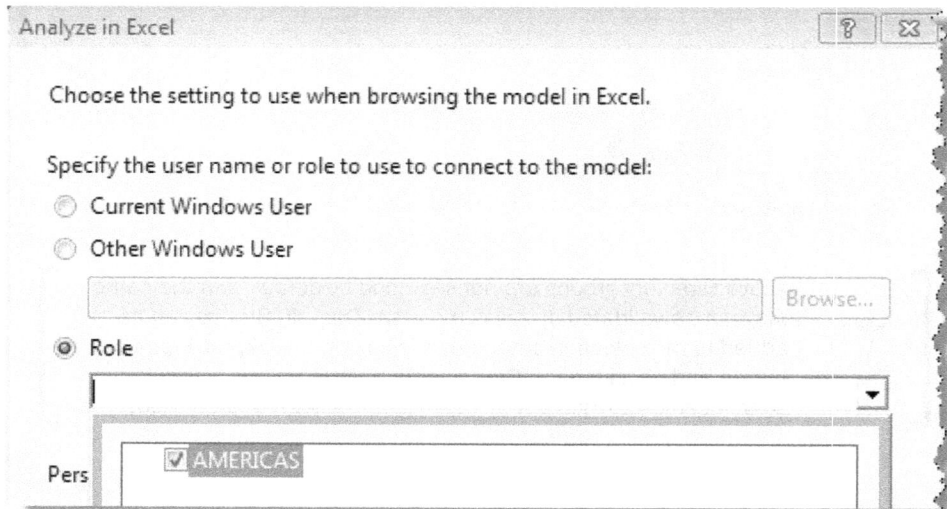

Analyze in Excel

Choose the setting to use when browsing the model in Excel.

Specify the user name or role to use to connect to the model:

○ Current Windows User

○ Other Windows User

[   ] Browse...

◉ Role

[▼]

Pers   ☑ AMERICAS

7. Excel will open with a Pivot Table connected to the tabular model. Drag the
   Geography by City hierarchy of the `Geography` table on to the Pivot's rows to confirm
   that only the countries **Canada** and **United States** are shown. The **Rows** column
   will look like the. following screenshot. Note that any attribute displayed on rows
   (for example, `City`) will also restrict to attributes relating to these countries.

	A
1	**Row Labels** ▾
2	⊞ Canada
3	⊞ United States
4	**Grand Total**

How it works...

We have discussed the general concept using which security is applied. That is, when the user
(domain member) connects to the model, they are allocated to whatever role(s) their domain
credentials specify. Their access permissions are then defined by the addition of all security
permissions and row filters that are defined by those role(s). The row filters simply evaluate
data according to the predicate of the DAX filter statement.

The addition of security roles should not be taken lightly because there is no way to explicitly
deny permissions to data. This means that a role can never specify a denied permission that
will take precedence over an allowed permission.

Consider the situation where we create a new role ALL_NOT_UNITED_STATES (for all
countries other than the United States). This may have a DAX filter as follows:

    [Country]<>"United States"

When an account is a member of this and the AMERICAS role, they will see United States in
their data. Perhaps it is easier to consider the not equals expression (<>) as meaning everything
other than what has been listed and not as a denied permission against United States.

The other permissions for the model (None, Read and Process, Process, and Administrator)
should be self-explanatory. However, they are included here for completeness.

Permissions	Description
None	Members cannot make any modifications to the model schema and cannot query data. This permission should be used to exclude users from the model.
Read	Members are only allowed to query and not change the model schema. The users with this permission cannot process the model.
Read and Process	Members are allowed to query data and process the model. No changes can be made to the model schema

Permissions	Description
Process	Members can process the model but cannot query data. The permission cannot alter the model schema.
Administrator	The user with this permission has (essentially) full control over the model.

There's more...

It is expected that roles should be added to the model in the development environment. However, once the model is in production, roles can be added and edited directly to the SSAS server using SQL Server Management Studio (SSMS). To do this, simply expand the Database's node to expose the roles, right-click on the node and select **New Role...** from the pop-up window. Alternatively, an existing role can be edited by double-clicking on its name.

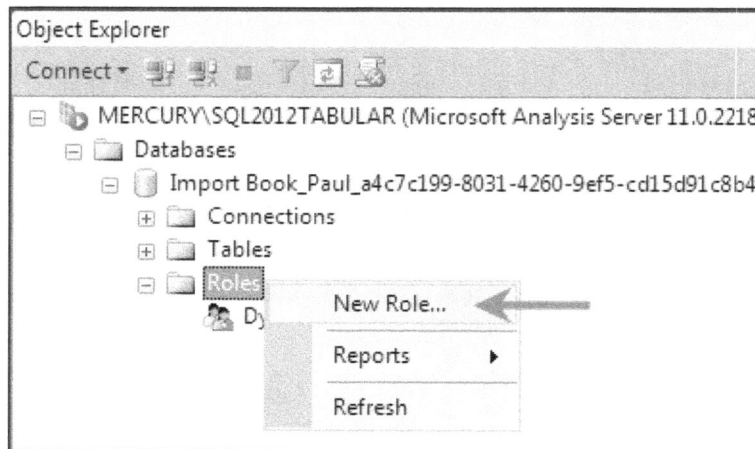

Changes made to the workspace database will not be reflected in the SSDT project.

Implementing dynamic security

Implementing security through roles that contain hardcoded row filters is a very convenient way to manage data access to the model. It's also relatively easy to understand.

However, some downsides of that method are that the roles require creation and maintenance. Imagine a situation where hundreds or thousands of detailed roles have to be created; this would require a lot of work! Further, while the use of Active Directory groups is convenient from a model's administration perspective, it removes a large amount of control from the BI environment (and the BI department). Often, this is not desirable (especially in smaller departments and agile environments) as the BI team is solely responsible for administering security.

One way of allowing the BI team to administer security is to create the security model as an artifact of the model and have security applied by reference to that artifact. This is commonly referred to as dynamic security because the model implements security by reference to its own data (and structure). Any changes to the (security) data are automatically applied in the model when the data is processed (refreshed).

This recipe implements dynamic security.

Getting ready

This recipe builds from the solution that was developed in the *Developing models in SQL Server Data Tools* recipe. Users and countries that each user can view are shown in a file, which is present in the code bundle of this book available at http://www.packtpub.com. The file is titled SecurityProfiles.txt and its content appears as shown in the following screenshot:

As a CSV file, the first column contains the user login (account), which includes the domain (or machine) name. In this recipe, the domain name used should refer to your machine or the domain that you work from; if you are working on a domain.

How to do it...

Start by importing the SecurityProfiles.txt file into the model.

1. Import the file SecurityProfiles.txt into the model. The download also includes a schema.ini file, which should be saved in the same location as the file.

2. Create a new role (titled Dynamic Security) with read permissions and set the role's members as **Authenticated Users**.

> To apply dynamic security, an Active Directory Account group is commonly used to group users in a Domain group. When a dynamic security is implemented you need not worry about Active Directory groups and can refer to individual users in the `Security` table.

3. Apply two row filters to the role. The first is created against the `SecurityProfiles` table with the condition `FALSE()`. The second is applied against the `Geography` table with the following syntax:

```
='Geography'[Country]=LOOKUPVALUE(
    SecurityProfiles[country], SecurityProfiles[user_login],
    USERNAME())
```

The **Row Filters** tab should look like the following screenshot:

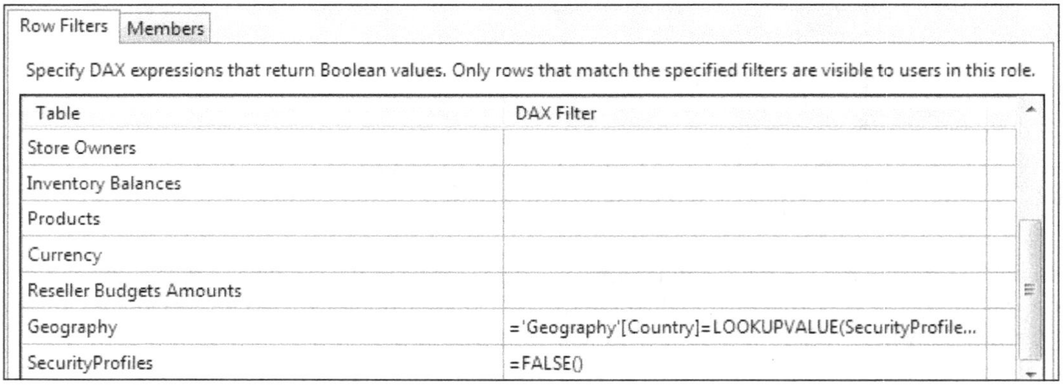

Table	DAX Filter
Store Owners	
Inventory Balances	
Products	
Currency	
Reseller Budgets Amounts	
Geography	='Geography'[Country]=LOOKUPVALUE(SecurityProfile...
SecurityProfiles	=FALSE()

Row Filters | Members

Specify DAX expressions that return Boolean values. Only rows that match the specified filters are visible to users in this role.

4. Create a Pivot Table to explore the model under both accounts (as in the *Securing data with roles* recipe). Examine how data from the `Geography` table is restricted by the user (that is, the user who is connected). Also notice that there is no data for the `SecurityProfile` table visible in the Pivot Table.

> Instead of testing security through SSDT using the option **Analyze** in Excel (and specifying the user account to test as), you may choose to run several instances of Excel running each instance as a different user. This can be achieved by using a command-line program `runas`. For example, to open Excel as the user `Mercury\Tabular Tester`, we will simply enter the following command into a new command window:
>
> ```
> runas /user:"Mercury\Tabular Tester"
>     "C:\Program Files\Microsoft Office\Office14\
>     Excel.exe"
> ```
>
> You are then prompted for the user's password.

5. Finally, hide the table `SecurityProfile` from client tools (because we do not want an end user to see the structure of the `SecurityProfile` table).

How it works...

The application of the row filter on the `Geography` table is the main mechanism that implements security in this recipe. Here, the predicate on the `Geography` table permits the `Country` value (data element) only if it exists in the `SecurityProfile` table with a match against the connected domain user.

The use of the `LOOKUPVALUE` function (see the *Linking fields between tables* recipe in *Chapter 1, Getting Started with Excel*) is that it associates a user with countries that are specified in the table `SecurityProfile`. Previously, `LOOKUPVALUE` has been applied to return data by reference to a column in an existing table; that is, the `search_value` argument of the `LOOKUPVALUE` function has been a column within an existing table. In this formula, however, the search arguments are defined by the `USERNAME()` function. This function simply returns the connected user.

> If we wish to see the username, we could create a measure `CURRENT USER:=USERNAME()`.

It was stated that the role can be implemented without hiding or specifying the `FALSE()` predicate on the `SecurityProfile` table. However, there are several reasons why this predicate should be implemented. It should be noted that hiding a table from client tools does not restrict the table from being queried. A curious user who knows the structure of the table can query it even though it may be hidden within the model. To circumvent this possible breach, the use of the `FALSE()` predicate as a row filter effectively disables data access (even for curious users).

Creating perspectives

In the prior recipes, we have restricted what the user sees by hiding tables and columns from client tools. This can remove clutter from the model and hide information that the user never needs to see (for example, the `SecurityProfile` table). However, in situations where the model contains distinctive subject areas, there may be a desire to expose only tables in those subject areas as particular views. This is achieved through perspectives.

A perspective allows a virtual model to be created over the existing model, so that the user has a choice of views for the model. As a view, the perspective inherits all security from the underlying model. Only the tables and columns that are shown in the view can be controlled. Further, data security cannot be applied directly against a perspective and visibility of the perspective cannot be defined by role. That is, the perspective cannot implement its own data security profile.

Getting ready

This recipe builds on the model that was developed by the *Model development in SQL Server Data Tools* recipe in this chapter. We will create a perspective to show only that information which relates to exchange rates (exchange rate values by date and currency).

How to do it...

The three steps for creating a perspective are to create it, name it, and set its table and column visibility.

1. Create a new perspective by launching the **Perspectives** dialog. Click on the **Perspectives** button (or click on **Perspectives** from the **Model** menu) as shown in the following screenshot:

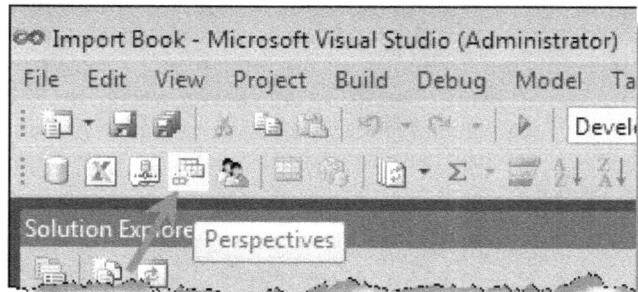

2. After the **Perspectives** window opens, click on the **New Perspective** button. This window shows any existing perspectives in the model. Name the new perspective `Exchange Rates` by overwriting the **New Perspective** caption. This is shown in the following screenshot:

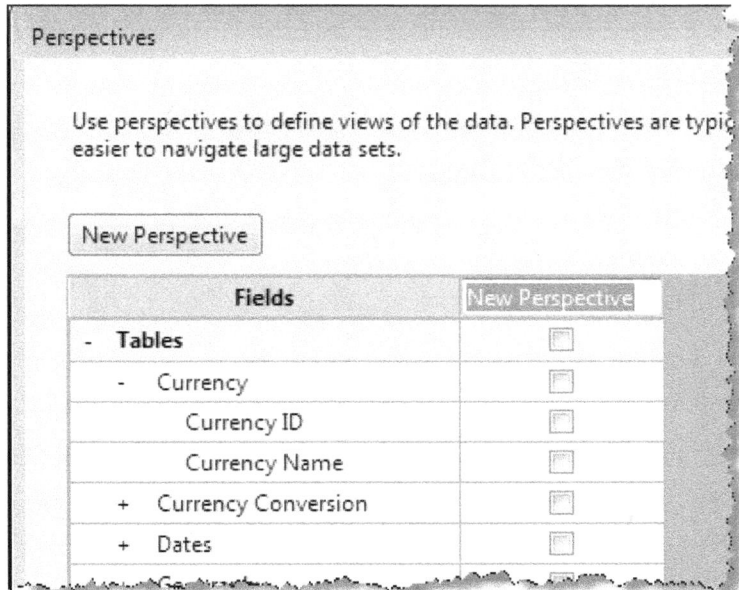

Perspectives

Use perspectives to define views of the data. Perspectives are typic easier to navigate large data sets.

| New Perspective | |

Fields	New Perspective
- Tables	☐
- Currency	☐
Currency ID	☐
Currency Name	☐
+ Currency Conversion	☐
+ Dates	☐

3. Select the fields, hierarchies, and measures that will be visible in the perspective. Expand each table and check each of the following items:

Table	Field/Measure
Currency	Currency ID
Currency Conversion	AVG Rate
Currency Conversion	EOD Rate
Currency Conversion	AVG EOD Rate
Currency Conversion	AVG Ex Rate
Dates	Day

4. Save the perspective by clicking on **OK**.

5. The perspective can then be reviewed through the **Analyze in Excel** function. The **Perspective** drop-down lists all perspectives in the model as shown in the following screenshot. Select the **Exchange Rates** perspective and click on **OK**.

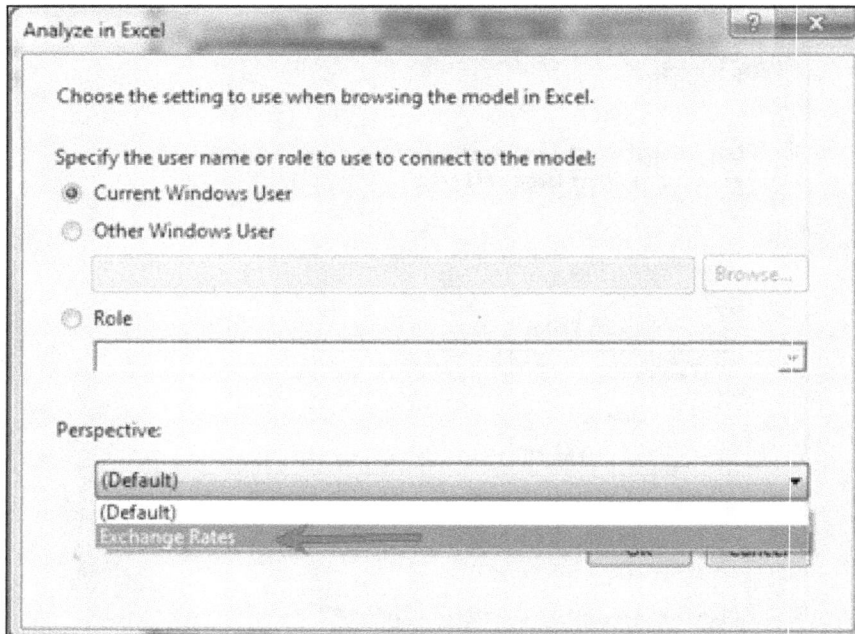

6. When the **PivotTable Field List** is displayed, only those items that are exposed through the perspective and are visible to client tools can be seen. Observe the following screenshot, the measure `AVG Rate` cannot be seen in the field selection list despite being checked when the perspective was created. This is because the measure is hidden from client tools in the model.

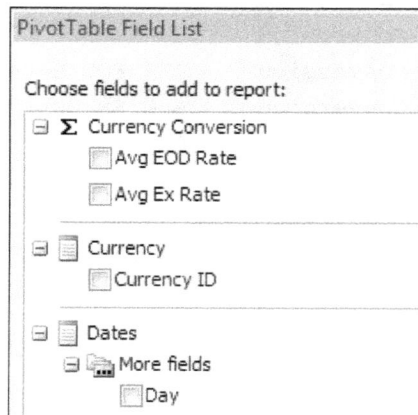

How it works...

There is no explanation required here, as the perspective is simply a derived view from the model. It cannot have any security applied to it and inherits the underlying model's security (and visibility). Perspectives are, for all intents and purposes, a representation mechanism.

There's more...

Perspectives can also be created in PowerPivot. Do this by clicking on the **Perspectives** button on the **Advanced** tab of the PowerPivot Ribbon. The user interface is the same as that of SSDT.

When analyzing in a Pivot Table, the perspective can be chosen from the field list as shown in the following screenshots:

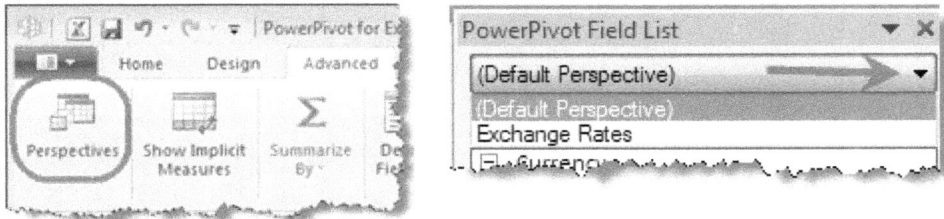

8

Enterprise Management

In this chapter, we will cover:

- ▸ Deploying models from SSDT
- ▸ Deploying models with the Deployment Wizard
- ▸ Creating and managing partitions
- ▸ Processing the data
- ▸ DirectQuery and real-time solutions

Introduction

When an Excel user creates a PowerPivot model, they have the luxury of managing all the data from within PowerPivot. They can update table data when needed in an ad hoc manner as they see fit.

However, the same situation is not true for enterprise models—tabular models that are deployed to an **SQL Server Analysis Server** (**SSAS**) server. Here, there is an expectation from all users that data is updated and refreshed according to an agreed schedule. Further, there are often restrictions on developers that limit the activity they can perform on production servers.

This chapter examines how models are managed against SSAS servers and includes deployment methods, management, and processing.

Deploying models from SSDT

The prior recipes in *Chapter 7, Enterprise Design and Features*, that deal with **SQL Server Data Tools** (**SSDT**), create a workspace database on a tabular server. This is used by SSDT as a temporary database (or model) for display and as a database that Excel can use (when you choose to analyze the data in Excel through SSDT). When SSDT is closed, the database is lost.

In order to persist the database, so that it is constantly available to end users, it must be deployed to an SSAS (tabular) server.

Getting ready

This recipe continues from the *Creating perspectives* recipe in *Chapter 7, Enterprise Design and Features*.

How to do it...

Let's start by examining the deployment properties for our project:

1. Confirm the deployment options of the **solution** by right-clicking on the solution and selecting **Properties**. The window opens as shown in the following screenshot. Change the **Deployment Server** settings if desired. These include the tabular server, the database (the name of the database that the model will be deployed to) and the cube name (the name of the cube).

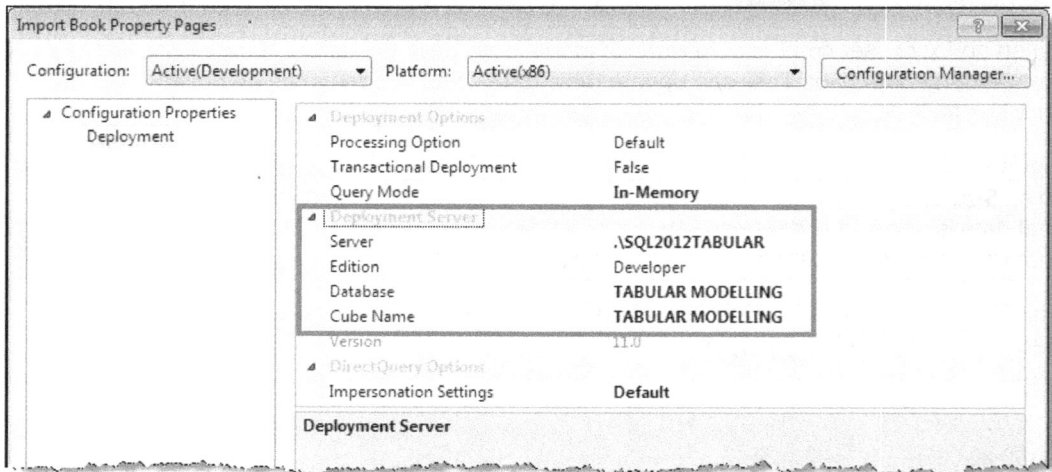

> The tabular model is synonymous to the **Database** and **Cube Name** settings in the prior screenshot and these settings have relatively little impact to the end user. In a tabular model, the model is published to a database (there can only be one model in the database) and the database contains the cube (the model).
>
> These definitions are inherited from the multidimensional model. In that model, the objects are disconnected (dimensions are separate objects from cubes) and there can be many cubes in each database.

2. Deploy the model by right-clicking on the solution and selecting **Deploy**.

3. **SQL Server Data Tools** (**SSDT**) will open a new dialog showing the steps and rows of the processing operation. This is shown in the following screenshot:

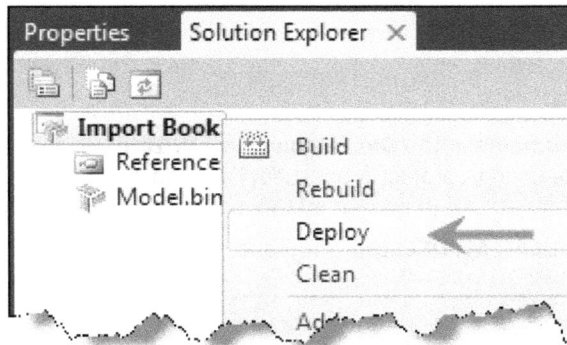

Details:

Work Item	Status	Message
Deploy metadata	Success. Metadata deployed.	
Reseller Sales	Success. 60,855 rows transferred.	
Resellers	Success. 701 rows transferred.	
Currency Conversion	Success. 14,264 rows transferred.	

4. Click on **Close**.

5. Confirm the deployment by connecting to the model through Excel. Go to **Data | From Other Sources | From Analysis Services**.

6. From an Excel workbook, connect to the model by inserting a new data source.

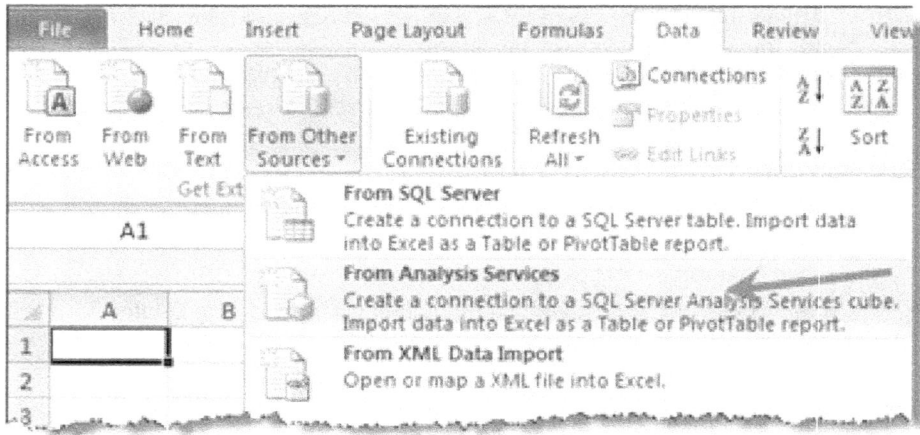

7. Enter the server name in the **Data Connection Wizard** window. This is the same server that was used in project properties. For example, in this project the server was \SQL2012TABULAR (a named instance on the localhost). Click on **Next**.

8. Select the **TABULAR MODELLING** database from the drop-down list.

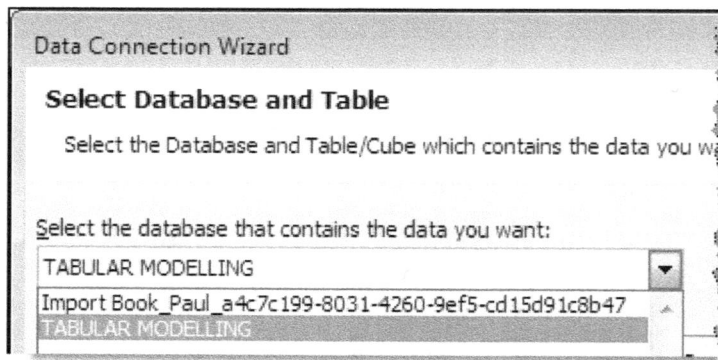

If SSDT is still open (and you have deployed to the same server as the workspace database), you should also see the workspace database. Remember that this is a temporary database used by SSDT to show the model.

9. Now, select the **TABULAR MODELLING** cube and click on **Next**. Then click on **Finish** to complete the wizard. Note (as shown in the following screenshot) that we can see and identify the model (which is called cube) and perspective:

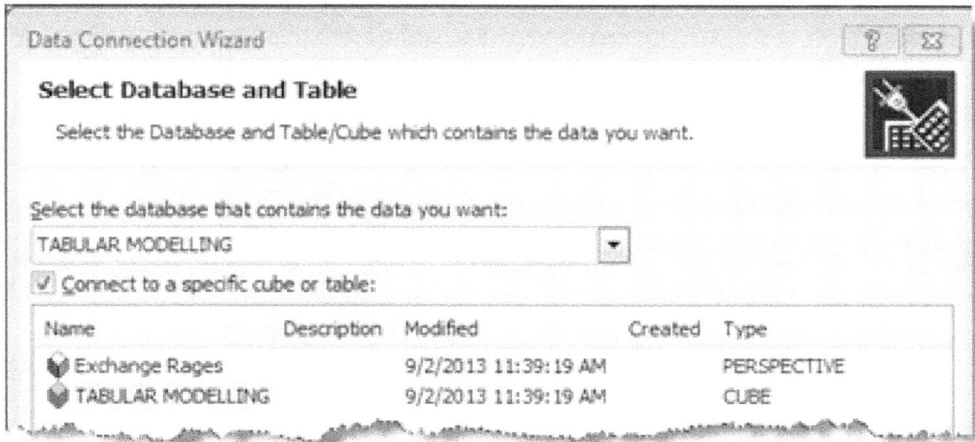

10. A pivot table will be inserted with a connection to the tabular (server-based) model. This is used as another pivot table (client-based connection). See the *Creating model calculations* recipe in *Chapter 1, Getting Started with Excel*, for the comparison of client versus the PowerPivot tables.

How it works...

Deploying from SSDT in this manner actually involves a two-step process that is managed by SSDT. The first step creates the database (model) on the server. If the database exists, it is updated for the new structure. The second command processes the database (data) that has been created on the tabular server (that is the database created in the prior step).

Before the model's data can be queried by the client tool, the database must be flagged as **processed**. The method of processing is specified in the deployment options of the solution (noting that the first step of this recipe was to confirm these options). Here, the **Processing Option** can specify how processing occurs after creation. These options are shown in the following screenshot:

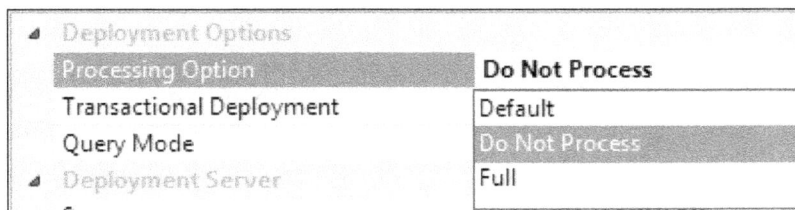

These options cover a range of processing, from no processing to full processing and are described in the following table:

Modes	Description
Default	SSAS determines the processing that is required for each table. A table will only be processed if it has been altered (or is new).
Do Not Process	No tables are processed.
Full	All tables in calculations are processed.

When the model is deployed with a processing option of **Do Not Process**, only metadata is deployed. This can be checked with the help of the following screenshot which shows deployment of the same model with the **Do Not Process** option. Note that no partition processing occurs.

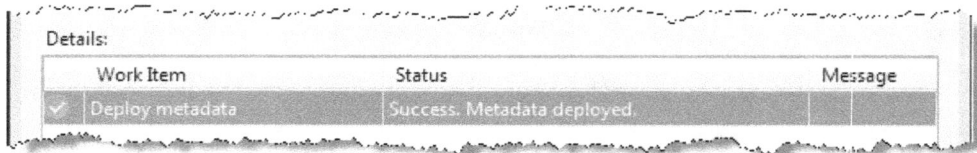

Details:

Work Item	Status	Message
✓ Deploy metadata	Success. Metadata deployed.	

Since the workspace database includes the all model data, one may question why the **Do Not Process** option should be considered as a part of deployment? This option has been chosen when the data used by the model is sample data and needs to be changed in production. This will require the deletion, alteration, and creation of additional partitions (data stores) and, therefore, reprocessing. See the *Creating and managing partitions* recipe.

Deploying models with the Deployment Wizard

Some organizations do not allow the developers to deploy their projects directly into production, this change must be managed by a different group that does not use SSDT. In this situation, the developer needs to provide an alternative method to the model.

This recipe examines how this can be achieved by using a deployment utility that is installed with SSAS. The tool can provide two methods for deployment and we will investigate both. Note that both the methods only differ in the final stage of deployment.

When using the Deployment Wizard, the wizard analyzes files that are created as part of a project build to create an output action. This action can either be the execution of a script from within the tool or the creation of a script—the XMLA file (**XMLA** stands for **XML for Analysis**) that can be executed against the (tabular) server. In order to deploy with these methods, only the output files need to be created from SSDT, everything else is managed through the Deployment Wizard.

Getting ready

This recipe continues with the model from the *Deploying models from SSDT* recipe.

How to do it...

When we deploy a model (with the Deployment Wizard) there are three things that happen—the solution is built (creating a database file), then the Deployment Wizard is used to configure the database file (this configuration is also saved in its own file), and then both files are executed against the server.

Start by building the solution as follows:

1. Build the solution by right-clicking on the solution in the **Solution Explorer** pane and selecting **Build** from the pop-up menu. Alternatively, click on the **Build Project XXX** button from the **Build** menu. This is shown in the following screenshot:

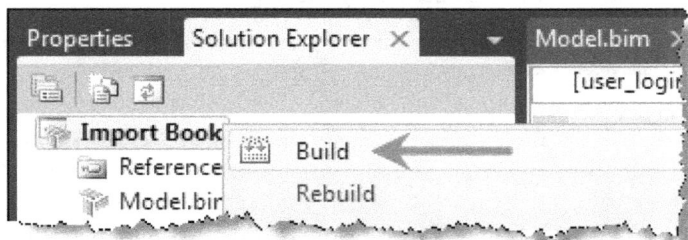

2. Close SSDT. Start the Deployment Wizard from the **All Programs** menu. It is located in the **Analysis Services** folder within the **Microsoft SQL Server 2012** program group.

3. Navigate past the wizard's welcome screen. The wizard will then ask for a file with the extension `.asdatabase` to open. The default location for this file is in the bin directory of the solution (files). This file is named `Model.asdatabase`; locate the file and click on the **Open** button.

> The build of the solution also creates two other files that are used by the Deployment Wizard. The first file `Model.deploymenttargets` specifies the current deployment server options—the server and the database name. The other file `Model.deploymentoptions` specifies the other default options for the model (such as whether partitions and roles will be created).
>
> The default settings in these files can be configured through the Deployment Wizard.

4. Specify the target server and target database that the model will be deployed to. Since the server and the database name have been configured, we can accept the defaults and move to the next screen by clicking on **Next**.

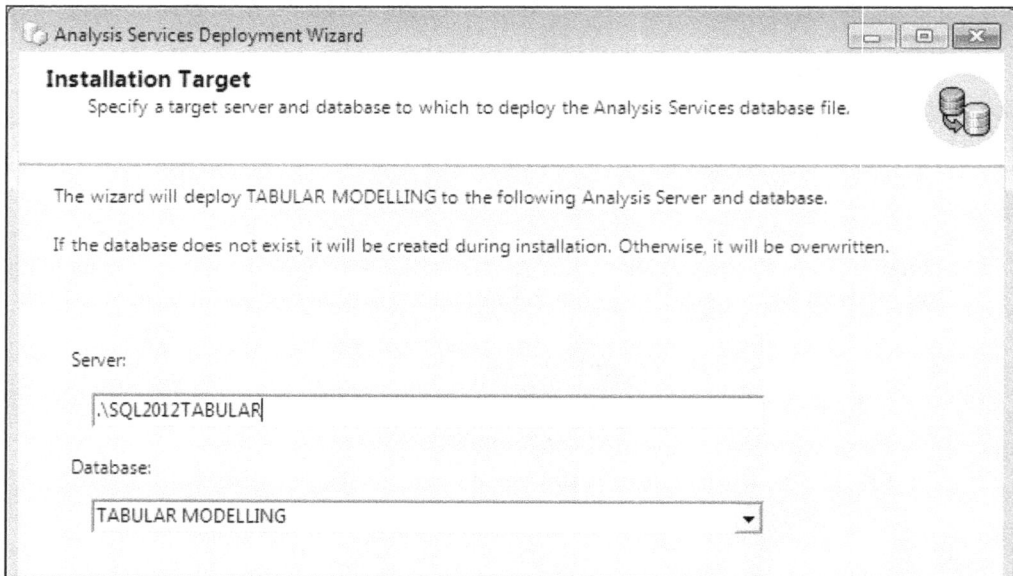

```
Analysis Services Deployment Wizard

Installation Target
    Specify a target server and database to which to deploy the Analysis Services database file.

The wizard will deploy TABULAR MODELLING to the following Analysis Server and database.

If the database does not exist, it will be created during installation. Otherwise, it will be overwritten.

Server:
    .\SQL2012TABULAR

Database:
    TABULAR MODELLING
```

> The deployment target settings are inherited from the `Model.deploymenttargets` file. The server and the database can be edited from this file, if needed.

5. Leave the default values for the **Partitions** option and **Role and members** option and click on **Next**.

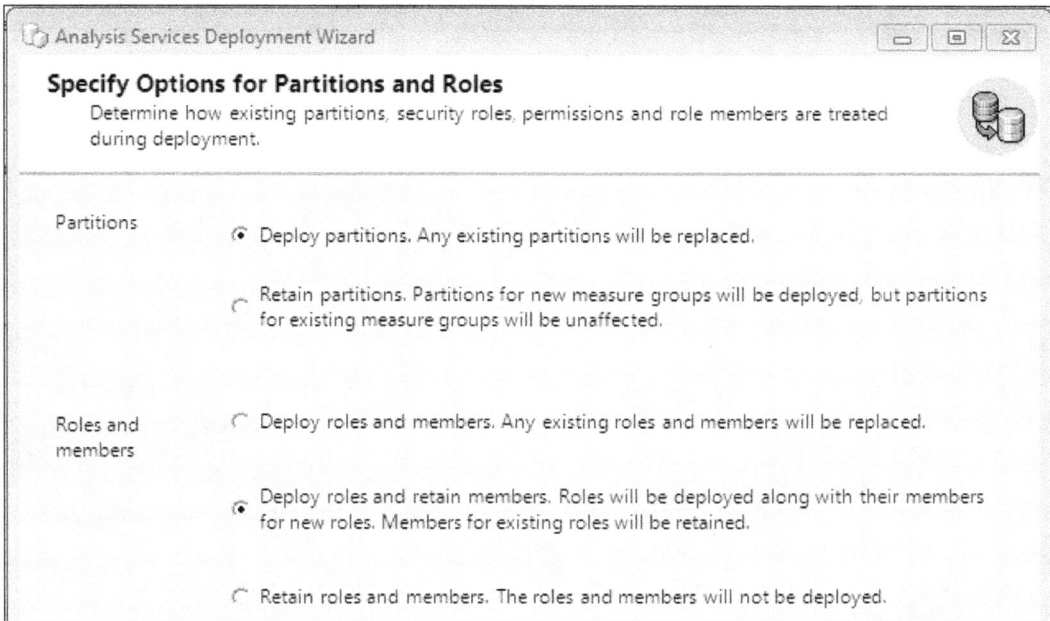

6. Finally, we can specify (if required) additional connection and impersonation information for each connection within the model. Accept the defaults (since the prior recipe, *Deploying models from SSDT*, is deployed with these values) and click on **Next**.

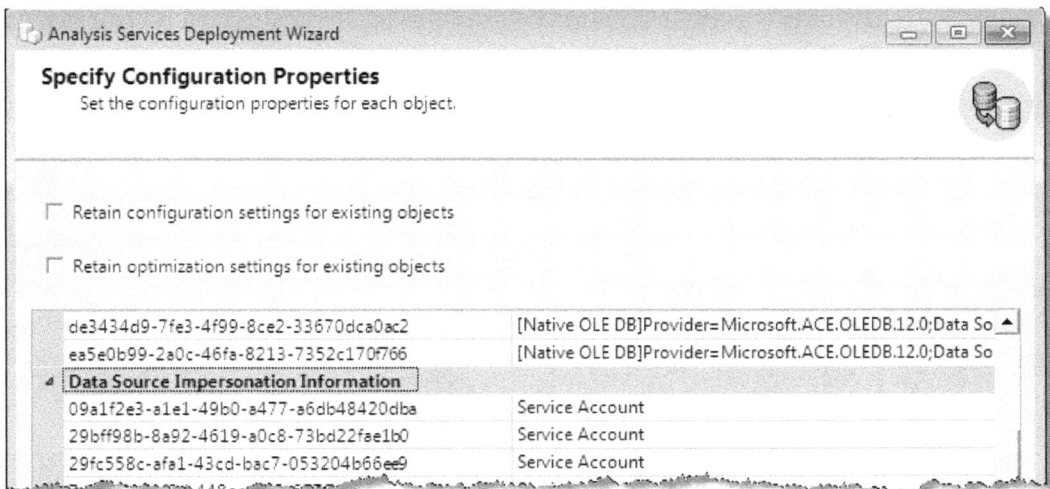

7. Finally, specify the processing option for the model after deployment. Leave this as **Default processing** and click on **Next**.

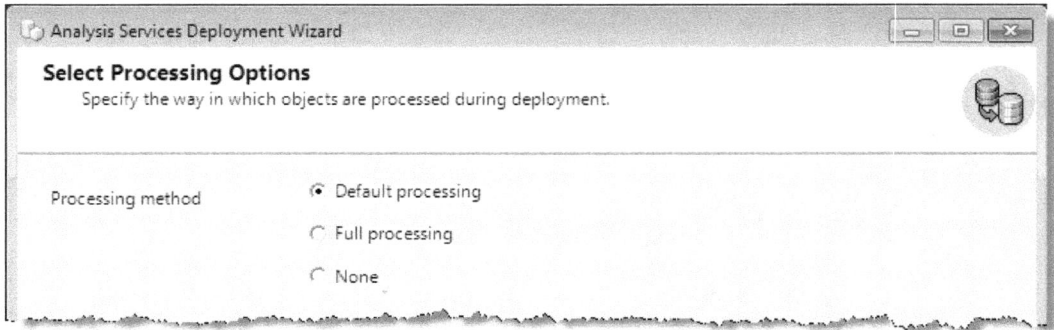

Analysis Services Deployment Wizard

Select Processing Options
Specify the way in which objects are processed during deployment.

Processing method
- (•) Default processing
- ( ) Full processing
- ( ) None

---

8. Finally, we can specify whether or not a deployment script will be created (and the name of that script). If a script's filename is provided, the Deployment Wizard will close after the script has been created. If no filename is given, the wizard will simply deploy the model and process it. In this recipe, we will choose the latter option and fully process the model from within the Deployment Wizard. Leave the **Script Location** field blank and click on **Next**.

9. The wizard will deploy and process the model; a sample output of this is shown in the following screenshot:

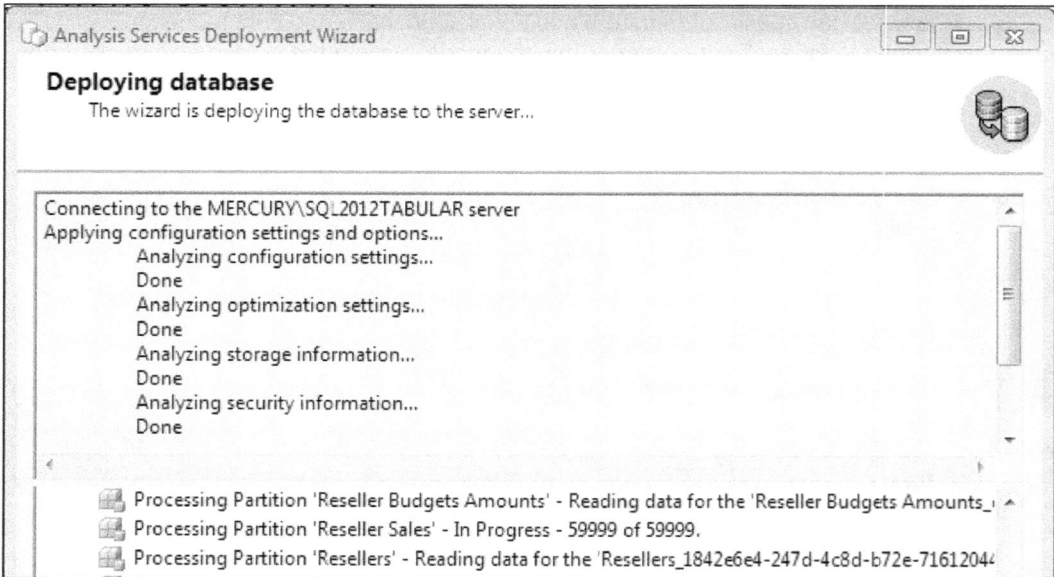

Analysis Services Deployment Wizard

Deploying database
The wizard is deploying the database to the server...

```
Connecting to the MERCURY\SQL2012TABULAR server
Applying configuration settings and options...
        Analyzing configuration settings...
        Done
        Analyzing optimization settings...
        Done
        Analyzing storage information...
        Done
        Analyzing security information...
        Done
```

Processing Partition 'Reseller Budgets Amounts' - Reading data for the 'Reseller Budgets Amounts_
Processing Partition 'Reseller Sales' - In Progress - 59999 of 59999.
Processing Partition 'Resellers' - Reading data for the 'Resellers_1842e6e4-247d-4c8d-b72e-71612044

---

10. Click on **Next** for the confirmation screen or on **Finish** to close the wizard.

How it works...

There is no additional information about deployment using the wizard. It is important to reiterate that the target settings (both server deployment and processing) are inherited from the two additional files that are created when the model was built. Both of these files are XML based and therefore the values (such as the processing option) can be set from within the files.

To demonstrate deployment using the script generation output, perform the following steps:

1. Complete the recipe using the **Create deployment script** option. By default, the output file will be created in the same location as that of the .asdatabase file and will be suffixed with an .xmla file extension. Of course, the location can be changed, but leave the default values. Finally, close the wizard.

2. Open **SQL Server Management Studio** (**SSMS**) and connect to the tabular server.

3. Open the deployment script that was created in step 1.

4. Execute the script. When the script is running, the **Messages** tab will show progress as shown in the following screenshot:

```
Messages
Executing the query ...
<Subscribe xmlns="http://schemas.microsoft.com/analysisservices/2003/engine"/>
<Subscribe xmlns="http://schemas.microsoft.com/analysisservices/2003/engine"/>
READS, 0
READ_KB, 0
WRITES, 0
WRITE_KB, 0
CPU_TIME_MS, 0
ROWS_SCANNED, 0
ROWS_RETURNED, 0

<Batch Transaction="false" xmlns="http://schemas.microsoft.com/analysisservices
  <Alter AllowCreate="true" ObjectExpansion="ExpandFull">
    <Object>
```

5. When the execution of the script is complete, the output results will show an empty result set for success, as shown in the following screenshot:

```
Messages   Results
<return xmlns="urn:schemas-microsoft-com:xml-analysis">
  <results xmlns="http://schemas.microsoft.com/analysisservices/2003/xmla
    <root xmlns="urn:schemas-microsoft-com:xml-analysis:empty" />
    <root xmlns="urn:schemas-microsoft-com:xml-analysis:empty" />
  </results>
</return>
```

There's more...

The use of the Deployment Wizard removed reliance on SSDT. However, deployment can still be a manual process because of the required interaction with the interface. Since the additional deployment files can be overridden in the wizard, one might also question their purpose.

One of the useful features about the Deployment Wizard is that it can execute executables from the command line and fully deploy the build. This can then be executed in a number of scheduled ways (for example, as a scheduled task or through an Integration Services package). Here, the use of the additional files becomes apparent as they specify the deployment options and target.

There are a number of parameters that can be set for deployment; however, consider the situation where we simply wish to deploy the model (with values specified in the additional files). Executing the following command will deploy the model and leave the log showing the steps that the deployment took:

```
Microsoft.AnalysisServices.Deployment.exe
"C:\BOOK\Import Book\Import Book\bin\Model.asdatabase"
   /s:"C:\BOOK\Import Book\Import Book\bin\deployment.log"
```

> In this situation, my `bin` directory is located at `C:\BOOK\Import Book\Import Book\bin\`.
>
> The code file that accompanies this chapter (available from the online content) includes the fully-qualified name of the `Deployment.exe` file. By default, this is found in the following directory: `C:\Program Files (x86)\Microsoft SQL Server\110\Tools\Binn\ManagementStudio`.

Further information about running the Deployment Wizard from the command line can be found at `http://tinyurl.com/nzn878y`.

Creating and managing partitions

The tabular model is an in-memory engine meaning that the data in the model (all models on the tabular server) is compressed and stored in the RAM while the server is running. The tabular server also stores data on the disk (storage for when the SSAS engine is not running)—however, the rule is generally that all queries against the model are performed on cached data. The exception to this, of course, is when there is not enough RAM for the engine to use, and paging occurs.

This is a stark contrast to **Multidimensional Online Analytical Processing** (**MOLAP**) storage, which stores data on the disk (notwithstanding aggregations that may have been cached). This storage requires an effective partitioning strategy as a performance consideration. That is, a strategy to physically store the data on the disk.

Aside from performance implications, partitioning is also used as a management function—it defines what data is available in the model. A common example of this is the application of a sliding window where; for example, data is held in monthly partitions and rolling data for the past 12 months is required. As monthly partitions are filled, the older and nonneeded partitions can be deleted without impacting the entire dataset.

This recipe examines how to implement partitioning on the tabular server at both design (in SSDT) and administration (using SSMS). Unlike MOLAP storage, partitioning can occur on any table (MOLAP SSAS restricts partitioning to measure groups). Additionally, since storage is in-memory, the use of a partitioning strategy becomes more of a management issue.

Getting ready

This recipe continues from the model that has been developed and deployed in the *Deploying models from SSDT* recipe. Our goal is to create yearly partitions for the `Reseller Sales` table that constrains data by the financial year. The partition names span financial years (for example, `Reseller_Sales_2006` spans records with order dates between `1-July-2005` and `30-Jun-2006`).

How to do it...

This recipe is completed in two steps. Firstly, we alter the current partition for `Reseller Sales` to apply for `Reseller_Sales_2006`. This is done in the design mode. Secondly, we alter the deployed model as it resides on the server (through SSMS).

Let's start by reviewing the current partition:

1. In SSDT, activate the `Reseller Sales` table in **Grid View Mode** and click on the **Partitions** button.

2. The **Partition Manager** window opens. Note that the values in the **Connection** and **Source Name** textboxes cannot be edited but the value in **Partition Name** can; modify the value in the **Partition Name** textbox to `Reseller_Sales_2006`. This is shown in the following screenshot:

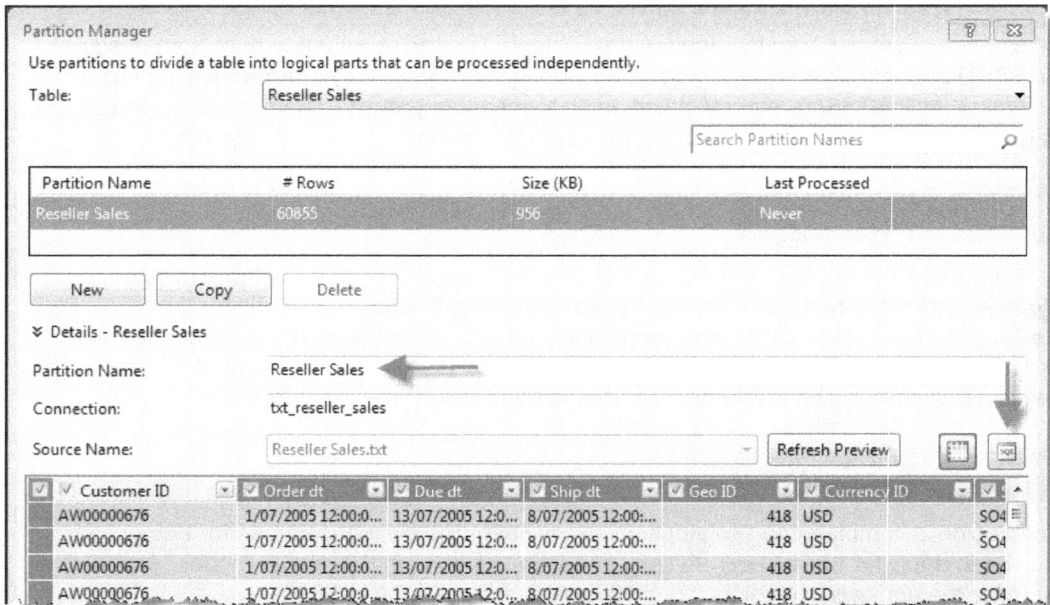

3. Click on the SQL definition button for the Partition. Replace the current SQL command with the following (note the inclusion of the `WHERE` clause). Remember that this data was sourced from the text file—this is why the `WHERE` condition includes #:

```
SELECT [Reseller Sales#txt].*
FROM [Reseller Sales#txt]
WHERE
[Order dt] between  #2005-07-01 00:00:00#
and #2006-07-01 00:00:00#
```

4. Validate the syntax and then close by clicking on **OK**.

5. Note that the current row count of the partition (before changes) is **60,855** records. Process the table (there is only one partition in the table) by clicking on the **Process** button and selecting the **Process Table** option, as shown in the following screenshot:

6. Observe the new row count of **8,459** records. Then, deploy and process the model to the server.

7. Now that the model has deployed to the server, we can consider it in a production state where further development is not possible, partitions must be managed from SSMS. The remaining part of this recipe adds a partition from SSMS.

8. Open SSMS and connect to the tabular server. Expand the TABULAR MODELLING database and then expand the **Tables** node. Right-click on the Reseller Sales table and select the **Partition...** option. A new window will open as shown in the following screenshot:

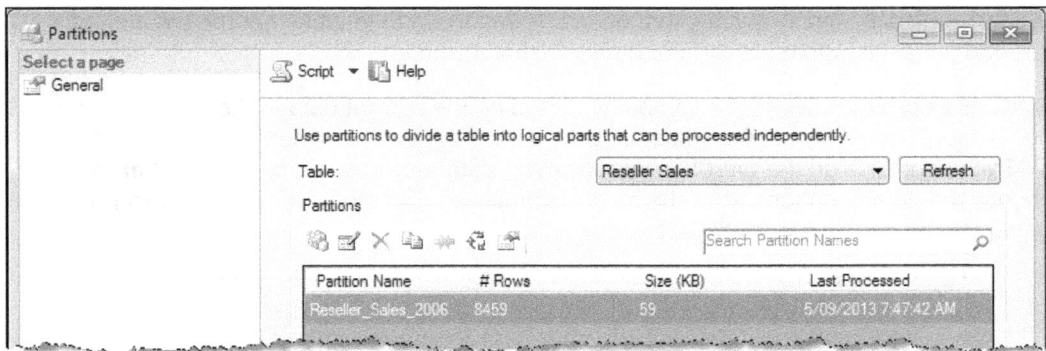

9. Copy the partition for 2006 by highlighting the partition in the grid and clicking on the **Copy** button.

> If there are more than one partitions in the grid, the one that is active (selected partition) in the grid is copied.

10. The **New Partition** dialog opens. Rename the partition to `Reseller_Sales_2007` and adjust the years of the dates so that the values in `[Order dt]` lies between 2006 and 2007, as shown in the following screenshot:

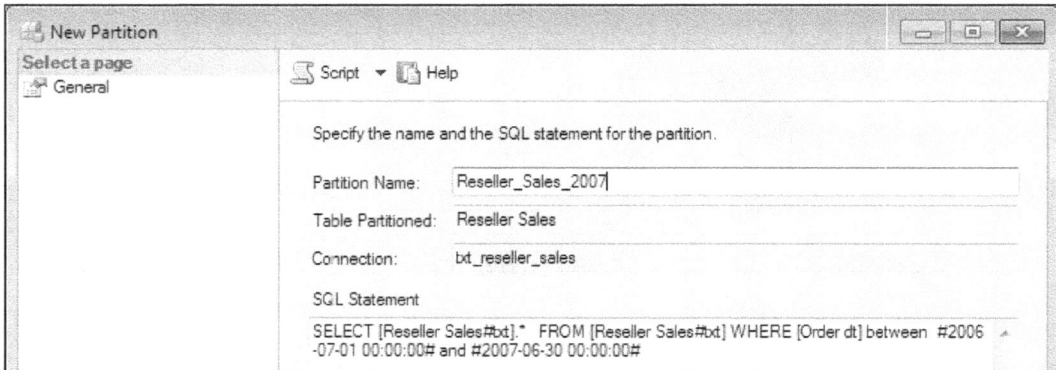

11. Confirm the creation of the new partition by clicking on the **OK** button.

How it works...

A partition is a logical definition of a data segment for a table, and the creation of a partition (in SSDT or SSMS) simply defines that data. It is important to identify that the creation of a partition does not automatically load data into that partition.

Consider a specific reseller (tire company), based on the current data in the model (as the model should currently be) the value of `[USD Sales Total]` for them should be $12,864. In SSMS, right-click on the `TABULAR MODELLING` database and select **Process Database** (choose the default option). After the model is processed, sales will now be $13,334 due to the additional data in the 2007 partition.

	A	B			A	B	
1	Customer ID	AW00000162		1	Customer ID	AW00000162	
2	Customer Name	Tire Company		2	Customer Name	All	
3				3			
4	**Row Labels**			4	**Row Labels**		
5	$12,864			5	$13,334		
6	**Grand Total**			6	**Grand Total**		

> Partition processing is examined in the next recipe—*Processing the data*.

There's more...

There are two issues associated with the user interface for creating partitions. Firstly, you cannot create a bulk set of partitions using some iterative process. For example, creating 70 partitions would be very troublesome and not easily reproducible if we wished to deploy to another environment! What is needed in this situation is a reusable method of generating a partition that can fully define the partition by changes to its structure (for example, its data source, query, and name). Secondly, the user interface does not allow the creation of a partition that uses a different data source to the *base* partition (the source used to create the table initially). For example, we could not specify the SQL Server connection in the previous part of the recipe.

Creating partitions through XMLA can solve both of these problems. Here, all we have to do is create a statement that is executed against the database. This process (and the iteration) can be easily managed through Integration Services. The remainder of this recipe looks at the generation of the XMLA command.

Before continuing, it is important to recognize the multidimensional representation of a tabular database. In the multidimensional view, each table in the tabular model can be shown in two ways—one as a **dimension** and the other as a **measure group**. Additionally, in multidimensional view, partitions are only created against measure groups. Further, the tabular model contains only one cube when compared to OLAP.

Finally, we need to recognize that all objects have an ID and a name. For example, the cube object has an ID (model) that may not be the same as its name (TABULAR MODELLING). We can identify the ID for a table (and therefore, the OLAP versions of the measure group) by right-clicking on it in SSMS and selecting **Properties**. Here, we can see that the Resellers Sales table's ID is different from its name.

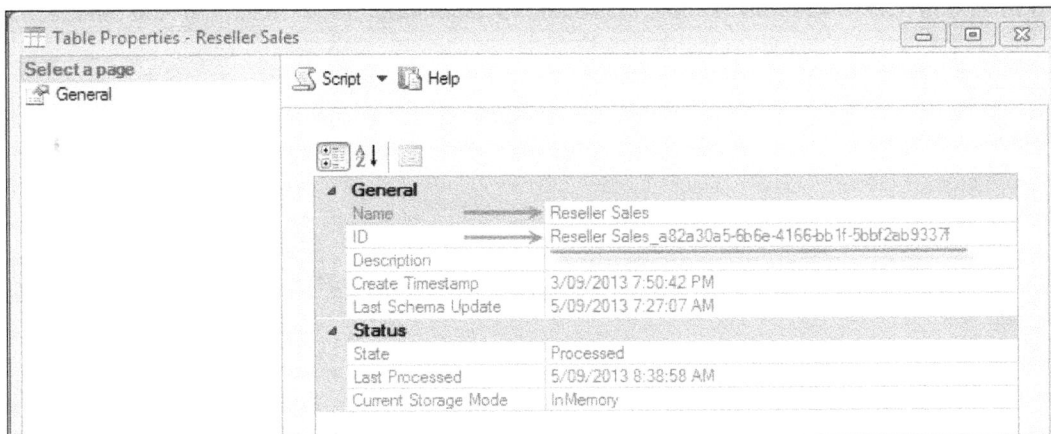

Our goal is to create a new partition for the `Reseller Sales` table that relates to 2009 and sources its data from the SQL database. Firstly (since there is no connection to our SQL Server in the model), we need to define the connection. The following code snippet will achieve this:

```
<Create xmlns="…">
  <ParentObject>
    <DatabaseID>TABULAR MODELLING</DatabaseID>
  </ParentObject>
  <ObjectDefinition>
    <DataSource xmlns:xsd="http….. ">
      <ID>sql_dw</ID>
      <Name>sql_dw</Name>
      <ConnectionString>ConString</ConnectionString>
      <ImpersonationInfo>
        <ImpersonationMode>ImpersonateServiceAccount
        </ImpersonationMode>
      </ImpersonationInfo>
      <Timeout>PT0S</Timeout>
    </DataSource>
  </ObjectDefinition>
</Create>
```

> For brevity, namespace declarations and the connection string details have been removed from the code snippet. The full code for all sections of this recipe is available in the resources accompanying this chapter available on the Packt Publishing website.

The CREATE statement defines the connection (data source) by name and ID as a child of the parent database. Additional information (impersonation and timeouts are also specified); however, the main criteria here is the name and ID. Both must be unique within the database otherwise an error will occur as shown in the following screenshot:

```
Messages
Executing the query ...
The datasource with the name of 'sql_dw' already exists in the 'TABULAR MODELLING' database.
Execution complete
```

If this is successful, the program will return an empty result, as shown in the following screenshot:

```
Messages   Results
<return xmlns="urn:schemas-microsoft-com:xml-analysis">
  <root xmlns="urn:schemas-microsoft-com:xml-analysis:empty" />
</return>
```

Now that the SQL connection has been created (refreshing the **Connections** node in SSMS will confirm this), we can define the script for the partition.

There are two ways to achieve this. Firstly, just as the connection, we can script the partition as the CREATE command. When the script is executed, it will fail if it already exists. The code snippet for the create is as follows:

```
<Create xmlns="…">
  <ParentObject>
    <DatabaseID>TABULAR MODELLING</DatabaseID>
    <CubeID>Model</CubeID>
    <MeasureGroupID>Reseller Sales-??? </MeasureGroupID>
  </ParentObject>
  <ObjectDefinition>
    <Partition xmlns:xsd="..">
      <ID>Reseller_Sales_2008</ID>
      <Name>Reseller_Sales_2008</Name>
      <Source xsi:type="QueryBinding">
        <DataSourceID>sql_dw</DataSourceID>
        <QueryDefinition>
          @sql
        </QueryDefinition>
      </Source>
      <StorageMode ..>InMemory</StorageMode>
      <ProcessingMode>Regular</ProcessingMode>
      <DirectQueryUsage>InMemoryOnly</ DirectQueryUsage>
    </Partition>
  </ObjectDefinition>
</Create>
```

Note here that the partition is a child of the measure group. The partition is defined by the ID and name (both must be unique). Further, the source (data) of the partition refers to a query against the one previously defined in the data source.

Secondly, the partition can be created through an ALTER command. In doing so, we specify that if the object does not exist, it should be created. The code snippet for ALTER is as follows:

```
<Alter AllowCreate="true" ...>
  <Object>
    <DatabaseID>TABULAR MODELLING</DatabaseID>
    <CubeID>Model</CubeID>
    <MeasureGroupID>Reseller Sales_</MeasureGroupID>
    <PartitionID>reseller_sales_2009</PartitionID>
  </Object>
  <ObjectDefinition>
    <Partition xmlns:xsd="...">
      <ID>Reseller_Sales_2009</ID>
      <Name>Reseller_Sales_2009</Name>
```

```
        <Source xsi:type="QueryBinding">
          <DataSourceID>sql_dw</DataSourceID>
          <QueryDefinition>
@query
          </QueryDefinition>
        </Source>
        <StorageMode>InMemory</StorageMode>
        <ProcessingMode>Regular</ProcessingMode>
        <DirectQueryUsage>InMemoryOnly</ DirectQueryUsage>
      </Partition>
    </ObjectDefinition>
  </Alter>
```

Notice whether the two statements `CREATE` and `ALTER` are defined in a similar way. The definition for the object (see the tag `<ObjectDefinition>`) is exactly the same, only the command and (parent) object definition differ.

The `ALTER` commands can be used to change any element of an existing object. Consider, for example, that we will like to define the `SecurityProfiles` table to reference the new `sql_dw` data source and the `security_profiles` table within it. Without impacting the operation of the current database, we can change the table's source:

```
    <Alter AllowCreate="true" ..>
      <Object>
        <DatabaseID>TABULAR MODELLING</DatabaseID>
        <CubeID>Model</CubeID>
        <MeasureGroupID>SecurityProfiles_</MeasureGroupID>
        <PartitionID>SecurityProfiles_</PartitionID>
      </Object>
      <ObjectDefinition>
        <Partition xmlns:xsd="..">
          <ID>SecurityProfiles_3</ID>
          <Name>SecurityProfiles_3</Name>
          <Source xsi:type="QueryBinding">
            <DataSourceID>sql_dw</DataSourceID>
            <QueryDefinition>
              select
              user_login
              , country
              from dbo.security_profiles
            </QueryDefinition>
          </Source>
        </Partition>
      </ObjectDefinition>
    </Alter>
```

It is important to remember that partition changes are only reflected as a change in data once the processing has occurred. Processing is examined in the next recipe—*Processing the data.*

Processing the data

Creating a partition (as explained in the *Creating and managing partitions* recipe) creates a definition of the partition (in model metadata). Once this is done, the data must be loaded into the partition if it has to become viewable. Furthermore, changes to the underlying data are not reflected in the model until the partition is processed.

Consider the situation where data is partitioned at the source database. This could be by table, partitions within tables, or views (or various combinations of these). For example, assume that we have the sales data separated in views by year, as shown in the following screenshot:

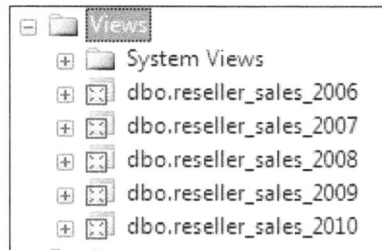

The partitioning strategy of the model also follows this structure because sales are recorded on the date that the order is placed (assume that this is a business rule) and, therefore, only the values in dbo.reseller_sales_2010 are expected to change in the source data when the data is updated (in a nightly batch). The least resource-intensive operation to update the model is, therefore, to update only the 2010 partition. So, rather than trying to fully process the model, we wish to only update the sales data for 2010.

> The time required to process the model can be a consideration for a number of reasons. Notwithstanding large databases (they naturally take longer to process), the demand for near real-time data implies small processing windows. Models that are built over OLTP systems and have an update frequency of *less* than 5 minutes are a real-world example of a targeted processing and partitioning strategy.

This recipe shows how to achieve that task by scheduling the model refresh with SQL Server Agent.

Getting ready

This recipe builds on the model that was created in the *Creating and managing partitions* recipe. For convenience, all the Reseller Sales partitions now reference the database. We assume that a user (in this case, Mercury\ProcessOperator) has permissions to process the model with read access to the relational database.

A backup of the tabular model for this recipe is also available (as an *.abf file) in the source files for this chapter. This backup has all connections referring to the SQL Server source. To restore the database simply use the following code snippet:

```
<Restore
xmlns="http://schemas.microsoft.com/analysisservices/2003/engine">
  <File>File Directory\TABULAR MODELLING.abf</File>
  <DatabaseName>TABULAR MODELLING</DatabaseName>
</Restore>
```

Note that when the database is restored, you will need to edit the sql_dw connection.

How to do it...

This recipe is broken into two components. Firstly, the creation of the code to process the partition and, secondly the creation of SQL Server Agent Job and schedule to execute the partition refresh. The following are the steps:

1. Open SSMS, connect to the TABULAR MODELLING database, and create an XMLA command.

2. Paste the following code into the code window and execute it:

```
<Process xmlns="http://schemas.microsoft.com/
analysisservices/2003/
engine">
  <Type>ProcessFull</Type>
  <Object>
    <DatabaseID>TABULAR MODELLING</DatabaseID>
    <CubeID>Model</CubeID>
    <MeasureGroupID>Reseller Sales_a82a30a5-6b6e-4166-bb1f-
5bbf2ab9337f</MeasureGroupID>
    <PartitionID>Reseller_Sales_2010</PartitionID>
  </Object>
</Process>
```

The code should execute correctly and display the following message:

```
Messages    Results
<return xmlns="urn:schemas-microsoft-com:xml-analysis">
  <root xmlns="urn:schemas-microsoft-com:xml-analysis:empty" />
</return>
```

If not, confirm the measure group ID by examining the properties of Reseller Sales (see the *Creating and managing partitions* recipe for an explanation on how to do this).

3. Create a credential to impersonate the processing user MERCURY\
   ProcessOperator:

```
USE [master]
GO
CREATE CREDENTIAL [ProcessOperator]
WITH IDENTITY = N'MERCURY\ProcessOperator'
GO
```

4. Create a proxy:

```
USE [msdb]
GO
EXEC msdb.dbo.sp_add_proxy @proxy_name=N'ProcessOperator',@
credential_name=N'ProcessOperator',
    @enabled=1
GO
EXEC msdb.dbo.sp_grant_proxy_to_subsystem @proxy_
name=N'ProcessOperator', @subsystem_id=10
GO
```

5. Create a job (that executes Analysis Service Command) that is run by the proxy.
   Connect to SQL Server and expand the SQL Server Agent. Right-click on **Jobs** and
   select **New Job...** from the pop-up menu, as shown in the following screenshot:

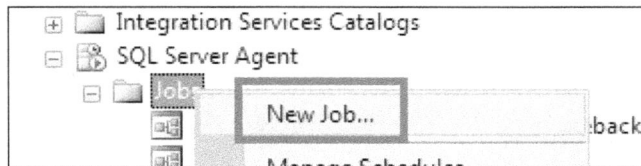

6. Name the job Process Tabular Model Partition. This is a general setting of
   the job (marked point **1** in the following screenshot):

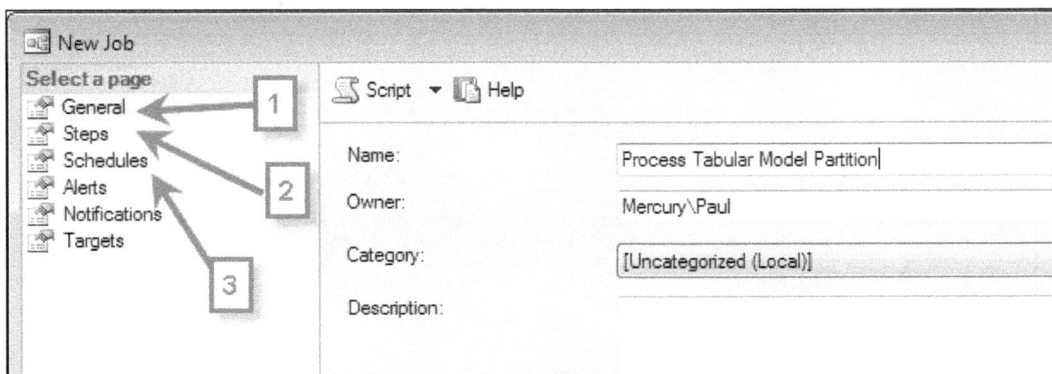

7. Select the **Steps** option from the **Select a page** pane (marked in red as point **2** in the prior screenshot). When this is clicked, a new pane opens on the right-hand side of the window. Create a new step by clicking on the **New** button.

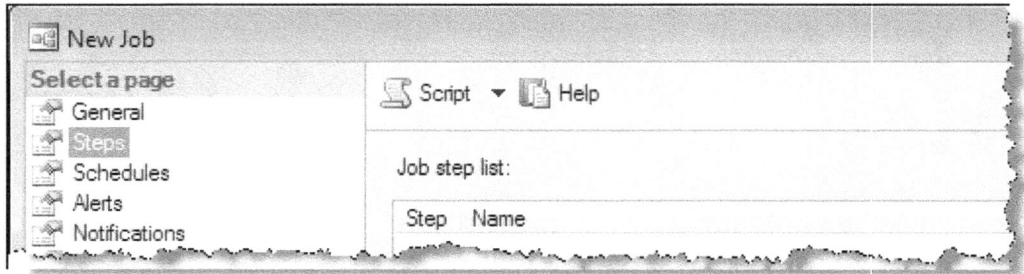

8. Name the step `Process Reseller Sales 2010 Partition`, select the **SQL Server Analysis Services Command** option from the **Type** drop-down and the **ProcessOpeartor** option from the **Run as** drop-down.

9. Then, specify the tabular server (in this case, `localhost\SQL2012TABULAR`) and paste the process command from the one that was created in step 1. The window should look like the following screenshot:

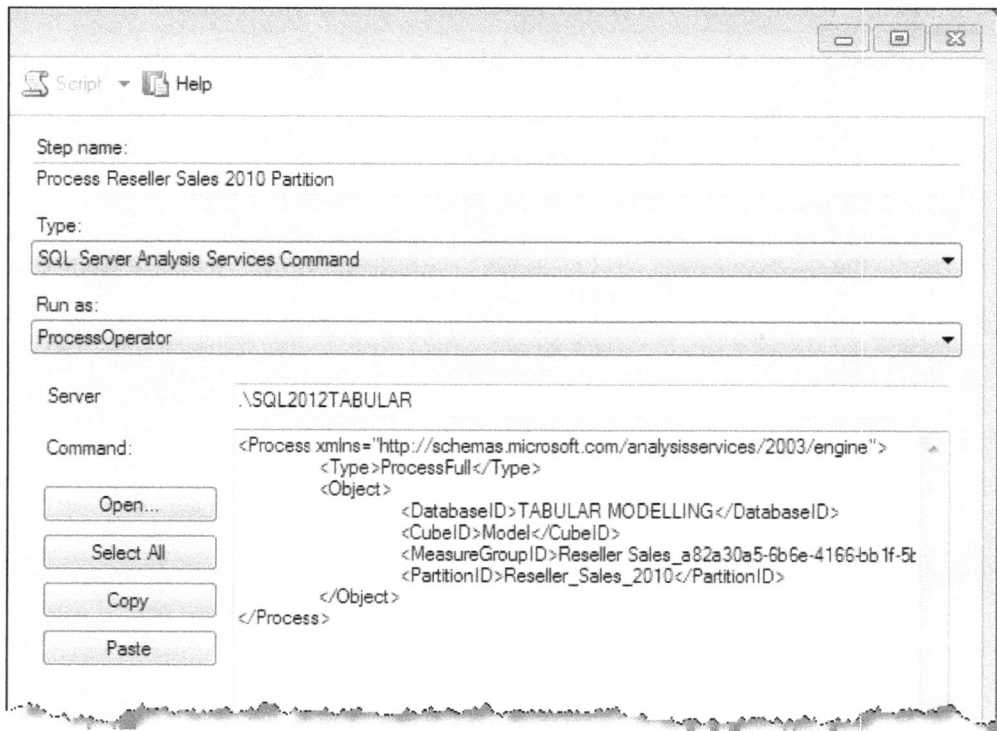

10. Click on the **Advanced** page. Now, ensure that the success action is **Quit the job reporting success** and the failure action is **Quit the job reporting failure**. The screen should look like the following screenshot:

11. Click on **OK** to confirm the step.

12. Click on the **Schedules** page. Create a new schedule (to run every 5 minutes during business hours (8:00 A.M. to 7:00 P.M.) by clicking on the **New...** button.

13. In the **Name** textbox, enter 5 Minute Intervals Business Hours.

14. Select the **Recurring** option in the **Schedule type** drop-down list.

15. Under the **Frequency** heading, select **Daily** in the **Occurs** drop-down list.

16. And finally, set it to occur every 5 minutes between 8:00 A.M. and 6:59 P.M. The following screenshot will give you a better idea:

17. Confirm the job schedule by clicking on **OK**.

> Although the user interface may imply that the schedule is attached to the job, the two items are separated and exist as objects in their own right. Deleting the job will not delete the schedule. You can re-use an existing schedule by clicking on the **Pick...** button in the **Schedules** page.

18. Confirm the job by Clicking on the **OK** button.

19. If the job is not shown in the job list, refresh the list by selecting the job's node and pressing *F5*.

20. Leave the job for some time (more than 5 minutes). Return to SSMS, right-click on the job (Process Tabular Model Partition) and select **View History** from the Pop-up menu. A new window will open showing the outcome of those executions stating that the job has completed. Failed jobs are indicated with a red cross mark.

	Load Log	Export	Refresh	Filter ...	Search ...	Stop	Delete ...	

Log file summary: No filter applied

Date ▽	Step ID	Server	Job Name
⊞ ✓ 9/09/2013 6:55:00 PM		MERCURY\SQL2012	Process Tabular Model Partitio
⊞ ✓ 9/09/2013 6:50:00 PM		MERCURY\SQL2012	Process Tabular Model Partitio
⊞ ✓ 9/09/2013 6:45:00 PM		MERCURY\SQL2012	Process Tabular Model Partitio
⊞ ✓ 9/09/2013 6:40:00 PM		MERCURY\SQL2012	Process Tabular Model Partitio
⊞ ✓ 9/09/2013 6:35:00 PM		MERCURY\SQL2012	Process Tabular Model Partitio
⊞ ✓ 9/09/2013 6:30:00 PM		MERCURY\SQL2012	Process Tabular Model Partitio
⊞ ✓ 9/09/2013 6:25:00 PM		MERCURY\SQL2012	Process Tabular Model Partitio

How it works...

There are two considerations in this recipe. Firstly, the XMLA command to process the required partition and secondly, the Agent Job that schedules and manages the process.

The processing XMLA for a single partition is straightforward. The partition is specified by its hierarchical association to its parent objects (that is, database, cube, and measure group). The other option (Type) specifies how the object will be processed. Have a look at the following code:

```
<Process ...>
  <Type>ProcessFull</Type>
  <Object>
```

```
      <DatabaseID>TABULAR MODELLING</DatabaseID>
      <CubeID>Model</CubeID>
      <MeasureGroupID>@Measure Group ID</MeasureGroupID>
      <PartitionID>Reseller_Sales_2010</PartitionID>
    </Object>
  </Process>
```

Further information about processing types can be found at `http://tinyurl.com/ozvldpk`. For this situation, we need to remember that the sales data is used to create calculations in other tables (that is, values in the `Resellers` table). Since there is a dependency between the two tables, it makes sense that one cannot be updated without impacting the other. Processing the partition using a data command (that is, `ProcessData`) will violate this dependency since calculations in the `Customers` table will not be updated. Should such a situation occur (where all the data is processed, however the model is unusable), a `ProcessRecalc` command can be applied to the entire database, so that only calculations are updated. As the name implies, this type only recalculates measures and does not load any data. Further, the operation can only be applied at the database level:

```
<Process
xmlns="http://schemas.microsoft.com/analysisservices/2003/engine">
  <Type>ProcessRecalc</Type>
  <Object>
    <DatabaseID>TABULAR MODELLING</DatabaseID>
  </Object>
</Process>
```

As an overview explanation of SQL Agent Job (remembering of course that the agent is not a part of Analysis Services or the tabular model), we effectively create an identity within SQL Server to execute the `Process` command.

From a security perspective, this identity raises several issues. Firstly, they need an authority to execute the command (on the SSAS subsystem) within SQL Server Agent. This was included after the credential and proxy (which effectively recognizes the user on the system) with the `sp_grant_proxy_to_subsystem` command. Secondly, as an identity processing the tabular model, the identity needs access to perform the operation within SSAS and access to read data from SQL Server. It should be noted that SQL Server Agent (usually) runs as its own account (SQL 2012 creates these accounts during installation) and the account is not likely to have any permissions on SQL or SSAS.

Finally, the job is essentially a batch process that is managed by SQL Server Agent (an independent Windows service). I say batch process because the job is a series of sequential steps (although we only had one) that are executed by the agent.

DirectQuery and real-time solutions

The ability to routinely process data with SQL Server Agent (see the *Processing the data* recipe) gives the model designer a large degree of flexibility to determine when data in the model is refreshed. In fact, the standard practice for Business Intelligence solutions is that data is updated on a nightly basis and therefore model processing becomes part of the nightly refresh.

However, where the source data is rapidly changing, there may be a requirement to implement a **DirectQuery** solution. This is an environment that is conceptually similar to **Relational Online Analytical Processing** (**ROLAP**). Here, the model passes all queries through to the relational database (rather than querying its own data store).

A DirectQuery solution may seem like an extremely attractive option for real-time data access since the model is essentially a semantic definition used to define the model structure. Further, there is no requirement for the model to process data since all queries are passed back to the relational engine. This also makes deployment very fast. However, there are some restrictions for the use of DirectQuery, which should be considered as a part of the development strategy:

- ▸ A DirectQuery option is applied in entirety to the model (you can not specify a query mode by partition as you can do with OLAP measure groups). This means that any query will be converted into SQL. In practice, this severely limits the performance of the model.

- ▸ There are modeling restrictions because some functions and DAX expressions are not supported.

- ▸ The source of data is restricted to SQL Server.

- ▸ Only DAX queries can be executed against the model. This will limit the client tools that can be used to query the model.

Getting ready

This recipe creates a simple model that shows the sales data by `Geographic`, `Customer`, and `Date` attributes. We demonstrate the implications of a model that supports DAX-only-queries in comparison to the de facto pivot table interface.

How to do it...

Start by creating a new project, the steps are as follows:

1. Create a new SSAS tabular project titled `Direct Query Solution`.

2. In the **Solution Explorer** pane, right-click on the `Model.bim` file, and select **Properties**. Then set the **DirectQuery Mode Property** option to **On** (it is **Off** by default). These configurations are shown in the following screenshot:

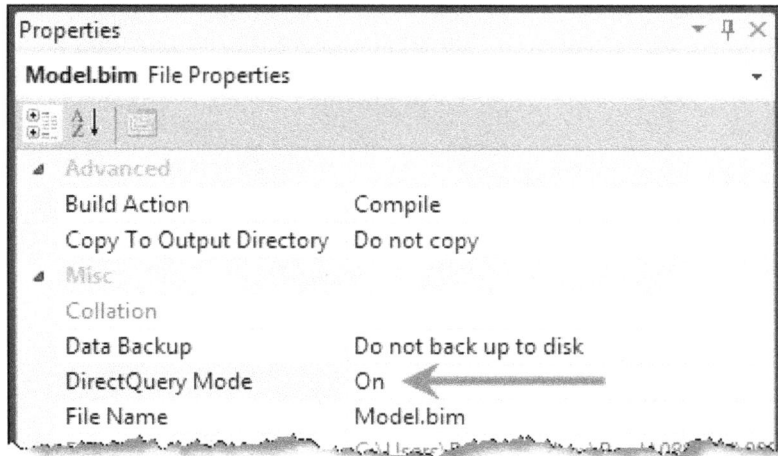

3. Return to the **Solution Explorer** pane, right-click on the solution name (`Direct Query Solution`), and select **Properties** from the pop-up menu.

4. Set the **Query Mode** option to **DirectQuery**.

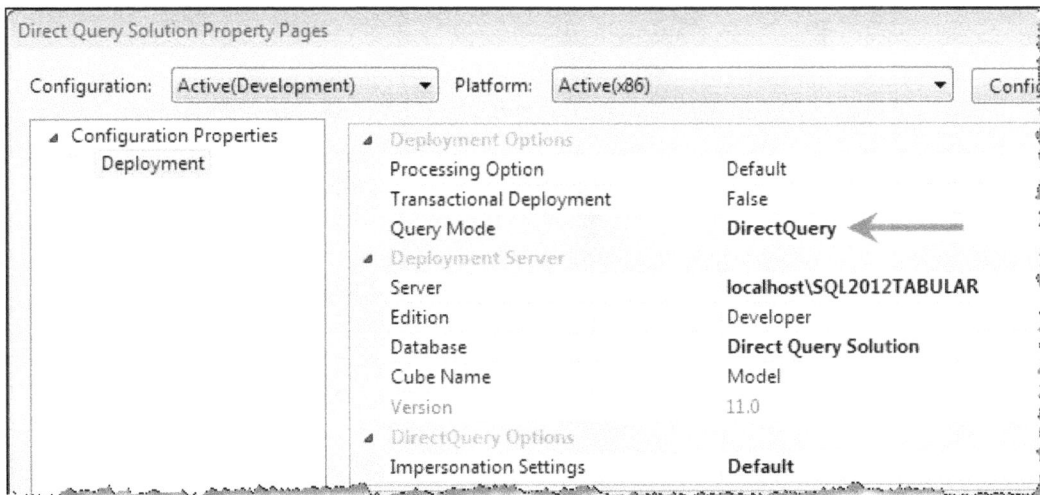

5. Select **OK** to accept the changes.

6. Click on the **Import From Data Source** button. Note that only **Microsoft SQL Server** connections are allowed. Click on **Next** to use the SQL Server data source.

7. Specify the **Server (Friendly) connection name** as `sql_dw` and specify the server. Finally, select the `tabular_modelling` database and test the connection.

8. Specify the impersonation (service account is allowable where the account has access). After all, this is a demonstration!

9. Select the following tables from the list of available tables (all tables are in the `dbo` schema). Specify the friendly names as indicated. For the `reseller_sales` table, filter the records to only import rows where the `currency_id` value is USD.

Tables	Friendly names
Dates	Dates
Products	Products
reseller_sales	Sales
Resellers	Stores
Geography	Geography

10. Click on **Finish** to import the data.

11. Switch to the diagram view. Note that most relationships have been created. Ensure that the relationship between `order_dt` in the `Sales` table is the primary relationship to the `Dates` table. Finally, create a relationship between `product_id` in the `Products` table and `product_id` in the `Sales` table.

12. Hide the `Sales` table from client tools.

13. Create a measure in the `Stores` table with the following formula:

```
Gross Sales:=sumx('Sales', [quantity]*[price])
```

14. Specify the format for `Gross Sales` as a decimal number with two decimal places. This is done by selecting the measure and with the **Properties** window open.

15. Finally, create a hierarchy in the `Dates` table (`Year`, `Month Name`, and `Day`). Specify the sort column for `Month Name` as `Month Number` and hide the `Month Number` column from client tools.

16. Click on the **Analyze in Excel** button and create a pivot that shows `Years` on the rows and `Gross Sales` as values. The pivot will look like the following screenshot (note that numbers have been formatted):

	A	B
1	Row Labels ▾	Gross Sales
2	2005	6,555,475
3	2006	18,541,506
4	2007	22,350,237
5	2008	10,622,435
6	**Grand Total**	**58,069,653**

17. Deploy the solution in SSDT. The progress window should show that only the metadata has been deployed; it will look like the following screenshot:

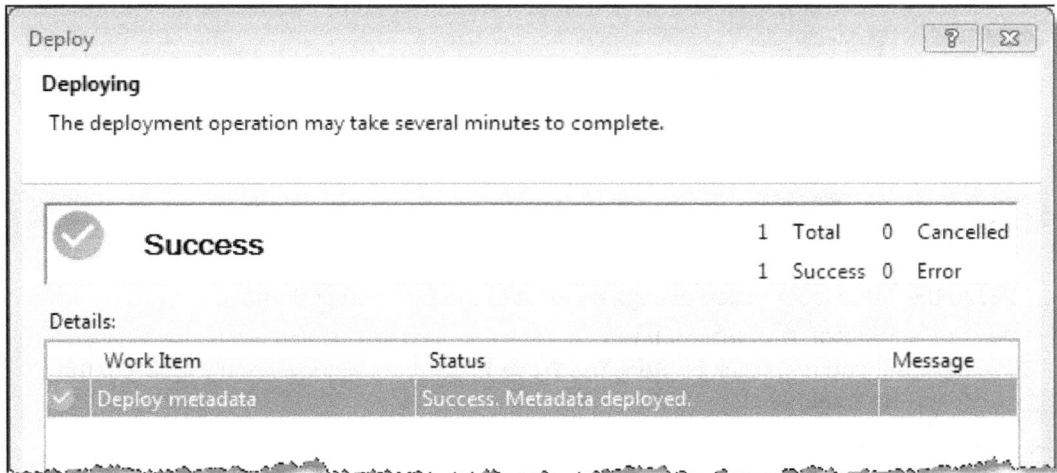

18. Connect to the deployed solution through Excel, that is, follow this menu path **Data | From Other Sources | From Analysis Services**.

19. Specify the appropriate tabular server and connect to the `Direct Query Solution` database (not to be confused with the workspace database).

20. After specifying the location for the pivot table, the following Error/Information box will be displayed:

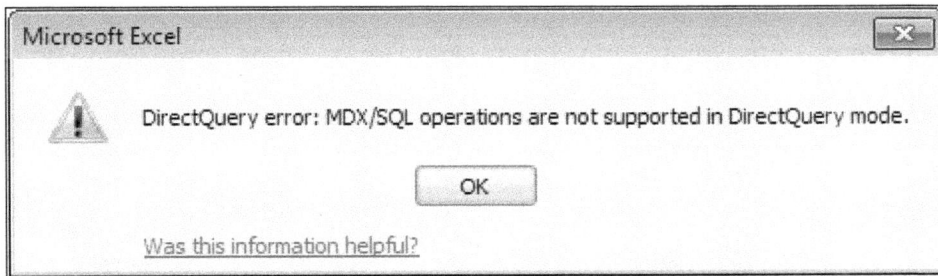

21. Clicking on **OK** will return to the pivot table (insert) location dialog. Click on **Cancel** to terminate the creation of the pivot table.

22. Create **SQL Server Trace** by clicking on the **SQL Server Profiler** option from the **Tools** menu in SSMS.

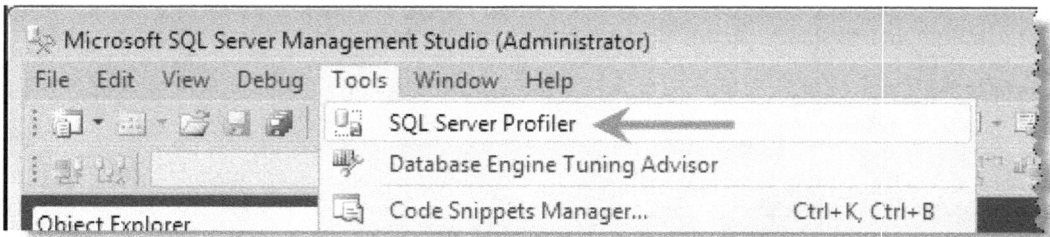

23. In the Trace (connection dialog), connect to the SQL Server database.

24. Check the **SQL:BatchCompleted** checkbox under **TSQL**, which will be the only event selected and then click on **Run**. The **Trace Properties** window should look like the following screenshot:

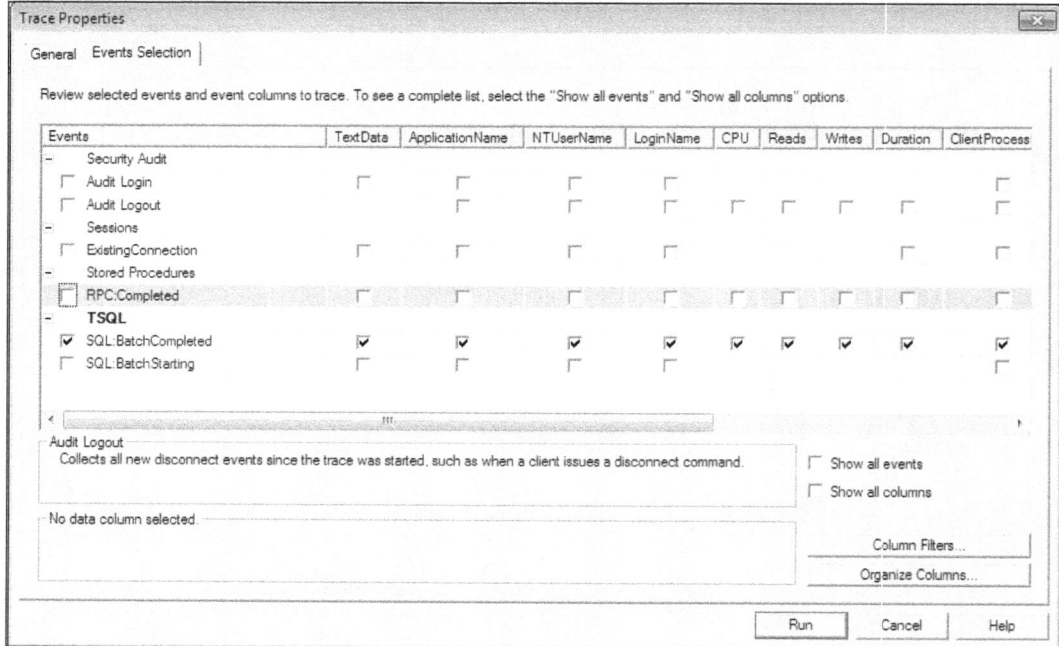

You can restrict the trace activity to the `tabular_modelling` database by checking the **Show all Columns** checkbox and then clicking on the **Column Filters** button. Then, select the **DatabaseName** filter group and specify the name `tabular_modelling`. The filter should look like the following screenshot:

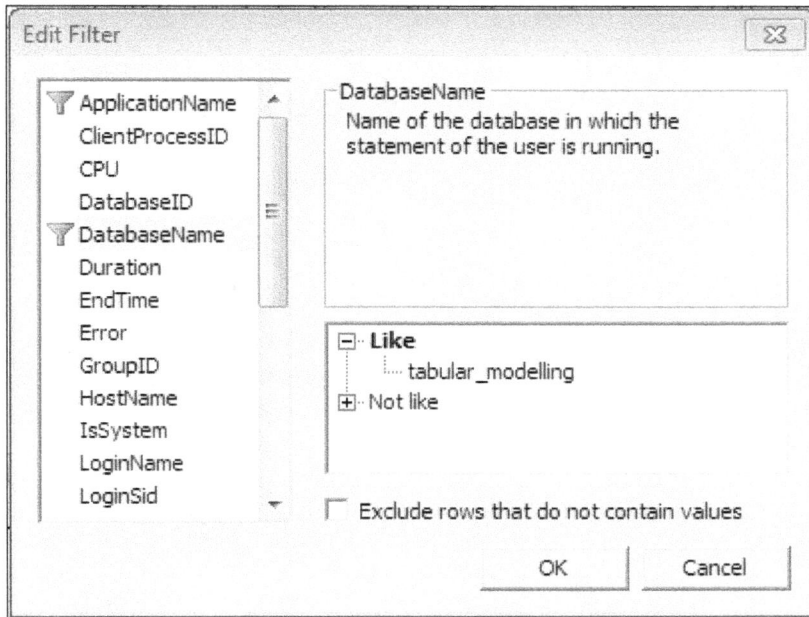

Click on **OK** to apply the filter.

25. Create a new MDX query against the tabular model and the `Direct Query Solution` database. The query is as follows:

```
define measure 'Stores'[SalesValue]
=  sumx('Sales', [quantity]*[price])
evaluate
(
  addcolumns
  (
    Values(Dates[Year])
    , "SalesValue",  'Stores'[SalesValue]
  )
)
```

26. Return to the trace window and note the outcomes. Stop the trace and close profiler.

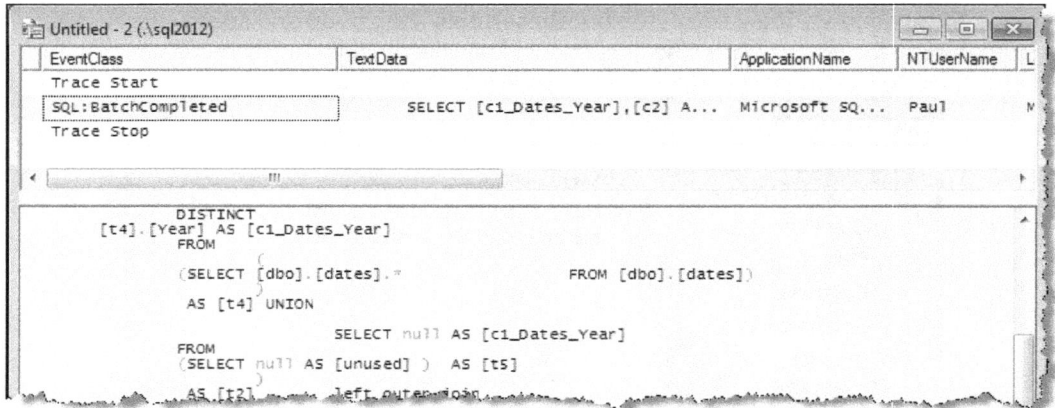

```
Untitled - 2 (.\sql2012)
EventClass                              TextData                                    ApplicationName      NTUserName    L
Trace Start
SQL:BatchCompleted                      SELECT [c1_Dates_Year],[c2] A...  Microsoft SQ...    Paul          M
Trace Stop
                  DISTINCT
      [t4].[Year] AS [c1_Dates_Year]
                  FROM
              (
              (SELECT [dbo].[dates].*               FROM [dbo].[dates])
              )
              AS [t4] UNION

                          SELECT null AS [c1_Dates_Year]
              FROM
              (SELECT null AS [unused] )   AS [t5]
              )
              AS [t2]         left outer join
```

27. Finally, expand the **Dates** and **Geography** nodes in the MDX query designer. An error **Error occurred retrieving child nodes:** .... is shown under each node as shown in the following screenshot:

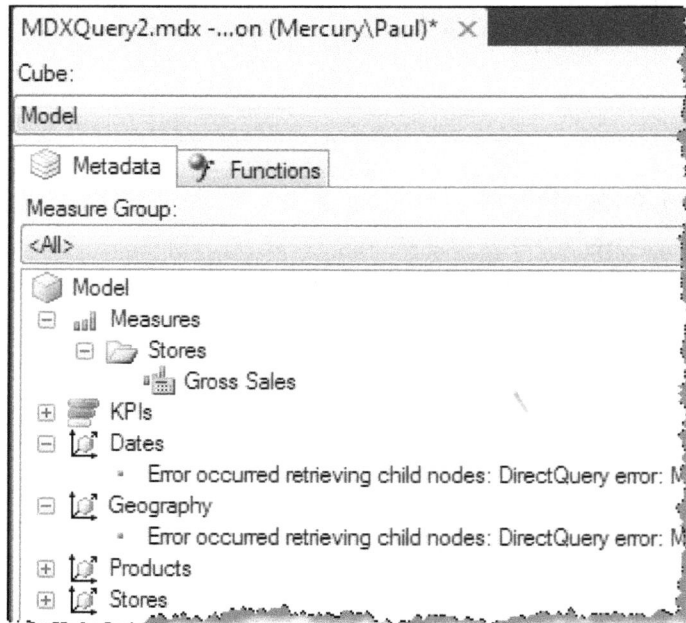

```
MDXQuery2.mdx -...on (Mercury\Paul)*   ✕
Cube:
Model
   📦 Metadata    🔧 Functions
Measure Group:
<All>
   📦 Model
   ⊟ 📊 Measures
       ⊟ 📁 Stores
           🏭 Gross Sales
   ⊞ 📊 KPIs
   ⊟ 📐 Dates
       ▪ Error occurred retrieving child nodes: DirectQuery error: M
   ⊟ 📐 Geography
       ▪ Error occurred retrieving child nodes: DirectQuery error: M
   ⊞ 📐 Products
   ⊞ 📐 Stores
```

The completed solution for this recipe is available from the online resources on the Packt Publishing website.

How it works...

This recipe demonstrates the nature and implications of the DirectQuery solutions.

Firstly, we can see the real time application of DirectQuery through the trace output (step 26 of the recipe). When a query is made to the tabular database, it is transformed into SQL and executed against the relational database.

The limited ability of the model to operate with existing client tools is also demonstrated. Naturally, this should be a major consideration for any model developer. Since most client tools are MDX-based (as seen with the pivot table and SSMS MDX browser), the existing tools may not be useable. Currently, only Power View (which is examined in the next chapter) is supported (other third-party tools may also exist).

Step 16 (*Analyzing the model in Excel*) shows that the pivot table can connect to the model but it is important to remind the reader that in this case, the model is the workspace database (which has storage in xVelocity mode).

9
Querying the Tabular Model with DAX

This chapter covers querying the tabular model with DAX. We'll be covering:

- ▸ Retrieving data from a single table
- ▸ Using projection to combine data from different tables
- ▸ Restricting data with filters and where conditions
- ▸ Deriving tables and selecting top n records

Introduction

Regardless of the amount of effort that has been applied in planning and building a model, it is likely that it will be required to answer a question that has not been anticipated. In this situation, the model must be queried.

Throughout this book, we have separated the concepts of the tabular model from the client tool that queries the model. This is because the client interprets the model and displays it to the user under a defined set of assumptions. Moreover, because the tabular model supports MDX (multidimensional) queries, the representation of the tabular model in most client tools is that of the multidimensional model (actually, Microsoft does not currently have a browser-style interface to query tabular models).

Because most client tools (including SQL Server Management Studio) show the tabular model in a multidimensional style, querying the tabular model with DAX can be extremely difficult because you cannot see the underlying tabular schema (and therefore, do not know the structure of the model). For example, consider the following two screenshots. The first shows a multidimensional representation, whereas the second shows the tabular representation:

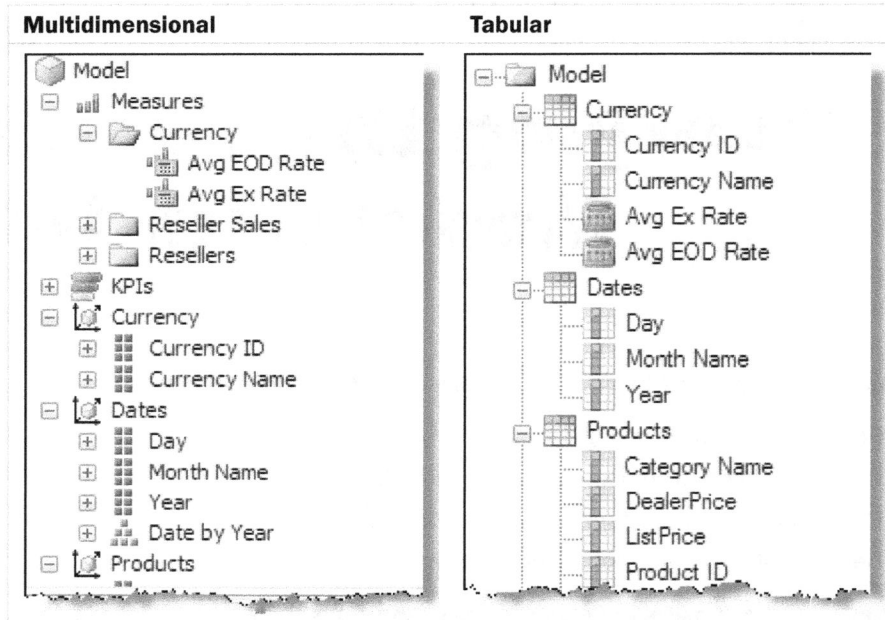

There are two main differences between the tabular and multidimensional view of the model, which are summarized as follows:

> ▸ There is no concept of a measure group in tabular modeling. Tabular models associate measures (or calculations) within the tables that they are defined in. Notice that in the multidimensional representation, the currency conversion measures are displayed in a measure group (**Currency**), whereas in the tabular representation, they are attached to the Currency table.

> ▸ There is no concept of hierarchies within a tabular model. The Date by Year hierarchy (even though it is defined in the tabular model) is not visible (or an object) in the tabular model.

While querying the model with MDX is user friendly (and provides a richer client experience), formulas must be written in DAX and may require debugging; therefore, it's better if the model is evaluated and queried with DAX.

> The recipes in this chapter are presented using a tool called DAX Studio. This is a free add-in for Excel that can be used to connect to PowerPivot and Tabular Servers, and is available at `https://daxstudio.codeplex.com/`.

Retrieving data from a single table

The first recipe in this chapter examines how to display results from a table in the model; keep in mind that the table may contain calculated columns and these are also included in its structure. The base script includes several alterations, so that segments of the table may be retrieved.

The workbook (with the associated model) is available from the online resources at `http://www.packtpub.com`.

Getting ready

The model used in this chapter is available from the online resources at `http://www.packtpub.com`. We have installed DAX Studio so that the model within the workbook can be queried. Alternatively, the model can be imported to a tabular server and queried through SSMS (SQL Server Management Studio) although you would not see the model schema definition.

> While using DAX Studio to query an embedded model (that is, a PowerPivot model stored in the workbook), ensure that the active cell is found on a pivot table that relates to the tabular model (while launching DAX Studio). An introduction to DAX Studio can be found at `http://wp.me/p1rCld-7e`.

How to do it...

Let us start by retrieving all the data available from the `Resellers` table:

1. Open DAX Studio and enter the following statement:

```
evaluate('Resellers')
```

2. The result (a table), that is shown will list the contents of the `Resellers` table, for example, the following screenshot shows the grid output:

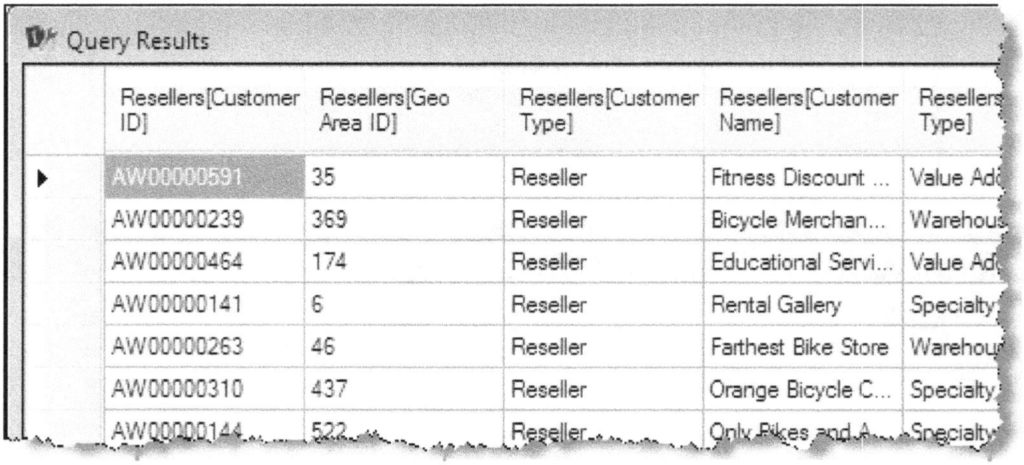

Resellers[Customer ID]	Resellers[Geo Area ID]	Resellers[Customer Type]	Resellers[Customer Name]	Resellers Type]
AW00000591	35	Reseller	Fitness Discount ...	Value Add
AW00000239	369	Reseller	Bicycle Merchan...	Warehous
AW00000464	174	Reseller	Educational Servi...	Value Ad
AW00000141	6	Reseller	Rental Gallery	Specialty
AW00000263	46	Reseller	Farthest Bike Store	Warehou
AW00000310	437	Reseller	Orange Bicycle C...	Specialty
AW00000144	522	Reseller	Only Bikes and A...	Specialty

3. Notice that the list is not in the proper order. To change this, so that the list appears ordered, add an `Order By` clause to the `evaluate` statement.

```
evaluate('Resellers') order by [customer Id]
```

How it works...

The `evaluate` statement returns the table that has been defined as its argument, and is the essential requirement to return a query. In this example, the table definition is like that of an existing table (that is, the `Resellers` table).

The syntax of the DAX query allows a high degree of flexibility and includes the ability to define measures and specify the ordering of results. The full syntax is as follows:

```
[DEFINE { MEASURE <tableName>[<name>] = <expression> }
EVALUATE <table>
[ORDER BY {<expression> [{ASC | DESC}]}[, …]
[START AT {<value>|<parameter>} [, …]]]
```

So far, the `table` argument for `EVALUATE` has been an existing table; however, the definition can be any DAX syntax that returns a table. Most probably, this could be an existing table that has been filtered. Consider the `Sales Group` calculation in the `Resellers` table, which assigns each `Reseller` to a group based on their sales value (see the *Grouping by binning and sorting with ranks* recipe in *Chapter 5, Applied Modeling*). The values for this field can be easily seen by creating a Pivot based on the field, but let's consider the situation where we want to show `Resellers` that have high sales (these are in the `$800K - $900K` bin range). As `filter` returns a table, we can use this within the `evaluate` statement.

```
evaluate
(
   filter('Resellers', 'Resellers'[Sales Group]="$800K - $900K")
)
```

The result of the preceding `evaluate` statement is as shown in the following screenshot:

Resellers[Customer ID]	Resellers[Geo Area ID]	Resellers[Customer Type]	Resellers[Customer Name]	Resellers[Reseller Type]	Rese Sales
AW00000170	567	Reseller	Excellent Riding ...	Value Added Res...	85385
AW00000328	591	Reseller	Totes & Baskets ...	Value Added Res...	81712
AW00000502	254	Reseller	Metropolitan Bicy...	Warehouse	82812
AW00000697	601	Reseller	Brakes and Gears	Value Added Res...	88227

There's more...

The use of the predicate `'Resellers'[Sales Group]="$800K - $900K"` in the previous query allows us to retrieve the data, which meets the filter condition, from the `Resellers` table. While this achieves our immediate goal, it relies on the prior knowledge that the highest group is in the `$800K - $900K` range and a hardcoded value in the query. In order to overcome this, we can create a DAX calculation within the `filter`, or define a calculation for the model and then use this (model calculation) within the query.

Descriptive text fields are notoriously poor identifiers for ordering. In fact, [Sales Group] has a `Sorted By` field of [Round Down Order] to achieve the required order. This field can, therefore, be used to determine the highest element of [Sales Group]. More specifically, the highest [Sales Group] element is determined by the lowest [Round Down Order]. If we wish to dynamically determine the resellers of the highest group, we could embed a calculation to determine the minimum value of [Round Down Order] (remembering that this needs to be evaluated over all the `Resellers` table's rows) and use this instead of the hard coded value. Our query would then become:

```
evaluate
(
  filter('Resellers', [Round Down Order] =
    (calculate (Min('Resellers'[Round Down Order]),
    ALL('Resellers')))
  )
)
```

Alternatively, we may want to define the minimum value as a measure for the query, and then use it instead of an embedded calculation. In this situation, we could utilize the `define measure` clause of the syntax and use the query as follows:

```
define measure 'Resellers'[lowest Order] =
  calculate(Min('Resellers'[Round Down Order]), ALL('Resellers'))

evaluate
(
  filter('Resellers',
  'Resellers'[Round Down Order]=[lowest order]
  )
)
```

Using projection to combine data from different tables

The evaluation of an entire table (as shown in the previous recipe, *Retrieving data from a single table*) excludes the wider concept of projection, because the example returns all the columns from a single table. More often than not, we wish to return only a subset of columns (or perhaps even derived columns) from one or more tables. Unlike SQL, which allows projection in its syntax, DAX has no succinct projection equivalent.

Consider the following SQL statement, which selects column_a from table_a and column_b from table_b.

```
Select table_a.column_a, table_b.column_b From …
```

Using DAX, we cannot specify a projection in the same manner (as follows):

```
Evaluate('table_a'[column_a], 'table_b'[column_b])
```

If we wish to mimic this activity using DAX, we must define the table as part of the `evaluate` statement. This recipe examines how to do that.

Getting ready

This recipe shows the concepts of projection by answering a common type of question (from our tabular model):

What were the total sales, by country, for the bike category in 2008 and what proportion of bike sales does each country have?

How to do it...

Create a new query with the following syntax:

```
define measure 'Reseller Sales'[2008 Sales] =
  calculate('Reseller Sales'[Local Gross Sales],
  'Dates'[Year] = 2008)

measure 'Reseller Sales'[2008 Bike Sales] =
  calculate('Reseller Sales'[2008 Sales],
  'Products'[Category Name] = "Bikes")

measure 'Reseller Sales'[2008 Bike Ratio] =
  'Reseller Sales'[2008 Bike Sales]/'Reseller Sales'[2008 Sales]

evaluate(addcolumns(summarize('Geography', 'Geography'[Country]),
  "Total Sales", 'Reseller Sales'[2008 Sales], "Bike Sales",
  'Reseller Sales'[2008 Bike Sales], "Bike Ratio",
  'Reseller Sales'[2008 Bike Ratio]))
```

The result of this query will be displayed, as shown in the following screenshot:

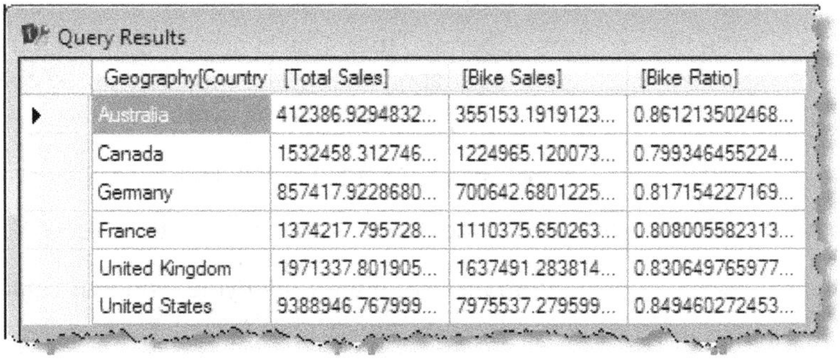

Geography[Country	[Total Sales]	[Bike Sales]	[Bike Ratio]
Australia	412386.9294832...	355153.1919123...	0.861213502468...
Canada	1532458.312746...	1224965.120073...	0.799346455224...
Germany	857417.9228680...	700642.6801225...	0.817154227169...
France	1374217.795728...	1110375.650263...	0.808005582313...
United Kingdom	1971337.801905...	1637491.283814...	0.830649765977...
United States	9388946.767999...	7975537.279599...	0.849460272453...

How it works...

The query is essentially broken down into three steps. These steps are broadly defined as measure creation, base table definition, and table extension (adding additional columns).

Firstly, the measures required for the model are defined. The definition of a measure (as far as the calculation is concerned) is essentially the same as the calculation of a measure in the model. For example, 2008 sales are defined by the following formula:

```
calculate('Reseller Sales'[Local Gross Sales],
  'Dates'[Year] = 2008)
```

Here, the existing sales measure within the model (`[Local Gross Sales]`) is filtered by the year 2008. Note that DAX does not include a clause for `WHERE` (as would be the case in SQL), so the filter is applied in the measure definition. In running the query, the statement is evaluated over the bounds of the model (that is, the table bounds).

The value for bike sales in 2008 (`[2008 Bike Sales]`) leverages the defined measure for the sales of the year 2008 with an additional restriction for products belonging to the bike category. While we could achieve the same outcome by fully defining bike sales of the year 2008 in a single measure (as follows), the measure definition for `[2008 Bike Sales]` shows how a measure created in the query can be re-used. The same outcome would be achieved with `[2008 Bike Sales]` being defined as follows:

```
calculate('Reseller Sales'[Local Gross Sales],
  'Products'[Category Name] = "Bikes", 'Dates'[Year] = 2008)
```

Next, we focus on the table definition that is embedded in `evaluate`. Here, the table is defined in two stages. Firstly, a base table is defined as a distinct list of countries, and secondly, the base table has columns appended to it with the additional measures that we have defined.

The `SUMMARIZE` syntax has been used to define the base table (that is, the list of countries). The `SUMMARIZE` syntax shown, as follows, essentially groups the data that is in a table. This is equivalent to the `GROUP BY` statement (SQL) applied to a single table.

```
SUMMARIZE(<table>, <groupBy_columnName>, <groupBy_columnName>)
```

Secondly, the base table has columns appended to it. This is achieved through the use of the `ADDCOLUMNS` function. The `ADDCOLUMNS` function simply appends calculated columns to a table by defining its name and expression. It has the following syntax:

```
ADDCOLUMNS(<table>, <name>, <expression>[, <name>, <expression>]...)
```

Therefore, the base table (as a list of countries) has been extended to include the measures.

It is important to recognize that the relationships in the underlying model are still being used by the query.

There's more...

In this recipe, the use of SUMMARIZE produces a single column table. An alternative to this is to use the VALUES function. The VALUES function returns a list of distinct values based on the column reference and has the following syntax:

```
VALUES(<column>)
```

Therefore, the body of the evaluate statement could also be written as follows:

```
evaluate
(
  addcolumns
  (
    values('Geography'[Country]), "Total Sales",
      'Reseller Sales'[2008 Sales], ….
  )
)
```

Using SUMMARIZE would only be required when there is more than one column from the same table to return.

Restricting data with filters and where conditions

In the *Using projection to combine data from different tables* recipe, we stated that there is no WHERE clause in DAX. If this type of restriction is to be applied to a result set, it must be defined by a query, and this is the focus of this recipe. Here, we seek to answer the question:

Which customers had sales in 2008 and what was their sales value (for that year)?

Getting ready

The model used in this recipe is the sales data that has been used in this chapter (see the workbook Model.xlsx, which is available from online resources at http://www.packtpub.com).

How to do it...

This recipe examines two queries. Firstly, listing customers and their sales value in 2008, and secondly, listing customers that had sales in 2008 with their sales value.

1. Create a new query to show the 2008 sales values of customers. The query is as follows:

```
define measure 'Resellers'[Sales] =
  calculate('Reseller Sales'[USD Gross Sales],
  'Dates'[Year]=2008)

evaluate
(
  addcolumns
  (
    values('Resellers'[Customer ID]), "Sales",
      'Resellers'[Sales]
  )
)
```

2. Execute the query and note that the result lists 701 customers.

3. Create a query to show the customers who had sales in 2008 and the associated value of their sales (for that year). The query is as follows:

```
define measure 'Resellers'[Sales 2008] =
  calculate('Reseller Sales'[USD Gross Sales],
  'Dates'[Year]=2008)

measure 'Resellers'[Sales 2008 Rows] =
  calculate(countrows('Reseller Sales'),
  'Dates'[Year]=2008)

measure 'Resellers'[Sales] =
  'Reseller Sales'[USD Gross Sales]

evaluate
(
  filter
  (
    addcolumns
    (
      values('Resellers'[Customer ID]), "Sales",
        'Resellers'[Sales 2008], "Sales (all)",
        'Resellers'[Sales]
    ), 'Resellers'[Sales 2008 Rows] > 0
  )
)
```

4. Execute the query and note the result. There are now 466 rows in the result set, the measure [Sales 2008] shows the sales for 2008, and the [Sales (all)] measure shows the sales for all years.

How it works...

Although there is no equivalent of WHERE in DAX, evaluate returns the table that has been defined. This definition can include a filter context (that restricts the table), so that the rows returned are reduced according to a condition; this is effectively a WHERE clause as most of the results are restricted (as would be the case with a WHERE clause in SQL).

In the second query, we achieve this by filtering based on customers that had sales in 2008, that is, the rows in the Sales table relating to the year 2008.

However, the use of a filter context in this way does not limit the evaluation of other measures that are defined within the query. There has been no restriction to the Sales table's data; only the customers are shown. Other measures are evaluated over the entire model (or the table bounds of the model).

There's more...

Should we wish to implement a more "classical" WHERE condition (that is, restricting the rows of the underlying table), calculations need to be applied when the table is filtered. This can be achieved by extending the use of summarize to include calculations. For this, we could execute the following query:

```
evaluate
(
  summarize(
    filter('Reseller Sales', related('Dates'[Year])=2008),
      [Customer Id], "Sales", 'Reseller Sales'[USD Gross Sales]
  )
)
```

Note how the filter is applied through the related Year in the Dates table.

Deriving tables and selecting top n records

As a comparison to DAX, SQL is a mature language that has a variety of mechanisms for temporarily defining and using tables. One of the reasons for using this type of feature is that a result may need to be pre-computed before it is applied in the outer constructs of a query.

Consider the situation of accumulating sales based on the sales values' ranks, as shown in the following screenshot:

Resellers[Customer ID]	[Sales]	[Rank]	[cum sales]
AW00000448	246662.8495754...	1	246662.8495754...
AW00000085	220496.6580000...	2	467159.5075754...
AW00000599	211318.9469000...	3	678478.4544754...
AW00000016	202644.1140716...	4	881122.5685471...
AW00000520	200652.9307579...	5	1081775.499305...
AW00000546	189204.4222000...	6	1270979.921505...
AW00000433	187964.844	7	1458944.765505...

This type of query must pre-compute values before they can be used. Logically, the query must determine each customer's sales value, then rank the customers based on that value, and then (finally) determine (on a row-by-row basis) the total value of sales for all rows with a lower rank. Clearly, there is an order to implement this type of query because one set of values cannot be calculated before the other is complete. Using temporary structures is an excellent method for achieving this.

Unfortunately, there is no declaration to derive a temporary table in DAX. The query must utilize a nesting functionality to incrementally build the output. This recipe looks at how to achieve that with a DAX query.

Getting ready

The goal of this recipe is to rank our resellers based on their 2008 sales and then produce an accumulating total. This involves two steps, firstly ranking them and then accumulating sales based on that rank. The RANK function was examined in the *Grouping by binning and sorting with ranks* recipe in *Chapter 5, Applied Modeling*.

The model used in this recipe is the same that has been used in prior recipes of this chapter, and is available from the online resources at http://www.packtpub.com.

How to do it...

Start by defining a base table:

1. Create a new query that defines customers, their sales (for 2008), and rank (based on those sales). We also order the results by that rank (so that the output is more visually meaningful).

```
define measure 'Resellers'[Sales 2008] =
  calculate('Reseller Sales'[USD Gross Sales],
  'Dates'[Year]=2008)

measure 'Resellers'[Sales Rank] = rankx(all('Resellers'),
  'Resellers'[Sales 2008])

evaluate
(
  addcolumns
  (
    values('Resellers'[Customer ID]), "Sales",
      'Resellers'[Sales 2008], "Rank",
      'Resellers'[Sales Rank]
  )
)

order by [Rank] asc
```

The result of this query will be displayed, as shown in the following screenshot:

Resellers[Customer ID]	[Sales]	[Rank]
AW00000448	246662.84957548417	1
AW00000085	220496.65800000002	2
AW00000599	211318.94690000007	3
AW00000016	202644.11407166766	4
AW00000520	200652.93075796368	5
AW00000546	189204.42220000003	6
AW00000433	187964.844	7
AW00000502	187702.26705881933	8

2. Now, extend this query to add the accumulating sales:

```
define measure 'Resellers'[Sales] =
  calculate('Reseller Sales'[USD Gross Sales],
  'Dates'[Year]=2008)

measure 'Resellers'[Rank] = rankx(all('resellers'),
  'Resellers'[Sales])

evaluate
(
  addcolumns
  (
    addcolumns
    (
      values('Resellers'[Customer ID]), "sales",
        'Resellers'[Sales], "Rank", 'Resellers'[Rank]
    ), "cum sales", calculate('Resellers'[Sales],
      filter(all('Resellers'),
      'Resellers'[Rank] <= [Rank]))
  )
)

order by 'Resellers'[Sales] desc
```

The result of this query will be displayed, as shown in the following screenshot:

Resellers[Customer ID]	[Sales]	[Rank]	[cum sales]
AW00000448	246662.8495754...	1	246662.8495754...
AW00000085	220496.6580000...	2	467159.5075754...
AW00000599	211318.9469000...	3	678478.4544754...
AW00000016	202644.1140716...	4	881122.5685471...
AW00000520	200652.9307579...	5	1081775.499305...
AW00000546	189204.4222000...	6	1270979.921505...
AW00000433	187964.844	7	1458944.765505...

How it works...

It has already been stated that there is no method of defining and manipulating a temporary table in DAX. In order to solve this problem and use the results of a previously generated query, we need to incrementally build the result set by sequentially adding columns to the previous table's output. This is seen in the use of the nested `addcolumns` statements, where each `addcolumns` statement is used to extend the previous table's results.

For example, we define a base table (defined with the innermost `addcolumns` statement) and extend that with another `addcolumns` statement. Here, the results of the inner table can be used in much the same way as a correlated subquery would be used in SQL. The outer statement is executed for each row of the inner context, or perhaps more appropriately, the outer calculation is applied under the filter context of the inner one.

This can be better represented in a pseudo code with the following statement:

```
For each
Record as { Customer, Sales, Rank }
List { Record, { sum (sales) where Rank <= Record.Rank }}
```

The use of `For each` in the preceding statement specifies that the `sum` function (which is appended to the `Record` table in the `List {}` line) should be applied in the context of the records' row. This makes sense when we consider that each row has a rank that determines its order (based on sales) and we need to sum all the records with a lower (or equal) rank.

Note that it is not enough to apply the accumulating sum calculation without considering the current row's `Rank`. For example, the `evaluate` section of the query should nest `addcolumns`, as shown in the following snippet:

```
evaluate
(
  addcolumns
  (
    values('Resellers'[Customer ID]), "sales", 'Resellers'[Sales],
      "Rank", 'Resellers'[Rank], "cum sales",
      calculate('Resellers'[Sales], filter(all('Resellers'),
      'Resellers'[Rank] <= [Rank]))
  )
)
```

The result of this query is not accumulating sales, but the total sales for the year on each row (that is, all sales for 2008). Why? This is because the following calculation removes any filter that exists in the table (with the statement `all('Resellers')`):

```
calculate('Resellers'[Sales], filter( all('Resellers'),
  'Resellers'[Rank] <= [Rank]))
```

Trying to reapply a filter with the predicate `'Resellers'[Rank] <= [Rank]` always evaluates to true as each row's rank is equal to itself. No rows are restricted and the calculation `'Resellers'[Sales]` is applied to all rows.

There's more...

There are two variations to this type of query, which are common business additions to the implementations of rank and accumulating values. The first is the **TOP N** query, which returns a given number of records (for example, the highest selling five customers), and the second is the **TOP** % query, which returns the number of records based on a threshold value (for example, the customers that are contributing 80 percent of the sales value).

DAX provides a `TOPN` function, which returns a specified number of records based on a sort condition. The `TOPN` function has the following syntax:

```
TOPN(<n_value>, <table>, <orderBy_expression>,
  [<order>[, <orderBy_expression>, [<order>]]…])
```

Implementing this function directly against the `Resellers` table (`Resellers` has an existing column for sales rank) to return the five highest selling customers could be achieved with the following query:

```
evaluate(topn( 5, 'Resellers', 'Resellers'[Sales Rank], true))

order by 'Resellers'[Sales Rank]
```

Here, the n_value argument of `5` represents the top five records. The orderBy_ expression argument is the (existing) column `[Sales Rank]` with the `order` argument set to ascending. Valid values for the order are `0` (or `FALSE`) for descending and `1` (or `TRUE`) for ascending. The default value, if the `order` argument is omitted, is `FALSE`.

It is unlikely that a model does not contain a convenient column that can apply the TOP N query. For example, we need to find who the top five bike sellers for 2008 are. For this, the measure needs to be defined for the bike sales of 2008 and applied to a table. This table is then filtered in with the `TOPN` function. The query would be as follows:

```
define measure 'Resellers'[Bike Sales 2008] =
  calculate('Reseller Sales'[USD Gross Sales], 'Dates'[Year]=2008,
'Products'[Category Name]="Bikes")

evaluate
(
  topn
  (
    5,
    /* table */
    addcolumns
```

```
      (
        values('Resellers'[Customer ID]), "Bike Sales 2008",
          'Resellers'[Bike Sales 2008]
      ), 'Resellers'[Bike Sales 2008], false
    )
  )


    order by 'Resellers'[Bike Sales 2008] desc
```

As an alternate approach to TOPN, we could simply implement a filter based on a derived rank. In this situation, the evaluate syntax of the previous query would be:

```
evaluate
(
  filter
  (
    addcolumns
    (
      values('Resellers'[Customer ID]), "sales",
'Resellers'[Sales], "Rank", 'Resellers'[Rank]
    ), [Rank] <= 5
  )
)
```

Finally, we examine the implementation of a TOP % query. To do this, we apply the **Pareto** principle, which is a common way to analyze data. This principle roughly states that only 20 percent of elements account for 80 of the total worth. Using our sales data, we would suggest that 20 percent of the customers contribute to 80 percent of the total sales value. Rather than validating this on the data, a more appropriate DAX related question might be "Which of the customers account for 80 percent of sales?" The query is shown as follows:

```
define measure 'Resellers'[Sales] =
calculate('Reseller Sales'[USD Gross Sales], 'Dates'[Year]=2008)

measure 'Resellers'[Rank] =
  rankx(all('resellers'), 'Resellers'[Sales] )

measure 'Resellers'[Total Sales] =
  calculate('Resellers'[Sales], all('Resellers'))

evaluate
(
  filter
  (
    addcolumns
    (
```

```
        addcolumns
        (
          values('Resellers'[Customer ID]), "sales",
            'Resellers'[Sales], "Rank", 'Resellers'[Rank]
        ), "cum sales", calculate('Resellers'[Sales],
          filter( all('Resellers'), 'Resellers'[Rank] <= [Rank])),
          "cum sales %", calculate('Resellers'[Sales],
          filter( all('Resellers'), 'Resellers'[Rank] <= [Rank]))
        / 'Resellers'[Total Sales]
      ), [cum sales %]<0.8
    )
  )


    order by 'Resellers'[Rank] asc
```

Here, the base query used in the recipe has been extended to include a column [cum sales %], which calculates the accumulating percentage of sales (naturally, this is based on the rank position of each customer). The purpose of this column is to show the ratio of the accumulated sales to the total sales (or each additional customer's contribution to the sales in terms of the percentage). Then, we can simply apply a filter to show the first 80 percent of customers (which is automatically implied as [cum sales %] is determined based on the rank).

10
Visualizing Data
with Power View

In this chapter, we will cover:

- ▶ Creating a Power View report
- ▶ Creating and manipulating charts
- ▶ Using tiles (parameters)
- ▶ Using and showing images
- ▶ Automating the table fields with default field sets
- ▶ Working with table behavior and card control
- ▶ Using maps
- ▶ Using multiples (Trellis Charts)

Introduction

Throughout this book, we have discussed tabular modeling with respect to the models and the client tools that interpret the models and display them to the enduser. Tabular models support MDX-based clients, and therefore, current clients can still be used against tabular models with the same look and feel as they had for multidimensional cubes. Examples of this have been demonstrated in the use of pivot tables, which are shown to the user in a multidimensional format.

However, the tabular model contains some settings that are designed for tabular clients. Exposing these features is the focus of this chapter. Here, we continue with the self-service theme of this book and introduce **Power View** (based in Excel 2013) as a reporting tool to present information to the enduser. We show how the model can be managed to present information to the user. To this end, the chapter is also an introduction to Power View. Power View has a different approach to traditional reporting. In traditional reporting (tools), the user designs a report (based on a metadata and structure) and then executes (or renders) the report to see the results. In contrast, Power View is designed to be a real-time analysis solution where users interact directly with a canvas. When any change is made to that canvas, the results are immediately reflected in the report.

Power View is available as a **SharePoint** (reporting) service or a feature in certain editions of Excel 2013 (Office 365 and Professional Plus).

The model in this chapter is similar to the `Sales Model` that has been presented in prior chapters. However, in this chapter, the model sources its data from a data mart, which is based on a star design. This can be seen in the `Products` (and `Customers`) table where the `ID` field is no longer the unique identifier for the table. These tables are modeled as Type II dimensions (or slowly changing dimensions). Here, the dimension row is uniquely identified by the surrogate key (in each table, the field is suffixed by `class_dk`). It is the surrogate keys that join the `Sales` data. Also, note that the `Sales` data has been flattened (and has no header—detail relationship). This schema is shown in the following screenshot:

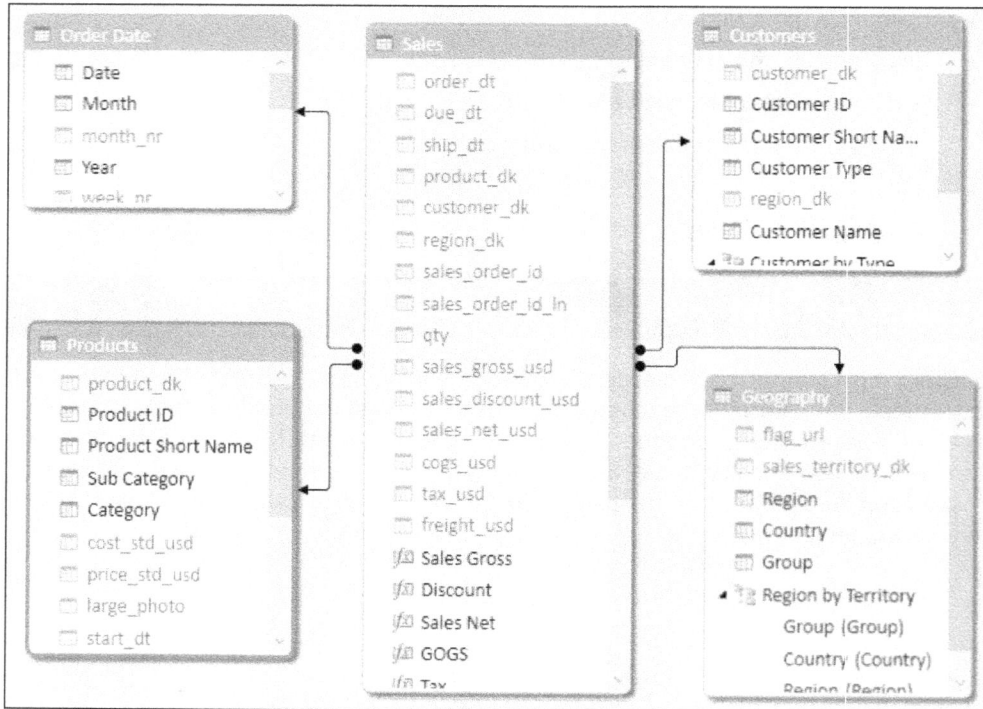

> Although there are some subtle changes in the operation of PowerPivot in the Excel 2013 model when compared to the 2010 model (for example, the calculated values are shown with function icons, rather than calculations), the creation of the model and its design is identical to Excel 2010.

Creating a Power View report

The first recipe examines how to create a Power View report and navigate the reporting surface. Our goal is simple, we have been asked to investigate trends in sales by `Product Category`, `Month`, and `Country`. This is done by creating a grid on the design surface and then manipulating it.

Getting ready

This recipe is based on the PowerPivot model shown above—the model in the workbook (`Sales Model 2013.xlsx`) is available from the online resources. Once a tabular model has been converted to an Excel 2013 format, the model is no longer compatible with the Excel 2010 add-in (and cannot be opened or used in Excel 2010).

All the tabular modeling features that relate to Power View can be set in Excel 2010 (the same menu paths are used); however, the results are only visible in Excel 2013 (since this is the only version of Excel that has Power View available). An Excel 2010 version of this file is also available from the online resources.

The Power View and PowerPivot add-ins may also require activation in Excel 2013 (this needs to be done only once). To check if these add-ins are active (or confirm if they are available in your version of Excel), perform the following:

1. Open Excel (so that there is no workbook open). Depending on how you have opened Excel, the following are two views available to you:

    ❑   If you opened Excel from an icon (on the Windows workspace), you will see the following screen. Click on the **Open Other Workbooks** option as shown in the following screenshot:

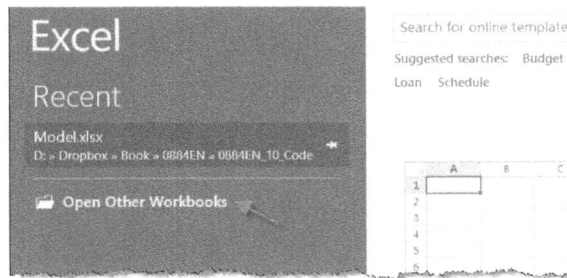

      ❏   If you closed all the workbooks that you had opened in Excel (and the screen looks like the following), simply click on the **FILE** option as shown in the following screenshot:

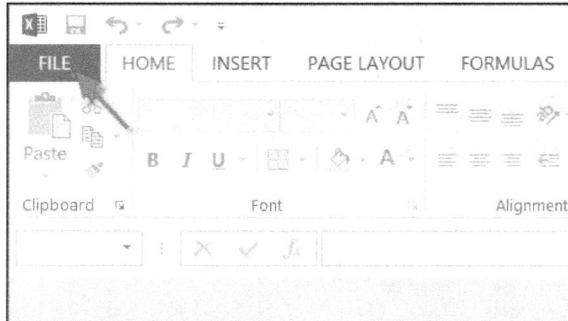

2. Click on **Options** from the list.

3. Click on **Add-Ins** from the navigation panel and confirm that the **Power Pivot for Excel** add-in and the **Power View** add-in appears under the **Active Application Add-ins** (as shown in the following screenshot):

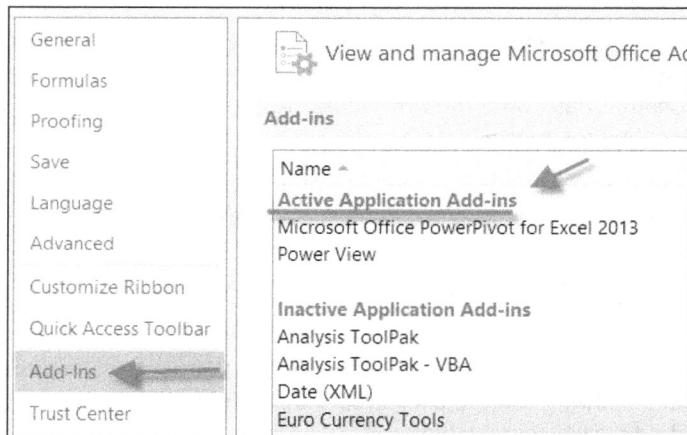

4. If the add-ins do not appear (as active), they have not been activated—they will need to be activated now. Select **COM Add-ins** from the **Manage** drop-down list (at the bottom of the window), then click on the **GO** button.

5. A new window will open displaying **COM Add-Ins**. Ensure that the PowerPivot and **Power View** add-ins are checked(as shown in the following screenshot) and then click on the **OK** button:

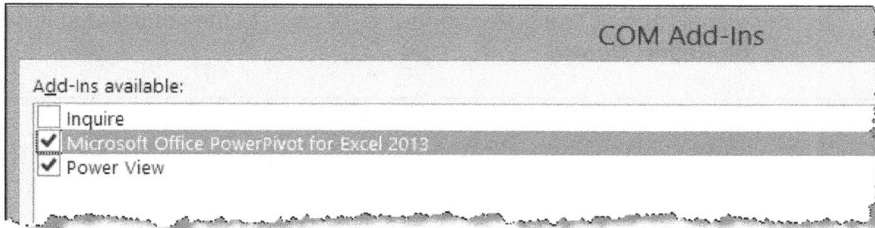

How to do it...

Open the `Sales Model 2013.xlsx` workbook and create a new Power View report. Reports appear in the same manner as worksheets, with a tab at the bottom of the Excel window.

1. Insert a new Power View report by clicking on the **Power View** button from the **Insert** Tab as shown in the following screenshot:

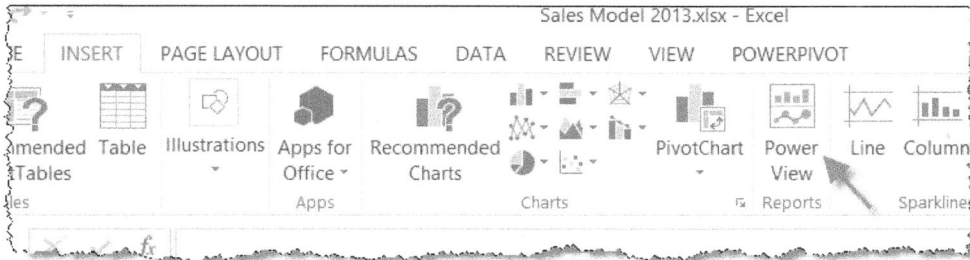

> If this is the first time that Power View has run, Excel may ask permission to install **Silver Light**. If this occurs, permit the installation (this is required only once).

2. A new Power View report is inserted. The design canvas consists of four sections, shown in the following screenshot. These are described as follows:

   ❑ The **Report Canvas** (the report) displays the data to the user.

   ❑ The **Filters Pane** applies a global (report-wide) filter (also titled a view filter) to the data, without the need to filter a control on the report.

   ❑ The Power View **Field List** shows the tables and fields in the model.

□ The **Control Content** shows what model fields are used in the active control (that is, the one that is selected on the **Report Canvas**). The **Control Content** also allows the user to add and remove fields from the active control and therefore, change the format and appearance of that control (or visualization). The active control is (of course) the control that is selected in the **Report Canvas**.

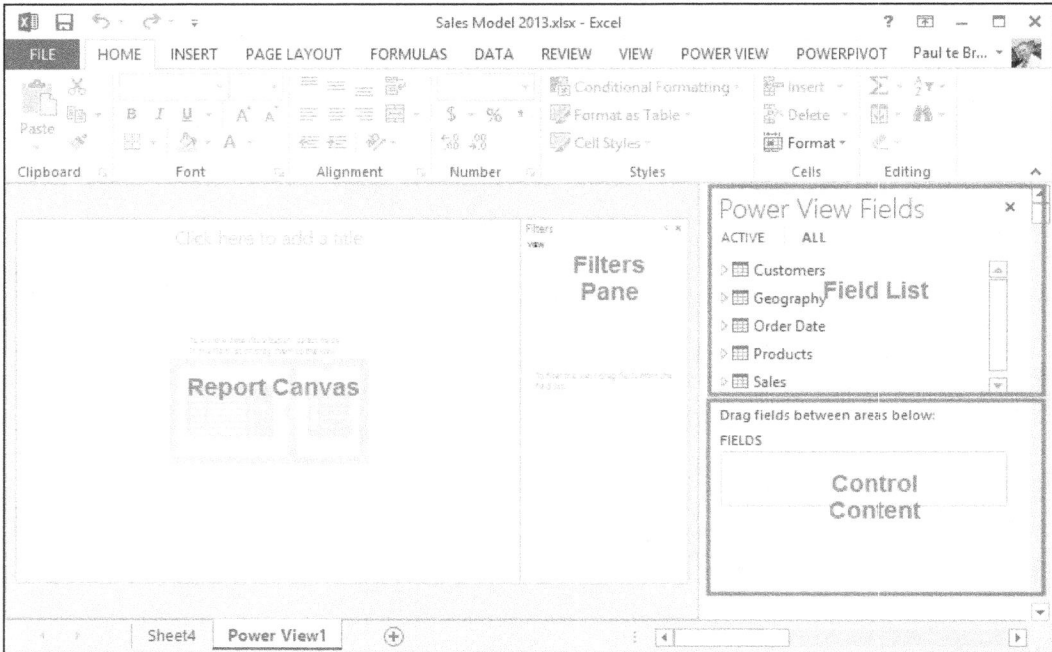

It may be helpful to think that anything displaying the data on the **Report Canvas** is done so through with a control. For example, a grid is a control that groups the data into a single object.

Also, note that the sheet name for the Power View report can be changed just as any Excel sheet—either double-click the name or right-click and select **Rename** from the pop-up window.

3. Add a table to the canvas by dragging the `Month` field from the `Order Date` table onto the canvas. The months will expand (showing each month of the year). Add the measure `Sales Gross` (found in the `Sales` table) to the `Reports` table (the control) by dragging the field onto the table (when the field hovers over the table, it gets a darker dotted border, as shown in the following screenshot):

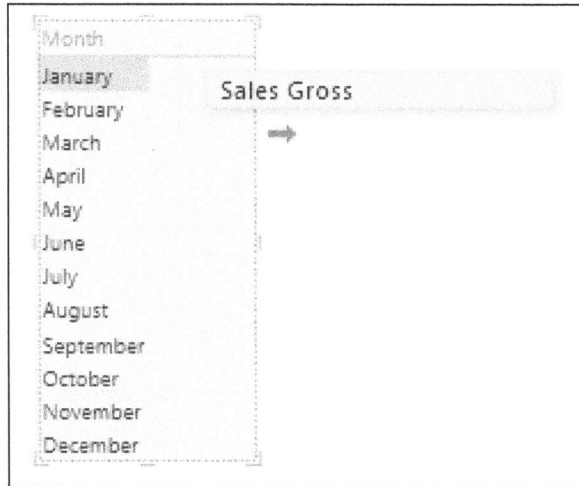

4. The table in the canvas has its edges surrounded by a light border. This indicates that the control is active. The control can be deactivated by clicking on any part of the canvas that is not in the control's border area. Activate the table and drag the **GOGS** measure into the **FIELDS** section of the **Control Content** section to add GOGS to the `Reports` table, as shown in the following screenshot:

5. The active control can be moved and resized by dragging its borders on the canvas. When the mouse hovers over the border boundaries (the gray lines of the border), the mouse pointer changes to an arrow to indicate that the border can be resized. The entire control can be moved when the mouse changes to a hand pointer. Ensure that the control is large enough to cover all the months of the year.

6. Add a new table to the canvas that shows `Country Sales` by `Product Category`. Drag the `Country` field to a new section of the canvas (that is, not on the `Month` table) so that a new table is added to the canvas.

7. Convert this new table to a matrix control (a matrix groups data into rows and columns) by activating the control and selecting **Matrix** from the **Table** drop-down, as shown in the following screenshot:

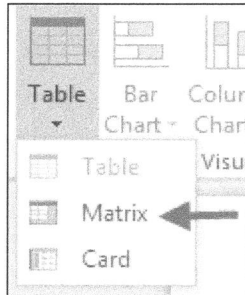

8. After the control has changed to a matrix, the available fields in the **Control Content** changes. We can now drag the `Category` field (from the `Products` table) into the **COLUMNS** section and the `Sales Gross` into the ∑ **VALUES** section. The controls content section should look like the following screenshot:

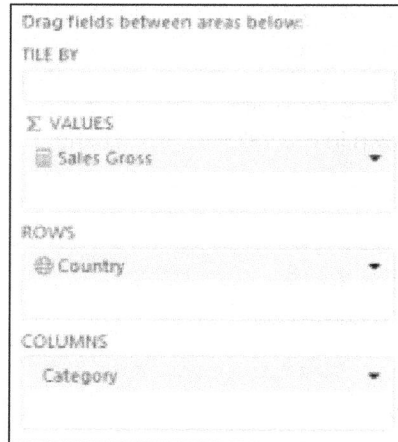

The number of boxes available (and their names) in the Control Content section is determined by the type of visualization that is used. That is, whether the control is a table, matrix, card, chart, or map.

9. Resize the control, so that all data fits onto the canvas.

10. Name the report by clicking on the grayed heading section (which displays the text **Click here to add a title**) and name the report `Sales Summary by Year`.

11. The controls currently show data for all the years in the model. We want to restrict the report to show only specific years and want to apply this filter to all the controls that are on the canvas. In the **Filters** pane, click on the **VIEW** label to apply the filter to the entire report (alternatively, you can select any area of the canvas that does not activate a control.). Then, drag the `Year` field into the **Filters** section. The section will immediately change and will look like the following screenshot:

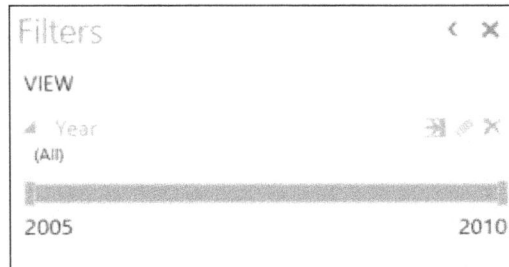

12. The filter can now be applied to the report by dragging the ends of the slider bar. When this is done, a text description is added to the view (as shown in the following screenshot):

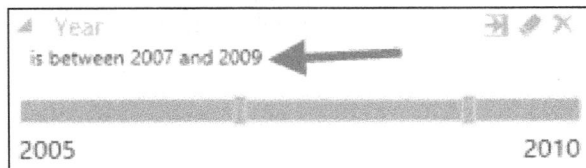

How it works...

The addition of controls to the canvas and the application of a (global) filter are straightforward and do not require further explanation.

There's more...

There are a few additional points that should be included to the recipe concerning the introduction of the report. These are discussed in the following section.

When a control on the canvas is selected, the **Filters** section changes to include the type of the control that is active (currently, there is no method available to name the control, so only the type of control is shown.). For example, if the Month table is selected (the one we initially created), the **Filters** pane will include a **TABLE** label as shown in the following screenshot. We can now click on the **TABLE** label to show the filters that are applicable to the active control.

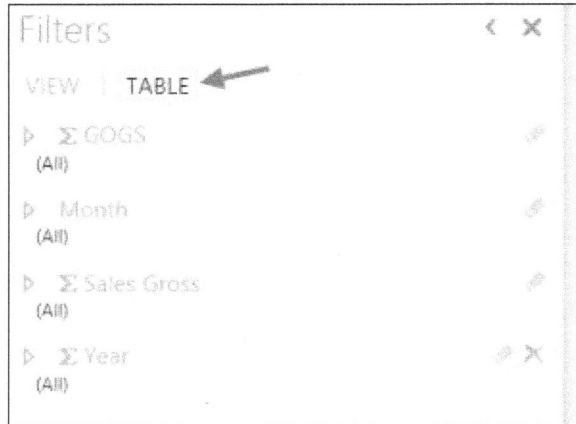

Now, any field that is added as a filter will only be applied to the active control and not the entire report. Clicking on the **VIEW** label will change the control back to the global filters.

A filter can be removed by clicking on the delete button for the filter (the button with a cross as highlighted in the following screenshot). Hovering over a button will show a tool tip for the item.

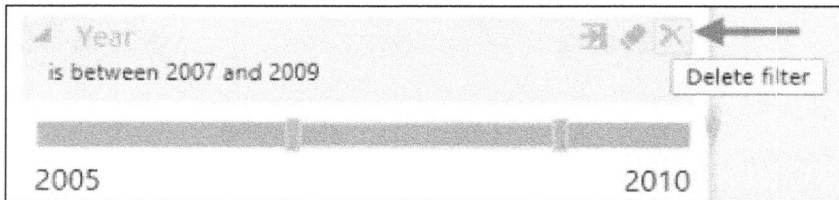

The way that the filter is presented in Power View is dependent on the type of data that the filter is based on. Since year is a number, Power View expects you to filter based on a range. But this need not be the case—you may desire a check-box list or some text based query. Clicking on the filter mode will change how the filter is presented (and of course, how you interact with it). These choices are shown in the following screenshot:

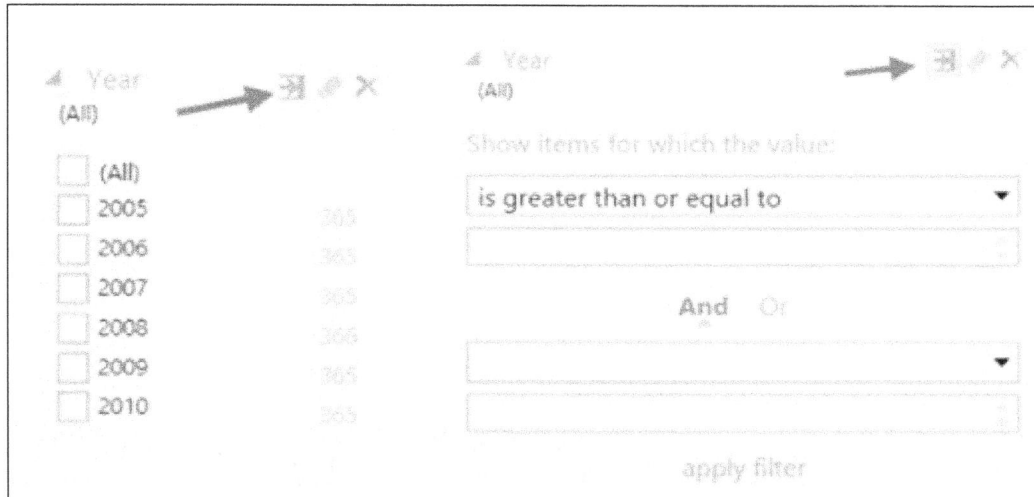

The controls in Power View work in a similar manner as a pivot table. That is, they hide information when there is no data for the selected view. This can be seen by applying a filter to `Year` for 2010. When this is done, the table control provides a no data message as shown in the following screenshot:

This may be a novel feature for visualization; however, there may be situations where you want to see the range of dimension members available (just like the **Show rows with no data** feature in a pivot table). To do this (and show all month labels), perform the following steps:

1. Activate the table, so that the Control Content shows the fields in the table.

2. Select the drop-down arrow for the `Month` field and select the **Show items with no data** option.

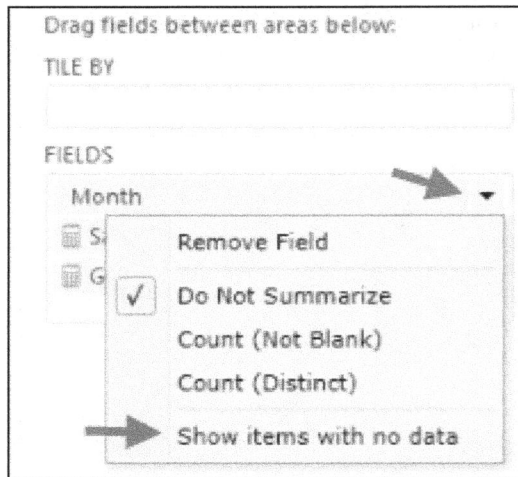

Drag fields between areas below:

TILE BY

FIELDS

Month

☐ S|

☐ G

	Remove Field
✓	Do Not Summarize
	Count (Not Blank)
	Count (Distinct)
→	Show items with no data

Creating and manipulating charts

When an enduser is shown data in tables and matrix controls, their subconscious mind thinks about the relationships between the data that they are presented with. For example, consider the table created in the prior recipe, *Creating a Power View report*, as shown in the following screenshot:

Month	▲ Sales Gross
January	1,242,605
February	2,311,803
March	1,473,826
April	1,734,404

Here, we recognize the month as a sequence of consecutive periods and associate performance and the change in values from month to month (for example, February is almost twice as good as January).

This analysis requires a bit of thought from the user and is not the most efficient way to present the month-on-month trend—a visual representation is much more effective. This recipe examines the creation and manipulation of charts in Power View.

Getting ready

This recipe uses the same workbook that was used in the prior recipe (`Sales Model 2013.xlsx` is available from the online resources). Unlike worksheets, Power View reports cannot be copied with the workbook. They must be created from scratch. Create a new report (titled `Charts`) and add a table that shows `Months` and `Sales Gross` (as in the preceding screenshot).

How to do it...

Let's start by converting a table to a chart.

1. Activate the table by selecting any cell in it.

2. Convert the table control to a stacked bar chart by selecting the **Stacked Bar** option from the **Bar Chart** button as shown in the following screenshot:

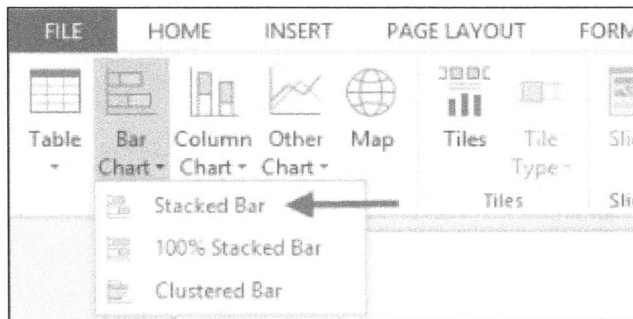

3. When this is done, the control converts to a chart with the same structure as the table (`Months` on rows), however, the values are now bars of the chart, as can be seen in the following screenshot:

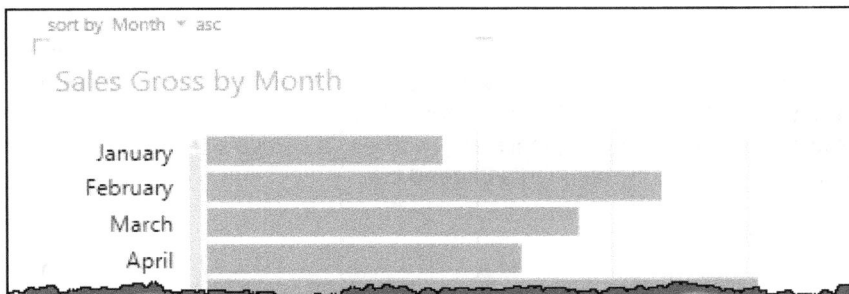

> When the chart cannot fit into the physical bounds of the control, the chart's axes are not compressed to fit into the control. Note that all the months are not shown (in the preceding screenshot) and there is a slider between the months and data bars. This allows the months to be scrolled with the chart.
>
> Alternatively (of course), the chart control can be resized so that all months fit into it.

4. Convert the control to a stacked column chart by selecting **Stacked Column** from the **Column Chart** button. A column chart (as the name suggests) displays the axis on the columns. Resize the chart so that it fits into the page.

5. Add the Category field from the Products table to the **Legend** box in the Control Content section. Each monthly bar is now broken down into sections that show category groupings. The chart and Control Content section should look like the following screenshot:

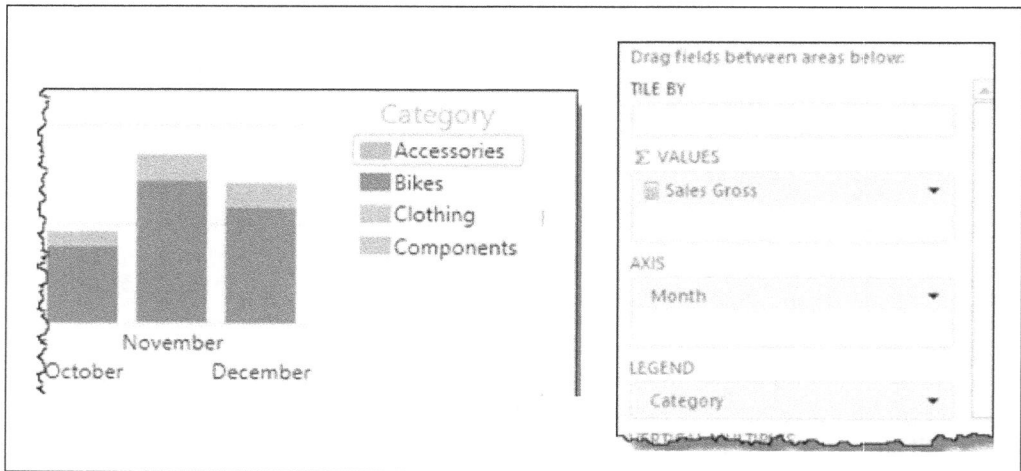

6. Currently, all Category stacks in columns are equally transparent. We (that is, the user) can draw attention to an individual category by selecting it in the **Legend** box on the chart. When this is done, all other categories in the chart will become dull. To return the chart to the original state (with equal category transparency), simply re-click the category in the chart's **Legend** box.

7. Convert the chart to a clustered column (chart) by selecting **Clustered Column** from the **Column Chart** button. The chart changes so that a data bar is shown for each category by month, as shown in the following screenshot. Individual categories can be emphasized by selecting the category name from the **Legend** box.

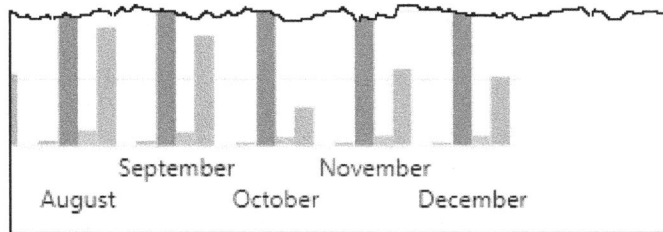

[A common use of a stacked chart is to show proportional values within a month. For example, the chart shows how a monthly sales value is broken down by category. However, one flaw of this type of visualization is that the proportions within a month are not comparable between months. A clustered chart is much more suitable for this type of analysis.]

8. Hide the title of the chart (which describes the chart as `Sales Gross by Month` and `Category`) by selecting the **None** option from the **Title** button from the **LAYOUT** tab, as shown in the following screenshot:

9. Add value labels to the chart by selecting **Outside End** from the **Data Labels** button (the **Layout** tab).

10. Move the **Legend** box to the bottom of the chart by selecting the **Show Legend at Bottom** option from the **Legend** button (the **Layout** tab).

Using tiles (parameters)

Regardless of the reporting tool, the use of parameters is a common feature for allowing user interaction with report data. The typical way that these are implemented is through the population of a control (usually a drop-down list) that allows the user to select a value, and this value dictates what data is seen on the report. When parameters are used, it is often necessary to explicitly define the parameter and its data before it can be used in the report (and subsequent datasets).

Power View does not have parameters in the traditional sense. Instead, the report is based on all of the data within the model. The user can filter controls through a special type of control called a **tile**. The tile lists available values for the field chosen, allowing the user to select a value which is applied to other report controls.

Getting ready

This recipe continues from the Power View report created in the previous recipe, *Creating and manipulating charts*.

How to do it...

Adding a tile can be achieved in a number of ways. In this recipe, we add it to an existing control and then manipulate it.

1. Activate the `Reports` table so that the Control Content (section) is visible.

2. Drag the `Year` field (from the table `Order Date`) into the box labeled **TILE BY**. The section should look like the following screenshot:

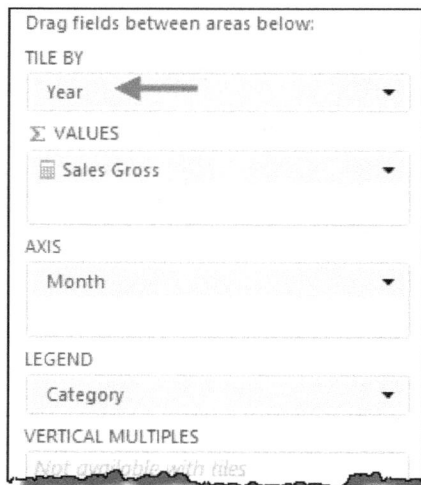

3. Immediately, the tile is added above the chart. Selecting different years (as shown in the following screenshot) from the tile will change the values:

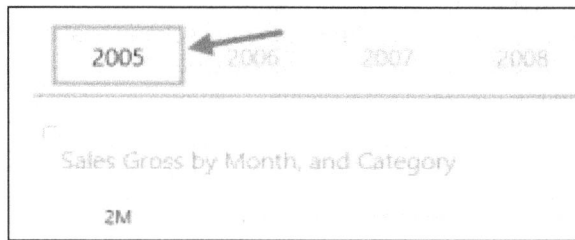

4. The tile is bound by a blue border (above and below) that covers the area that is applicable to the tile. In the preceding screenshot, we can see the upper bound; the lower bound (which is not shown) is below the chart. Resize the tile control so that it fills the canvas. When this happens, the existing chart will also move some of its borders (within the tile's boundary of course).

5. Add a new pie chart to the tile control by dragging the `Category` field onto the canvas between the tile's boundary lines (that is, place the field under the existing chart).

6. When this is done, a new table will be added to the canvas.

7. Add the `Sales Gross` measure to the table and convert it to a pie chart by selecting it from the **Other Chart** button.

8. Resize the pie, so that it is positioned in the center of the page.

9. Select a `Category` field from the bar chart. Note that the transparency of the segments also changed to reflect the targeted `Category`.

10. Change the `Year` in the tile. Note that the existing (selected) category remains active.

How it works...

There is nothing extra to explain here. The tile may be thought of as an additional control that has its own bounds. Any other control placed within those bounds are controlled by the tile.

There are two positions that the tile can occupy within the canvas. The first (as we have seen) is at the top of the control and is called a **Tab Strip**. The second is at the bottom with a slightly focused visualization (called a **Tile Flow**). Change the type by selecting **Tile Flow** from the **Tile Type** button as shown in the following screenshot:

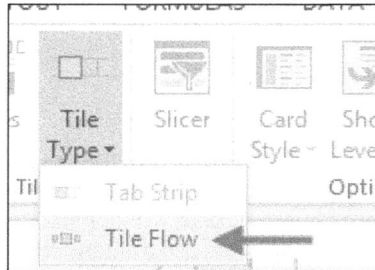

Once the previously described steps have been performed, our canvas should now look like the following screenshot:

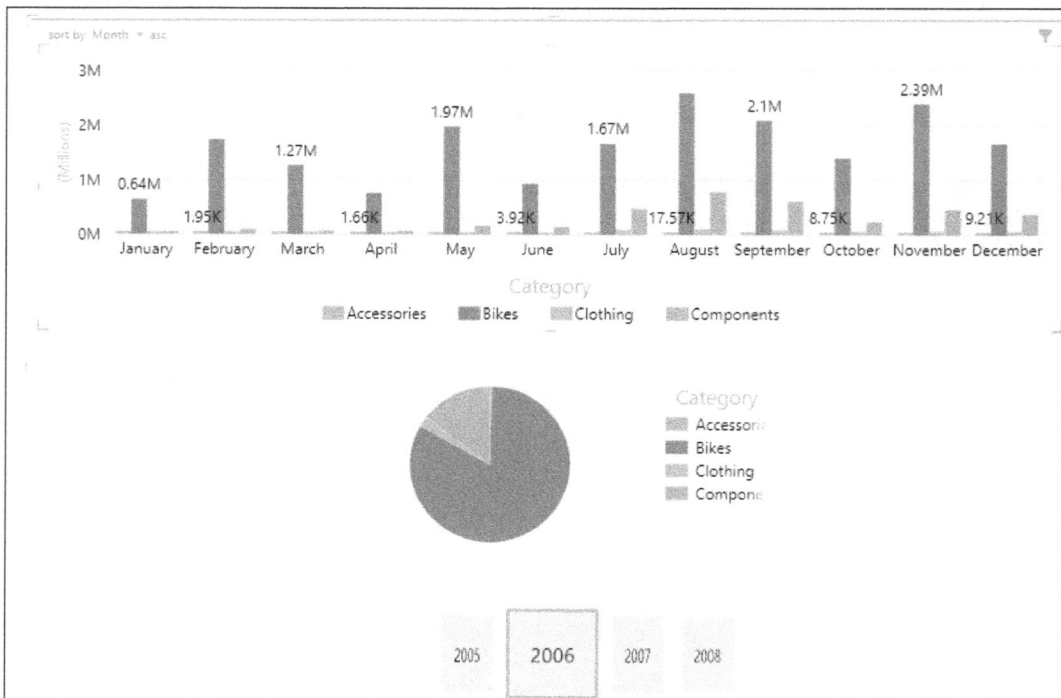

Using and showing images

There is an old adage that a picture is worth a thousand words. While we can naturally assess data more easily if it is presented in the correct visual format, pictures and images in reports add a style that add recognition to data. Consider the use of KPIs (KPIs were addressed in the *Creating and using Key Performance Indicators* recipe in *Chapter 3, Advanced Browsing Features*) that visually display performance. On seeing a set of KPIs, we can immediately assess the position.

Images are an attractive inclusion in reports because they are visually appealing and improve user understanding. This is because an image is immediately identifiable as a symbol—it holds a predetermined meaning for the user.

This recipe looks at what the tabular model requires for displaying data as images in Power View.

Getting ready

This recipe uses the `Sales Model 2013.xlsx` workbook available from the online content. There is no dependency on prior recipes.

How to do it...

The `Country` table of the model list's sales areas that include a `Country` field and a `Country Flag` field. The `Country` field aggregates regions into countries with the `Country Flag`, providing a URL image of that country's flag.

1. Unhide the `Country Flag` field from client tools on the `Geography` table.

2. Observe that the field is actually a fully qualified **Uniform Resource Locator** (**URL**) that requests an image (note the `.gif` extension) as shown in the following screenshot:

https://www.cia.gov/library/publications/the-world-factbook/graphics/flags/large/us-lgflag.gif			
Country	Group	Country Flag	*Add Column*
United States	North America	https://www.cia.gov/li...	
United States	North America	https://www.cia.gov/li...	
United States	North America	https://www.cia.gov/li...	
United States	North America	https://www.cia.gov/li...	

3. To verify the location of the URL, copy it from the formula bar and paste it into Internet Explorer. Instead of a web page, the following screenshot will be displayed:

4. Ensure that the **Data Category** for the field is set to **Image URL**. This may be automatically detected by PowerPivot. To confirm this, examine the **Reporting Properties** option in the **Advanced** Tab. The **Data Category** should be set to **Image URL** as shown in the following screenshot. If it is not, select it from the drop-down list.

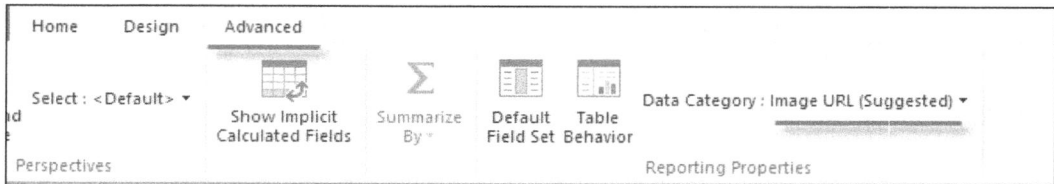

5. Click on the **Table Behavior** button and set the **Default Image** (field) to **Country Flag (optional)**.

> We can also use a URL as an image by specifying its **Data Category** as **WEB URL**. However, if this option is used, setting the default image property for the table will raise an error when Power View tries to read the model.

6. Return to Excel and insert a new Power View report (named `Images`). Drag the `Country Flag` field onto the canvas. Observe that the flags are shown in the place of text (as in the following screenshot). Generally, this field can be used just as any other field in Power View (for example, as a tile or as rows in a table).

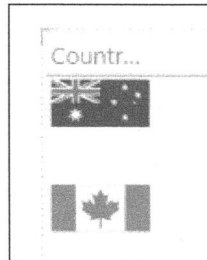

> Excel may display a warning that external content is required—if this is shown, allow Excel to access the external content.

There's more...

In addition to using the **WEB URL** feature, tabular models allow fields of binary data (type). This allows an image to be stored in the field, rather than a pointer to an external resource (that is, a URL). The `Photo` field in the `Products` table is an example of this type of data.

A recipe of how to load this data is outside the scope of the book (other than the loading of the table from the database); however, Power View can interpret the binary data and display it as an image. There are no additional settings or properties that need to be set to use an image, however, it is recommended that the **Data Category** be set to **Image**.

Automating the table fields with default field sets

There is often a set of standard views that users like to see when they use a model, for example, we might expect any user that uses the `Products` table would automatically like to see only the `Category` and `Sub Category` fields. Of course, they are not restricted from adding other fields to a control, however, when they use the table, we might like to give them the option of automatically adding those fields.

This recipe looks at how that can be achieved (and used).

Getting ready

This recipe uses the `Sales Model 2013.xlsx` workbook available from the online content. There is no dependency on prior recipes.

How to do it...

Let's start by examining Power View's behavior before the model is configured for this action.

1. Create a new Power View report. Double-click on the `Products` table (note that nothing happens).

2. Launch the PowerPivot window and activate the `Products` table.

3. Click the **Default Field Set** button to launch the **Default Field Set** dialogue.

4. Add the `Category` and `Sub Category` fields to the **Default fields, in order:** box by selecting them from the **Fields in the table:** box and clicking on the **Add** button as shown in the following screenshot:

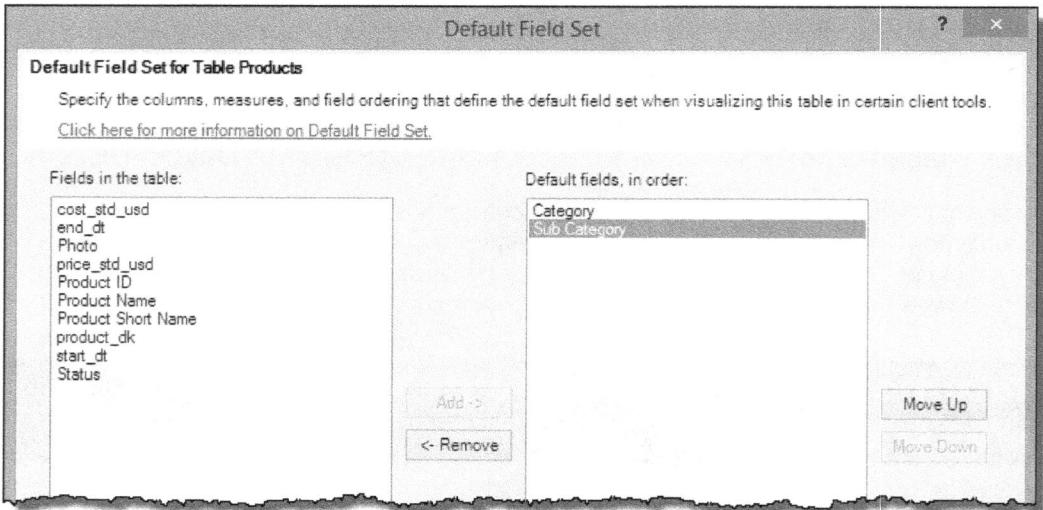

> You can specify the order in which the fields will be added to the table by specifying the order in the **Default fields, in order:** box. To change the order, simply highlight the field (in that box) and click on the **Move Up** or **Move Down** button.

5. Close the dialogue by clicking on the **OK** button.

6. Return to Power View and click on **OK** to refresh Power View's cache of the data model.

7. Double-click on the Products table. This time, the two fields are added to a new table.

> You can also use this (double-click) technique to add the default fields to an existing control (this does not apply to all controls). Simply ensure that the control is active before you double-click on the table in the Power View field list.

Working with table behavior and card control

PowerPivot is very flexible for summarizing and aggregating data—most of the time, we want to see that data at an aggregated level and at other times, it may be required at a detailed level. This recipe looks at how to specify table properties so that data is listed distinctively.

Finally, the recipe introduces a **Card control** that lists data into a distinctive group for display.

Getting ready

This recipe uses the Sales Model 2013.xlsx workbook available from the online content. There is no dependency on prior recipes.

How to do it...

This recipe commences on the assumption that there is no table behavior set on the Products table. First, we ensure that any formats from prior recipes are discarded.

1. Launch the PowerPivot window and activate the Products table.

2. Click on the **Table Behavior** button in the **Advanced** tab to launch the **Table Behavior** dialog. Ensure that the table has no behaviors set. It should look like the following screenshot. Click on **OK** to confirm the properties.

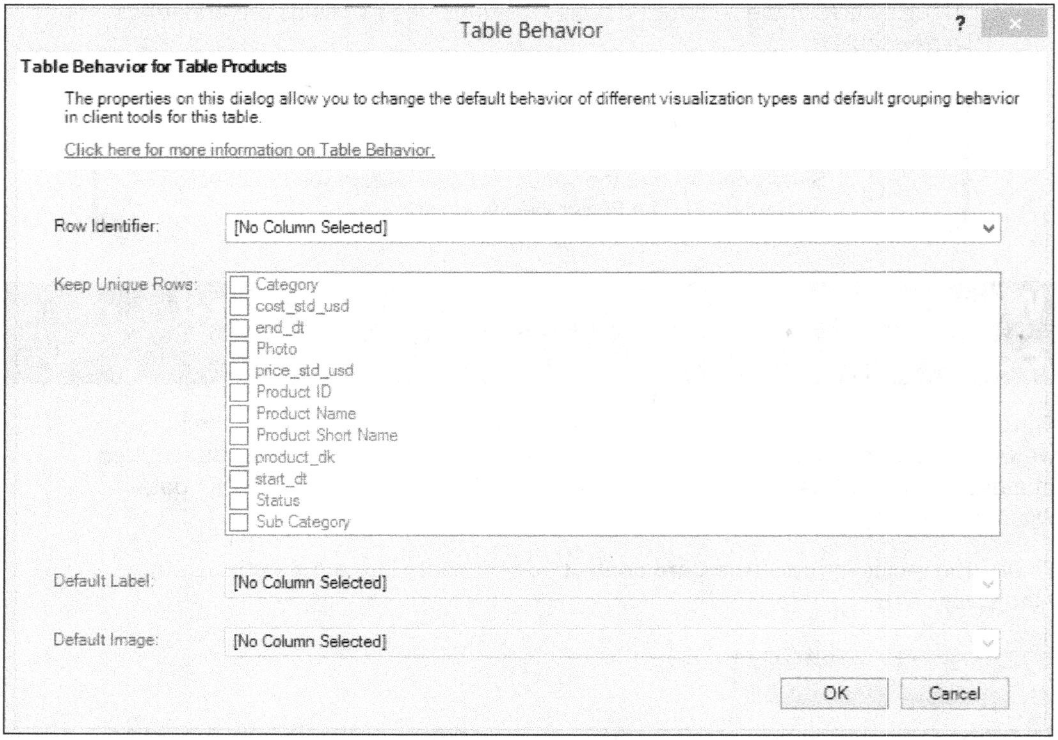

3. Create a new Power View report using a table control that includes the Product ID, Category, and Sub Category fields from the Products table.

4. Add a filter to the report so that only product **HL-U509** is shown. Drag Product ID to the **Filter** section, then use a string filter for product **HL-U509** (searching for product 509 will list similar products to 509). Check the product **HL-U509** in the **Filter** section to check if the details are displayed in one row (as in the following screenshot):

Product ID	Category	Sub Category
HL-U509	Accessories	Helmets

5. Return to the **Table Behavior** dialogue and set the **Row Identifier** field to the product_dk field.

Each table should have a **Row Identifier** assigned (assuming that there is a field in the table that can act in this capacity—sometimes this may not be the case). This materializes the (primary) key for the table and will stop the tabular model from creating an arbitrary unique identifier for each row.

6. Return to Power View and refresh the report (update the cache of Power View); there is no change to the report.

7. Return to the **Table Behavior** dialog for the `Products` table. Check the box next to `Product ID` in the **Keep Unique Rows** list.

8. Return to Power View (refresh the cache). Since the change has been made to `Product ID`, you will also need to re-apply a filter to `Product ID`.

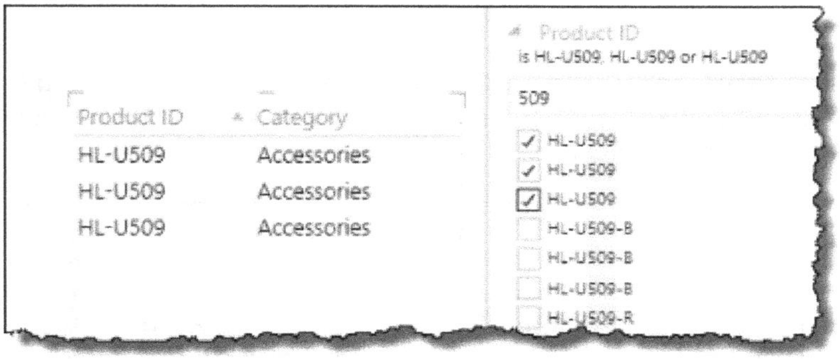

Product ID	▲ Category
HL-U509	Accessories
HL-U509	Accessories
HL-U509	Accessories

Product ID
Is HL-U509, HL-U509 or HL-U509

509

☑ HL-U509
☑ HL-U509
☑ HL-U509
☐ HL-U509-B
☐ HL-U509-B
☐ HL-U509-B
☐ HL-U509-R

9. Return to the **Table Behavior** dialog for the `Products` table. This time, set the **Default Label** to `Product ID` and the **Default Image** to **Photo** (this is the only choice available). The **Table Behavior** dialog should look like the following screenshot:

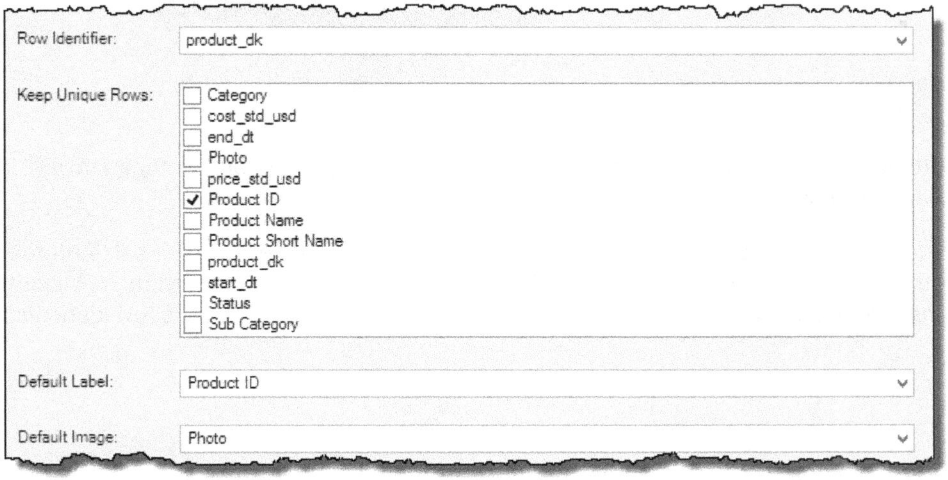

Row Identifier: product_dk

Keep Unique Rows:
☐ Category
☐ cost_std_usd
☐ end_dt
☐ Photo
☐ price_std_usd
☑ Product ID
☐ Product Name
☐ Product Short Name
☐ product_dk
☐ start_dt
☐ Status
☐ Sub Category

Default Label: Product ID

Default Image: Photo

10. Save the changes to the model (by clicking on **OK**) and return to Power View.

11. Extend the table (control) by adding the `Photo` field and `Gross Sales`.

12. Change the table view to a card by selecting **Card** from the **Table** drop-down in the **Switch Visualization** group as shown in the following screenshot:

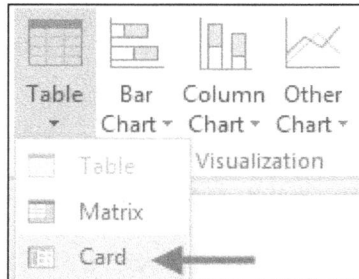

13. The table control changes to the **Card** layout. Note the placement and format of the `Product ID` field in the **Card**. It has a larger (attention-grabbing) font and is located in the top-left corner of each card, as in the following screenshot:

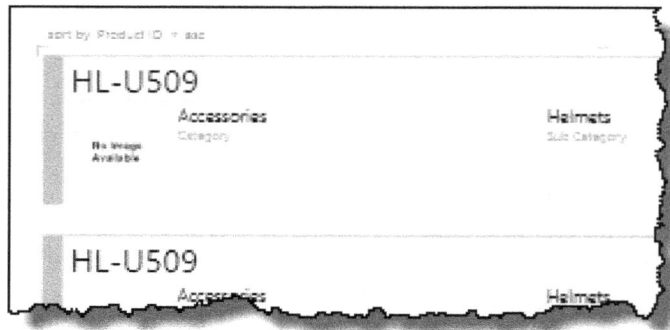

How it works...

The setting of table properties in this recipe is relatively straightforward. Setting a row identifier explicitly defines the unique field for the table.

Once the unique field has been set, the fields that require uniqueness can be set—naturally, things must be done in this order. This assigns a one-to-one relationship with the row identifier, meaning that each `Product ID` is repeated for each instance of the table's row identifier.

Finally, the table's default label is a property which is only applicable to the Card. This specifies the field that will be used as a label in the Card control. This can be thought of as a unique identifier for the Card (note duplicates are shown, even though we might not expect that behavior) and the more pronounced formatting.

> Setting a default label will force the field to be treated in the same manner as a **Keep Unique Rows** flag and force Product ID to be repeated in a Card (even if the **Keep Unique Rows** flag was not checked).
>
> If you wish to use the Card visualization in Power View, the model needs to be physically structured, so that the Product ID is unique.

Using maps

Humans absorb data more easily if it is presented in a visual format—consider how quickly trends can be assessed when a line chart is used rather than a data table. The same argument applies to maps, where information related to geographic regions is used. The use of maps (or map reports) is an efficient way to display geography-related information because it adds context to data that would otherwise require thought. For example, imagine a table summarizing the sales by city. When you look at this table, you think about where the city is, and try to make comparisons between the values for each city. This is a lot for the user to do in their subconscious!. To analyze the relationships between cities, a more suitable approach would be to show the data values on a map, so that the user need not think about the location element of their data.

This recipe examines how to configure the tabular model for use with maps in Power View.

Getting ready

This recipe uses the Sales Model 2013.xlsx workbook available from the online content. There is no dependency on prior recipes.

How to do it...

Let us start by examining fields that can be used to refer to geographies.

1. Activate the Customer table in the PowerPivot window.

2. Ensure that the data categories for the geography-related fields are set to appropriate values. That is, the geography-related fields are tagged as geography. These are set in the **Advanced** tab under the **Reporting Properties** grouping when the field is selected (as in the following screenshot):

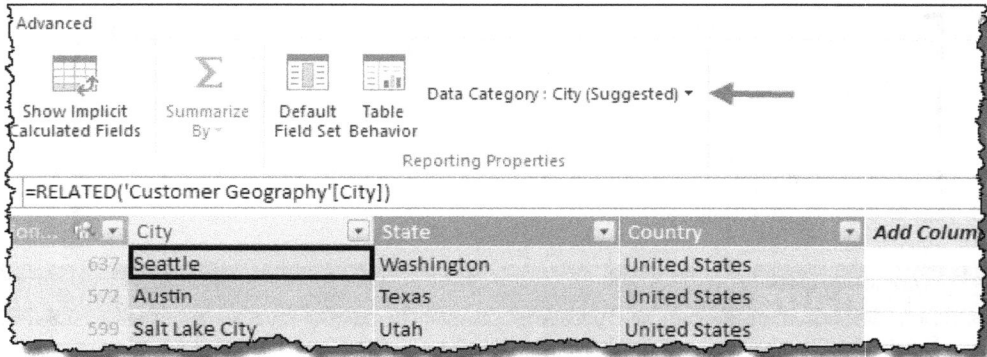

The Data Categories that should be set are as follows:

Field Name	Data Category
City	City (suggested)
State	State/Province
Country	Country/Region (suggested)

3. Return to Excel and create a new Power View report. Expand the `Customers` table and examine the fields `City`, `State`, and `Country`. Note that the fields have a globe icon (indicating that they play a geographic role), as is visible in the following screenshot:

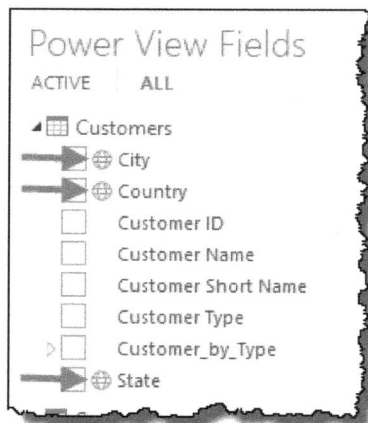

4. Create a new table by dragging the `City` attribute onto the report canvas. Extend the table to include the `Sales Gross` measure.

5. Convert the table to a map by clicking on the **Map** button (from the **Switch Visualization** group).

6. Immediately, the visualization changes. Resize the control so that it fits in the entire page.

> The map is interactive, and its view (that is, the actual map with data points) can be zoomed into by using the mouse roller or moved (left-click and dragging). Alternatively, the maps navigation controls can be used (as in the following screenshot):

7. Because the map is showing data at a city level, it appears cluttered. We can reduce this clutter in the following combination of ways:

   □ We could use a higher-level attribute in the `Location` field of the Control Content. This is done by dragging the `State` attribute to the **Location** box in the Control Content and removing `City`. As expected, the number of display points on the chart decreases (we could also use the `Country` attribute for a higher-level view).

   □ We could apply a Filter to show only data points that met a specific criteria (sales value). This is done by expanding the **Filters** section, ensuring that the **MAP** control is selected, and using the slider filter (or an alternate filter control, as discussed in the *Creating a Power View report* recipe).

8. Set the `Location` field to `State`, to examine the change in granularity.

How it works...

There is no requirement for additional explanations other than the reiteration, that the map is dependent on the data category setting for fields. The control section of the map also includes the longitude and latitude placeholders. These should be used in preference to field names.

There's more...

The size of the bubble on the map indicates sales value, however, we often want to add more meaning to those data points by adding a category to indicate how those sales are broken down. Do this by dragging the `Category` field into the **COLOR** box (in the map's Control Content). When this is done, the bubbles change to pie charts (to indicate the composition of sales), and a legend is added to the map.

[🔍 The legend is interactive. Selecting an individual entry from the legend will focus on each pie chart's segment in that category. Selecting it again will return the selection to the original state.]

Using multiples (Trellis Charts)

The use of charts is a common way to understand relationships between data—of course, this is not unique to Power View, but applicable to analytics in general. However, as more data fields are added to the chart and the number of fields exceeds the axis number of the chart, the chart becomes more complex and difficult to read. One solution that has been used to combat this situation, is to reproduce a template chart based on a dimension—for example, we might show various charts with each chart showing data for a specific country. When this functionality is included in the charting engine, the output is commonly referred to as **trellis charting**.

This recipe shows how to implement trellis charting in Power View. This functionality is possible for most Power View charts (including maps).

Getting ready

This recipe uses the `Sales Model 2013.xlsx` workbook available from the online content. There is no dependency on prior recipes.

How to do it...

1. The creation of a Trellis Chart (which is called **multiples** in Power View) is a configuration of the chart control (whether a chart or map). However, this behavior is consistent among all chart types. Create a Clustered Column chart that shows `Sales Gross` by `Category` (see the *Creating and Manipulating Charts* recipe in this chapter for information on how to do this).

[🔍 It is often preferred to show columns (or bars) in an ordered sequence based on data value (rather than the chart's axis category name). This can be achieved by setting the sort by field of the chart. This option is shown when the mouse hovers over the chart (as in the following screenshot). Set the sort by field to `Sales Gross`.]

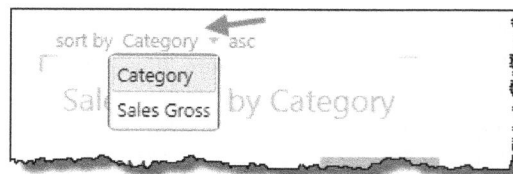

2. Drag the `Country` field to the chart's **Vertical Multiples** box in the chart's control section.

3. Resize the chart, so that it covers the full canvas (to see the full effect of the visualization).

How it works...

As mentioned in the recipe, the use of multiples (or Trellis's) technique is available in all charts (including maps). A vertical multiple will expand individual charts, so that they can appear over rows (column cells are first populated, and then individual charts overflow to rows—this is shown in the following screenshot). Horizontal multiples will only have one layer of charts and will not overflow to additional rows.

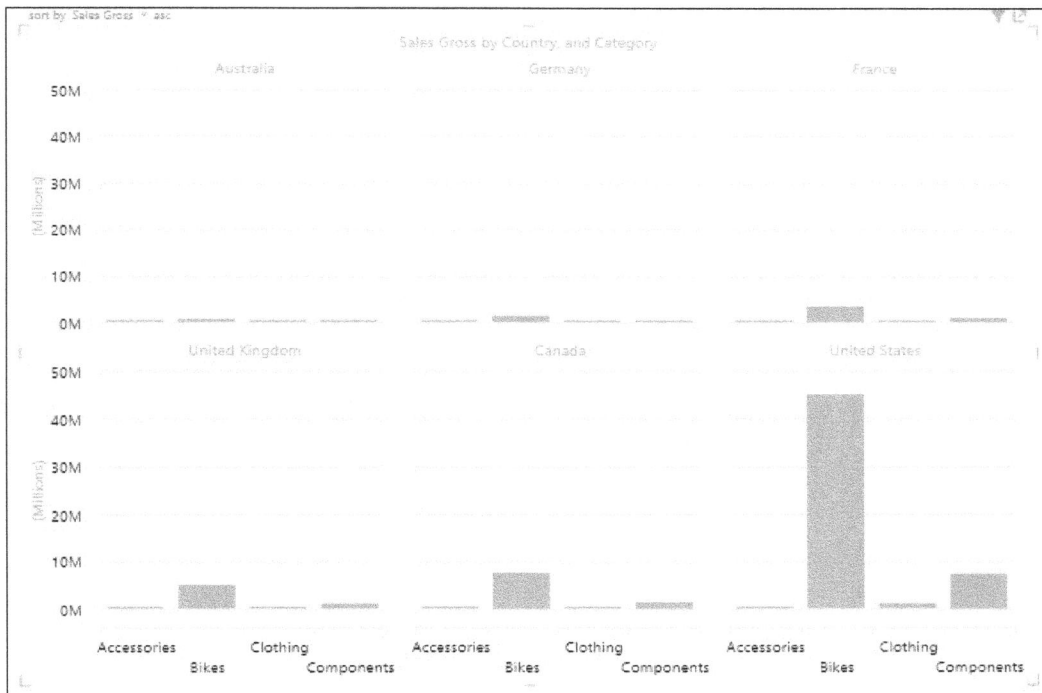

There's more...

Once multiples have been created on a chart, the format of the multiples (that is, the number of charts appearing in each row and column) can be adjusted, so that the Trellis Chart is more visually appealing. This is specified by the **Grid Height** and **Grid Width** settings in the **LAYOUT** tab of Power View (as shown in the following screenshot). Simply set the number of charts to appear in rows (**Grid Height**) and columns (**Grid Width**).

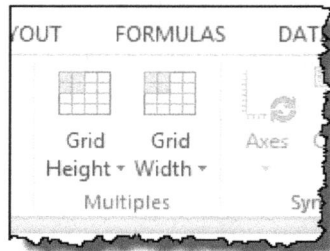

Installing PowerPivot and Sample Databases

In this appendix, we will discuss:

- ▶ Installing PowerPivot
- ▶ Creating the database

Installing PowerPivot

In Excel 2010, PowerPivot is an add-in that must be downloaded and installed. In Office 365 Pro and Excel 2013 Pro Plus, the add-in is a part of the default Excel installation setup (which means there is no requirement to install PowerPivot). However, the add-in must be activated before it can be used (see *Chapter 10, Visualizing Data with Power View*, for details on enabling the add-in in Excel 2013).

The 2010 add-in can be downloaded from the Microsoft download center (free of charge) using the following URL:

```
http://www.microsoft.com/en-us/download/details.aspx?id=29074
```

Although the installation is relatively straightforward once the installation file is obtained, the downloaded file must match the installed version of Excel (that is, whether Excel is operating in 32-bit or 64-bit mode). This can be checked by selecting the **Help** option from the **File** tab (in Excel), as shown in the following screenshot:

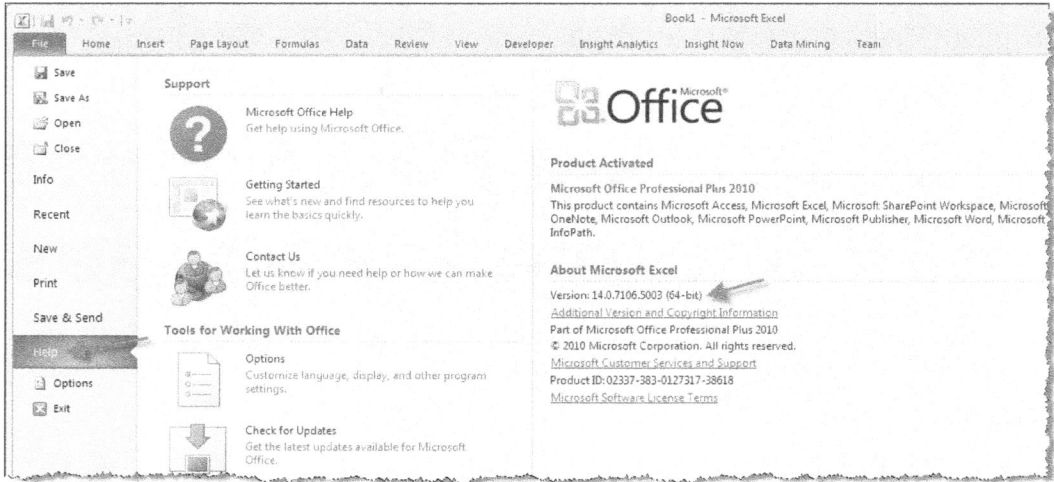

In the **About Microsoft Excel** section, we can see that this version of Excel is a **64-bit** version (and hence, we must install the 64-bit version of PowerPivot).

The download page (from the provided URL) will look like the following screenshot:

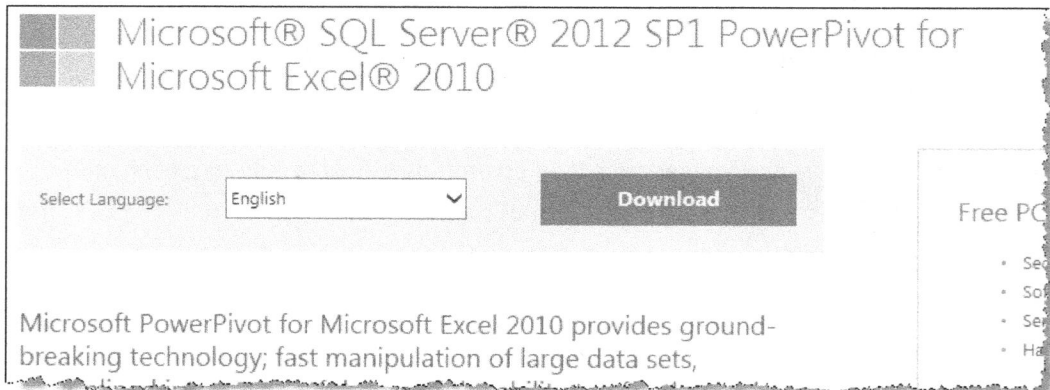

When the **Download** button is clicked, you are prompted to choose the file to download, as shown in the following screenshot.

The file with the name ending with _amd64.msi—the middle one in the following screenshot should be installed for the 64-bit version of Excel and the other file (_x86.msi) should be downloaded and installed on systems having the 32-bit version of Excel:

Choose the download you want

File Name	Size
☐ 1033\ReadMe_PowerPivot.htm	12 KB
☐ 1033\x64\PowerPivot_for_Excel_amd64.msi	130.0 MB
☐ 1033\x86\PowerPivot_for_Excel_x86.msi	98.5 MB

Once the file has been downloaded, we can execute it by double-clicking on it, however, Excel must be closed during the installation of PowerPivot. Note that, depending on your user account permissions, you may be prompted to run the installation process as an administrator, or the file will change the computer's settings. Run the file by simply clicking on the **Run** button.

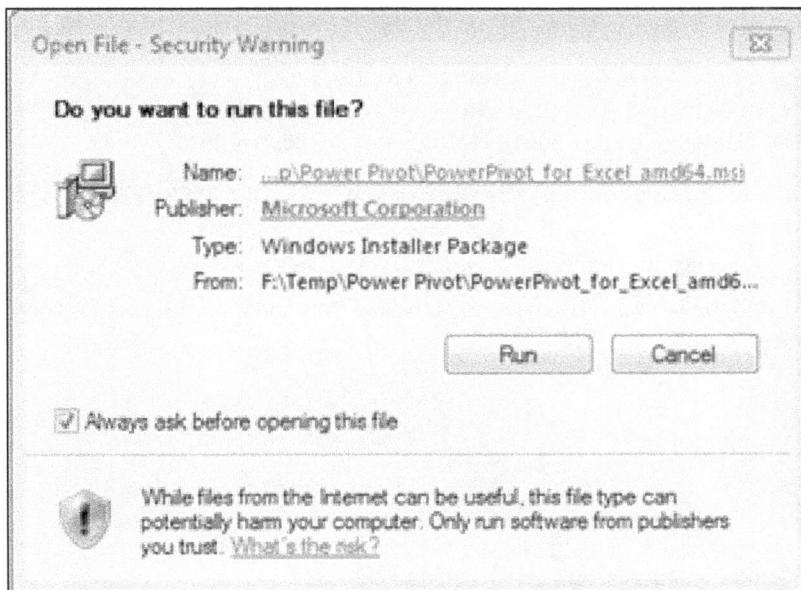

Open File - Security Warning

Do you want to run this file?

    Name: ...p\Power Pivot\PowerPivot_for_Excel_amd64.msi
    Publisher: Microsoft Corporation
    Type: Windows Installer Package
    From: F:\Temp\Power Pivot\PowerPivot_for_Excel_amd6...

[Run] [Cancel]

☑ Always ask before opening this file

While files from the Internet can be useful, this file type can potentially harm your computer. Only run software from publishers you trust. What's the risk?

The installation process does not require any advanced user interaction. All you have to do is accept the terms and license agreement and click on the **Install** button. Once the installation is successfully completed, the installer will provide a confirmation window, as shown in the following screenshot. Simply click on **Finish** to complete the process.

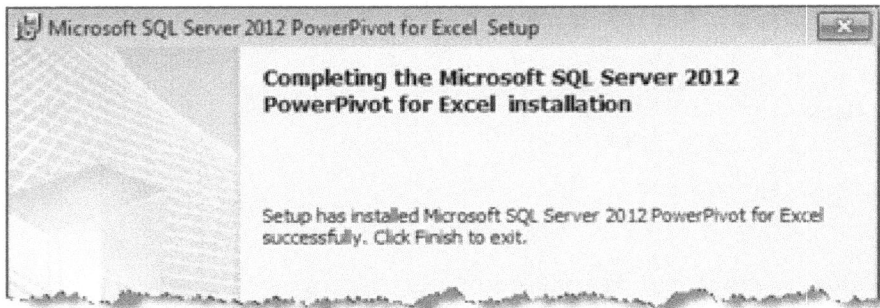

When Excel is opened, the **PowerPivot** tab will appear in Excel's menu bar.

Creating the database

The SQL Server database used in the prior recipes is available as a backup from the online content for this book on the Packt Publishing website. This backup can be restored to the SQL server instance (running SQL Server 2012).

We do not specify details for the installation of SQL Server (since they are outside the scope of this book). However, a brief overview of the database restore is discussed in this section.

An evaluation version of SQL Server is available for download at the following URL. This license will expire after 180 days. Alternatively, a free edition of SQL Server (SQL Server Express) is also available (with reduced features and no license expiry limit).

http://www.microsoft.com/betaexperience/pd/SQL2012EvalCTA/enus/
default.aspx

The online resources contain two files. Firstly, a file named `tabular_modelling.bak`, which is the database backup. The second is the file that contains the restore script. It is also reproduced as follows:

```
USE [master]

RESTORE DATABASE tabular_modelling
FROM   DISK = N'C:\BOOK\SQLDATA\tabular_modelling.bak'
WITH   FILE = 1
,  MOVE N'tabular_modelling' TO
   N'C:\BOOK\SQLDATA\tabular_modelling.mdf'
```

```
,   MOVE N'tabular_modelling_log' TO
    N'C:\BOOK\SQLDATA\tabular_modelling.ldf'
,   NOUNLOAD,  REPLACE,  STATS = 5

GO
```

This code assumes that the backup file has been stored in the `C:\BOOK\SQLDATA` directory. Additionally, the database files that are created will also be created in this directory. Running the code from SQL Server Management Studio will create the database and restore all its data.

The output of executing the script should look like the following screenshot:

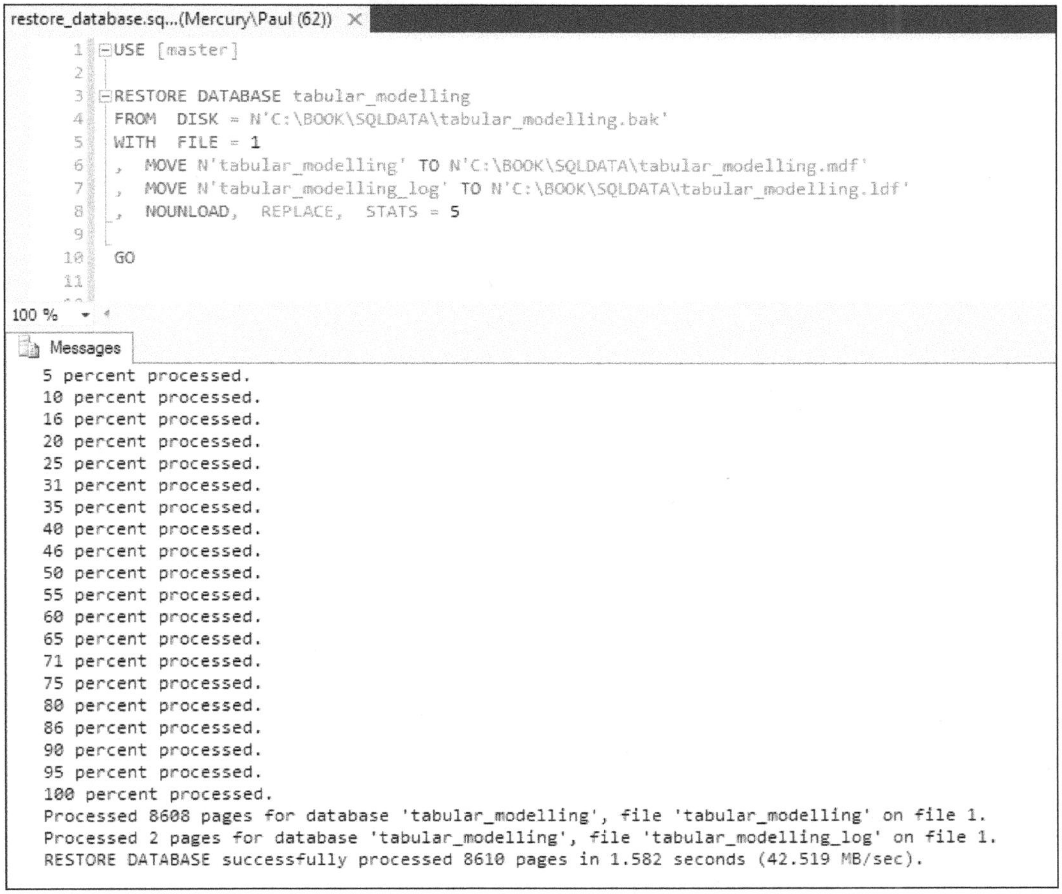

```
restore_database.sq...(Mercury\Paul (62))  ×
 1 ⊟USE [master]
 2
 3 ⊟RESTORE DATABASE tabular_modelling
 4  FROM DISK = N'C:\BOOK\SQLDATA\tabular_modelling.bak'
 5  WITH FILE = 1
 6  ,  MOVE N'tabular_modelling' TO N'C:\BOOK\SQLDATA\tabular_modelling.mdf'
 7  ,  MOVE N'tabular_modelling_log' TO N'C:\BOOK\SQLDATA\tabular_modelling.ldf'
 8  ,  NOUNLOAD,  REPLACE,  STATS = 5
 9
10   GO
11
100 %   ▼  ◂

 Messages
   5 percent processed.
  10 percent processed.
  16 percent processed.
  20 percent processed.
  25 percent processed.
  31 percent processed.
  35 percent processed.
  40 percent processed.
  46 percent processed.
  50 percent processed.
  55 percent processed.
  60 percent processed.
  65 percent processed.
  71 percent processed.
  75 percent processed.
  80 percent processed.
  86 percent processed.
  90 percent processed.
  95 percent processed.
 100 percent processed.
 Processed 8608 pages for database 'tabular_modelling', file 'tabular_modelling' on file 1.
 Processed 2 pages for database 'tabular_modelling', file 'tabular_modelling_log' on file 1.
 RESTORE DATABASE successfully processed 8610 pages in 1.582 seconds (42.519 MB/sec).
```

If the folders used on your computer are different, the directories in the script should be changed accordingly. It should also be noted that SQL Server does not require its data (or log files) to be stored in specific folders, so the choice of `C:\BOOK\SQLDATA` as a data folder may be suitable.

Index

Symbols

D

data
allocating, at different levels 144-150
importing, as text 38-43
importing, from databases 43-49
processing 227-233
restricting, with filters 251-253
restricting, with where conditions 251-253
retrieving, from single table 245-248
securing, with roles 193-198
sorting 58, 59
Data Analysis Expressions (DAX) 29
Database Management System (DBMS) 43
databases
creating 296, 297
data, importing from 43-50
Data Categories 288
data feeds
about 54
using 55
working 56
data filtering
tabular relationships, using for 18-28
datasets
customers list 8
date list 8
orders list 8
product categories list 7
product list 7
product subcategories list 7
DATEADD function 105
dates list 8
DAX 127
Deployment Wizard
using, for model deploying 212-218
Design button 53
dimension 223
dimensional table
manipulating 118-124
DirectQuery Mode Property option 235
DirectQuery solution
about 234
implications, demonstrating 241
new project, creating 234-240
restrictions 234

DISTINCTCOUNT function 131
Do Not Process option 212
Download button 294
dynamic security
implementing 198-201

E

Excel tabular model
promoting, methods 182
Existing Connections button 120
Export to Data Feed button 55

F

field appearance
managing 12-18
Field List button 35
fields
adding, to tables 28-30
linking, between tables 30
Filter 157
Filters Pane 265
FIRSTDATE function 101
Format as Table button 10
Formulas tab 10
From Data Feeds button 55

H

HideMemberIf property 71
hierarchies
creating, for drilldown interaction 60-62
hierarchy 121
Home Tab 12

I

ImageLoad command 185
images
displaying 279-281
using 279, 281
Import From Data Source button 190
Install button 296

K

Key Performance Indicators. *See* **KPI**

KPI
about 74
adding, to model 76, 78
creating 75, 76
measures, adding to model 78-80

L

LASTDATE function 101
last non-empty function
using 132-136
working 137, 138
last year value 101-105
levels 121
LOOKUPVALUE function 31

M

Manage Relationships button 22
many-to-many relationships
defining 127-130
working 131, 132
maps 287
MDX (Multidimensional Expressions) 89
measure group 223
Measure Settings window 27
Microsoft SQL Server 235
model calculations
about 32
creating 32-36
models
creating 8
deploying, Deployment Wizard used 212-218
deploying, from SSDT 208-212
deploying, in SSDT 189-192
importing, to SSDT 186-189
working 10, 11
Month to Date (MTD) aggregations 96-98
Multidimensional Online Analytical
Processing (MOLAP) 218
multidimensional view
differentiating, with tabular model 244
multiples 290

N

Name Box 160
Name Manager window 11

O

Online Transactional Processing (OLTP) 44
Open DataBase Connectivity (ODBC) 43
Open Data Protocol (OData) 54
orders list 8

P

parent-child hierarchies
about 65
creating 68-74
diagram 66
using 66, 68
Pareto principle 259
partitions
creating 218-226
managing 218-226
PATHITEM function 69
perspectives
creating 201-205
pipe symbol (|) 145
PivotTable button 12, 154
PivotTable Connections... option 157
PivotTable Field List window 36
pivot tables
connecting 153-158
PowerPivot
installing 293-296
PowerPivot Data Connections group 50
PowerPivot Field List 153
PowerPivot Field List panel 17
Power View
about 262
trellis charting, implementing 290
Power View report
Control Content 266
creating 263-271
Filters Pane 265
Power View Field List 265
Report Canvas 265
Preview Selected Table window 49
prior period value
about 101-103
forms 101, 102
working 103-105
processed 211
ProcessRecalc command 233

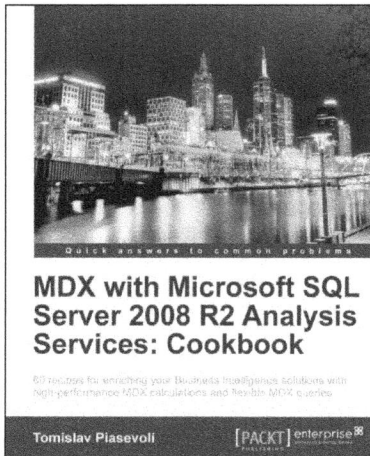

MDX with Microsoft SQL Server 2008 R2 Analysis Services: Cookbook

ISBN: 978-1-84968-130-8   Paperback: 480 pages

80 recipes for enriching your Business Intelligence solutions with high-performance MDX calculations and flexible MDX queries

1. Enrich your BI solutions by implementing best practice MDX calculations

2. Master a wide range of time-related, context-aware, and business-related calculations

3. Enhance your solutions by combining MDX with utility dimensions

4. Become skilled in making reports concise

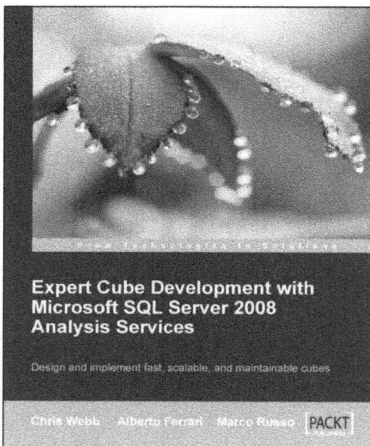

Expert Cube Development with Microsoft SQL Server 2008 Analysis Services

ISBN: 978-1-84719-722-1   Paperback: 360 pages

Design and implement fast, scalable, and maintainable cubes

1. A real-world guide to designing cubes with Analysis Services 2008

2. Model dimensions and measure groups in BI Development Studio

3. Implement security, drill-through, and MDX calculations

4. Learn how to deploy, monitor, and performance-tune your cube

Please check **www.PacktPub.com** for information on our titles

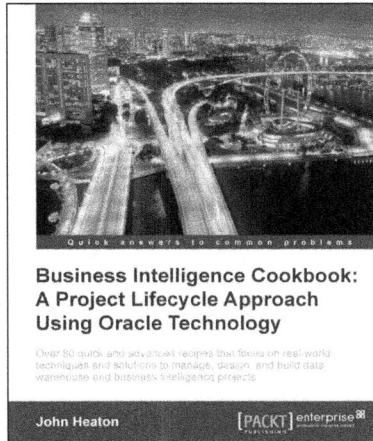

Business Intelligence Cookbook: A Project Lifecycle Approach Using Oracle Technology

ISBN: 978-1-84968-548-1   Paperback: 368 pages

Over 80 quick and advanced recipes that focus on real-world techniques and solutions to manage, design, and build data warehouse and business intelligence projects

1. Full of illustrations, diagrams, and tips with clear step-by-step instructions and real-time examples to perform key steps and functions on your project

2. Practical ways to estimate the effort of a data warehouse solution based on a standard work breakdown structure

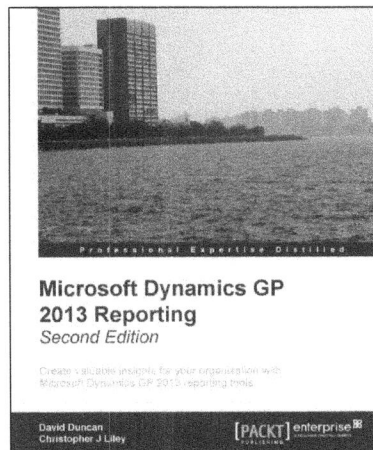

Business Intelligence Cookbook: A Project Lifecycle Approach Using Oracle Technology

Over 80 quick and advanced recipes that focus on real-world techniques and solutions to manage, design, and build data warehouse and business intelligence projects

John Heaton

Microsoft Dynamics GP 2013 Reporting *Second Edition*

ISBN: 978-1-84968-892-5   Paperback: 386 pages

Create valuable insights for your organization with Microsoft Dynamics GP 2013 reporting tools

1. Explore the new reporting features found in GP 2013

2. Add value to your organization by identifying the major reporting challenges facing your organization and selecting the most effective reporting tool to meet those challenges

3. Empower users from top to bottom in your organization to create their own reports

Microsoft Dynamics GP 2013 Reporting
Second Edition

Create valuable insights for your organization with Microsoft Dynamics GP 2013 reporting tools

David Duncan
Christopher J Liley

www.ingramcontent.com/pod-product-compliance
Lightning Source LLC
Chambersburg PA
CBHW080929220326
41598CB00034B/5733